Warranty and Preventive Maintenance for Remanufactured Products

Modeling and Analysis

Warranty and Preventive Maintenance for Remanufactured Products

Modeling and Analysis

By

Ammar Y. Alqahtani, PhD and
Surendra M. Gupta, PhD, PE

CRC Press
Taylor & Francis Group
Boca Raton London New York

CRC Press is an imprint of the
Taylor & Francis Group, an **informa** business

CRC Press
Taylor & Francis Group
6000 Broken Sound Parkway NW, Suite 300
Boca Raton, FL 33487-2742

First issued in paperback 2021

ISBN-13: 978-0-367-78061-6 (pbk)
ISBN-13: 978-1-138-09751-3 (hbk)

Library of Congress Cataloging-in-Publication Data

Names: Alqahtani, Ammar Y., author. | Gupta, Surendra M., author.
Title: Warranty and preventive maintenance for remanufactured products : modeling and analysis / Ammar Y. Alqahtani and Surendra M. Gupta.
Description: Boca Raton, FL : CRC Press/Taylor & Francis Group, 2018. | Includes bibliographical references.
Identifiers: LCCN 2018030268| ISBN 9781138097513 (hardback : acid-free paper) | ISBN 9781315104805 (ebook)
Subjects: LCSH: Remanufacturing--Reliability. | Recycled products--Reliability. | Recycled products--Maintenance and repair. | Warranty.
Classification: LCC TS183.8 .A47 2018 | DDC 363.72/82--dc23
LC record available at https://lccn.loc.gov/2018030268

Visit the Taylor & Francis Web site at
http://www.taylorandfrancis.com

and the CRC Press Web site at
http://www.crcpress.com

Dedicated to our families:

Nojood Alqahtani, Yahya Alqahtani, Farah Alqahtani and Lana Alqahtani

-Ammar Y. Alqahtani

Sharda Gupta, Monica Gupta, and Neil Gupta

-Surendra M. Gupta

Contents

List of Figures

List of Tables

Preface

The aim of this book is to describe the practical implementation of an advanced after sales management framework devoted to warranty and preventive maintenance management of remanufactured products. This framework is useful for facilities producing either remanufactured components or products. The framework allows for easy organizational improvement and supports innovative decision-making processes for technical assistance in warranty claim rectification.

The exponential increase in the development of modern technological advances and devices, coupled with the customers' immense desire to possess the newest technological models and products on the market makes for truncated product lifespans, which instigates a substantial upsurge in their rate of disposal. Consequently, landfill areas and natural resources reach a critical tipping point, which compels governments to invoke mandates and environmental regulations on product manufacturers. Therefore, at the culmination of a product's life, some companies permit the return of their used products in order to conform to the newly integrated regulations and to encourage customer awareness of the environmental issues involved. Attempts have been made to establish specialized product recovery facilities with the intention of diminishing the volume of accumulated waste delivered to landfills by retrieving materials, parts, and components from the 'end-of-life' (EOL) products through procedures such as recycling, refurbishing, and remanufacturing. The economic benefits produced by these facilities also portray the role of product recovery in a more attractive light.

The quality of a remanufactured product is still uncertain for some consumers. Therefore, these consumers possess insecurities in deciding whether or not the remanufactured products will render the same expected performance. This ambiguity regarding a remanufactured product could result in the consumer deciding against its purchase. With such consumer apprehension, remanufacturers often seek market mechanisms that provide reassurance as to the stable durability that these products still maintain. One strategy that the remanufacturers often use is the utilization of the premise of offering product warranties with preventive maintenance on their products.

The analysis of warranty policies and cost models associated with one-dimensional or two-dimensional policies has received significant attention from academic researchers and practitioners. A significant amount of academic research has been conducted in modeling policies and costs for brand-new products' warranties. In contrast, remanufactured products' warranty policies have not been studied or published widely. This has motivated the authors to write this book.

The book is divided into 12 chapters. Chapter 1 presents an introduction to the book by providing a brief overview of the text, a description of the motivation for writing the book, a statement of the scope of the book, a statement on the contribution the book is expected to make to the field, and an outline of the book. Chapter 2 provides a review of the literature in four different areas, namely, environmentally conscious manufacturing and product recovery (ECMPRO), sensor-embedded products, warranty analysis and maintenance analysis. The scope of the literature review supports the subject matter covered in the subsequent chapters of this book. Chapter 3 provides an introduction to product warranty and preventive maintenance for remanufactured products. Also addressed are the problem statement, definitions of warranty, warranties and preventive maintenance for remanufactured products, and the objectives of the book. Chapter 4 introduces 27 different warranty policies for remanufactured products with a preventive maintenance strategy. They range from non-renewing to renewing, simple to combined and one-dimensional to two-dimensional policies. Chapter 5 presents mathematical models to analyze warranty costs with preventive maintenance for the remanufactured products when failures occur at system and component levels. Chapter 6 presents the description and analysis of a representative remanufacturing facility, called the Advanced Remanufacture-To-Order (ARTO) system, which is considered throughout the book. Also presented is the information on the characteristics and precedence relationships of the components disassembled and remanufactured at different stations of the remanufacturing line. Chapter 7 provides analyses of two of the most popular non-renewing warranty policies, namely, Free-Replacement Warranty (FRW) and Pro-Rata Warranty (PRW), for remanufactured product. Chapter 8 presents analyses of eight non-renewing warranty policies, namely, Specified Parts Excluded (SPE), Lump-Sum Cost-Sharing (LCS), Labor or Material Cost Shared (LMS), Limit on Individual Cost (LIC), Individual Cost Deductible (ICD), Limit on Total Cost (LTC), Total Cost Deductible (TCD) and Money Back Guarantee (MBG), for remanufactured product. Chapter 9 provides analyses of nine combination warranty policies, namely, Combination of Free-Replacement Warranty and Pro-Rata Warranty (FRW-PRW), Limits on individual and total cost policy (LITC), Combination of Free-Replacement Warranty & Limit on Individual Cost Warranty (FRW-LIC), Combination of Free-Replacement Warranty & Lump-Sum Cost-Sharing Warranty (FRW-LCS), Combination of Free-Rreplacement Warranty & Labor/Material Cost-Shared Warranty (FRW-LMS), Combination of Money-Back Guarantee & Free-Replacement Warranty (MBG-FRW), Combination of Money-Back Guarantee & Pro-Rata Warranty (MBG-PRW), Combination of Money-Back Guarantee & Limit on Individual Cost Warranty (MBG-LIC), Combination of Money-Back Guarantee & Limits on Total Cost Warranty (MBG-LITC), for remanufactured products. Chapter 10 provides analyses of three of the most popular renewing warranty policies, namely, Renewing Free-Replacement Warranty (RFRW), Renewing Pro-Rata Warranty (RPRW) and their combination (RFRW-RPRW), for remanufactured products. Chapter 11 provides analyses of six two-dimensional warranty policies, namely, Non-Renewing 2D Free-Replacement Warranty (2D FRW), Non-Renewing 2D Pro-Rata Warranty (2D PRW), Renewing 2D Free-Replacement Warranty (2D RFRW), Renewing 2D Pro-Rata Warranty (2D RPRW), Combination (2D FRW-PRW) and Combination (2D RFRW-RPRW), for remanufactured products. In all the cases discussed in Chapters 7 through 11, the expected warranty, corrective maintenance (CM) and preventive maintenance (PM) costs, from both the buyer's and remanufacturer's perspectives, are also discussed. Finally, conclusions are presented in Chapter 12.

This book is concerned with the theory and practice of warranty management and preventive maintenance, particularly in relation to remanufactured product warranties. Models developed in this book can be used for making the correct decision in offering renewable, nonrenewable, one- and two-dimensional warranty policies, and for managerial decision making when considering maintenance contracts or outsourcing maintenance for remanufactured components and products.

Acknowledgments

The knowledge in this book is a collective effort of many people working in the remanufacturing and warranty areas. In this regard, we thank hundreds of researchers from whose work we have benefited and many of whom we have had the good fortune to meet and interact with at conferences around the world. We want to thank Taylor & Francis Group for their commitment to publish and stimulate innovative ideas. We express our appreciation to Cindy Renee Carelli and the Taylor & Francis Group staff for providing unwavering support at every stage of this project. Finally, we acknowledge our families, to whom this book is lovingly dedicated, for their unconditional love and support for making this book a reality.

Ammar Y. Alqahtani, PhD
King Abdulaziz University
Jeddah, Saudi Arabia

Surendra M. Gupta, PhD, PE
Northeastern University
Boston, Massachusetts

Authors

Ammar Y. Alqahtani, PhD, is an assistant professor of Industrial Engineering at King Abdulaziz University in Jeddah, Saudi Arabia. He received his BS degree with first honors from the Industrial Engineering Department of King Abdulaziz University, Jeddah, Saudi Arabia, in May 2008. Being awarded with a full scholarship by the King Abdulaziz University (KAU), he received his MS degree in Industrial Engineering from Cullen College of Engineering, University of Houston. In September 2012, he started his PhD studies in Industrial Engineering at Northeastern University, Boston, Massachusetts. He received his PhD degree in 2017. He has been employed as a faculty member by King Abdulaziz University since December 2008. His research interests are in the areas of environmentally conscious manufacturing, product recovery, reverse logistics, closed-loop supply chains (CLSC), sustainable operations and sustainability, simulation and statistical analysis and modeling with applications in CLSC and multiple life-cycle products. He has coauthored several technical papers published in edited books, journals and international conference proceedings.

Surendra M. Gupta, PhD, is a professor of Mechanical and Industrial Engineering and the Director of the Laboratory for Responsible Manufacturing at Northeastern University in Boston, Massachusetts. He received his BE in Electronics Engineering from Birla Institute of Technology and Science, his MBA from Bryant University and his MSIE and PhD in Industrial Engineering from Purdue University. He is a registered professional engineer in the State of Massachusetts. Dr. Gupta's research interests span the areas of Production/Manufacturing Systems and Operations Research. He is mostly interested in environmentally conscious manufacturing, reverse and closed-loop supply chains, disassembly modeling and remanufacturing. He has authored or coauthored 12 books and over 600 technical papers published in edited books, journals and international conference proceedings. His publications have received over 11,800 citations (with an h-index of 54) from researchers all over the world in journals, proceedings, books and dissertations. He has traveled to all seven continents, namely, Africa, Antarctica, Asia, Australia, Europe, North America and South America and presented his work at international conferences on six continents. Dr. Gupta has taught over 150 courses in such areas as operations research, inventory theory, queuing theory, engineering economy, supply chain management and production planning and control. Among the many recognitions he has received are the outstanding research award and outstanding industrial engineering professor award (in recognition of teaching excellence) which he received from Northeastern University and a national outstanding doctoral dissertation advisor award.

List of Notations

W	Warranty period [For all policies]
W_1	Sub-interval of warranty period [Policies 6, 8, 9(i), 9(ii), 10, 13, 14, 15, 16]
α	Cost-sharing parameter [Policies 2(ii), 9(i)]
k	Limit on number of failures for Money-Back Guarantee [Policies 12, 13, 14]
$C_s(RL)$	Sale price of item, remaining life *RL* [Policies 5, 11, 14]
$C_j(RL)$	Cost of replacement/repair the jth claim, j = 1, 2, …
C_{jM}	Material cost of replacement/repair the jth claim, j = 1, 2, …
C_{jL}	Labor cost of replacement/repair the jth claim, j = 1, 2, … [Note: $C_j = C_{jM} + C_{jL}$]
TC_j	Total cost of replacement/repair the first j claims, j = 1, 2, … [Note: $TC_0 = 0$]
c_I	Cost limit on individual replacement/repair cost [Policies 3(i), 7. 8, 15, 16]
c_E	Cost limit with deductibles [ICD Policy]
c_T	Limit on total (over the warranty period) replacement/repair cost [Policies 4(i), 7, 16]
c_x	Limit under a deductible policy [TCD Policy]
$S(X)$	Refund function [policies 5, 11, 14]
n	Number of components in an item
S	Set of all the components in an item
I	Sub-set of S covered under the warranty [SPE Policy]
E	Sub-set of S not covered under the warranty [SPE Policy], [Note: $S = I \in E$]
RL	Remaining life of item at sale, return or fail
RL_i	Remaining life of component i ($1 \leq i \leq n$)
C_E	Cost per minimal repair for item failures due to component (s) $\in E$
C_I	Cost per minimal repair for item failures due to component (s) $\in I$
C_1	Labor cost per minimal repair for an item
C_m	Material cost per minimal repair for an item
$C_0(RL; \tau)$	Cost of improvement τ on item of remaining life *RL*
C_r	Cost per minimal repair for an item
$E[.]$	Expected value of expression within [.]
$F_i(x)$	Failure distribution of a new component i
$F_{i1}(x)$	Distribution function for times to first failure of component i subsequent to the sale of item

$F_{i2}(x)$	Distribution function for times to subsequent failures of component i subsequent to the sale of item
$F_{ir}(\mathrm{x})$	Distribution function for times to failure of component i subsequent to the sale of item
$F_{iu}(x)$	Distribution function for times to failure of remanufactured component used in replacement
$G(c)$	Distribution function for C_J
$G_E(c)$	Distribution function for C_E
$G_I(c)$	Distribution function for C_I
$G_i(rl)$	Distribution function for RL_i (for repairable components) when remaining life is unknown
$G_L(c)$	Distribution function for C_L
$G_M(c)$	Distribution function for C_M
$H(rl)$	Distribution function for RL when remaining life is unknown
$H_i(rl)$	Distribution function for RL_i (for replacement components) when remaining life is unknown
$N(W; RL)$	Number of failures over the warranty period when remaining life, RL, is known
$N_E(W; RL)$	Number of failures over the warranty period when item remaining life, RL, is known and failed component (s) $\in E$
$N_I(W; RL)$	Number of failures over the warranty period when item remaining life, RL, is known and failed component (s) $\in I$
$N_i(W; RL_i)$	Number of failures for component, i, over the warranty period when component remaining life, RL_i, is known
$N(W)$	Number of failures over the warranty period when item remaining life, RL, unknown
$N_E(W)$	Number of failures over the warranty period when item remaining life, RL, is unknown and failed component (s) $\in E$
$N_I(W)$	Number of failures over the warranty period when item remaining life, RL, is unknown and failed component (s) $\in I$
$N_i(W; RL_i)$	Number of failures for component, i, over the warranty period with component remaining life, RL_i, unknown
$\bar{C}$	Expected cost per minimal repair for an item
$\bar{C}_E$	Expected cost per minimal repair for an item and failed component (s) $\in E$
$\bar{C}_I$	Expected cost per minimal repair for an item and failed component (s) $\in I$
$\bar{C}_L$	Expected cost of labor per minimal repair for an item
$\bar{C}_M$	Expected cost of material per minimal repair for an item
C_{in}	Cost of replacement by a new component for component i
C_{im}	Cost of replacement by an working used component or by a new component when used component is not available for component i

C_{io}	Cost of overhaul for component *i*
C_{ir}	Cost of minimal repair for component *i*
C_{iu}	Cost of replacement by working remanufactured component for component *i*
$h(rl)$	Density function associated with $H(rl)$
$h_i(rl)$	Density function associated with $H_i(rl)$
$g(c)$	Density function associated with $G(c)$
$g_E(c)$	Density function associated with $G_E(c)$
$g_I(c)$	Density function associated with $G_I(c)$
$g_i(rl)$	Density function associated with $Gi(rl)$
$g_l(c)$	Density function associated with $G_l(c)$
$g_m(c)$	Density function associated with $G_m(c)$
$r_i(x)$	Failure rate for component *i*
$\Lambda(t)$	Intensity function for system failure
$\Lambda_I(t)$	Intensity function for system failures due to component (s) $\in I$
$\Lambda_E(t)$	Intensity function for system failures due to component (s) $\in E$
$\Lambda_0(t)$	Intensity function for system failure of overhauled item
τ	Remaining life upsurge after an upgrade
θ	Degree or level of improvement with $\theta = 0$ means no upgrade or minimal repair/cosmetic change and $\theta = 1$ means as good as new repair/replacement by new
ψ, ξ	Parameter of cost function for upgrade action
B_j	Cost to buyer for replacement/repair jth failure, $j \geq 1$ [Note: $C_j = D_j + B_j$]
$C_b(W; RL)$	Total warranty cost to buyer with *RL* known
$C_b(W)$	Total warranty cost to buyer with *RL* unknown
$C_d(W; RL)$	Total warranty cost to remanufacturer with *RL* (System remaining life) known
$C_d(W)$	Total warranty cost to remanufacturer with *RL* unknown
C_i	C_d (*W*: *RL*) for the ith independent simulation run
$C_i(W; RL_i)$	Total warranty cost for component i with RL_i (component remaining life) known
$C_i(W)$	Total warranty cost for component i with RL_i unknown
C_j	Cost of replacement/repair jth failure, $j \geq 1$
$C_p(RL)$	Purchasing cost to remanufacturer for a remanufactured item of remaining life, *RL*
$\bar{C}(n)$	Estimate of E [C_d (*W*; *RL*)] based on n independent simulation run
D_j	Cost to remanufacturer for replacement/repair jth failure, $j \geq 1$
$E[\,]$	Expected value
$G(c)$	Distribution function for C_j, $j \geq 1$
Q	Parameter for LCS Policy

Y_j	Binary random variable associated with jth failure for analysis of SPE Policy
$\overline{c}_b$	Expected cost to buyer per warranty claim in cost limit policies
$\overline{c}_d$	Expected cost to remanufacturer per warranty claim in cost limit policies (3(i), 3b, 4(i) 4(ii))
$C_d(W_1; RL)$	Warranty cost to the remanufacturer in the period $[0, W_1)$ for an item of remaining life, *RL*
$C_b(W–W_1; Y)$	Cost to the buyer in the period $[W_1, W)$ for an item of excess remaining life, *Y*
$C_d(W–W_1; Y)$	Warranty cost to the remanufacturer in the period $[W_1, W)$ for an item of excess remaining life, *Y*
$C_b(W_1. W; RL)$	Cost to the buyer for an item of remaining life, *RL*
$C_d(W_1,W; RL)$	Total warranty cost to the remanufacturer for item of remaining life, RL
$C_b(W_1, W)$	Cost to the buyer for an item of remaining life, RL unknown
$C_d(W_1, W)$	Total warranty cost to the remanufacturer for item of remaining life, RL unknown
$F_w(x)$	Distribution function for the first failure in the period $[W_1, W)$ given by the excess remaining life of renewal process associated with failures in the period $[0, W_1)$ with first failure given by $F_{i1}(x)$ for remaining life known [or $F_{iu}(x)$ for remaining life unknown] and subsequent failures given by $F_{iu}(x)$
Y	Excess remaining life of renewal process associated with failures in the period $[0, W_1)$ with first failure given by $F_{i1}(x)$ for remaining life known [or $F_{iu}(x)$ for remaining life unknown] and subsequent failures given by $F_{iu}(x)$
$J_d(W; RL)$	Total after sale cost to remanufacturer for an item of remaining life, *RL* sold with warranty (*W*).
$J_d(W_1, W; RL)$	Total after sale cost to remanufacturer for an item of remaining life, *RL* sold with combination warranty (W_1,W).
$J_b(W_1, W; RL)$	Total after sale cost to buyer for an item of remaining life, RL sold with combination warranty (W_1,W).
n	Number of failures
k	Parameter of policy
$\overline{c}_{bb}$	Expected cost of buyback to remanufacturer (may be full sale price if the item has to be scrapped and the difference between sale price and salvage value otherwise)
$P_n(RL, RL+W)$	Probability of n failures over [0,W) given the remaining life of the item is RL
γ	Probability that buyer will execute money-back option

Acronyms

EOL	End-of-Life
SEPs	Sensor-Embedded Products
CP	Conventional Products
RFID	Radio Frequency Identification Device
ARTO	Advance Remanufacture-to-Order
BW	Based Warranty
CM	Corrective Maintenance
PM	Preventive Maintenance
FRW	Free-replacement warranty
CSW	Cost-sharing warranty
SPE	Specified parts excluded
LCS	Lump-sum cost-sharing
LMS	Labor or material cost shared
CLW	Cost-limit warranty
LIC	Limit on individual cost
ICD	Individual cost deductible
LTC	Limit on total cost
TCD	Total cost deductible
PRW	Pro-Rata Warranty
FRW-PRW	Combination of Free-replacement warranty and Pro-Rata Warranty
LITC	Limit on individual and total cost policy
FRW-LIC	Combination of Free-replacement warranty & Limit on individual cost warranty
FRW-LCS	Combination of Free-replacement warranty & Lump-sum cost-sharing warranty
FRW-LMS	Combination of Free-replacement warranty & Labor/ Material cost-shared warranty
RFRW	Renewal Free-replacement warranty policy
RPRW	Renewal Pro-Rata warranty policy
RFRW-RPRW	Combination of Renewal Free-replacement warranty & Renewal Pro-Rata warranty
2D FRW	Two-Dimensional Free-replacement warranty policy
2D PRW	Two-Dimensional Pro-Rata warranty policy
2D RFRW	Two-Dimensional Renewal Free-replacement warranty policy
2D RPRW	Two-Dimensional Renewal Pro-Rata warranty policy
2D RFRW-RPRW	Two-Dimensional Combination of Renewal Free-replacement warranty & Renewal Pro-Rata warranty

1

Introduction and Overview

1.1 Overview

Nowadays, the high rate of technology development and customers' desire for newer models and products result in shorter product life cycles and an increase in the disposal rate. As a result, landfill areas and natural resources have started to reach a critical point which has forced many governments to mandate environmental regulations on manufacturers. The result is that, at the end of products' useful lives, many firms take back their own products to comply with these new regulations. They build special facilities for product recovery to minimize the amount of waste sent to landfills by retrieving materials, parts and components from the end-of-life (EOL) products through recycling, refurbishing and remanufacturing processes. Additionally, the economic benefits from such facilities make the role of product recovery more attractive.

In product recovery, disassembly is the most important operation: it separates the desired components, subassemblies and materials from EOL products using non-destructive, semi-destructive or destructive operations. The main objective of disassembly is to support the goal of recovery processes by minimizing manufacturers' dependency on natural resources and their rates of depletion. There are different ways to perform the disassembly operations, such as at a single workstation, in a disassembly cell or on a disassembly line. While a single workstation and disassembly cell is more flexible, the highest productivity rate is provided by a disassembly line which is also suitable for automated disassembly (Güngör & Gupta, 2001).

The main issue in the product recovery process is the uncertainty in the number of components and their quality due to the lack of any information about the condition of components prior to disassembly. The obvious solution is to test each component after disassembling it. However, this impairs the profitability of the remanufacturer, depending on the testing time and the testing costs. Furthermore, if the tests reveal that the component is non-functional, then all that time and resources spent on disassembly and testing is wasted.

The use of sensor-embedded products (SEPs) is a way to mitigate the uncertainty in disassembly yield. SEPs involve implanting sensors in the product during their production process. By monitoring critical components of a product, these sensors facilitate the data collection process. The data collected through sensors can be used to predict the components and/or product failures during the product's life while allowing for accurate estimation of remaining lives and conditions of components at the EOL of the product. Moreover, the information provided by sensors regarding any nonfunctional, replaced or missing component prior to the disassembly of an EOL product provides important savings in testing, disassembly, disposal, backorder and holding costs (Ilgin & Gupta, 2010, 2011a, 2011b).

1.2 Motivation

The quality of a remanufactured product is still uncertain for consumers. Therefore, the consumers are unsure if the remanufactured products will render the expected performance. This ambiguity about a remanufactured product could lead the consumer to decide against buying it. With such apprehension held by consumers, remanufacturers often seek market mechanisms that provide assurance about the durability of the products. One strategy that the remanufacturers often use is to offer warranties on their products (Murthy & Blischke, 2006; Alqahtani & Gupta, 2017).

Thus, the motivation for and purpose of this book is to study the impact of offering non-renewing and renewing warranties on remanufactured products. We will analyze various warranty scenarios by making use of the information provided by SEPs during their life cycles. Finally, we will minimize the cost associated with warranty, maximize remanufacturer's profit and determine an attractive price for offering the warranty.

1.3 Scope and Contribution of this Book

To deal with the high level of complexity and uncertainty associated with the remanufacturing process, the scope of this book is limited to the following situations. EOL products and demand for components arrive at the remanufacture facility according to a Poisson process. The disassembly time at each station is exponentially distributed. Backorders are allowed by imposing a cost calculated based on the duration of the backorder. Excess EOL products and components are disposed of regularly according to the disposal policy. A pull type production control mechanism is used in all disassembly line settings considered in this book. Comparison of warranty cost and period is provided between different warranty policies.

The primary contribution of this book is the quantitative assessment of the effect of offering warranty on the cost of remanufacturing from the remanufacturer's perspective and an attractive price from the buyer's perspective. While there are books and studies on the development of warranty policies for brand-new products, and a few on secondhand products, there is no comprehensive book that evaluates the potential benefits of warranty quantitatively for remanufactured products. In the studies presented in this book, the improvement in profit achieved by offering warranty using different policies forms the basis for determining the amount of money that can be invested in offering the warranty in a cost-effective manner.

1.4 Outline of the Book

There are 12 chapters in this book.

Chapter 1 (this chapter) gives an introduction and overview of the book.

Chapter 2 reviews the literature associated with environmentally conscious manufacturing and product recovery, sensor-embedded products, warranty analysis and maintenance analysis.

Chapter 3 provides an introduction to warranty and preventive maintenance.

Chapter 4 introduces a variety of warranty policies for remanufactured products with preventive maintenance strategy.

Chapter 5 presents mathematical models to analyze warranty costs with preventive maintenance for remanufactured products.

Chapter 6 introduces a representative remanufacturing facility used for the analysis of various warranty and preventive maintenance models discussed in the rest of the book.

Chapter 7 and Chapter 8 present the cost analysis of simple non-renewing warranties.

Chapter 9 presents the cost analysis of combination warranties.

Chapter 10 presents the cost analysis of renewing warranties.

Chapter 11 presents the cost analysis of two-dimensional warranties.

Finally, Chapter 12 presents some conclusions.

2

Review of Product Recovery, Sensor-Embedded Products, Warranty and Maintainability

2.1 Environmentally Conscious Manufacturing and Product Recovery (ECMPRO)

In the modern world, environmental importance originating mostly from consumers, governments and businesses have made sustainability a key issue. Sustainability is comprised of social, environmental and economic elements of responsibility in business. In the literature that spans the fields of management, operations and design, sustainability has become an increasingly popular subject. Beyond theory, sustainability is also increasingly prevalent in practice, as manufacturers are rapidly adopting related practices. According to the definition offered by the World Commission on Environment and Development in 1987, sustainability is the "development that meets the needs of the present without compromising the ability of future generations to meet their needs." Sustainability is an issue of global importance in both the industrial and the developing world, and is driven by the environmental impact of economic activity (Ehrlich & Ehrlich, 1991; 1993). The impact of business on the environment is particularly tangible in terms of the exploitation of non-renewable resources and the conservation efforts employed to secure those (Whiteman & Cooper, 2000).

The increasing importance allocated to sustainability is due to a variety of factors, driven largely by the growing awareness related to the impact of human activities on the environment. Greater transparency is being demanded of the organizations pertaining to their operations environment and social impact.

As the impact of organizations on the environment has increased in concert with demands linked to transparency and regulations, manufacturers must increasingly heed the importance of sustainability. Customers, regulatory entities and internal employees are mutually and increasingly demanding that manufacturing organizations address and manage the environmental and social impact of their operations. The supply chains exploited by manufacturers are especially impactful upon the sustainable character of operations. The supply chains employed may have positive or negative impacts upon the social or physical environment, and thus the selection of suppliers and assessment of their methods is particularly important to ensure the character of the manufacturer.

To address the growing regulations imposed by governments to address the impact of commerce on the environment, environmentally conscious manufacturing (ECM) is increasing in study and practice. ECM is rooted in green principles and concerned with the development of methods for product manufacturing that encompass the full cycle from conceptual design to final delivery, as well as end-of-life (EOL) disposal, so as to satisfy environmental standards of practice. Within the context of ECM, products are returned to the Original Equipment Manufacturers (OEMs) or product recovery facilities at their ends-of-life (EOLs). A key goal of ECM is to minimize the volume of end-of-life products (EOLPs) that are disposed of in landfills. Through the ECM process, the negative effect of product manufacture on the environment is minimized, and product recovery processes such as recycling, remanufacturing and reuse are implemented.

Three types of returns may be experienced over the course of the product life cycle, namely, end-of-use (EOU), EOL, and repair/warranty return. EOU returns are realized when a functional product is returned in exchange for an upgraded device. The EOL is realized when the product becomes out-of-date or lacks utility for current users. The smartphone provides a valuable example to consider given the many reasons behind returns over the product life cycle. In the United States, consumers are generally provided a 30-day period during which they may return the device for any reason following the purchase. Beyond this period, some 80% of smartphone users opt to upgrade their phones for newer versions prior to technological utility necessity, exhibiting an EOU return. When phones are no longer supported by a network provider, and thus use is discontinued, the EOL return is realized.

Repair and warranty returns may be experienced at any point in the product life cycle. Within the realm of consumer electronics, millions of products are returned annually in the United States. These returns represent significant potential value in terms of recovery.

Numerous review papers, as shown in Table 2.1, have appeared in the literature that cover various subjects within the general area of ECMPRO in varied depth. What follows next is a brief literature review on the subjects within environmentally conscious manufacturing and product recovery (ECMPRO) that are of interest to us in this book and are organized into three subsections, namely, reverse and closed-loop supply chains, product recovery and product design.

TABLE 2.1

Previous Reviews

Review	Scope
Fleischmann et al., 1997	Reverse Logistics
Moyer & Gupta, 1997	Recycling/Disassembly Efforts In The Electronics Industry
Zhang et al., 1997	Environmentally Conscious Design And Manufacturing
Carter & Ellram, 1998	Reverse Logistics
O'Shea et al., 1998	Disassembly Planning
Bras & McIntosh, 1999	Remanufacturing
Guide et al., 1999	Production Planning And Control For Remanufacturing
Güngör & Gupta, 1999	Environmentally Conscious Manufacturing And Product Recovery
Fleischmann et al., 2000	Reverse Logistics
Guide, 2000	Production Planning And Control, Inventory Management And Control, Disassembly, Reverse Logistics
Ferguson & Browne, 2001	Product Recovery And Reverse Logistics
Lee et al., 2001	Disassembly Planning And Scheduling
Tang et al., 2002	Disassembly Modelling, Planning And Application
Desai & Mital, 2003	Disassembly Algorithms And DFD Guidelines
Dong & Arndt, 2003	Disassembly Sequence Generation And Computer-Aided Design For Disassembly
Lambert, 2003	Disassembly Sequencing
Dong et al., 2005	Inventory Management In Reverse Logistics
Prahinski & Kocabasoglu, 2006	Reverse Logistics
Williams, 2006	Electronics Remanufacturing Processes
Kim et al., 2007	Disassembly Scheduling
Sbihi & Eglese, 2007	Green Logistics
Srivastava, 2007	Green Supply Chain Management
Williams, 2007	Computer Integrated Remanufacturing, Recycling, Disassembly
Rubio & Corominas, 2008	Reverse Logistics
Sasikumar et al., 2008a, 2008b, 2009	Reverse Logistics
Akcali et al., 2009	Network Design For Reverse And Closed-Loop Supply Chains
Chanintrakul et al., 2009	Reverse Logistics Network Design
Pokharel & Mutha, 2009	Reverse Logistics
Subramoniam et al., 2009	Strategic Planning Factors For Automotive Aftermarket Remanufacturing
Akcali & Çetinkaya, 2011	Inventory And Production Planning In Closed-Loop Supply Chains
Ilgin & Gupta, 2010	Environmentally Conscious Manufacturing And Product Recovery
San and Pujawan, 2012	Closed-Loop Supply Chain With Remanufacturing
Ilgin & Gupta, 2012a	Physical Programming

(*Continued*)

TABLE 2.1 (CONTINUED)

Previous Reviews

Review	Scope
Souza, 2013	Closed-Loop Supply Chain
Morgan & Roger, 2013	Remanufacturing Scheduling
Govindan et al., 2015	Reverse Logistics And Closed-Loop Supply Chain
Agrawal et al., 2015	Reverse Logistics
Ilgin et al., 2015	Multi-Criteria Decision Making In Environmentally Conscious Manufacturing And Product Recovery
Curkovic & Sroufe, 2016	Environmentally Responsible Manufacturing
Esmaeilian et al., 2016	Sustainable Manufacturing And Remanufacturing
Matsumoto et al., 2016	Remanufacturing
Jena & Sarmah, 2016	Acquisition Management In Closed-Loop Supply Chain
Barange & Agarwal, 2016	Green Supply Chain Management
Diallo et al., 2016	Quality, Reliability, Maintenance In Closed-Loop Supply Chains/Remanufacturing
Musa and Dabo, 2016	RFID In Supply Chain Management
Priyono et al., 2016	Disassembly For Remanufacturing
Rubio and Jiménez-Parr, 2017	Reverse Logistics
Thöni and Tjoa, 2017	Sustainable Supply Chain
Govindan & Soleimani, 2017	Supply Chain Network
Govindan et al., 2017	Reverse Logistics
Correia et al., 2017	Supply Chain Sustainability
Abbey et al., 2017	Closed-Loop Supply Chain

2.1.1 Reverse and Closed-Loop Supply Chains

Reverse supply chain (RSC) refers to all activities linked to the collection, recovery and disposal of EOLPs. Due to the decrease in raw material resources and growing environmental regulations issued by governments, RSC is an increasingly important practice with rising benefits. Consumer awareness related to environmental and corporate responsibility on behalf of organizations are on the rise, underscoring the value of RSC. In addition, RSC operations improve operational profitability by reducing costs associated with transportation, inventory and warehousing. RSC operations also support the optimization of forward supply chain performance measures such as storage space occupancy and transportation capacity.

Closed-loop supply chains (CLSC) are simultaneously concerned with forward and reverse supply chains, and are becoming an increasingly employed and cost-effective solution for the management of forward and reverse supply chain operations. Much of the literature on reverse and closed-loop supply chains is focused on the design problem. Other subjects explored in the literature include transportation problems, selection of used products, selection and evaluation of suppliers, performance measurement, marketing related issues, EOL alternative selection and product acquisition management.

RSCs and CLSCs are of growing value and are applicable in the strict regulatory environment of the modern world in which social awareness of related issues is likewise on the rise. In the European Union, legislation is underlining the importance of alternative supply chain options. Such practices are more prevalent in the United States due to their potential profitability. RSCs and CLSCs involve the reclamation of used products from customers through varying means, followed by the recovery of value from the used products. This is accomplished through the reuse, refurbishment and remanufacture of either the entire product or select sub-systems, components, parts and materials.

Beyond the environmental benefits, the effective management of RSC operations leads to higher profitability through a reduction in the costs associated with transportation, inventory and warehousing. The key challenges of RSC and CLSC are in the areas of disassembly, EOL component selection, performance measurement, selection of used products and remanufacturing. Additional challenges beyond physical EOLP and component selection include marketing issues, network design, the selection and evaluation of suppliers and transportation.

The remanufacturing phase is home to many opportunities through which profitability may be increased. As noted by Blackburn et al. (2004), RSC and CLSC deserve equal attention to forward supply chains given their profit potential and thus should be effectively deployed and managed as processes through which value can be created. The prospective profitability of RSC is mitigated by the type of product involved. As noted by Fisher et al. (1997), there are two RSC strategies from which to choose: 'efficient' or 'responsive'. Efficient RSC is a supply chain designed to minimize product costs. A responsive RSC is a supply chain designed to optimize speed.

The appropriate matching of products to the varying supply chain strategies available optimizes profit. Efficient RSCs are most valuable for functional products, while RSCs are best for innovative products. The product classification of 'functional' refers to products with low marginal values of time, while the 'innovative' product classification refers to products with high marginal values of time. Products that are innovative, such as laptop computers or smartphones, generally have short life cycles and thus a high marginal value of time, while functional products such as power tools or utensils are less time-sensitive and thus have lower marginal values of time.

A key point of differentiation between efficient and responsive RSCs is the point in the supply chain at which testing and evaluation is conducted to determine the condition of the product and its components. When cost-efficiency is the central focus, the evaluation activity is generally centralized in the returns supply chain. Should responsiveness be the focus, a decentralized evaluation activity is generally employed to minimize time delays associated with processing returns (Blackburn et al., 2004).

Blackburn et al. (2004) highlight the importance of noting the potentially substantial value present in product returns and their sensitivity in time. Effectively heeding these factors supports the effective design of RSCs, particularly for maturing markets like consumer electronics. Such markets may realize significant profits yet face many threats thereto, including declining margins, poorly handled return streams and increasing return volumes. Such factors highlight the importance of not only effective planning but the identification of the most appropriate RSC configuration.

2.1.2 Product Recovery

Environmental concerns, including the ongoing depletion of natural resources and growing reduction in available landfill space for disposal, have led to legislative action. Legislators have undertaken efforts to hold OEMs responsible for their own EOLPs. To meet regulatory parameters while simultaneously seeking to optimize profit, OEMs have begun to invest in product recovery facilities. Product recovery facilities collect EOL products and process them through various means, including recycling, reuse and remanufacturing with the primary goal being a reduction in the volume ultimately disposed of in landfills. To contribute to the conservation of natural resources, OEMs engage in product development geared towards high reuse potential, remanufacture and recyclable character.

When products are returned to a product recovery facility, a variety of actions may be engaged in. Within the context of the product recovery facility, the least intensive and highest profit option is to resell the product as a used product, insofar as it meets particular quality standards. Sometimes, the product may be repaired through the fixing or replacement of damaged parts, leading to the product being sold as a refurbished rather than used product (Jayaraman et al., 1999). The process pursued depends on the measured condition of the object. Mitra (2007) developed a pricing model to maximize the expected revenue from the recovered products.

Refurbishment is a value-added process through which a used product is reconditioned to a functional state. Such state may or may not be equal to the condition of the original product, although technology is at times upgraded during the refurbishment process, adding further value. Remanufacture is the next level of refurbishment, and when products are not deemed appropriate for these options, disassembly and component retrieval is pursued to realize whatever value may remain in the reclaimed used product. Materials may be retrieved through recycling, while energy can be gained through incineration. Devices unsuited for these processes are disposed of (Jayaraman, 2006). There are a number of important product recovery processes explored in the subsections below.

2.1.2.1 Disassembly

Insofar as items are deemed unfit for resale as a used product, for remanufacture or for refurbishment, disassembly is the next step in the product recovery process. Brennan et al. (1994) define disassembly as the systematic separation of a device or assembly into its components, subassemblies or other groupings. Disassembly is a key element of the value reclamation process and facilitates the selective separation of desirable parts and materials (Moore et al., 1998; Pan & Zeid, 2001).

To optimize the disassembly process, it is essential that the degree and order of disassembly be carefully considered and strategized to provide desirable components. For the reverse logistics element of the EOL phase to be optimized, disassembly must be incorporated into process design. Following disassembly, the reclaimed items are cleaned and refurbished. Functional items are categorized for reuse or remanufacture, while items classified as nonfunctional are recycled, and residuals are disposed of. According to Lambert (1999), disassembly is pursued for a variety of reasons, including maintenance and repair, improving access to subassemblies and desired parts, to remove contaminants from materials, while complying with regulations for the removal of particular parts or materials for environmental and safety reasons, with a key goal being the reduction of residual waste.

The type of disassembly process that is chosen from the many available is determined by various criteria. There are two main types of disassembly processes, determined by the final use and condition of the components: destructive and non-destructive. Within destructive disassembly, it is accepted that damage may be realized upon subassemblies and components during the process, as the functionality and condition of the subassemblies and components is not critical to their value. Non-destructive disassembly is the opposite, in that damage is not accepted during the process, as the functionality and condition of the subassemblies and components are critical to their value. Non-destructive disassembly is a more cost-intensive process given the greater time it requires.

Disassembly processes may be further classified as either partial or complete. In partial disassembly, only particular items are disassembled to minimize the time and effort invested into separating the items, while complete disassembly is self-explanatory. To maximize the value that is realized through the disassembly operation, stopping the process at the appropriate time is important. The disassembly process may be halted at many points, although the two most important are the point of maximum profit or minimum loss, and the point of complete disassembly (Harjula et al., 1996).

Moore et al. (2001) highlight the systematic separation that the disassembly process entails. It is a key process within the context of material and product recovery, as it facilitates the selective separation of valuable parts and materials. Lambert & Gupta (2005) provided a thorough exploration of general disassembly and may be referenced for a more in-depth treatment of the subject.

Disassembly-to-order systems (DTOs) are undertaken to determine the optimal lot-sizes of EOLPs to disassemble to satisfy the demand for the components therein from a mix of various product types that have components and/or modules in common (Lambert & Gupta, 2002). Lambert & Gupta (2008) employed heuristics developed under the assumption of deterministic disassembly yield to develop a method called the tree network model. The tree network model was developed by modifying the disassembly graph method for a multi-product-demand-driven disassembly system with commonality and multiplicity. Kongar & Gupta (2002) proposed a single period integer goal programming model for a DTO system to identify the optimal combination for multiple products to selectively disassemble. The selective disassembly was undertaken to meet the demand for items and materials under physical, financial and environmental constraints and goals (Kongar & Gupta, 2006a).

Within the first line of research explored, Kongar & Gupta (2006b) employed fuzzy goal programming (FGP) to build upon the research of Kongar & Gupta (2002) to model the fuzzy aspiration levels of varying objectives. Langella (2007) offered a multi-period heuristic accounting for holding costs and the external procurement of items. Gupta et al. (2009) employed NN to solve the DTO problem, while Kongar & Gupta (2009a) proposed an LPP-based solution methodology to address tangible or intangible financial-, environmental- and performance-related measures of DTO systems. Building upon this, Kongar & Gupta (2009b) developed a multi-objective TS algorithm through a consideration of multiple-objective functions, including total profit maximization, resale/recycling percentage maximization and the minimization of the disposal percentage.

In the second line of research considered, the uncertainty associated with disassembly yield is explored. Two heuristic procedures – one-to-one and one-to-many – were developed by Inderfurth & Langella (2006) to investigate the effect of stochastic yields on the DTO system. These were employed by Imtanavanich & Gupta (2006) to address the stochastic elements of the DTO system, after which a Goal Programming (GP) procedure is applied to determine the number of returned products to satisfy specific goals.

The Advanced Repair-to-Order and Disassembly-to-Order (ARTODTO) model has been proposed by Ondemir et al. (2012). The ARTODTO model is concerned with products that have embedded-sensor and radio frequency identification (RFID) tags. The purpose of the ARTODTO is to determine how to process each EOLP on hand to meet used product and component demand in addition to recycled material demand. The model accounts for disassembly, repair and recycling options for each EOLP to satisfy material and remaining lifetime-based component/product demands, considered 'sophisticated', while minimizing the total cost.

Ondemir & Gupta (2012) presented the remanufacturing-to-order (RTO) system for end-of-life sensor-embedded products (SEPs). The researchers proposed an integer programming (IP) model to determine the optimal means of processing available EOLPs to meet quality-based product, component and recycled material demand while minimizing cost. Ondemir & Gupta (2013a; 2013b) proposed an ARTODTO model for EOL processing of SEPs under the constraints of demand and decision uncertainty. The model is formulated as a FGP model through which a number of financial, physical and environmental goals are supported. A linear physical programming (LPP) model has also been proposed to optimize the multi-criteria ARTODTO system (Ondemir & Gupta, 2014). Building upon Ondemir & Gupta (2013a), Alqahtani et al. (2014) employed the simulation discrete model.

Disassembly line is the most efficient way to disassemble products on a large scale. However, disassembly line balancing remains a challenging problem, as it is an NP complete problem (McGovern and Gupta, 2007). For more information refer to the book by McGovern and Gupta (2011) and the recent review paper on disassembly line balancing by Özceylan et al., (2018).

2.1.2.2 Reuse

Reuse is the utilization of the entire product without disturbing the existing product design. Reuse conserves the original structure and oftentimes the same purpose is maintained. Cleaning and minor repair may be undertaken prior to distributing the product to the consumer. Reuse is a particularly beneficial EOLP recovery strategy, as no additional resources are consumed. Reuse as a strategy, however, may only be implemented when product reuse is more advantageous than reselling. Generally, two types of products are reused, those for which value increases over time, such as antiques, and those that are durable, such as furniture. Such used products may be procured directly from a prior user or from a retail establishment that sells used objects for reuse.

2.1.2.3 Remanufacturing

Within the context of World War II, many manufacturing facilities converted from ordinary production into military production. When this occurred, many of the products that were in use were effectively remanufactured in order to maintain the momentum of society. As the 20th century progressed past World War II, the concept of remanufacturing diffused into a variety of sectors, including those comprised of appliances, electrical devices, machinery and toner cartridges. In the United States, Original Equipment Manufacturers (OEMs) account for some 5% of the total manufacturing activity of the nation (Guide, 2000). The situation in Europe is markedly different, with the market potential for remanufactured products having been recognized by OEMs, and thus remanufacture is on the rise (Seitz & Peattie, 2004).

Remanufacturing entails the complete disassembly of products, with some parts being machined to like-new condition, something entailing cosmetic operations. Generally, remanufactured products have shorter lead times, which complicate the deployment of traditional operations management techniques. Researchers have proposed new methodologies to address the operations management issues in remanufacturing, including capacity planning, effect of uncertainty, forecasting, inventory management, and production planning and scheduling. Ilgin & Gupta (2012b) have explored the many aspects of remanufacturing published at the outset of the 2010s. Remanufacturing is an industrial process through which worn-out products are converted into like-new condition (Aksoy & Gupta, 2005; Kim, K. et al., 2006; Kim et al., 2007).

A variety of definitions of remanufacturing have been offered, although they are generally variations of the concept of product recovery (Seaver 1994; Amezquita & Bras 1996; Bras & Hammond 1996; Lund 1998; Cox & Blackstone 2002). Through the literature, remanufacturing is being commonly referred to as the process of restoring useful life to discarded products (Lund, 1998). Through the application of literature studies and surveys, Bras & Hammond (1996) have noted similar generic manufacturing steps and condensed them into the following: Cleaning, damage correction (repair, refurbishment and replacement), quality assurance (testing and inspection) and part interfacing (disassembly and assembly).

Remanufacturing entails the complete disassembly of products and potential cosmetic improvement of used, yet still operable and functional, used items. Incorporating new and emerging methodologies such as capacity planning, inventory management, and production planning and scheduling, the challenges associated with managing remanufacturing activities within the context of operations management are being addressed.

As the concern over the impact of business on the environment has risen, principles have emerged through which profit may be maximized in concert with environmental savings and related benefits. Many of these principles are of value to OEM and third-party remanufacturers, with Jacobsson (2000) having developed various perceived advantages to remanufacturing by OEMs. The OEM of a particular product produced the original and is the only organization that has full access to the product's complete design, content and specifications. Given this, the OEM has the capacity to make the most informed decisions about the product's anticipated reliability and durability. Such information is necessary for the Original Equipment Remanufacturer (OER) to process the product through remanufacturing, as it provides the information related to what may be recovered from the product and how it can be altered throughout the process while still maintaining its functionality. Required maintenance decisions are also facilitated through this information, underlining the importance thereof.

OEMs have particularly strong positions from which to remanufacture products due to many reasons. OEMs have an established distribution network for the original product, and thus could apply this to remanufactured products, and for the collection of discarded products. The OEM, upon having decided to remanufacture the original device, becomes an OER, and realizes the capacity to build a better relationship with the end consumer by offering a remanufacturing operation with comprehensive information on what EOLPs may emerge, when to expect them and to what levels of volume.

OEMs and subsequently OERs have many advantages over independent remanufacturers, including the supplier network. OERs are able to access a supply of original parts which may be difficult to source outside the supply chain. This adds difficulty to independent remanufacturers who rarely have such access and thus must rely upon replicas or purchases from the OEM. Such elements represent advantages held by OEMs, advantages that are not capitalized upon should OER activity not be pursued. OEMs that accept discarded products for remanufacture have the added benefit of insight, in that the EOL phases of their designs may be better assessed through remanufacture, informing future design decisions through the data collected. This is known as design for remanufacturing (DfRem), and will be further explored below in the section on product design.

A key factor that differentiates remanufacturing from manufacturing is that of energy; remanufacturing a product requires markedly less energy than recycling the same product, insofar as the product meets the essential production characteristics for remanufacture (Lund, 1998). According to Lund (1998) the following characteristics must be incorporated into the remanufacturing process to support the profitability of the operation:

- The product has a core that is not consumed, discarded or does not function properly;
- The product can be restored to its original state using current technologies;
- The product can be mass-produced in a factory setting;
- The value of a remanufactured product is close to the original product market value;
- The cost associated with acquiring discarded or failed products is relatively low compared to the market value of the remanufactured product; and
- There are no rapid changes in the product technology, as it is difficult to mass-produce remanufacture-worthy products that constantly evolve.

Given the high rate of technological change in the modern market, the characteristics supported by Lund (1998) are of value to consider, although they are not essential given that they may be made irrelevant through technological progress. Ovchinnikov (2011) considered the pricing and remanufacturing strategy of a firm that decides to offer both new and remanufactured versions of its product in the market and is concerned with demand cannibalization.

The management challenges that are encountered in remanufacturing are markedly different than those of conventional manufacturing. Conventional manufacturers generally manage one generation of product variation at a time, with mass-production volumes allowing for production lines to be dedicated to single products. Remanufacturers, however, must manage small batches of products encompassing a range of product variants and generations, complicating tool changing, disassembly and assembly processes. Remanufacturers experience particular difficulty establishing the lean and mass-production systems that manufacturers depend on (Seitz & Peattie, 2004).

In some instances, the remanufacturing facility is required to order new spare parts, which may involve long lead times. To avoid bottlenecks in parts supplies, given the scale of the delivery times of ordered parts in concert with product variant proliferation and inability to predict product return character and volume, remanufacturers maintain high inventory levels (Seitz & Peattie, 2004). Uncertainties complicate recovery processes and the ability to manage them. Uncertainty linked to processing times and the many essential operations within the recovery process are compounded by uncertainty concerning the quantity, quality and timing of materials and components that are released through the recovery process. Further, the return flows that supply the recovery process are also uncertain in terms of quality, quantity and timing (Van Nunen & Zuidwijk, 2004).

A number of constraints in the supply loop for the recycling and reuse of products have been identified in research by Geyer & Jackson (2004). A supply loop is classified as being constrained when any of the processes therein experience difficulty with the output of the upstream process. There are two process groups within the context of the supply loop framework: collection and reprocessing. According to Geyer & Jackson (2004), collection and reprocessing may be subject to the following types of constraints:

- Limited access to EOL products leaving the use phase;
- Limited feasibility of EOL product reprocessing; and
- Limited market demand for the secondary output from reprocessing.

When a supply loop constraint is encountered, Geyer & Jackson (2004) note that there are two means of overcoming it. The first of these is to change the design of the products and processes that are within the primary supply chain. The second means of overcoming supply loop constraints is to adapt the processes in the supply loop to the constraints. Adopting a systems perspective, the first strategy emerges as the most advantageous and is generally practiced when both the primary supply chain and the secondary supply loop are owned and controlled by the same organization. Such findings align with research conducted by Jacobsson (2000).

2.1.2.4 Recycling

Recycling is a method through which components are processed into their materials or useful degraded materials. The purpose of recycling is to retrieve the material content of both nonfunctional and used products. The original structure of the product is not conserved through the process of recycling, and thus recycling is pursued largely for products that are ineligible for reuse or remanufacturing. The recycling process generally consists of the procurement of products and components from the product and then recycling them into materials that may be utilized to produce new components and products. Depending upon the prevalence of the recycling technology and material, the global market for recycled materials may be plentiful, particularly for recycled materials such as aluminum, copper and steel.

Recycled materials may be incorporated into the manufacture of the original product or a new product altogether. The use of recycled materials to manufacture the original product is often called upcycling, or closed-loop recycling. The use of upcycled materials precludes the need to utilize virgin resources, thereby managing the environmental impact of the manufacturer. Recycling processes account for approximately 10%-20% of recycling costs, with the design of the product determining much of the remaining cost structure and with the economic benefits of production and recycling determining the processes and product components utilized.

Product recovery operations are generally classified into two types: upcycling and downcycling. Through upcycling, an EOLP is processed into a product of equal or greater value, while downcycling entails the degradation of the EOLP into something of lesser value, such as the processing of unusable paper stock into toilet tissues. Remanufacturing and reuse fall beneath the umbrella of upcycling, while recycling and energy recovery are forms of downcycling. The life cycle of the product exhibits the importance of incorporating the process of product recovery during design, with the incorporation of future reusability or recyclability adding future value during the product recovery period.

2.1.3 Product Design

The key purpose of product development is the cost-effective design of products heeding the importance of manufacturability and functionality. Due to growing concerns related to the environment, the product design process has been compelled to incorporate environmental and resource-based concerns into the process. Incorporating environmental factors during design supports the social and environmental character and compliance of the organization and the devices produced through it. To support this, methodologies such as design for X, Life Cycle Assessment (LCA) and material selection may be utilized by designers, as explored below.

2.1.3.1 Design for X

Increasingly comprehensive rules and regulations issued by governments are being placed upon OEMs to produce and dispose of their own products while mitigating any negative impact upon the environment. Given the growing requirements placed upon them, OEMs are increasingly incorporating EOL recovery options into product design, with the adoption of the Design for X (DfX) concept supporting this. DfX is comprised of design specialties to ensure the fit of the process deployed, including design for environment, design for disassembly, design for recycling and design for remanufacturing (Veerakamolmal and Gupta, 2000).

According to Fiksel & Wapman (1994), Design for Environment (DfE) is the "systematic consideration during new product and process development of design issues associated with environmental safety and health over the full product life cycle". DfE is utilized to facilitate pollution prevention, resource conservation, waste management and environmental risk management. DfE designs products to minimize the environmental impact of products throughout their life cycle (Fiksel, 1996; Billatos & Basaly, 1997, Basaly & Billatos 1997; Giudice et al., 2006; Bevilacqua et al., 2007a). As noted by Horvath et al. (1995), the three main goals of DfE are to minimize the use of non-renewable resources, to manage renewable resources and to minimize the toxic release to the environment realized throughout the product life cycle.

A methodology proposed by Madu et al. (2002) involves a step-by-step approach to support the environmental character of manufacturing and remanufacturing operations alike. The first step is that of the Analytic Hierarchy Process (AHP) and is employed to prioritize customer requirements. Following this is Quality Function Development (QFD), through which design requirements are linked to customer requirements. Finally, a cost-effective design plan is developed through the application of Taguchi experimental design and the Taguchi loss function. Furthering this, Masui et al. (2003) developed a four-phase QFD-based methodology for DfE in the early stages of product development. The first two phases identify important components in product design, while the latter two phases determine the most appropriate designs to pursue in terms of their environmental impact, with suggestions made to improve existing designs when necessary.

Ramani et al. (2010) noted that many tools must be capitalized upon to effectively evaluate product designs for environmental criteria. The most commonly used technique in DfE methodologies to determine environmental impact is that of life-cycle assessment, as explored below (Veerakamolmal & Gupta, 1998). The Green Design Advisor (GDA) was proposed by Feldmann et al. (1999) to account for metrics linked to product information such as number of materials, materials used in the product and their character such as toxicity, and the disassembly and recyclability variables of a product, such as the time of disassembly. The ECoDE was developed by Lye et al. (2002) as a computer-based evaluation tool to assess the environmental impact of the components in a given product, employing AHD to compare and rank each criterion. Scores for each of the criterion employed are calculated through the use of a multi-criteria rating technique for the product and its components, with higher scores indicating a lesser impact on the environment. This was extended by Knight & Curtis (2002), who presented a software tool through which the environmental and economic effects of disassembly may be quantified.

Designers may incorporate DfE into products through a variety of methods. Common DfE practices include waste source reduction, substance use reduction, material substitution, energy use reduction and life extension. Simple shifts in design can be capable of achieving multiple goals, such was waste source reduction, which can reduce energy and material use, thereby supporting resource conservation. DfE is also valuable in the context of new product development, as incorporating it enables producers to be more responsive to corporate environmental laws. The inclusion of DfE into overall product design creates greater opportunity throughout the product life cycle to incorporate environmental quality improvements in a systematic fashion.

Design for Disassembly (DfD) is defined by Veerakamolmal & Gupta (2000) as the ease of disassembly in the context of the design process. Mok et al. (1997) have labeled the ease of disassembly as 'disassemblability'. The purpose of DfD is to design products that may be readily disassembled at the EOL in order to optimize the value for reuse or remanufacturing, or the recycling of products and/or harvesting of materials and components. To facilitate the disassembly process, particular assembly operations such as forming, pressing or welding are best not included in the design process.

Within the context of disassembly, three elements must be incorporated into the design process. The first of these is that of joint selection, with non-permanent joints being most supportive of disassembly; for example, bolts are simpler to disassemble than adhesives (Mabee et al., 1999). The type of disassembly must then be considered, with non-destructive disassembly being best to minimize component damage throughout the process (Bras & McIntosh, 1999). The final element to consider when optimizing the design process for disassembly is that of corrosion/rust, which represents a hindrance to the disassembly process, and thus preventative measures such as employing non-corrosive materials is beneficial (Charter & Gray, 2008).

Harjula et al. (1996) note that two key factors must be considered during DfD. The financial impact of disassembly for the various options must be considered, whether reuse, recycling, remanufacturing or disposal. The environmental impact is the next key facet of DfD, according to Harjula et al. (1996), which considers the amount of material, components and/or items disassembled that are ultimately disposed of.

Through the adoption of DfD, the complexity of the product structure is minimized through a reduction in the number of parts necessary by improving upon the use of common materials and optimizing the spatial alignment of the components. In doing so, it is necessary that such efforts do so without impacting ease of assembly, functionality or structural soundness of the product (Veerakamolmal & Gupta, 2001). Bogue (2007) advances that DfD is comprised of three key areas: the selection and use of materials; the selection and use of joints, connectors, and fasteners; and the design of components and the product architecture.

The incorporation of product recovery into the overall design, particularly in the early stages, has the potential to increase value. Disassembly is an active element of most of the product recovery processes and facilitates the separation of particular parts and materials, highlighting the importance of designing for disassembly. DfD determines the specifications of a product to reduce the complexity of the design through reducing the number of parts required, employing common materials in addition to easily removable fasteners and non-permanent joints.

Design for Recycling (DfR) is concerned with the factors of design that provide for the cost-effective recycling and disaggregation of the materials and components of the product (Masanet & Horvath, 2007). Kriwet et al. (1995) outlined the following aspects to consider when engaging in product DfR: to avoid the use of hazardous and environmentally harmful materials, to minimize the variety of materials employed, to prioritize reusable materials while avoiding those that are incompatible with standard recycling processes and to utilize fasteners/joints that are simple to disassemble.

Remanufacturing is a valuable form of sustainable production. Through remanufacturing, EOLPs are restored to working condition through the processes of disassembly, sorting, cleaning, reconditioning and reassembly, with challenges such as component damage and the unavailability of remanufacturing equipment and labor (Yang et al., 2016). Such challenges may be addressed through the inclusion of remanufacturing into the early stages of product design. According to Charter & Gray (2008), Design for Remanufacturing (DfRem) is "a combination of design processes whereby an item is designed to facilitate remanufacture".

DfRem is comprised of a number of design processes, including design for disassembly, product support for take-back decisions, design for multiple life cycles and modular design. DfRem may be viewed through the lenses of product strategy or engineering. The latter considers the detailed product and manufacturing data, while product strategy includes marketing, sales, service support and reverse logistics (Charter & Gray, 2008).

To support DfRem, the products and their modules and components must be evaluated to determine whether they are viable candidates for remanufacturing. According to Nasr & Thurston (2006), the evaluation considers the cost and value of the component, the recoverable value at EOL, the cost of remanufacture, the ease of disassembly in terms of extracting components without damaging them and disposal options accounting for related environmental impact and any legislation linked to it. Products must meet particular criteria to be considered for remanufacturing, such as holding standard interchangeable parts (Lund, 1998).

Charter & Gray (2008) underline the importance of a high value and durable core for the EOLP. Shu & Flowers (1999) value the upgrade potential of the EOLP, while sufficient customer demand for the remanufactured product is also a factor to be considered (Ayres et al., 1997). Many design tools and methodologies have been developed in research and applied in practice to support DfRem. Yang et al. (2009a), through an assessment of extant literature, have classified the many approaches into five categories: life-cycle thinking, design guidelines, disassembly strategy planning, adaptations from existing design tools and assessment tools.

2.1.3.2 Life-Cycle Assessment

Life-Cycle Assessment (LCA) is a method through which the environmental impact of a product throughout its entire life cycle is determined. The life cycle in terms of the environmental impact includes the extraction and processing of the necessary raw materials and the manufacturing, distribution, use, recycling and final disposal involved with the product. Many researchers have utilized LCA within a DfE methodological framework as a tool to quantify the environmental impact of a product design (Zhang, 1999; Mehta & Wang, 2001; Bovea & Wang, 2003, 2007; Bevilacqua et al., 2007b; Boks & Stevels, 2007; Sakao, 2007; Grote et al., 2007).

LCA, rooted in chemistry and technology, is an effective tool to quantify the environmental impacts of products and their related processes. It is simplest to apply on products that have already been made and to products being compared against each another. In pursuit of more environmentally friendly operations, LCA can be of value, in addition to determining the impact a product has upon the environment throughout its life cycle. Ryding (1999) presents a four-step LCA comprised of:

1. Goal definition and scoping;
2. Inventory analysis;
3. Impact assessment (classification, characterization and valuation); and
4. Improvement assessment.

The Global Warming Potential (GWP) and other indices help LCA tools in contrasting products or processes, although few continue into an evaluative phase (Simon et al., 1998). While presenting value, LCA is also costly and time-consuming, due in part to the prevalence of LCA software tools being stand-alone applications and thus not connected to other tools and product data management (PDM) solutions (Schluter, 2001). To address such concerns, abridged LCA methods have been developed that are less complicated and detailed, requiring less quantitative data while relying more upon qualitative information. This limits the reliability of the abridged LCA when compared to the full LCA, although oftentimes the results of both tests are similar and thus the value and time saved exhibit the benefits of the abridged version.

LCA first emerged in the 1960s, evolved in methodology during the 1970s and in the 1990s was the subject of increasing attention from within the environmental science sector. The concept is described in varying ways across the globe. In Austria, Germany, Japan and Switzerland 'eco-balancing' is applied, while in the United States the term is 'resource and environmental profile analysis', in addition to 'cradle-to-grave assessment' and 'environmental profiling' elsewhere. The Society of Environmental Toxicology and Chemistry (SETAC) advocates on behalf of increased knowledge and awareness of LCA. In concert with the US Environmental Protection Agency (USEPA), in the 1990s SETAC in North America sponsored projects and workshops to develop and promote a consensus towards a framework for engaging in life-cycle inventory analysis and impact assessment. SETAC-Europe engaged in parallel activities alongside the International Organization of Standardization (ISO) and global LCA practitioners. Through such efforts, consensus has been reached on an overall LCA framework built atop a well-defined inventory methodology (ISO, 1997).

The two most essential elements of LCA are goal definition and scoping. The direction of a study is determined by the statements and definitions established during the goal definition and scoping phase, including the expected product of the study, system boundaries and functional unit (FU) assumptions. Generally, the system boundary is illustrated by a general input and output flow diagram, in which all processes that contribute to the life cycle of the product, process or activity are included. The purpose of determining FU assumptions is to establish a reference unit to normalize inventory data on as a benchmark. The definition applied to the FU is determined by the environmental impact category and aims of the investigation, with the FU oftentimes being based on the mass of the product being studied. However, Cederberg & Mattsson (2000) note that the nutritional and economic values of products are also considered, in addition to land area.

The Life Cycle Inventory (LCI) analysis phase has the greatest levels of work intensity and time consumption, in contrast to the other phases in an LCA, due largely to the significant data collection undertaken during this phase. The data collection element may be less time-consuming insofar as good databases are available, and customers and suppliers facilitate the collection as well. Some existing LCA databases are included with LCA software. An LCA database is generally comprised of data on the extraction of raw materials, transport, processing of materials, disposal and production of oftentimes used-material sourced products such as plastic and cardboard. Such data may be applied to processes that are not applied to a particular product, such as general data on packaging or production. To acquire product-specific data, site-specific data is essential, including all inputs and outputs from the processes employed. Inputs include energy of both renewable and non-renewable sources, such as water or raw materials, while outputs are defined as the products and co-products, such as chemical oxygen demand (COD) and chlorinated organic compounds (AOXs), biological oxygen demand (BOD), solid waste generation (municipal solid waste (MSW) and landfill), and gaseous emissions to air, water and soil, such as total suspended solids (TSS).

The life-cycle impact assessment (LCIA) is undertaken to establish greater understanding and ability to evaluate the environmental impacts rooted in inventory analysis, within the framework of the scope and goals of the study. Within this particular phase, inventory results are assigned different impact categories based upon their anticipated impacts upon the environment. The impact assessment process is four-tiered and is generally comprised of classification, characterization, normalization and valuation.

Classification is the process through which the LCI data is assigned and aggregated into common impact groups. The characterization step assesses the extent of the environmental impact of each inventory flow into the corresponding environmental impact, such as establishing a model to quantify the impact of carbon dioxide and methane emissions on global warming. Characterization is important as it provides a means through which the LCI results from each category may be directly compared, with the factors therein commonly referred to as 'equivalency factors'. Potential impacts are presented in ways that can be compared through normalization, for example, comparing the impact on global warming from carbon dioxide and methane emissions from two available options. Valuation is the determination of the relative importance of environmental burdens that are identified within the scope of the classification, characterization and normalization stages through the assignation of weights, thereby allowing for simple comparison or aggregation.

The impact upon the environment, whether local or abroad, is important to consider. Impact categories include global effects, regional effects and local effects. Global effects include ozone depletion and global warming. Regional effects include photo-oxidant formation, eutrophication and acidification. Local effects include the effects of solid waste, working conditions, nuisance and the effects of hazardous waste.

The key goal of an LCA is to establish conclusions that may be applied to support the decision-making process, or to generate a readily understood LCA outcome. In the context of an LCIA, the inventory and impact assessments are discussed alongside one another, while in LCI only inventory is considered, with the significant environmental issues being identified for conclusions and recommendations in line with the goals and scope of the study. Such is an expression of a systematic technique to identify, quantify and evaluate information from the results of the LCI and the LCIA, and to subsequently communicate these outcomes effectively. The assessment may incorporate both qualitative and quantitative suggestions for improvement, including shifts in product, raw material use, consumer use, process and activity design, industrial processing and waste management.

2.1.3.3 Material Selection

The selection of materials for a particular application is influenced primarily by mechanical factors, including ease of processing and weight, although cost is also an important factor to take into account. Recently, environmental factors have become increasingly influential upon material selection. To address environmental criteria within the design process, many tools and methodologies have been presented. A conventional material selection technique, material selection charts, have been augmented by the addition of environmental concerns (Holloway, 1998). Giudice et al. (2005) developed a systematic method to minimize the environmental impact of the materials chosen while simultaneously satisfying the performance and functional requirements placed upon the materials. This is an important means of ensuring fit between materials deployed and the goals of the organization.

Chan & Tong (2007) developed a GRA-based multi-criteria decision-making (MCDM) approach that incorporated EOL product strategy with the economic and technical characteristics of the chosen materials. Teng et al. (2008) engaged in green material cost analysis to establish material recommendations through which less pollution is realized. Yu et al. (2009) linked neural network and genetic algorithms for material selection based upon factors such as the weight, cost and environmental impact of the products and components used in the study. Huang et al. (2008) developed a method that considers traditional design factors in concert with life-cycle environmental impact.

The recyclability of the materials that are ultimately selected is a key factor in quantifying the environmental impact of given products and related processes. Mathematical models have been developed that may be utilized for the recycling-based evaluation of the material content of product designs in early stages of design (Sodhi et al., 1999; Knight & Sodhi, 2000). A recyclability index has also been proposed to serve as a tool to evaluate product design for potential material recovery (Villalba et al., 2002; 2004).

Additional extant research has explored recycling infrastructure to support designers in selecting the most suitable materials for recycling. Goal Programming (GP) has been applied to investigate the effect of lighter materials on the profitability of the recycling infrastructure (Isaacs & Gupta, 1997). Boon et al. (2003) furthered the work of Isaacs & Gupta (1997) by expanding upon their mathematical formulation for the recycling infrastructure to facilitate the assessment of materials streams and process profitability rates by applying these to various clean vehicles and aluminum-intensive vehicles in an earlier study (Boon et al., 2000). Bandivadekar et al. (2004) have explored the material flows and economic exchanges within the context of the automotive recycling infrastructure. Research has been conducted to assess the sensitivity of a recycler's profitability to reprocessing and shipment decisions pursued with various ferrous and nonferrous metal prices as well as varying EOL vehicle compositions (Williams et al., 2007). Sutherland et al. (2008) present a comprehensive overview of studies on automotive recovery infrastructure while identifying future challenges including highlighting the growing importance of recycling.

2.2 Sensor-Embedded Products

Due to advances in technology, manufacturers now have the capacity to build sensors at lower cost and in smaller sizes. The utilization of sensor-based technologies on after sale product condition monitoring is an active subject of research and inquiry. Scheidt & Zong (1994) began the discourse with a study on varying methods of data acquisition from products during their use (Karlsson, 1997, 1998; Klausner et al., 1998a, 1999; Petriu et al., 2000; Simon et al., 2001). A generic embedded device was developed by Cheng et al. (2004) that may be installed into different types of equipment, including manufacturing equipment, automated guide vehicles and portal servers. The device is capable of retrieving, collecting and managing data with the assistance of an embedded real-time operation system supported by many software modules.

An intelligent product model has been developed for realizing product service systems for consumer products, including refrigerator appliances and even the PlayStation2. Within the model, an intelligent data unit (IDU) is installed on each product. The IDU is then employed to collect data during the use and distribution stages of the life cycle (Yang et al., 2009a; Yang et al., 2009b).

Acquiring essential life-cycle components with sensors embedded in them facilitates the tracking of the overall devices considered (Zeid et al., 2004; Vadde et al., 2008). Further research has explored the value of embedded-sensor utilization in terms of product life-cycle management efficacy. Pecht (2008) presented a comprehensive survey of commercial sensor systems that are utilized in the context of health management for electronic products and systems. Embedded sensors are increasingly prevalent, with Fang et al. (2015) exploring model practices related to embedding sensors in products and how sensor data is represented and interpreted.

Additional research is exploring the analysis of life-cycle data that is acquired through the use of varying sensor-based data acquisition methods. Mazhar et al. (2005) presented a two-stage integrated approach that effectively combined Weibull analysis and multiple linear regression in order to assess the reliability of components that are reused within refurbished products, employing life-cycle data for the analysis. Mazhar et al. (2007) extended this by integrating Weibull analysis with neural networks. The performance of several neural network variations has also been compared to facilitate the prediction of the residual life of machines and components.

While many studies, as exhibited above, focus upon the development of SEP models that facilitate the acquisition of product data during the life cycle and/or in the EOL phase, few researchers have explored a cost-benefit analysis. Klausner et al. (1998b) explored the perceived trade-off between greater initial costs of manufacturing realized through using an electronic data log (EDL) in products and the cost savings that are realized from the reuse of used motors. Simon et al. (2001) improved upon the cost-benefit analysis presented by Klausner et al. (1998b) through the incorporation of the limited life of a product design, demonstrating that servicing results in more reusable components than EOL part recovery.

The use of RFID tags to support the ease of retrieving, updating and managing information in the product life cycle is being increasingly studied (Kiritsis et al., 2003; Parlikad & McFarlane, 2007). Kulkarni et al. (2007) have explored the use of RFID in reducing the quality uncertainty that is associated with the remanufacturing process. Ferrer et al. (2000) explored the application of RFID technology to provide for efficient and simple identification and localization of components in a remanufacturing facility, noting that passive RFID tags may be permanently affixed onto the components of products with remanufacture potential at the beginning of their life to facilitate ongoing tracking and assessment. Ondemir et al. (2012) proposed an Advanced Repair-to-Order and Disassembly-to-Order (ARTODTO) system through which EOL management is optimized in closed-loop supply chains by employing sensors and RFID tags. The study applied the information retrieved through the sensor about the age and usage of EOLPs on warranty costs and periods of a remanufacturing system with distinct warranty policies and failure functions, thereby representing product failure likelihood during the warranty period.

2.3 Warranty Analysis

Warranty is defined by Berke & Zaino (1991) as a contractual obligation presented by the manufacturer in connection to the sale of a given product. The purpose of the warranty contract is to provide to the buyer assurance that the product can perform its intended functions, under particular conditions, for a specific period of time. In the event the product fails to meet the criteria outlined in the warranty, the vendor may either repair the product or provide a replacement of the product to the buyer. When the item is replaced, it may be replaced for free through a free-replacement warranty, or there may be a reduced cost as in the case of the pro-rate warranty. Anityasari et al. (2007)

elucidated the role of warranty in the reuse strategy by reviewing the functions of warranty and putting them into a reuse context. Since warranty analysis is heavily based on reliability and leads to potential additional future costs, a model for analyzing the reliability of reused products and the cost consequences was presented. Noh & Borges (2015) studied if the no-warranty condition can actually produce more favorable product evaluations and purchase intentions as opposed to a longer warranty offer.

The warranty in the modern environment has gained increasing currency as a marketing tool. Warranties generally provide circuitous information pertaining to the quality of the product and are meant to relieve uncertainty in the minds of the consumers related to product failure. Warranties are generally included with products at the time of sale. The key purpose of the warranty is to assure the customer that in the event the product experiences catastrophic failure, the product will be repaired or replaced within a particular window of time.

Customers realize value through the time-limited protection against catastrophic failure provided by warranty policies and may also utilize them as a source of information. The manufacturer values warranty policies due to their role as both a security measure and promotional tool, and thus warranties can prove to be sources of competitive advantage. There are two common types of warranty policies presented in the literature: free-replacement warranty (FRW) and pro-rate warranty (PRW). In the latter, replacements are provided in accordance to a cost proportional to the operating time of the product, while in FRW the manufacturer agrees to repair or replace the failed product at no cost to the consumer insofar as it is within the warranty period (Blischke & Murthy, 1992).

Nguyen & Murthy (1984) assessed two general warranty policies involving an initial free replacement period and a pro-rate period. Nguyen & Murthy (1989) additionally examined the combined FRW with fixed and renewed period of ages. Yeh et al. (2007) studied the impact of free repair warranty on optimal periodic replacement policies. The primary objective of product warranty analysis is to effectively model and estimate the cost of warranties. A key point of concern is the expected warranty cost or cost rate over the warranty period and life cycle of a given product (Chattopadhyay & Rahman, 2008; Chen & Chien, 2007; Jung et al., 2010).

Myriad warranty policies have been proposed and studied in the literature, with Blischke & Murthy (1992) presenting a comprehensive taxonomy of warranty policies. Heeding the many variables that may be employed to define a warranty policy, warranties can be split into two main categories: one-dimensional (1D) and two-dimensional (2D). The 1D policy is defined by a single variable such as age or usage, while the 2D policy is represented by a region within a 2D plane, in which one plane generally denotes usage while the other indicates age. New automobiles are generally covered by 2D warranties that address both age and usage, or years and miles, respectively.

Blischke (1995) presented a taxonomy through which the different one- and two-dimensional warranty policies may be contrasted. Kim & Rao (2000) explored two-attribute warranty policies for non-repairable items, producing an analytical expression for two-dimensional renewal functions and cost of warranty, assuming bivariate exponential failure distribution. Yang & Nachlas (2001) presented two approaches to two-dimensional failure modeling and employed a bivariate failure distribution to consider a two-dimensional renewal process model for a non-repairable system.

Iskandar & Murthy (2003) considered two repair-replace strategies for products sold with a two-dimensional failure-free warranty policy. Baik et al. (2004) presented a two-dimensional failure model in which system degradation is attributed to age and usage which implies that the one-dimensional minimal repair concept of unchanging failure rate may be extended into two-dimensional failures. Consumer behavior was modeled through a warranty execution function and employed to analyze warranty costs for repairable products with a two-attribute policy by Mitra & Patankar (2006a; 2006b).

Recently, substantial research has emerged exploring bivariate warranties (Chukova & Johnston, 2006; Corbu et al., 2008; Jung & Bai, 2007; Manna et al., 2006, 2007, 2008). Raja Jayaraman (2008) studied warranty models of one-dimension and two-dimensions with different options available to the manufacturer for repair-replacement upon product failure. Jack et al. (2009) developed a new servicing strategy based on the usage rates of products sold with a two-dimensional warranty. Huang & Yen (2009) explored a two-dimensional warranty model that incorporated preventative maintenance to identify a warranty policy that maximizes the profits of the manufacturer.

While the majority of extant literature on warranties is concerned with one- and two-dimensional warranty policies for new products, little research has been conducted on warranty cost analysis for secondhand products. Through technological innovation and improvement, the life of new products has been extended. To stimulate the sale of new products, the trading in of secondhand products has become common practice. However, the level of consumer uncertainty in purchasing used products is greater given their status, and thus the provision of warranties on secondhand products is a means to reduce this uncertainty and thereby increase secondhand sales. Chattopadhyay & Murthy (2000) developed probabilistic models through which the expected warranty cost of used products may be computed insofar as the items are sold with free replacement or pro-rate warranties. This would be built upon by the formulation of three new cost-sharing warranty policies for secondhand products to effectively analyze the cost of such warranty policies (Chattopadhyay & Murthy, 2001). Saidi-Mehrabad et al. (2010) explored the reliability of improvement strategies for used products sold under a number of differing types of warranty policies. Guerriero et al. (2010) considered the analysis of some failure data during the warranty period with regard to some electrical products. The goal was to define some innovative models for warranty forecasting which are transferable to the company where this study has been carried out.

Product warranties are means to serve three key purposes, beginning with insurance and protection, enabling consumers to transfer the risk of failure to the seller (Heal, 1977). Following this, product warranties are a means through which reliability is communicated to the consumer (Spence, 1977; Gal-Or, 1989; Soberman, 2003; Ferrer et al., 2011). The third and final key purpose of the product warranty is to enable the seller to realize greater profitability (Lutz & Padmanabhan, 1995). Considerable research has been conducted on basic warranty (BW) and extended warranty (EW) policies for the management of new product supply chains (Blischke, 1993; Blischke et al., 2011). Despite such research, little study has been conducted on warranties for remanufactured products' reverse and closed-loop supply chain management.

Limited research has emerged modeling the warranty cost analysis process for used products. Saidi-Mehrabad et al. (2010) have presented optimal upgrade strategies to be applied to remanufactured items through the virtual age and the screening test reliability development method. Shafiee et al. (2011) established a stochastic model to explore the optimal degree of investments to increase the reliability of remanufactured products within the context of free repair warranty (FRW) policies. The researchers concluded that greater investment results in larger declines in the virtual age of the upgraded product, in addition to greater reliability levels.

Naini & Shafiee (2011) conducted a study to identify the optimal upgrade, selling price and maximum expected profit, applying a restrictive assumption about the age distribution of used cores. The researchers established a mathematical model through which they implemented a parametric analysis on the historical ages of the items to determine the best policies to institute. Sarada & Mubashirunnissa (2011) developed two stochastic models, based on the characterization of the system failure and to compute the expected warranty cost for a secondhand product, when the products are sold with free-replacement and/or pro-rata warranties. A two-dimensional warranty, which focuses on both age and usage of the system, has been considered for the above warranty models. Chukova & Shafiee (2013) developed stochastic models for the evaluation of the expected warranty cost, from the dealer's viewpoint, for secondhand items sold under different warranty policies. Yazdian et al. (2014) took this further by adopting an integrated mathematical model that is independent of the specific age of the received item to identify the typically experienced remanufacturer choices.

Shafiee & Chukova (2013a) note that there are two key problems facing the user, those of uncertainty and durability in relation to secondhand products (SHPs), due largely to the unavailability of past maintenance and usage history. To reduce the risk and impact of malfunctioning products, dealers may offer generous warranty policies to satisfy consumer concerns. An integrated taxonomy and classification framework for maintenance and warranty models has been presented by Shafiee & Chukova (2013b). This research explores all concepts of maintenance models and assists the reader in understanding the basics of maintenance and warranty models for both new products and SHPs.

Chattopadhyay & Murthy (2000 & 2001) established a trio of various cost-sharing warranty policies. Through analysis, it was determined that the expected warranty costs increase as the SHP ages. The models identified may be utilized by SHP dealers to determine the warranty costs for medium- and heavy-duty transports, in addition to electronic and electrical goods. Researchers have developed a taxonomy for lifetime warranty policies and subsequently proposed a one-dimensional free replacement lifetime warranty. The researchers also proposed a framework for long-term warranty policies within the confines of their findings (Chattopadhyay & Rahman, 2008). An overview of warranty policies for secondhand products and the mathematical models, which have been developed for cost estimation of warranties for secondhand products, was conducted by Rahman & Chattopadhyay (2015).

Within the literature, lifetime warranties are generally classified into three primary types: simple free rectification, cost-sharing and trade-in lifetime warranty. Saidi-Mehrabad et al. (2010) proposed a method for reliability improvement for SHPs sold with various warranty policies, adopting the perspective of the dealer. The researchers proposed two cost models, the first based on Kijima's virtual age approach (1988; 1989), and the second on a screening test. Within the research conducted in this study, the three decision variables considered are those of past age, reliability improvement and warranty.

Naini & Shafiee (2011) proposed a joint upgrade level and optimal price model for a warrantied SHP. The researchers propose an optimal decision-making model to maximize the anticipated profits of the dealer. The primary marketing strategy is noted as being product pricing, as customer evaluation of products is oftentimes based upon the price. A similar model for the joint optimization of remanufacturing, pricing and warranty decision making for EOLPs was also presented by Yazdian et al. (2016).

An extended warranty policy for secondhand four-door sedan cars was developed by Aksezer (2011) in which four different warranty policies were considered: cost-sharing, free replacement, rebate and hybrid warranty policies. Shafiee et al. (2013a) presented a numerical two-dimensional repair/replacement warranty model for SHPs to provide an estimate of the dealer's warranty cost, based upon the product's past age, reliability, usage and service strategy. Shafiee et al. (2013b) explore two primary types of warranties, those of Rectangular and L-shaped warranties, with such models being of value for a variety of products, including electronic equipment and home appliances.

Diallo et al. (2014) introduced and studied the shape and the behavior of the failure rate of a mixture of two populations of components with the same distribution but different ages. This type of mixture is encountered in industrial settings when new and reconditioned systems are mixed together in remanufacturing or for maintenance operations. Chari et al. (2012) developed a mathematical model to find the cost-optimal production strategy that incorporates reconditioned components in the manufacturing effort. New and reconditioned components were used to carry out replacements upon failure in order to honor warranty commitments. A mathematical model to identify the ideal one-dimensional unlimited free-replacement warranty policy in which replacements are made with reconditioned products was developed by Chari et al. (2013). A framework was assembled by Chukova & Shafiee (2013) to support managerial decisions in the context of a one-dimensional warranty of SHPs, from the position of the SHP dealer. The researchers found that uncertainty related to the durability and performance of the product during past usage, and uncertainty pertaining to maintenance history, are the two primary issues encountered by remanufacturers.

Lo et al. (2013) presented a cost-sharing warranty policy targeted towards manufacturers and retailers alike, with the goal being a reduction in the risk realized by the manufacturer. The researchers explored a decentralized channel that employs a Stackelberg game model in which the manufacturer acts as the leader and the retailer as the follower, and an integrated channel in which both manufacturers and retailers are considered as equal partners. Through the presentation of a numerical example, it was demonstrated that the integrated channel is superior to the decentralized channel.

Mathematical models for two variations of extended warranty policies were presented by Kuik et al. (2015) to assist manufacturers in the evaluation of the benefits of utilizing remanufactured products. The optimization models in their study were numerically solved through the application of a sequential quadratic programming approach and demonstrated that a manufacturer's warranty type-I policy with time as a factor was generally preferable to a warranty type-II policy with failure accounting for the scenario put forward. While the models were not optimized for the consumer, they nevertheless provide them value by calculating the average warranty cost for buyers.

Liao et al. (2015) explored the impact of warranty policy upon consumer behavior. The model accounted for the warranty service and customer heterogeneity in the context of developing three marketing settings to provide for the examination of the impact of warranty on the profitability of the manufacturer. It was found that manufacturers can command higher prices for their products when they are accompanied by a warranty.

An optimization model for secondhand items sold with a non-renewing free repair warranty is proposed from the view of dealers, in which a secondhand product is subjected to upgrade action at the end of its past life, and during the warranty period preventive maintenance actions were carried out when the age of the product reaches a pre-specified threshold value. Su &

Wang (2014) jointly derived the optimal upgrade level and preventive maintenance policy so that the dealer's expected profit could be maximized. A pre-sale upgrade model for repairable used products sold with two-dimensional warranty policies was developed by Su & Wang (2016). The researchers applied the marginal approach to describe the effect of age and usage on the reliability of the product, considering usage as a random function of age. An optimal upgrade policy is identified to minimize the total expected servicing cost to the dealer. A five-step approach was also proposed to present flexible warranty contracts with optimized upgrade policies for SHPs, enabling the consumer to choose the most suitable warranty plan from among the options presented by the dealer.

Alqahtani & Gupta (2017a,b,c,d,e; 2018) have recently introduced warranty analysis for remanufactured products as a new field of research.

2.4 Maintenance Analysis

Parkinson & Thompson (2003) define maintenance as a series of actions that are undertaken during the use of a product to support its functioning at predetermined levels during the economic lifetime of the product. Given the lower reliability of SHPs, appropriate maintenance models are essential. Ait-Kadi et al. (1988) developed a block replacement policy (BRP) that relies upon old components for replacements. Yeh et al. (2011) presented two preventative maintenance (PM) strategies, the first of which held a fixed maintenance degree, while the second had an age threshold, with results demonstrating that PM reduces the total anticipated cost while increasing profitability.

Pongpech et al. (2006) presented an optimal upgrade and PM strategy for SHPs under lease. The researchers suggest that products be upgraded prior to leasing to optimize their value, with PM reducing the rate of failure and the total expected cost. Sheu & Grifith (2002) expanded upon the BRP through the inclusion of shock models. A new dynamic heuristic to support the optimization of opportunities to employ new and remanufactured spare parts in stochastic degradation was developed by Boudhar et al. (2014). Shafiee & Chukova (2013a) presented a taxonomy scheme through which maintenance and warranty models may be classified.

PM and warranties are interrelated, with the PM over the warranty period impacting the costs associated with warranty servicing (Kim et al., 2004). Chun (1992) assessed items sold with free replacement and modified warranty policies to identify the optimal number of PM operations to be performed during a given warranty period to minimize manufacturer costs. An additional model was developed by Chun & Lee (1992) to identify optimal replacement time for a system that is subject to imperfect PM actions in addition to minimal repair activity at failure. They determined that the optimal policy is that which minimizes the cost realized by the consumer within the specified warranty policy.

The first servicing model with minimal repair was presented by Nguyen & Murthy (1984). Therein, the warranty period is split into an initial replacement interval and then an interval for repair. The first interval's length is determined based upon anticipated warranty costs and the minimization thereof. This strategy was demonstrated to be sub-optimal by Jack & Van der Duyn Schouten (2000), with the optimal servicing strategy characterized by three distinct intervals, [0, x], [x,y] and [y, W] in which W is the warranty period. The optimal method is to perform minimal repairs in the first and last intervals and to employ minimal repairs or replacements with a new identical item during the interval [x,y], depending upon the age of the product at the time of failure. Murthy & Jack (2003) presented a review of the literature dealing with warranty and maintenance and suggest areas for future research.

Yun et al. (2008) explored two servicing strategies linked to minimal and imperfect repair. Within the context of both instances explored, a failed item is subjected to a minimum of one imperfect repair over the duration of the warranty period. The first strategy determines the level of improvement in reliability under imperfect repair based upon the age at which the imperfect repair was performed, while the second strategy functions independently of the age of the product. Jack & Dagpunar (1994) adopted the perspective that minimal repairs are made following failures and identified the optimal number of imperfect PM actions to be performed in addition to their timing, and the system age reduction that is experienced following each PM action during the period of the warranty.

The most common type of warranty that is applied to non-repairable products is that of the renewing free-replacement warranty (RFRW). Under an RFRW policy, a product that fails during the warranty period is replaced by one with a full warranty. The effects of an RFRW on an age replacement policy for a non-repairable product with an increasing rate of failure have been analyzed by Yeh et al. (2005). The researchers developed cost models for products with and without warranties, and then derived optimal replacement ages through analysis to minimize the long-run expected cost-rates of the products. The optimal warranty, and the optimal out-of-warranty replacement age from vendor and buyer perspectives for products with an increasing failure rate, is that RFRW (Chien, 2005).

Jain & Maheshwari (2006) presented a discounted PM cost model following the expiration of the adopted renewing pro-rate warranty (RPRW). PM policies allowing for buyers to negotiate over the warranty period have also been proposed (Pascual & Ortega, 2006). Murthy (2006) developed a framework needed for effective management of product reliability. Wu et al. (2011) considered a general periodic PM policy for the buyer, taking into account the value of maintenance and the cost thereof. The best PM strategies for the buyer are identified by considering the calendar time of the first PM action and the maintenance level that corresponds with it. Chien (2010) explored a warranty strategy that combined a fully renewable free-replacement warranty with a pro-rate warranty policy and based upon this analysis developed a model to identify the optimal preventive replacement age for non-repairable products within a combined warranty policy through the minimization of the long-run anticipated cost rate.

Further research has been conducted to explore the impact of imperfect maintenance rather than minimal repair or replacement by new items within the confines of the warranty period. Nguyen & Murthy (1986, 1989) explored a warranty policy in which a failed product during the warranty period is replaced by a repaired product, which generally has a lower rate of reliability than a new product. In the event such an imperfect replacement policy is adjoined to the RFRW, the 'imperfect RFRW strategy' is realized. Chien (2008) studied an imperfect RFRW strategy, in which it was assumed that manufacturers must provide RFRW, and that the warranty contract determines that the product sold must be replaced by a repaired one should the original one fail during the warranty period, with the replaced product itself also covered under an identical policy, thereby addressing the reduced reliability of the refurbished product.

Much of the extant literature on warranties considers those with a fixed period. While this is the case in research, in practice, many products are sold with the potential option of extending the warranty at the time of purchase, or in some instances at the end of the warranty period. Extended warranties provide a means through which manufacturers can maintain contact with consumers following the warranty period's expiration. Extended warranties and the link to consumer contact have been understudied in extant literature, although recently have become a greater focus. Padmanabhan (1995) applied an economic perspective to develop a mathematical model that considers consumer heterogeneity in usage habits. It was found that variations in consumer usage habits for products establishes variation in the demand of consumers for extended warranties (Padmanabhan, 1995).

An extended warranty model was presented by Lam & Lam (2001) that is comprised of a free warranty period and an extended warranty period. Within such a warranty, the consumer is provided the choice of renewing or not renewing the warranty at the end of the free repair period, with PM not being factored into the model. Various choices were presented, each with different cost implications for both manufacturer and consumer. Optimal policies for the consumer may be identified through the derivation of exact expressions of the total expected discounted cost and the long-run average cost per time unit.

Chen & Chien (2007) explored the instance of repairable products being sold under a free-replacement renewing warranty, in which minor and catastrophic failures were accounted for. Minor failures are solved through minimal repair, while catastrophic failures are addressed through replacement. Within the free-replacement renewing warranty policy, should a product fail due to a catastrophic failure, it is replaced with a new product alongside a new warranty, at no cost to the consumer. The expression of the expected total cost was assembled through the perspectives of both the buyer and manufacturer. The manufacturer's contractual obligation under the warranty per unit sold expires the moment the product passes the end-date of the warranty period without having experienced catastrophic failure.

Additional research has analyzed the life-cycle cost of a product with protection from both standard and extended warranty policies from the perspective of the consumer (Wu & Longhurst, 2011). It was assumed that the product in the study could have two types of failures, minor or catastrophic, corrected respectively by minimal repair and replacement. It was assumed that the length of the extended warranty may be selected from a prescribed list of choices. Optimal values of the opportunity-based age replacement were derived in addition to the duration of the extended warranty that minimizes the expected life cycle cost per time unit (Wu & Longhurst, 2011). Substantial extant research has been conducted on the various aspects linked to product warranty, such as warranty versus product, warranty versus maintenance, warranty versus costs analysis over the product life cycle and others (Murthy et al., 1990; Murthy & Wilson, 1991; Murthy et al., 2002, 2008;).

Product marketing in the modern environment is no longer solely concerned with performance, price and quality; it is also concerned with after sale services such as warranty and maintenance. The warranty is a contractual obligation on behalf of the manufacturer that is realized in connection with a product sale. The primary purpose of the warranty is to present the consumer with a post-sale remedy in the event the product fails to fulfill its intended function, within the scope of the warranty period (Blischke & Murthy, 1993). The warranty has been applied to meet many objectives, with increasing attention being paid to the practice from a variety of academic disciplines (Huang et al., 2008; Tong et al., 2014; Xie et al., 2014).

The provision of attractive warranty terms can promote the sale of items. While sales may be supported, manufacturers likewise realize additional cost as a result of servicing warranty claims. The costs associated with warranty servicing, depending upon the products and manufacturer, may range from 2%–15% of net sales (Djamaludin et al., 2001). An example of this is presented by General Motors (2014), with the 2014 annual report of the company representing total annual revenue of US$ 155.9 billion, with the warranty servicing cost on sold automobiles estimated at US$ 4.3 billion, amounting to approximately 2.8% of revenue. The total warranty servicing costs of US-based automobile manufacturers reached US$ 15.6 billion in 2014, the highest rate experienced since 2003 (Warranty Week, 2015). Due to the growing prevalence and cost of warranty servicing, manufacturers, particular those in the automotive industry, are prioritizing programs to reduce the cost of warranties and related servicing.

To reduce the servicing costs associated with warranties, appropriate preventative maintenance (PM) actions may be incorporated into the warranty policy. As opposed to corrective maintenance activities meant to restore a failed item to an operational state, PM activities are scheduled over the life cycle of the product to reduce the likelihood of item failures and/or to prolong the life of the product (Wu & Zuo, 2010). Whether failure is reduced or the life cycle of the product is extended, the manufacturer realizes reductions in cost.

From the consumer perspective, PM activities may reduce the number of failures experienced by a product and increase the availability thereof through a decrease in new product replacements. Given these facts, PM activities under warranty are beneficial to the consumer and manufacturer alike, although while purely beneficial to the consumer, they do represent an extra cost to the manufacturer. From the cost-benefit perspective of the manufacturer, PM programs are only worth incorporating insofar as the reduction of warranty servicing costs exceeds the additional costs incurred by the PM program (Djamaludin et al., 2001; Kim et al., 2004).

The pioneering research of Barlow & Hunter (1960) provided the foundation for the modern discourse, with the modeling and optimization of PM strategies becoming increasingly prevalent in modern research (Chang & Lo, 2011; Khatab et al., 2014; Zhou et al., 2015; Tarakci, 2016). The study being pursued herein is focused upon the optimization of PM strategies and warranty contracts through mathematical modeling and analysis. Much of the existing extant research focuses upon PM problems within the context of 1D warranties, such as: Djamaludin et al. (2001), Yeh & Lo (2001), Jack & Murthy (2002), Chen & Chien (2007), Wu et al. (2011), Bouguerra et al. (2012), Chang & Lin (2012), Shafiee et al. (2013c) and, Su & Wang (2014). Among these researchers, Kim et al. (2004) established a framework for analyzing costs through the interrelationship of warranty and PM policy, from a life-cycle perspective. Therein, it was noted that PM activities are performed at discrete time instants and that the impact of PM is characterized by the reduction in the virtual age of the product. This study will adopt a variation of the modeling framework offered by Kim et al. (2004) to support research.

Extant literature has further underlined the importance of developing warranty policies based on a 2D framework that accounts for the age and usage of items in order to build upon the competitive advantage of the manufacturer and satisfaction of the consumer (Huang & Yen, 2009). Two-dimensional warranties specify a usage limit in addition to an age limit and thus protect the manufacturer from experiencing high expenses from warranties due to high consumer usage alone (Moskowitz & Chun, 1994; Su & Shen, 2012). From the consumer perspective, the 2D warranty provides the capacity to be flexible in terms of the selected policy to ensure that the warranty chosen is most appropriate to the needs and/or usage patterns of the consumer (Moskowitz & Chun, 1994; Manna et al., 2006).

While many researchers have noted the importance of the 2D warranty and PM, few studies exist in which both concerns are integrated. To maximize the profit of the manufacturer, Huang & Yen (2009) generated optimal

2D warranty terms through a consideration of periodic PM activities that are assigned in terms of responsibility to the consumer. Shahanaghi et al. (2013) developed a mathematical model through which the optimal PM strategy may be identified within the context of 2D extended warranty contracts to support the minimization of the warranty provider's servicing cost. Cheng at al. (2015) proposed a warranty servicing strategy that combines imperfect PM and minimal repair, in which PM actions are implemented in a special sub-region of warranty coverage, with all failures being repaired minimally. Wang et al. (2015) endeavored to connect the 2D basic warranty and extended warranty to identify the optimal number of PM activities to perform during the basic and extended warranty periods. Jafar Raam & Mahsa (2015) compared the company's warranty cost and profitability by chooding between refurbished and remanufactured products as a strategy. Darghouth et al. (2015) presented a cost model to determine the optimal reliability improvement level for secondhand products sold with a free repair type of warranty (FRW). The secondhand product of age x is subjected to an upgrade action of a certain level u before it is sold. They look at determining the optimal upgrade level when not performing and when performing periodic preventive maintenance (PM) during the warranty period in order to reduce the risk of early failures. The optimal 2D PM strategy under fixed warranty terms was developed by Wang et al. (2015) to minimize the total expected warranty servicing cost from the manufacturer's perspective. Darghouth et al. (2017) presented a cost model for optimal reliability improvement of warranted secondhand production equipment. The secondhand production equipment of age x is subjected to an upgrade action of a certain level u before it is sold with a free repair warranty. They try to determine the optimal upgrade level when not performing and when performing periodic preventive maintenance (PM) during the warranty period. Two different PM strategies were considered: (a) periodic PM actions having the same efficiency level; (b) periodic multi-phase PM actions with a maintenance efficiency level which varies according to the phase. The model aims at helping the dealer to find the optimal upgrade level to perform before selling the secondhand equipment, and to assess whether performing PM actions during the warranty period, according to a specific maintenance strategy, is worthwhile in terms of cost reduction.

2.5 Conclusions

This chapter presented a thorough review of extant literature on environmentally conscious manufacturing and product recovery (ECMPRO), sensor-embedded products, warranty analysis and maintainability analysis. Due to the implementation of broader and stricter governmental regulations on businesses in concert with greater environmental awareness in society, it is essential that organizations be educated in terms of the environmental impacts of their operations. and learn to incorporate them effectively as a policy to increase their competitive advantage. To support this, professional education within relevant organizations is suggested in addition to the inclusion of such principles into engineering curriculums in programs of higher education.

3

Product Warranty and Preventive Maintenance

3.1 Introduction

The quality and reliability of a remanufactured product is uncertain for buyers. Therefore, buyers are unsure if the remanufactured products will provide the anticipated performance. This opacity about a remanufactured product could encourage the consumer to decide against buying it. With such buyer apprehension, remanufacturers often seek market mechanisms that provide assurance about the reliability of the products. One tactic that the remanufacturers often use is to offer warranties and recommend preventive maintenance (PM) on their products.

A warranty is a contractual obligation incurred by a manufacturer (vendor/seller) in connection with the sale of a product. The purpose of the warranty is to establish liability in the event of a premature failure of an item or the inability of the item to perform its intended function. The contract specifies the promised product performance and, when it is not met, provides some sort of recourse or compensation to the buyer (Blischke et al., 2011).

Product warranties have different major functions. First, a product warranty is insurance and protection, permitting buyers to transfer the risk of product failure to sellers (Heal, 1977). Then, product warranties can also signal product reliability to customers (Balachander, 2001), (Gal-Or, 1989), (Soberman, 2003), (Spence, 1977). Finally, the sellers use warranties to extract additional profitability (Lutz & Padmanabhan, 1995). There are a few articles and books that consider warranty policies for new products' supply chains. However, there are very few or none that consider the analysis of warranty and PM strategy for the remanufactured products' reverse and closed-loop supply chains (Blischke, 1995).

By offering a warranty, the manufacturer or remanufacturer gives a guarantee or assurance for the satisfactory performance of the product for a period of time, called the warranty period, when the product is used under specified operating conditions. In the case of product failure, the manufacturer carries out repairs, provides replacement at no or a fraction of the cost to the buyer or refunds full or part of the sale price to the buyer. The obligation of the manufacturer to protect the interest of the consumer against unsatisfactory performance of products by offering a warranty has become a major marketing tool. Servicing of a warranty results in additional costs to the manufacturer (between 1.0% and 15.0% of net sales – McGuire, 1980). However, it has marketing value also. By offering better terms or longer duration than competitors, the manufacturer gets a competitive advantage. Attractive warranty terms act as a marketing tool to boost sales. If the increase in revenue generated is greater than the cost of warranty servicing, then it is worthwhile to offer the warranty.

Preventative Maintenance (PM) has a variety of major functions, the first of which is that of insurance and protection. Through the insurance and protection offered by PM, the risk of product failure is transferred from the buyer to the seller (Heal, 1977).

Most new products are now sold with a warranty. Analysis of warranty cost for new and secondhand products has received a lot of attention. In contrast, the analysis of warranty and PM strategy cost for remanufactured products has not received any attention.

The rest of the chapter is organized as follows. Section 3.2 discusses the problem investigated in this book. A brief review of the different definitions of warranty are presented in Section 3.3. This is followed by a discussion on the warranties for remanufactured products in Section 3.4. Section 3.5 introduces preventive maintenance for remanufactured products. Finally, the scope and objectives of the book are given in Section 3.6.

3.2 The Problem Statement

In real life, there is a high level of variability and uncertainty associated with the conditions and versions of components that can be derived from an EOL product. These uncertainties create several problems in effectively controlling the warranty policy offered by the remanufacturer. There are some traditional ways to deal with such problems.

A common method to deal with the uncertainty associated with the functionality of a product is testing. Extensive testing times of some products and components result in high testing costs. In addition, the cost, time and other resources used in the testing of a nonfunctional component go to waste. Moreover, offering the wrong warranty policy will result in a high number of warranty claims.

Testing solves the uncertainty problem but increases the disassembly and remanufacturing costs. A cost-effective solution must have the ability to provide the required information regarding the version and the condition of the components prior to disassembly and remanufacture. Based on this information, the disassembly and remanufacture sequence of an EOL product could be determined at the beginning. This would eliminate the unnecessary disassembly and remanufacture of nonfunctional and unneeded components.

To this end, embedding sensors into products during their production offers a promising solution. These sensors could provide information on the version and the condition of the components prior to disassembly and remanufacture. However, there is a need for a quantitative assessment of the impact of using sensors on various performance measures of remanufacturing and warranty claims.

3.3 Definitions of Warranty

There are many different ways to define warranty. Thorpe & Middendorf (1979) defined warranty as "the representation of the characteristics or quality of product." The National Association of Consumer Agency Administration (1980) defined it as follows: "[A] warranty is an expression of the willingness of business to stand behind its products and services. As such, it is a badge of business integrity". Blischke (1993) defined it as follows: "[I]t offers protection when an item, properly used, fails to perform as intended or as specified by the manufacturer".

A warranty protects the consumer through repair or replacement of the product or return of full or partial amount of money by the manufacturer if the product is found defective or fails to perform as specified during the warranty period. Also, a warranty protects the manufacturer against any damage or failure of the product due to consumer misuse.

For remanufactured products, we can define a warranty in a somewhat similar fashion, that is, "[I]t is a contractual obligation offered by the remanufacturer or the seller and accepted by the buyer for a desired level of performance of the product during the warranty period". By "performance of the product", we mean those aspects of the product which are implicitly or explicitly covered by the warranty. Implicit obligations of the manufacturer are set out by regulatory laws and treated as unwritten and/or unspoken promises by the remanufacturer. The explicit coverage is the written or verbal undertaking against product failure.

3.4 Warranties for Remanufactured Products

In the process of deciding to purchase merchandise, buyers usually compare features of a product with other competing brands that are selling a similar product. The competing brands may have similar features such as cost, special characteristics, quality and brand credibility and even insurance from the provider. In these cases, other factors may differentiate the products, such as discount, warranty, availability of parts, repairs and other additional services. These factors, particularly the warranty, may be very significant to the buyer, since it further assures the buyer of the reliability of the product.

For new products, the warranty cost to the manufacturer (in a statistical sense) is the same for every new product if the manufacturer has good quality control. In contrast, each EOL product is different due to factors such as remaining life, usage and maintenance history. This makes the warranty cost to the remanufacturer statistically different for every remanufactured product derived from EOL items.

The importance of a warranty for remanufactured products is increasing because consumers want assurance they will be protected against potential lack of quality of remanufactured products and future costs of replacement/repair. Therefore, warranty management has become very important to remanufacturers. They need to estimate the warranty cost to factor it into the price structure. Failure to do so can result in the remanufacturers incurring loss with the sale of remanufactured items. Analysis of warranty cost for remanufactured products is more complex when compared to new and secondhand products because of the uncertainties in usage and maintenance history. Moreover, warranty policies similar to new and secondhand products may not be economically acceptable to the remanufacturer. Therefore, there is a need to test and compare these warranty policies for remanufactured products and estimate the expected warranty cost associated with these policies. There are other related issues, such as the servicing strategies involving the use of remanufactured spare parts during the warranty period.

3.5 Preventive Maintenance for Remanufactured Products

The remanufacture of a product through the application of used components is considered to be one of the most advantageous means of protecting the environment. Remanufacturing conserves natural resources, saves on the production cost of equivalent new goods, and also protects the environment through preventing the used products from being converted into waste instead of usable components. Despite such advantages, the remanufactured product market has not developed at the anticipated rate, influenced largely by consumer uncertainty pertaining to remanufactured products. Consumers generally prefer new products, particularly those with warranties, to insulate themselves from the risk of product failure. To address such concerns, many nations have enacted laws to protect the consumer from the early failure of secondhand products through the institution of mandatory warranty requirements. Anityasari et al. (2007) advance that the two central quality dimensions that must be addressed for remanufactured product are functionality and reliability.

The functionality of a remanufactured product is represented by the condition of the product at the beginning of its second life. The reliability of a remanufactured item is determined through an assessment of the probability of survival during the second life of the product. Within this book, remaining life of the remanufactured product will be employed to represent the general condition of the remanufactured product. To facilitate product upkeep and to slow the degradation process of the product, thereby mitigating the failure rate, preventative maintenance (PM) will be adopted.

PM policies of varying iterations have been proposed, implemented and studied under a variety of circumstances, including finite or infinite horizons, perfect or imperfect maintenance and periodical or sequential maintenance (Barlow & Hunter, 1960; Chun, 1992; Jack & Dagpunar, 1994; Pham & Wang, 1996; Yeh & Lo, 2001; Yeh & Chen, 2006a,b). The level of preventative maintenance performed is described or defined in terms of the age reduction or failure rate reduction that is realized through the process (Yeh et al., 2009).

An imperfect PM model was presented by Nakagawa (1981) and Nakagawa & Kowada (1983) for repairable products in which an element of the PM is determined by the reduction in age of the product. Given the relative mathematical simplicity and accessibility of age reduction as a measure of preventative maintenance, it is one of the most widely adopted maintenance policies (Guo et al., 2001). When failure is experienced with a product, minimal repair is the most commonly deployed corrective maintenance method applied to return the product to the prescribed functional state. Following a minimal repair, products are operational, although the failure rate is unaffected.

Having conducted an exhaustive review of the literature on the subject, it is clear that research on maintenance policies for secondhand products (SHPs) is limited. Chattopadhyay & Murthy (2000) developed models to estimate the anticipated warranty costs for SHPs sold with either free-replacement warranty policies or pro-rate warranty policies, delimiting PM action from the consideration. Two additional models were presented by Chattopadhyay & Murthy (2004) to determine the reliability improvement strategy to employ for items sold with a free-replacement warranty policy. Within the strategies presented, reliability improvement activities are undertaken only once prior to the sale of the product, and not during the usage period of the second life of the SHP.

Pongpech et al. (2006) considered lease contracts for used equipment and the maintenance performed upon related SHPS. The researchers found that within such contracts, an upgrade action prior to leasing the equipment, in addition to PM during the lease period itself, was performed to reduce the costs associated with corrective maintenance and penalties as a result of equipment failures. The majority of the literature on maintenance policies for SHPs, however scant, to this date is largely concerned with maintenance policies for used products from the perspective of the seller or leaser of the equipment.

3.6 Objectives of the Book

The overall objective of this book is to analyze the impact of offering non-renewing and renewing warranties on the cost of remanufacturing products. The goal is to test and examine the impact of using various warranty policies with PM for sensor-embedded remanufactured products. To this end, the following specific objectives are addressed.

The first objective is to quantitatively analyze the impact of offering a one-dimensional non-renewing base warranty (BW) policies with PM strategy for SEPs on the performance of a relatively simple remanufacturing facility. In this facility, one product type is remanufactured.

The second objective is to quantitatively analyze the impact of offering a one-dimensional renewing BW policy with PM strategy for SEPs on the performance of a relatively simple remanufacturing facility. In this facility, one product type is remanufactured.

The third objective is to quantitatively analyze the impact of offering a two-dimensional non-renewing BW policy with PM strategy for SEPs on the performance of a relatively simple remanufacturing facility. In this facility, one product type is remanufactured.

The fourth objective is to quantitatively analyze the impact of offering a two-dimensional renewing BW policy with PM strategy for SEPs on the performance of a relatively simple remanufacturing facility. In this facility, one product type is remanufactured.

The last objective involves comparing the different warranty policies (one-dimensional, two-dimensional, non-renewing and renewing) with PM considering a remanufacture line designed for remanufacture of multiple product types. Each product type has its own precedence relationships.

4

Warranty Policies for Remanufactured Products with Preventive Maintenance Strategy

4.1 Introduction

This chapter introduces a variety of one-dimensional and two-dimensional warranty policies for remanufactured products sold jointly as a part of the product price (basic warranty) or separately (Exteneded Warranty). Some of these are currently offered by manufacturers of brand-new products and some are offered for secondhand products.

A basic warranty (BW) is generally referred to as a 'warranty', and is commonly associated with products sold. A warranty (or BW) is a contractual agreement between the manufacturer (or remanufacturer) and a consumer that is established through the sale of a product. Within the warranty contract, the means of correction or compensation available to the buyer should the performance of the product be deemed unsatisfactory are defined. The warranty is an element of the overall sale, and the cost thereof is factored into the price charged to the consumer of the product. By contrast, the extended warranty (EW) is a voluntary contract that is entered into by the buyer through the separate purchase of a warranty contract, at times from a vendor other than the manufacturer (or remanufacturer).

This chapter is organized as follows: The sensor-embedded remanufactured products are introduced in Section 4.2. Section 4.3 briefly discusses the classification of warranty policies. The details of the various warranty policies studied in this book are given in the subsequent sections. Section 4.4 and Section 4.5 deal with simple warranty policies. Section 4.6 presents combination warranty policies. Section 4.7 discusses renewable warranty policies. Section 4.8 discusses two-dimensional warranty policies. Maintenance strategies for remanufactured products are the subject of Section 4.9. Section 4.10 summarizes all the policies presented in the chapter using two tables.

4.2 Sensor-Embedded Remanufactured Product

Remanufactured products are built using components retrieved from end-of-life (EOL) products and restored to good working condition. From the warranty point of view, each remanufactured item is unique in terms of its remaining life (RL) and condition. The RL of a product is influenced by the remaining lives, past usage and maintenance history of the EOL components. The remanufacturer can have comprehensive knowledge about the EOL components' condition if EOL products are Sensor-Embedded Products (SEPs). SEPs contain sensors that are implanted during the production of SEPs. These sensors monitor the critical components of SEPs. By facilitating data collection during product usage, these embedded sensors enable the prediction of product or component failures and estimation of the RL of components as the products reach their EOL.

SEPs, when used in concert with preventive maintenance (PM) and corrective maintenance, can improve the product's performance, effectiveness, reliability, maintainability, serviceability, recyclability and warranty costs. SEPs can also reduce the costs associated with product design, product operations and product retirement using the comprehensive in-depth data that is collected during their operation. SEPs, when effectively utilized, present the following major advantages:

Marketing. Data on patterns of product usage of SEPs may be collected and used to design products that better satisfy customer needs and address common usage patterns.

Design for Reliability. SEPs' main value source is data. The data on failure modes and their frequency enable designers to collect information beyond what can be collected using laboratory tests or field trials. This information helps in improving the reliability of the product.

Servicing. Through the data-tracking benefits of SEPs, repair/service personnel may readily obtain data on the likely causes of any failures encountered. This information may then be used to improve diagnosis and servicing decisions, and to order spare parts in advance of future failure or replacement, which saves time.

Preventive Maintenance. The ability of SEPs to facilitate monitoring of product condition can provide the data necessary to perform PM to avoid catastrophic product breakdowns, enabling convenient and cost-saving repairs over replacement costs or more substantial catastrophic repair costs should the problem be allowed to exacerbate.

End-of-Life Take-Back. Products' full life histories, including servicing data, can be accessed and utilized to optimize their EOL processing operations. The parts or components that are removed for disassembly may then be individually classified for treatment according to their life history.

4.3 Classification of Warranty Policies

A variety of warranty policies could be offered by remanufacturers. This book studies warranty policies for remanufactured products in a general setting and develops simulation models to study a variety of issues in warranty analysis in remanufactured products from the remanufacturer's perspective. We examine many different warranty policies which might be of potential interest to remanufacturers in the future. The warranty policies for remanufactured products can be divided into two broad categories:

1. One-dimensional (1D)
2. Two-dimensional (2D)

A classification of the different types of warranty policies for remanufactured products is shown in Figure 4.1. The policies in each category can be divided into two sub-groups based on whether the policies are renewable or not. Policies without renewing options indicate that if a remanufactured product fails during the warranty period, it is replaced/repaired by the remanufacturer and returned to the buyer without any change of the original warranty terms. Policies with renewing warranty options indicate that if a remanufactured product fails during the warranty period, it is replaced/repaired by the remanufacturer and returned to the buyer with a new warranty either identical to the original warranty terms or some other modified policy terms.

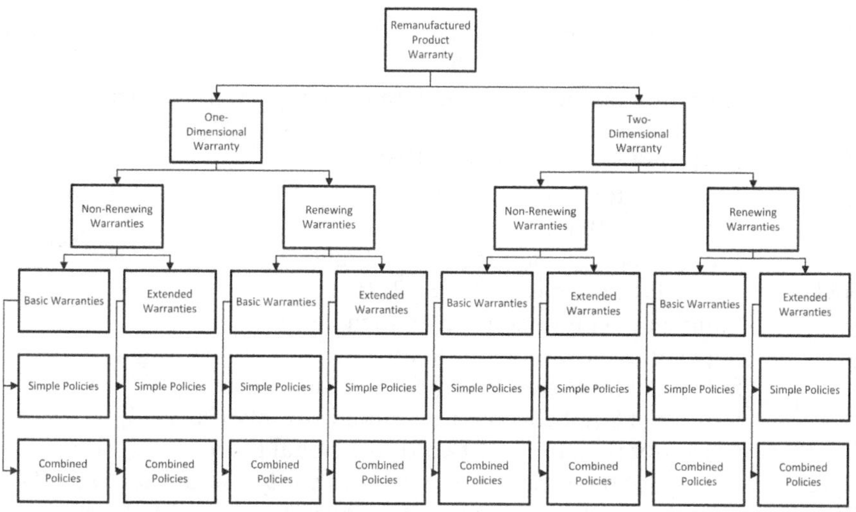

FIGURE 4.1
Classification for remanufactured products warranty policies.

Such policies may be further divided into BW policies and EW policies as described at the beginning of this chapter.

Each of these (that is, BW and EW) can be further subdivided into two subgroups: simple policies and combined policies. There are two famous simple policies, namely, the Free-Replacement Warranty (FRW) and the Pro-Rata Warranty (PRW) policies. A combined policy is a policy that incorporates the terms of two or more simple policies. The classification of remanufactured products warranty policies is shown in Figure 4.1. The rest of the chapter gives details of a large number of warranty policies belonging to this classification using the following notations.

Notations

W — Warranty period [For all policies]

W_1 — Sub-interval of warranty period [Policies 12, 13, 14, 15, 16, 17, 18, 19, 20, 21]

α — Cost-sharing parameter [Policies 4, 14]

k — Limit on number of failures for Money-Back Guarantee [Policies 11, 16, 17, 18, 19]

$C_s(RL)$ — Sale price of item with remaining Life RL [Policies 2, 17, 21]

$C_j(RL)$ — Cost of replacement/repair the jth claim, j = 1, 2, …

C_{jM} — Material cost of replacement/repair the jth claim, j = 1, 2, …

C_{jL} — Labor cost of replacement/repair the jth claim, j = 1, 2, … [Note: $C_j = C_{jM} + C_{jL}$]

TC_j — Total cost of replacement/repair the first j claims, j = 1, 2, … [Note: $TC_0 = 0$]

c_I — Cost limit on individual replacement/repair cost [Policies 6, 10, 13, 18, 19]

c_E — Cost limit with deductibles [Policy 7]

c_T — Limit on total (over warranty period) replacement/repair cost [Policies 8, 10, 19]

c_x — Limit under a deductible policy [Policy 9]

$S(RL)$ — Refund function [Policies 2, 12, 21]

n — Number of components in an item

S — Set of all the components in an item

I — Sub-set of S covered under the warranty [Policy 3]

E — Sub-set of S not covered under the warranty [Policy 3]

Ω — Warranty region in the two-dimensional plane

Ω_1 & Ω_2 — Subsets of the warranty region with $\Omega_1\ \Omega_2 = \Omega$ and $\Omega_1 \cap \Omega_2 = \emptyset$

RL_i — Remaining life of remanufactured component i at failure.

X_i — Usage of remanufactured component i at failure.

4.4 Simple Warranty Policies for Remanufactured Products (Group 1)

In this section, the first group of simple warranty policies are introduced. This group contains two well-known policies, namely, FRW and PRW.

4.4.1 Free-Replacement Warranty Policy (FRW)

POLICY 1 Free-Replacement Warranty [FRW]: Under the FRW policy, the remanufacturer replaces/repairs all failures over the warranty period at no cost to the buyer. The warranty expires after time *W* from the time of sale.

4.4.2 Pro-Rata Warranty Policy (PRW)

POLICY 2 Pro-Rata Warranty [PRW]: Under the PRW policy, the remanufacturer refunds a fraction of the sale price if an item fails within the warranty period. The buyer is not forced to buy a replacement item. Let *RL* denote the remaining life left in the item when he item fails after sale. The fraction refunded is given by a function *S*(*RL*), which is given by:

$$S(RL) = \begin{cases} C_s(RL)\left(1 - \dfrac{X}{W}\right) & \text{for } 0 \leq X \leq W \\ 0 & \text{for } X > W \end{cases} \tag{4.1}$$

where C_s (*RL*) is the sale price of the item with remaining life *RL*.

4.5 Simple Warranty Policies for Remanufactured Products (Group 2)

This section introduces the second group of simple warranty policies. This group contains three policies, namely, Cost-Sharing Warranty, Cost-Limit Warranty and Buyback Warranty.

4.5.1 Cost-Sharing Warranty (CSW) Policies

Under the cost-sharing warranty, the buyer and the remanufacturer share the replacement/repair cost. The rule for sharing can vary as follows:

POLICY 3 Specified Parts Excluded [SPE]: Under this policy, the remanufacturer replaces/repairs failed components if they belong to the covered set *I* at no cost to the buyer throughout the warranty period. On the other hand, if the failed components belong to the excluded set E, the cost of replacement/repairs is borne by the buyer. The warranty agreement will specify which components or parts are in each of the set I or E.

POLICY 4 Lump-Sum Cost-Sharing [LCS]: Under this policy, the total cost to rectify any claim during the warranty period, C_j, is shared by both the remanufacturer and the buyer. The buyer pays a percentage (α%) of the total cost of each replacement/repair and the remanufacturer covers the rest (100-α%). As a result, the cost to the remanufacturer and buyer are (100-α%) C_j and (α%) C_j for the jth claim, respectively.

POLICY 5 Labor or Material Cost-Sharing [LMS]: Under this policy, the remanufacturer pays for the labor cost of each replacement/repair (C_{jL} for the jth replacement/repair), and the cost of materials needed for the replacement/repair (C_{jM} for the jth replacement/repair) is paid by the buyer or vice versa.

4.5.2 Cost-Limit Warranty (CLW) Policies

Under the cost-limit warranty policy, the remanufacturer's responsibilities are determined by cost limits on either individual claims or total claims over the warranty period. There are four different limit policies, as follows:

POLICY 6 Limit on Individual Cost [LIC]: Under this policy, the cost of replacement/repair during the warranty period is subject to a cost limit, c_I. If the rectifying cost is below c_I, then it is totally covered by the remanufacturer and there is no cost to the buyer. But if it exceeds c_I, then the buyer will cover only the extra cost.

POLICY 7 Individual Cost Deductible [ICD]: Under this policy, the buyer pays for each replacement/repair up to a limit c_E, and any cost beyond c_E is covered by the remanufacturer. This implies that if a replacement/repair cost is c_E, then the cost to the remanufacturer is zero and if the cost is more than c_E, then the cost to the buyer is c_E and to the remanufacturer is the difference between the cost of replacement/repair and c_E.

POLICY 8 Limit on Total Cost [LTC]: Under this policy, the remanufacturer's obligation ceases when the total repair cost over the warranty period exceeds c_T. As a result, the warranty ceases at W or earlier if the total repair cost, at any time during the warranty period, exceeds c_T.

POLICY 9 Total Cost Deductibles [TCD]: Under this policy, the remanufacturer's obligation starts when the total repair cost over the warranty period exceeds c_x. As a result, the remanufacturer charges full costs of repair to the buyer if the total cost of repair during the warranty period is less than c_x. If the total repair cost in the warranty period exceeds c_x, then the remanufacturer pays the excess until the warranty expires.

4.5.3 Buyback Warranty (BBW) Policies

Under the buyback warranty policy, the buyer could return the remanufactured product during the warranty period and get a full or partial refund of the sale price from the remanufacturer. There are two types of a refund, either unconditional (money-back guarantee) or conditional on predetermined events such as if the number of failures over the warranty period exceed some specified limit.

POLICY 10 Money-Back Guarantee [MBG]: Under the Money-Back Guarantee Policy, all failures during the warranty period are replaced/repaired free of charge to the buyer. If the number of failures during the warranty period exceeds a predetermined value, *k*, then the buyer has the option of returning the item for 100% money-back. The warranty ceases either when the buyer returns the remanufactured product or the product reaches the end of the warranty period.

4.6 Combination Policies for Remanufactured Products

This section introduces nine different combination policies. As mentioned earlier, a combination policy involves terms of one or more simple policies discussed in Sections 4.4 and 4.5. Under these policies, the warranty period is split into two sub-periods. Each period represents one simple warranty policy. The two sub-periods may or may not be equal periods and are subjected to pre-specification in the warranty agreement.

POLICY 11 Limits on Individual and Total Cost [LITC]: Under this policy, the cost to the remanufacturer has an upper limit, c_I, for each replacement/repair. The warranty ceases when the total cost to the remanufacturer exceeds c_T or at time W, whichever occurs first. The difference in the actual cost of replacement/repair and the cost carried by the remanufacturer is paid by the buyer.

4.6.1 FRW-PRW Combination Policy

POLICY 12 [FRW-PRW]: Under this policy, the warranty period, W, is divided into two sub-periods $[0, W_1)$ and $[W_1, W)$. The remanufacturer replaces failed items at no cost to the buyer up to time W_1 (FRW). After that, if a failure occurs in the interval $[W_1, W)$, the remanufacturer refunds a fraction of the sale price and the warranty terminates (PRW).

4.6.2 Combination Policies with Cost-Limit Warranty (CLW)

POLICY 13 [FRW-LIC]: Under this policy, the remanufacturer repairs all failures in the interval $[0, W_1)$ at no cost to the buyer (FRW). The replacement/repair of a failure in the interval $[W_1, W)$ results in no cost to the buyer if it is less than or equal to c_I. If not, the buyer is responsible for the excess cost amount (LIC).

4.6.3 Combination Policies with Cost-Sharing Warranty (CSW)

POLICY 14 [FRW-LCS]: Under this policy, the remanufacturer repairs failures in the interval $[0, W_1)$ at no cost to the buyer (FRW). The replacement/repair cost of each failure in the interval $[W_1, W)$ is shared by both the remanufacturer and the buyer. The buyer pays a percentage of the cost (α%), and the remanufacturer pays a (100- α%) portion of the replacement/repair cost (LCS).

POLICY 15 [FRW-LMS]: Under this policy, the remanufacturer repairs all failures in the interval $[0, W_1)$ at no cost to the buyer (FRW). For failures occurring in the interval $[W_1, W)$, the replacement/repair costs are shared. The buyer pays for the labor cost, and the remanufacturer pays for the material cost (LMS).

4.6.4 Combination Policies with Buyback Warranty Policies (BBW)

This section defines four combination policies where the buyback option is combined with one or more of the non-buyback policies.

POLICY 16 [MBG-FRW]: Under this policy, if the number of failures during $[0, W_1)$ exceeds a specified value k, the buyer has the option of returning the item for 100% money-back and the warranty ceases (MBG). All failures during $[W_1, W)$ are replaced/repaired at no cost to the buyer (FRW).

POLICY 17 [MBG-PRW]: Under this policy, if the number of failures during $[0, W_1)$ exceeds a specified value k, then the remanufacturer refunds the full sale price (MBG). If the item fails during $[W_1, W)$ then the remanufacturer refunds a fraction of the sale price (PRW).

POLICY 18 [MBG-LIC]: Under this policy, all failures are replaced/repaired at no cost to the buyer during $[0, W_1)$ and on a cost-sharing basis over $[W_1, W)$. If the number of failures during $[0, W_1)$ exceeds a specified value k, then the buyer has the option of returning the item for 100% money-back (MBG). If the number of failures during $[0, W_1)$ does not reach the maximum number of failures, k, then the remanufactured product is covered with a cost limit on each individual claim during $[W_1, W)$, with the buyer paying the excess of any replacement/repair cost above c_I per claim (LIC).

POLICY 19 [MBG-LITC]: Under this policy, all failures are replaced/repaired at no cost to the buyer during $[0, W_1)$, and on a cost-limiting basis over $[W_1, W)$. If the number of failures in the period $[0, W_1)$ exceeds a specified value k, then the buyer has the option of returning the item for 100% (MBG). If the number of failures during $[0, W_1)$ does not reach the maximum number of failures, then the remanufactured product is covered with a cost limit on each individual claim and on the total repair cost during $[W_1, W)$. The buyer pays the excess of any replacement/repair cost above c_I per claim, and the financial responsibility of the remanufacturer ends when the total repair cost to remanufacturer during $[W_1, W)$ exceeds c_T or at W, whichever occurs first (LITC).

4.7 Renewable Policies

POLICY 20 Renewing Free-Replacement Warranty [RFRW]: Under this policy, the remanufacturer replaces/repairs all failures in the interval [0, *W*) at no cost to the buyer and supplies the user with a new warranty of duration *W*. This implies that the warranty ends only when there is no failure in a duration, *W*.

POLICY 21 Renewing Pro-Rata Warranty [RPRW]: Under this policy, the remanufacturer provides a replacement remanufactured product at a reduced price if a failure occurs during the warranty period *W*. Under this policy, the buyer is required to use the refunded amount to buy the replacement item from the remanufacturer. The amount refunded is dependent on how much *RL* is left and is given by a function *S* (*RL*) similar to the one in PRW Policy. The replacement item comes with a new warranty identical to the original one.

4.8 Two-Dimensional Warranty Policies for Remanufactured Products

Two-dimensional warranty policies can be viewed as an extension of the one-dimensional warranty policies. In a two-dimensional warranty, a two-dimensional plane is used to characterize the warranty region, with one axis representing RL and the other representing usage. Different warranty regions define different warranty policies.

4.8.1 Simple Two-Dimensional Warranty

POLICY 22 Two-dimensional Free-Replacement Warranty [FRW]: Under this policy, if an item fails in Ω, the failed item is replaced by another remanufactured item free of charge. The replacement item is warranted for the remaining region of warranty. Should this item fail again under warranty, the process is repeated until failure occurs outside the warranty region for the first time.

Depending on the shape of Ω, different warranty policies can result. This book considers four different shapes of Ω resulting in the following four policies.

POLICY 22(a) Rectangle Two-Dimensional FRW: The warranty region is characterized by the rectangle $[0, W_a) \times [0, U_a)$ as shown in Figure 4.2(a). The warranty terminates the first time a failure occurs outside the rectangle. The policy assures the buyer coverage for a maximum of W time units and/or U units of usage.

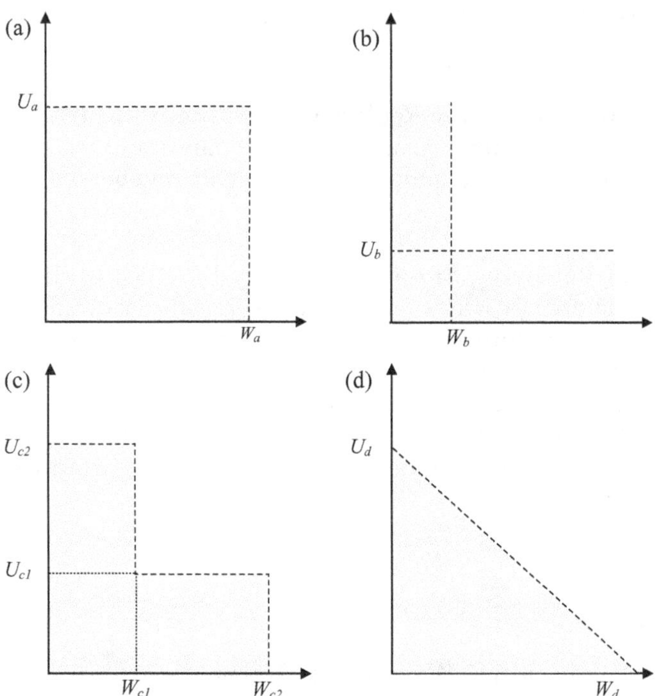

FIGURE 4.2
Warranty regions for policies 22(a)–22(d).

If the average usage rate (usage per unit time) is approximately U_a/W_a, then the RL and total usage when the warranty ceases are very close to W_a and U_a, respectively. If the average usage rate is low (less than U_a/W_a), then the warranty expires at time W_a subsequent to the sale, with the total usage at expiry less than U_a. On the other hand, if the average usage rate is high (greater than U_a/W_a), then the warranty expires before time W_a due to the total usage exceeding the limit W_a. As a result, for consumers with either high or low average usage rate, the warranty is not very attractive and tends to favor the remanufacturer as opposed to the consumer.

POLICY 22(b) Infinite Dimensional Strips FRW: The warranty region Ω is defined by two infinite dimensional strips, as shown in Figure 4.2(b). Under this warranty region, the consumer is guaranteed a minimum coverage for W_b time units and for U_b units of usage. The warranty expires when both time and usage exceed the limits W_b and U_b, respectively.

Under the policy, a consumer with a low average usage rate gets warranty coverage for more than W_b units of time, and a consumer with a heavy usage rate is covered for a time period W_b, with a total usage excess of U_b before the warranty ceases. As a result, this warranty tends to favor the low and high usage consumers rather than the remanufacturer.

POLICY 22(c) Four Parameters Two-Dimensional FRW: The warranty region Ω is characterized by four parameters, namely, lower warranty time limit (Wc_1), upper warranty time limit (W_{c2}), lower usage limit (U_{c1}) and upper usage limit (U_{c2}), as shown in Figure 4.2(c). Under this policy, a consumer is assured of warranty coverage for a minimum of W_{c1} time units and for a minimum usage U_{c1}, and for a maximum time period W_{c2} and a maximum usage U_{c2}.

The rectangle $[0, W_{c1}) \times [0, U_{c2})$ results in better coverage for a heavy user, while the rectangle $[0, W_{c2}) \times [0, U_{c1})$ results in a better coverage for a light user. In contrast to Policy 22(b), upper limits on time and usage protect the remanufacturer from excessive warranty costs.

POLICY 22(d) Triangle Two-Dimensional FRW: The warranty region is defined by a triangle, as shown in Figure 4.2(d). Here, there is a trade-off between the period of coverage and the usage.

Policy 22(c) and (d) offer a trade-off between the remanufacturer's and the consumer's interests.

POLICY 23 Two-Dimensional Renewing FRW: Under this policy, whenever a remanufactured item fails in the warranty region Ω, the failed item is replaced by a new remanufactured item free of charge. The replacement comes with a new warranty identical to that of the original one. As with the Non-renewing FRW policy 22, here, too, there are four different policies for the four different warranty regions shown in Figure 4.2, which are similar to policies 22(a)–22(d).

POLICY 24 Two-Dimensional Pro-Rata Warranty [PRW]: Under this policy, the buyer is refunded a fraction of the original sale price when the failure occurs in the warranty region Ω. The amount of refund is a function of the combination of RL and usage of the remanufactured item at the time of failure. The refund is unconditional, as the buyer has no obligation to buy a replacement item.

If the RL at the time of failure is given by rl and the usage at failure by x, the amount refunded is given by a function $R(rl, x)$, which is non-increasing in rl and x for $(rl, x) \in \Omega$.

Here, the warranty policy depends not only on the shape of Ω but also on the form of $R(rl, x)$. Depending on the shape of Ω and the form of $R(rl, x)$, there is a family of warranty policies possible. This book limits the discussion to the following two special cases.

POLICY 24(a) Rectangle Two-Dimensional PRW: The warranty region Ω is a rectangle similar to that for Policy 22(a), and the refund function is given by:

$$R(rl,x)=\begin{cases}\left(1-\frac{rl}{W}\right)\left(1-\frac{x}{U}\right) & \text{if}\,(rl,x)\in\Omega \\ 0 & \text{otherwise}\end{cases} \tag{4.2}$$

POLICY 24(b) Infinite Dimensional Strips PRW: The warranty region Ω consists two infinite dimensional strips similar to that for Policy 22(b), and the refund function is given by:

$$R(rl,x)=\begin{cases}\left[1-\text{Min}\left(\dfrac{rl}{W},\dfrac{x}{U}\right)\right]\times C_s & \text{if}\,(rl,x)\in\Omega\\ 0 & \text{otherwise}\end{cases} \tag{4.3}$$

POLICY 25 Two-Dimensional Renewing PRW: Under this policy, if the remanufactured item fails in the warranty region Ω, a replacement item is supplied at reduced price. This can be viewed as a conditional refund since the refund is tied to a replacement purchase.

Similar to Policy 24, different forms for Ω and $R(rl, x)$ define different warranty policies, and we consider the following two special cases.

POLICY 25(a) Rectangle Two-Dimensional Renewing PRW: The warranty region Ω is a rectangle similar to that for Policy 22(a), and the refund function is given by (4.2).

POLICY 25(b) Infinite Dimensional Strips Renewing PRW: The warranty region Ω consists of two infinite dimensional strips similar to that for Policy 22(b) and the refund function is given by (4.3).

4.8.2 Combination Two-Dimensional Warranties

In combination warranties, the warranty region Ω consists of two disjoint sub-regions Ω_1 and Ω_2, with different warranty terms for each region.

POLICY 26 Combined Non-Renewing FRW & Non-Renewing PRW Policy [FRW-PRW]: Under this policy, if a failure occurs in Ω_1, the failed remanufactured item is replaced by a new remanufactured one free of charge, and if the failure occurs in Ω_2, the buyer receives a partial refund. Here, the refund is full and conditional when the item failure occurs in Ω_1 and partial and unconditional if it occurs in Ω_2. The replacement item is warranted for the remaining warranty coverage.

Similar to Policy 24, depending on the shape of Ω and the form of $R(rl, x)$, a family of warranty policies is possible. The following two policies are considered.

POLICY 26(a) Two Rectangles Regions Non-Renewing FRW-PRW: The warranty regions are both rectangles as shown in Figure 4.3(a). Ω_1 and Ω_2 are given by:

$$\Omega_1=[0,W_1)\times[0,U_1) \tag{4.4}$$

and

$$\Omega_2=\{[0,W_2)\times[0,U_2)\}/\Omega_1 \tag{4.5}$$

and the refund function is given by:

$$R(rl,x)=\begin{cases}\left(1-\dfrac{rl}{w_2}\right)\left(1-\dfrac{x-U_1}{U_2-U_1}\right)\times C_s & \text{if } 0<rl\le W_1;U_1<x\le U_2\\ 1-\dfrac{(rl-W_1)}{W_2-W_1}\left(1-\dfrac{x-U_1}{U_2-U_1}\right)\times C_s & \text{if } W_1<rl\le W_2;U_1<x\le U_2\\ 1-\dfrac{(rl-W_1)}{W_2-W_1}\left(1-\dfrac{x}{U_2}\right)\times C_s & \text{if } W_1<rl\le W_2;0<x\le U_1\end{cases} \quad (4.6)$$

POLICY 26(b) Two Infinite Dimensional Strips Non-Renewing FRW-PRW: The warranty region Ω and the sub-regions Ω_1 and Ω_2 are infinite dimensional strips as shown in Figure 4.3(b). Ω_1 and Ω_2 are given by:

$$\Omega_1=\{[0,W_1)\times[0,\infty)\}\cup\{[W_1,\infty)\times[0,U_1)\} \quad (4.7)$$

$$\Omega_2=\{[W_1,W_2)\times[U_1,\infty)\}\}\cup\{[W_2,\infty)\times[U_1,U_2)\} \quad (4.8)$$

and the refund function is given by:

$$R(rl,x)=\begin{cases}\left[1-\text{Min}\left(\dfrac{t-W_1}{W_2-W_1},\dfrac{x-U_1}{U_2-U_1}\right)\right]\times C_s & \text{if}(rl,x)\in\Omega_2\\ 0 & \text{otherwise}\end{cases} \quad (4.9)$$

This policy reduces to Policy 22 when $\Omega_1=\Omega$ and $\Omega_2=\text{Ø}$ and Policy 24 when $\Omega_1=\text{Ø}$ and $\Omega_2=\Omega$.

POLICY 27 Combined Renewing FRW & Renewing PRW Policy [FRW-PRW]: If a failure occurs in Ω, the failed remanufactured item is replaced with a new remanufactured item at no cost to the buyer, and if a failure

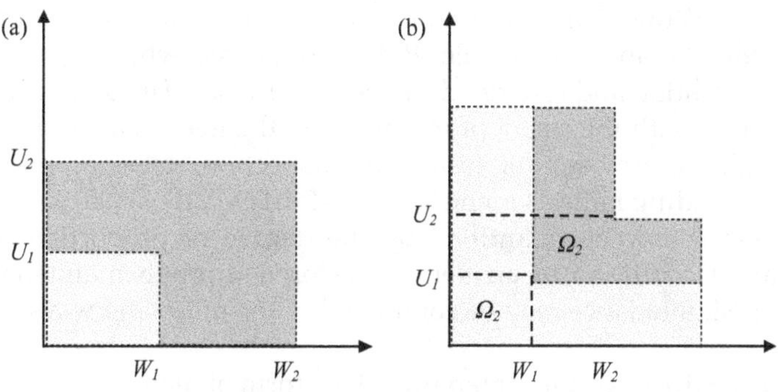

FIGURE 4.3
Warranty regions for policy 26 and policy 27.

occurs in Ω, the buyer is provided with a new remanufactured one at reduced price. The replacement item is covered with a new warranty identical to that of the original item. Any failure in Ω results in the remanufacturer refunding an amount $R(rl, x)$ if the RL and usage at failure is $(rl. x)$, and the refund is conditional as it is tied to a purchase.

Similar to Policy 25, depending on the shape of Ω and the form of $R(rl, x)$, a family of warranty policies is possible. The following two policies are considered.

POLICY 27(a) Two Rectangles Regions Renewing FRW-PRW: The warranty regions are both rectangles, as shown in Figure 4.3(a), and the refund function $R(rl, x)$ is given by (4.6).

POLICY 27(b) Two Infinite Dimensional Strips Renewing FRW-PRW: The warranty region Ω and the sub-regions Ω_1 and Ω_2 are infinite dimensional strips, as shown in Figure 4.3(b) and the refund function $R(rl, x)$ is given by (4.9). This policy reduces to Policy 23 when $\Omega_1 = \Omega$ and $\Omega_2 = \emptyset$ and Policy 25 when $\Omega_2 = \emptyset$ and $\Omega_2 = \Omega$.

4.9 Maintenance Strategies for Remanufactured Products

Product maintenance is split into two major categories: corrective and preventive. Corrective maintenance (CM) is conducted in response to a failure of the product or an inherent component. CM is often referred to as 'repair', with CM and 'repair' being used interchangeably herein. CM is defined by the *Military Standard: Definition of Terms for Reliability and Maintainability* as all actions performed in response to a failure to restore the item to a specified condition ("MIL-STD-721B", 1995). Given that CM is a response to a failure, it is unpredictable.

CM is typically performed in three steps: diagnosis of the problem, repair and/or replacement of the faulty component/s and the verification of the repair action. While CM is unpredictable and performed at random times, PM is systematic and predictable. PM is conducted while a product is in operating condition and is defined by the *Military Standard* as all actions that are performed with the intent of maintaining the item in a specified condition through the provision of systematic inspection, detection and prevention of any pending failures identified ("MIL-STD-721B", 1995).

Maintenance may be quantified by the degree or proportion to which the operating condition of an item is restored through maintenance (see Figure 4.4). Maintenance may be conducted in the following ways:

Perfect repair/perfect maintenance. This form of maintenance returns a product to operating condition that is 'as good as new'. Upon having achieved perfect maintenance, a product holds the same lifetime

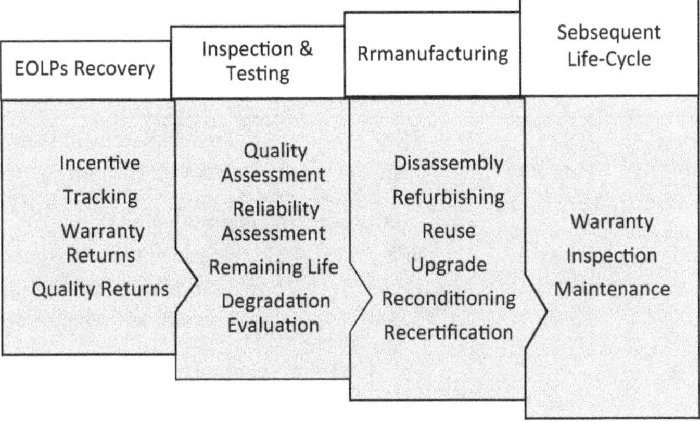

FIGURE 4.4
Preventive maintenance activities for remanufactured products.

distribution of failure rate function as a new product. In general, the replacement of a failed component or system with an entirely new one is classified as a perfect repair.

Minimal repair. Under minimal repair, the least possible maintenance actions are undertaken to restore the product to the failure rate it possessed at the time of failure. Barlow and Hunter (1960) pioneered the research on minimal repair, with the condition of the product labeled 'as bad as old' within the literature.

Imperfect repair/imperfect maintenance. These maintenance actions bring a system near 'as good as new' to a younger product age than the time when the maintenance was performed. Generally, imperfect maintenance is thought to restore products to an operating state between 'as good as new' and 'as bad as old'.

Worse repair/worse maintenance. Such maintenance action accidentally results in system failure, or an increase in RL without system failure but still falls earlier than expected. Worse repair or maintenance may or may not address the problem, but nonetheless decreases the overall life of the product rather than restoring it to the pre-repair state.

Worst repair/worst maintenance. Worst repair and maintenance results in the accidental failure or breakdown of the product. In line with the classifications presented above, PM is a minimal, perfect, imperfect, worse or worst form of maintenance. CM may likewise be classified as minimal, perfect, imperfect, worse or worst. The role of imperfect CM and PM as imperfect maintenance will be explored later in this book in concert with the types and degrees of maintenance that are employed in practice, determined by the variables of system type, cost, reliability and safety.

TABLE 4.1

One-Dimensional Warranty Policies for Remanufactured Products

Class	Policy	Abbreviation	Policy Name
Non-Renewing Simple Warranty Policies	Policy 1	FRW	Free-Replacement Warranty
	Policy 2	PRW	Pro-Rata Warranty
		Cost-sharing warranty (CSW)	
	Policy 3	SPE	Specified Parts Excluded
	Policy 4	LCS	Lump-Sum Cost-Sharing
	Policy 5	LMS	Labor or Material Cost-Shared
		Cost-limit warranty (CLW)	
	Policy 6	LIC	Limit on Individual Cost
	Policy 7	ICD	Individual Cost Deductible
	Policy 8	LTC	Limit on Total Cost
	Policy 9	TCD	Total Cost Deductible
		Money-Back Guarantee (MBG)	
	Policy 10	MBG	Money-Back Guarantee
Non-Renewing Combined Warranty Policies		**Combined Policies**	
	Policy 11	LITC	Limits on Individual and Total Cost
		Combined with-Free-Replacement Warranty (FRW)	
	Policy 12	FRW-PRW	Combination of Policies 1 & 2
	Policy 13	FRW-LIC	Combination of Policies 1 & 6
	Policy 14	FRW-LCS	Combination of Policies 1 & 4
	Policy 15	FRW-LMS	Combination of Policies 1 & 5
		Combined with Buyback Warranty (BBW)	
	Policy 16	MBG-FRW	Combination of Policies 11 & 1
	Policy 17	MBG-PRW	Combination of Policies 11 & 2
	Policy 18	MBG-LIC	Combination of Policies 11 & 6
	Policy 19	MBG-LITC	Combination of Policies 11 & 10
Renewing Policies		**Renewing Warranty Policies**	
	Policy 20	RFRW	Renewing Free-Replacement Warranty
	Policy 21	RPRW	Renewing Pro-Rata Warranty

The reliability of recovered EOL products and their components is an important factor within the context of the remanufacturing decision-making process. Upon having been refreshed, remanufactured or anything in between, the product must survive a second lifetime while performing at satisfactory levels for the consumer. To ensure fit, it is important that any warranty and maintenance policies offered are aligned with the actual levels of reliability of the remanufactured product.

TABLE 4.2

Two-Dimensional Warranty Policies for Remanufactured Products

Class	Policy	Abbreviation	Policy Name
Non-Renewing Policies	Policy 22	2D FRW	Non-Renewing 2D Free-Replacement Warranty
	Policy 23	2D PRW	Non-Renewing 2D Pro-Rata Warranty
Renewing Policies	Policy 24	2D RFRW	Renewing 2D Free-Replacement Warranty
	Policy 25	2D RPRW	Renewing 2D Pro-Rata Warranty
Combination Policies	Policy 26	2D FRW- PRW	Combination of Policies 22 & 23
	Policy 27	2D RFRW- RPRW	Combination of Policies 24 & 25

Maintenance is a significant determinant of product reliability and lasting quality (Wang, 2002; Garg & Deshukh, 2006; and Sharma et al., 2011). Nakagawa (2006) provided valuable and detailed information on the general field of maintenance theory and provided an extensive review of modeling maintenance policies (Nakagawa, 2008).

According to Shafiee & Chukova (2013b), maintenance policies for second-life (remanufactured) products during the warranty period has been understudied. Despite this, Yeh et al. (2011) presented two periodic age reduction PM models positioned to decrease the high failure rate of secondhand products. Kim et al. (2011) explored the optimal periodic PM policies of a secondhand product following the expiration of warranty. From the perspective of the manufacturer, PM activities are economically worthwhile insofar as they save on warranty servicing costs. Insofar as the warranty servicing costs exceed the costs realized through PM, they are profitable and worthwhile for the manufacturer. Given these facts, further research into remanufactured products and related PM policies is needed, as will be suggested in this book.

4.10 Conclusions

The warranty policies introduced in this chapter for remanufactured products are summarized in Table 4.1 and Table 4.2. These policies will be studied in the remainder of this book.

5

Modeling Warranty Costs with Preventive Maintenance for Remanufactured Products

5.1 Introduction

This chapter presents mathematical models to analyze warranty costs with preventive maintenance (PM) for remanufactured products. The first step is to model the failure claims over the warranty period. Here, the number of failures over the warranty period is a random variable that is affected by three factors:

1. The remaining life of the components derived from end-of-life (EOL) products
2. The total remaining life of the remanufactured products at the time of sales or repairs, and
3. The maintainability actions taken for the remanufactured products.

One can view a remanufactured product as a system composed of several remanufactured components. Therefore, failures could be modeled at the system level or the component level. Consequently, together with the three factors mentioned above, this can lead to a variety of possibilities for modeling failures over the warranty period. This chapter presents various models for analyzing remanufactured product failures over the warranty period with PM.

The rest of the chapter is organized as follows. Section 5.2 discusses the modeling of the failures of remanufactured products. Section 5.3 presents the modeling of PM and the effect of PM on the failures of remanufactured products. The modeling of failures at system and component levels are presented in Sections 5.4 and 5.5. respectively. Sections 5.6 and 5.7 discuss the modeling of the cost of the warranty and the cost of maintenance, respectively. The conclusions are presented in Section 5.8.

5.2 Modeling the Failures of Remanufactured Products

In general, products are complex and multipart, so that a remanufactured product can also be viewed as a system consisting of several components. Failure in a product occurs due to the failure of one or more components. Therefore, a remanufactured product or component can be categorized as either working or functionality failed. The times between two consecutive failures are modeled as random variables with proper distribution functions.

The action taken to make a failed product operational depends on whether the failed component(s) is (are) repairable or not. If a component is repairable, the remanufacturer has the option of repairing or replacing it with another remanufactured working component. If the repairing option is chosen, there are different types of repairs possible, namely, minimal repair, imperfect repair, perfect repair. These types of repair will affect the subsequent failures. Similarly, if a component is non-repairable, the remanufacturer can replace it with a remanufactured working component to make the product operational.

This book considers 12 different models. Four models deal with system-level failures and eight deal with component-level failures. Models Sl and S3 deal with failures at the system level for Sensor-Embedded Products (SEPs). In both models, the replacement/repair action is through minimal repair. Model S1 presents the case where the remanufacturer performs only corrective maintenance (CM). Model S3 presents the case where the remanufacturer performs PM plus CM, if necessary. Models S2 and S4 are similar to models Sl and S3, respectively, but deal with failures at the system level for conventional products (instead of SEPs).

Models Cl through C8 deal with modeling failures at the sub-system or component level. Models Cl through C4 deal with the situation where the failed components are non-repairable. Models Cl and C3 deal with SEPs. In model C1, the remanufacturer performs only CM, and the failed component is replaced with a new component (in case of shortage, it is replaced with a remanufactured component) and model C3 presents the case where the remanufacturer performs PM plus CM, if necessary, and the failed component is replaced with a remanufactured component. Models C2 and C4 are similar to models C1 and C3, respectively, but deal with conventional products (instead of SEPs).

Models C5 through C8 deal with repairable components and with two different types of repair actions (minimal and imperfect). Models C5 and C7 deal with SEPs. In model C5, the remanufacturer performs only CM, and the failed component is repaired using minimal repair action. Model C7 presents the case where the remanufacturer performs PM plus CM, if necessary, and the failed component is repaired using imperfect repair action. Models C6 and C8 are similar to models C5 and C7, respectively, but deal with conventional products (instead of SEPs).

The significant features of these models are summarized in Figure 5.1.

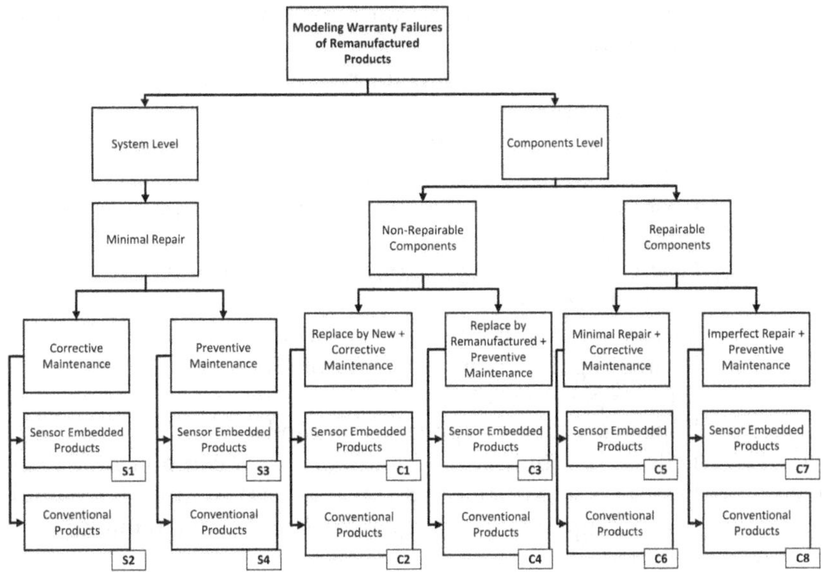

FIGURE 5.1
Models for warranty failures of remanufactured products.

The following assumptions have been made to simplify the analysis:

1. The failures are statistically independent.
2. The failure of a remanufactured item is only a function of its remaining life.
3. The time to carry out the replacement/repair action is relatively small compared to the mean time between failures.
4. Every item failed under warranty period results in a claim.
5. All claims are valid.
6. The remaining life of a product is always greater than the warranty period.

Notations

In addition to notations introduced in Chapter 4, the following additional notations will be used:

RL Remaining Life of remanufactured product at sale, return or fail
RL_i Remaining Life of remanufactured component i $(1 \leq i \leq n)$

C_E Cost per minimal repair for remanufactured product failures due to component (s) $\in E$

C_I Cost per minimal repair for remanufactured product failures due to component (s) $\in I$

C_1 Labor cost per minimal repair for a remanufactured product

C_m Material cost per minimal repair for a remanufactured product

$C_0(RL; \tau)$ Cost of improvement τ on remanufactured product of Remaining Life, RL

C_r Cost per minimal repair for a remanufactured product

m Level of PM effort

ν Virtual remaining life after performing PM activity

δ Remaining life increment factor of PM with effort m

T_n Time of performing the n PM

$E[.]$ Expected value of expression within [.]

$F_i(x)$ Failure distribution of a remanufactured component i

$F_{i1}(x)$ Distribution function for times to first failure of remanufactured component i subsequent to the sale of a remanufactured product

$F_{i2}(x)$ Distribution function for times to subsequent failures of remanufactured component i subsequent to the sale of a remanufactured product

$F_{ir}(x)$ Distribution function for times to failure of remanufactured component i subsequent to the sale of a remanufactured product

$F_{iu}(x)$ Distribution function for times to failure of remanufactured component used in replacement

$G(c)$ Distribution function for C_J

$G_E(c)$ Distribution function for C_E

$G_I(c)$ Distribution function for C_I

$G_i(rl)$ Distribution function for RL_i (for repairable remanufactured components)

$G_L(c)$ Distribution function for C_L

$G_M(c)$ Distribution function for C_M

$H(rl)$ Distribution function for RL

$H_i(rl)$ Distribution function for RL_i (for replacement remanufactured components)

$N(W; RL)$ Number of failures over the warranty period when Remaining Life, RL, is known using embedded sensor

$N_E(W; RL)$ Number of failures over the warranty period when failed remanufactured component (s) $\in E$

$N_I(W; RL)$ Number of failures over the warranty period when failed remanufactured component (s) $\in I$

$N_i(W; RL_i)$ Number of failures for component, i, over the warranty period

$N(W)$	Number of failures over the warranty period
$N_E(W)$	Number of failures over the warranty period when failed component (s) $\in E$
$N_I(W)$	Number of failures over the warranty period when remanufactured item remaining life, A, is unknown and failed component (s) $\in I$
$N_i(W; RL_i)$	Number of failures for remanufactured component, *i*, over the warranty period with component Remaining Life, RL_i
$\bar{C}$	Expected cost per minimal repair for a remanufactured item
$\bar{C}_E$	Expected cost per minimal repair for an item and failed remanufactured component (s) $\in E$
$\bar{C}_I$	Expected cost per minimal repair for an item and failed remanufactured component (s) $\in I$
$\bar{C}_L$	Expected cost of labor per minimal repair for a remanufactured item
$\bar{C}_M$	Expected t of material per minimal repair for a remanufactured item
C_{in}	Cost of replacement by a new component for component *i*
C_{im}	Cost of replacement by a working remanufactured component or by a new component when a remanufactured component is not available for component *i*
C_{io}	Cost of overhaul for component *i*
C_{ir}	Cost of minimal repair for component *i*
C_{iu}	Cost of replacement by working remanufactured component for component *i*
$h(rl)$	Density function associated with $H(rl)$
$h_i(rl)$	Density function associated with $H_i(rl)$
$g(c)$	Density function associated with $G(c)$
$g_E(c)$	Density function associated with $G_E(c)$
$g_I(c)$	Density function associated with $G_I(c)$
$g_i(rl)$	Density function associated with $G_i(rl)$
$g_l(c)$	Density function associated with $G_l(c)$
$g_m(c)$	Density function associated with $G_m(c)$
$r_i(x)$	Failure rate for component *i*
$\Lambda(rl)$	Intensity function for system failure
$\Lambda_I(rl)$	Intensity function for system failures due to remanufactured component (s) $\in I$
$\Lambda_E(rl)$	Intensity function for system failures due to remanufactured component (s) $\in E$
$\Lambda_0(rl)$	Intensity function for system failure of overhauled remanufactured item

5.3 Modeling Preventive Maintenance and Its Effect

Preventive maintenance (PM) activities normally involve a set of maintenance tasks, such as cleaning, systematic inspection, lubricating, adjusting and calibrating, replacing different components and so on (Ben Mabrouk et al., 2016). The right set of PM activities has the ability to reduce the number of failures and as a result reduce the warranty cost and increase customer satisfaction. Here, we adopt the modeling framework proposed by Kim et al. (2004) to model PM activities.

A series of PM activities are performed on remanufactured items at remaining life RL_1, RL_2, … RL_j, …, with $RL_0 = 0$. Here, the effect of PM results in the restoration of the item so that the item's virtual remaining life is effectively increased. The concept of virtual remaining life was introduced in Kijima et al. (1988) and then extended in Kijima (1989). In this book, the jth PM only reimburses the damage accrued during the time between the $(j-1)$th and the jth PM activities; as a result, an arithmetic reduction of virtual remaining life can be obtained (Martorell et al., 1999). Therefore, the virtual remaining life after performing the jth PM activity, v_j, is given by:

$$v_j = v_{j-1} + \delta(m)\left(RL_j - RL_{j-1}\right) \tag{5.1}$$

where m is the level of PM effort and $\delta(m)$, $m = 0, 1, \ldots, M$, is the remaining life increment factor of PM with effort m. Note that the effect of PM depends on its level m, $0 \le m \le M$, and its relationship with the remaining life is characterized by the remaining life-incremental factor $\delta(m)$, as shown in Figure 5.2. A larger value of m represents greater PM effort, hence $\delta(m)$ is an increasing

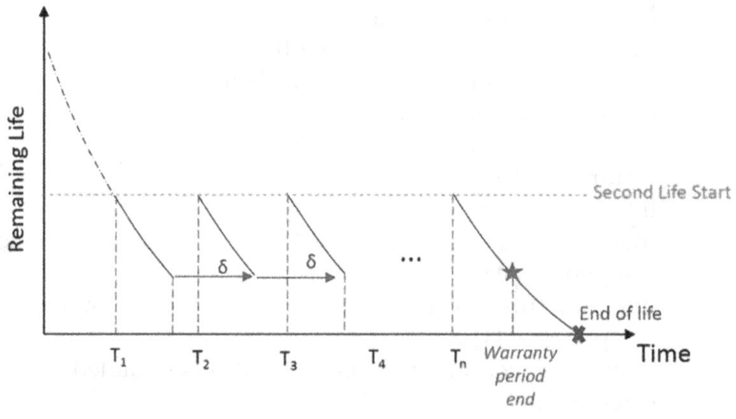

FIGURE 5.2
Scheme for PM policies for remanufactured products.

function of m with $\delta(0) = 0$ and $\delta(M) = 1$. More specifically, if $m = 0$, then $v_j = RL_j$, $j \geq 1$, which means that the item is restored to as bad as old (ABAO). If $m = M$, the item is restored back to as good as new (AGAN), while in a more general case $m \in (0, M)$, the item is partially restored, that is, the PM activity is imperfect. This concept will be used in the next section to derive the expected cost of warranty and maintenance.

5.4 Modeling Failures at System Level

This section discusses the models of remanufactured product failures at the system level.

5.4.1 Model S1 (SEPs with Corrective Maintenance)

The sensors embedded in the remanufactured products provide the remanufacturer with an estimation of the remaining life of the item at the time of sale, return or failure. The remanufactured product failure is modeled by a point process – a type of random process for which any one realization consists of a set of isolated points in time – with intensity function Λ (*rl*) where *rl* represents the remaining life of the item. Λ (*rl*) is a decreasing function of *rl*, which indicates that the number of failures increases as remaining life decreases. The failures over the warranty period occur according to a non-stationary Poisson process – a non-stationary (non-homogeneous) Poisson process is similar to an ordinary Poisson process, except that the average rate of arrivals is allowed to vary with time – with intensity function Λ (*rl*). This implies that the number of failures over the warranty period is a random variable with

$$P\{N(W:RL)=n\}=\left\{\int_{RL-W}^{RL}\Lambda(rl)drl\right\}e^{-\int_{RL-W}^{RL}\Lambda(rl)drl}\Big/n! \tag{5.2}$$

The expected number of failures over the warranty period is given by:

$$E\left[N(W;RL)\right]=\int_{RL-W}^{RL}\Lambda(rl)drl \tag{5.3}$$

In this model, a remanufactured SEP failure occurs due to one or more component failures. The remanufactured SEP is made operational through CM to repair or replace the failed components. No action is taken on the other working components. Thus, the failure rate after a CM is nearly the same as that just before failure. In this case Λ (rl) is the failure rate associated with the failure distribution for the item after performing the CM, as shown in Figure 5.3.

A simple form for Λ (*rl*) is as follows:

$$\Lambda(rl) = \lambda\beta(\lambda rl)^{(\beta-1)} \tag{5.4}$$

with the two parameters $\beta > 1$ and $\lambda > 0$ of Weibull distribution. This is an increasing function of *rl*. A value of $\beta > 1$ indicates that the failure rate increases with time. This happens because the remaining life of the product reduced with time, so remanufactured parts are more likely to fail as time goes on. The expected number of failures over the warranty period is given by:

$$E\left[N(W;RL)\right] = \lambda^{\beta}\left\{(RL-W)^{\beta} - RL^{\beta}\right\} \tag{5.5}$$

5.4.2 Model S2 (Conventional Remanufactured Product with Corrective Maintenance)

In this model, a conventional (without sensors) remanufactured product fails due to one or more component failures. The remanufactured conventional product is made operational through CM to repair or replace the failed components. No action is taken on the other working components. Thus, the failure rate after a CM is nearly the same as that just before failure. In this case Λ (rl) is the failure rate associated with the failure distribution for the item after performing the CM as shown in Figure 5.4.

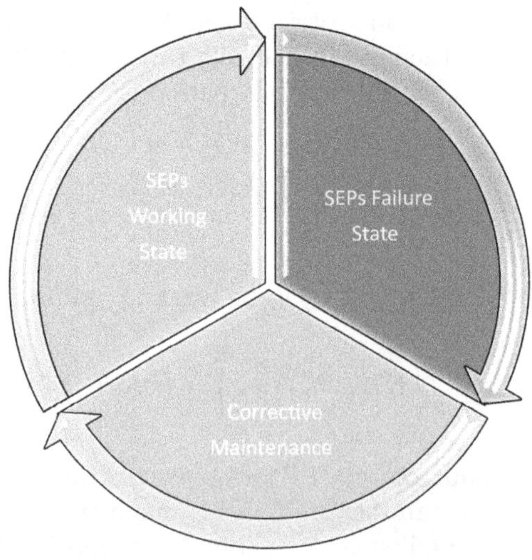

FIGURE 5.3
Model S1 for SEPs with corrective maintenance.

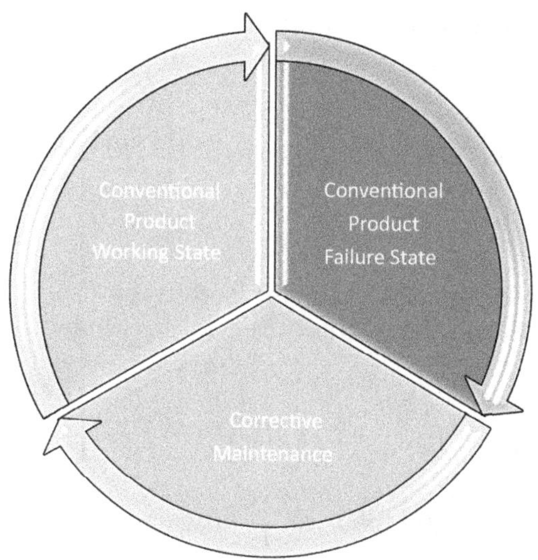

FIGURE 5.4
Model S2 for conventional remanufactured products with corrective maintenance.

In this model, there is no sensor embedded in the remanufactured product (conventional product) which leads to an unknown RL for the remanufactured product at time of sale. Therefore, the RL of the conventional remanufactured product is totally random and could be modeled with a distribution function, $H(rl)$. The RL of a remanufactured conventional product could be represented by estimated upper limit (U) and lower limit (L), depending on the product type with $H(L) = 0$ and $H(U) = 1$. Consequently, the density function associated with $H(rl)$ is given by:

$$H(rl) = \left[e^{-\rho L} - e^{-\rho a}\right] / \left[e^{-\rho L} - e^{-\rho U}\right] \tag{5.6}$$

This implies that the RL is given by a truncated exponential distribution with the mean value of the RL given by:

$$\mu = E[RL] = \left[(Le^{-\rho L} - Ue^{-\rho U}) + \left(e^{-\rho L} - e^{-\rho U}\right)/\rho\right] / \left[e^{-\rho L} - e^{-\rho U}\right] \tag{5.7}$$

As in Model S1, the failures occur according to a point process with an intensity function $\Lambda(rl)$. The number of failures over the warranty period is a random variable with:

$$P\{N(W) = n\} = \int_L^U \left[\left\{ \int_{rl-W}^{rl} \Lambda(t)dt \right\}^n e^{-\int_{rl-W}^{rl} \Lambda(t)dt} \Big/ n! \right] h(rl)\,drl \tag{5.8}$$

The expected number of failures over the warranty period is given by:

$$E\left[N(W)\right]=\int_{L}^{U}\left\{\int_{RL-W}^{RL}\Lambda(rl)\,drl\right\}h(RL)\,dRL \tag{5.9}$$

When Λ (rl) is given by (5.4) and H (rl) is given by (5.6), then from (5.9) the number of failures over the warranty period is given by:

$$\begin{aligned}E\left[N(W)\right]=&\left[\lambda^{\beta}/\left(e^{-\rho L}-e^{-\rho u}\right)\right]\left[e^{-\rho L}\left\{(L+W)^{\beta}-L^{\beta}\right\}\right.\\&-e^{-\rho U}\left\{(U+W)^{\beta}-U^{\beta}\right\}+\beta/\rho\left\{\left[e^{-\rho L}(L+W)^{\beta-1}-L^{\beta-1}\right\}\right.\\&\left.-e^{-\rho U}\left\{(U+W)^{\beta-1}-U^{\beta-1}\right)\right\}\\&\left.+\beta(\beta-1)\Big/\rho\left\{\int_{L}^{U}(rl+W)^{\beta-2}-e^{-\rho rl}\,drl-\int_{L}^{U}rl^{\beta-2}e^{-\rho rl}\,drl\right\}\right]\end{aligned} \tag{5.10}$$

5.4.3 Model S3 (SEPs with Preventive Maintenance)

In this model, a remanufactured SEP fails due to one or more component failures. The remanufactured SEP is made operational through CM to repair or replace the failed components. PM action is taken on all the working components. Thus, the failure rate after a PM is reduced, and the RL for the components is increased. In this case, Λ (v) is the failure rate associated with the failure distribution for the item after performing the PM, as shown in Figure 5.5.

Here, the remanufactured components of the SEPs are grouped into two sets, namely, Included (I) components and Excluded (E) components. Under the remanufacturer's policy, set I corresponds to all the components that are covered by the warranty. Set E corresponds to all the components which are not covered by the warranty. Let N_I $(RL;\ W)$ denote the number of failures over the warranty period which are covered and N_E $(RL;\ W)$ denote the number of failures over the warranty period which are not covered under warranty for a given SEP. There are two different ways to represent the attributes of Model S3.

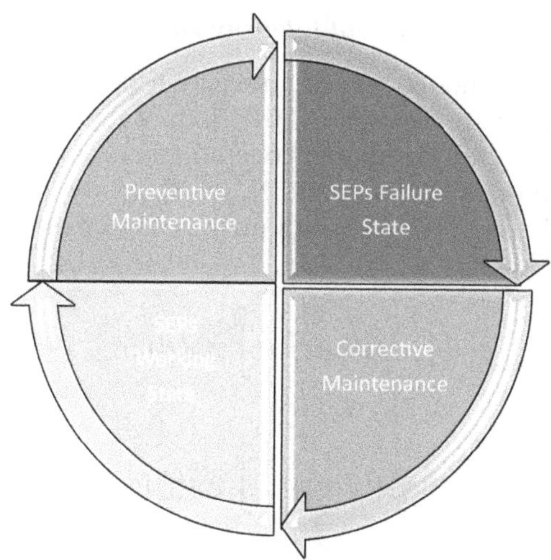

FIGURE 5.5
Model S3 for SEPs with preventive and corrective maintenance.

5.4.3.1 Method 1: Using Binary Random Variable

In this method, the failures are modeled as in Model S1 (Sensor-Embedded, Corrective Maintenance) by a point process with intensity function Λ (*rl*). Still, with each point (corresponding to a failure) there is an indicator in the SEP which specifies whether the remanufactured components failure is covered by warranty or not. This indicator could be modeled by a binary random variable Y with $Y = 1$ or 0 indicating that the failure is covered when $Y = 1$ or not covered under warranty when $Y = 0$. Let:

$$P\{Y=0\}=p \text{ and } P\{Y=1\}=1-p \tag{5.11}$$

Here, the expected number of covered failures over the warranty period is given by:

$$E\big[N_I(W;v)\big]=(1-p)\int_{v-W}^{v}\Lambda(rl)drl \tag{5.12}$$

Similarly, the expected number of not covered failures over the warranty period is given by:

$$E\big[N_I(W;v)\big]=p\int_{v-W}^{v}\Lambda(rl)drl \tag{5.13}$$

5.4.3.2 Method 2: Using Different Intensity Functions

Here, set I failures are modeled by an intensity function $\Lambda_I\,(rl)$, and set E failures by another intensity function $\Lambda_E\,(rl)$. Both of these are increasing functions in rl. Then expected number of covered and excluded failures over the warranty period, namely, $N_I\,(W; v)$ and $N_E\,(W; v)$, are distributed according to a non-stationary Poisson process with intensity functions $\Lambda_I\,(rl)$ and $\Lambda_E\,(rl)$, respectively, as follows:

$$E\left[N_I\left(W;v\right)\right] = \int_{v-W}^{v} \Lambda_I\left(rl\right)drl \tag{5.14}$$

$$E\left[N_I\left(W;v\right)\right] = \int_{v-W}^{v} \Lambda_E\left(rl\right)drl \tag{5.15}$$

5.4.4 Model S4 (Conventional Product with Preventive and Corrective Maintenance)

In this model, a remanufactured conventional product fails due to one or more component failures. The remanufactured conventional product is made operational through CM to repair or replace the failed components. PM action is taken on all the working components. Thus, the failure rate after a PM is reduced, and the RL for the components is increased. In this case, $\Lambda\,(v)$ is the failure rate associated with the failure distribution for the conventional item after performing the PM, as shown in Figure 5.6.

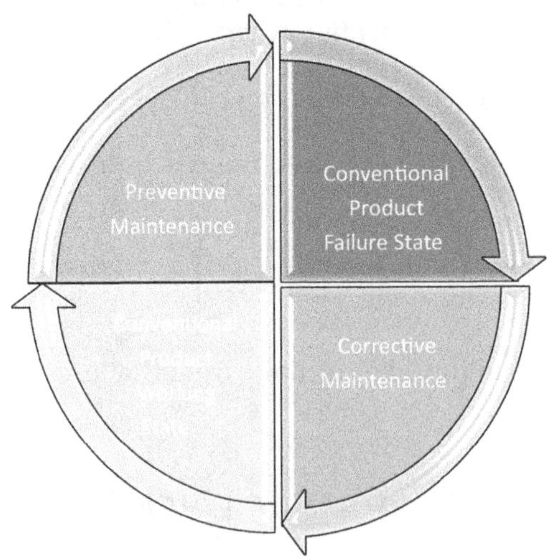

FIGURE 5.6
Model S4 for conventional products with preventive and corrective maintenance.

Here, the components are grouped into two sets, namely, I (Included) components and E (Excluded) components, as in Model S3. Let N_I (W) represent the number of failures over the warranty period which are covered and N_E (W) for not covered components under warranty. There are two different ways to represent the expected values of Model S4, as follows:

5.4.4.1 Method 1: Using Binary Random Variable

Here, the expected number of covered failures over the warranty period is given by:

$$E\left[N_I(W)\right]=(1-p)\int_{L}^{U}\left\{\int_{v-W}^{v}\Lambda(rl)drl\right\}h(v)dv \tag{5.16}$$

Similarly, the expected number of not covered failures over the warranty period is given by:

$$E\left[N_E(W)\right]=p\int_{L}^{U}\left\{\int_{v-W}^{v}\Lambda(rl)drl\right\}h(RL)dRL \tag{5.17}$$

5.4.4.2 Method 2: Using Different Intensity Functions

The expected number of covered and excluded failures over the warranty period are given by:

$$E\left[N_I(W)\right]=\int_{L}^{U}\left\{\int_{v-W}^{v}\Lambda_I(rl)drl\right\}h(RL)dRL \tag{5.18}$$

$$E\left[N_E(W)\right]=\int_{L}^{U}\left\{\int_{rl}^{rl+W}\Lambda_E(t)dt\right\}h(rl)drl \tag{5.19}$$

5.5 Modeling Failures at Component Level

This section describes the failure at the component level. Here, the first failure needs to be distinguished from the subsequent failures over the warranty period because all subsequent failures depend on the type of rectification action that is used to deal with the previous failure. In the case of a non-repairable remanufactured component, the failed component is replaced by a remanufactured or a new one, if necessary (due to a shortage in the remanufactured component), to make the remanufactured product functional again. In the case of a repairable remanufactured component, the remanufactured product can be made operational by repairing the failed remanufactured component. Three types of repairs are possible.

1. Minimal Repair, which restores the remanufactured product in a functional state to a condition similar to the one prior to the failure of the product without any change in the failure rate of the remanufactured product.
2. Imperfect Repair, which restores the remanufactured product in a functional state to a condition that is better than the one prior to the failure of the product but not as good as new, with a reduction in the failure rate of the remanufactured product.
3. Perfect Repair, which makes the item as good as new.

In this book, only minimal and imperfect repairs are used to rectify the warranty claim.

5.5.1 First Failure

Time to first failure of a remanufactured component depends on the RL of the component at the time of the sale of the remanufactured product. If the sensor information indicates that the original component (the component when the item was new) never failed or was always minimally repaired, then the RL of the component at sale, return or failure is considered to be the same as that of the item. Usually, the RL of a remanufactured component at sale, return or failure differs from that of a new component because the replacement or repair actions in the past are different from minimal repair. Therefore, the time to first failure under warranty needs to be defined. Let RL_i denote the remaining life of remanufactured component. There are two cases: either RL_i is known because of SEPs (Models C1, C3, C5 and C7) or RL_i is unknown in case of conventional remanufactured products (Models C2, C4, C6 and C8).

5.5.2 Succeeding Failures

The succeeding failures depend on the type of actions taken to repair/replace failed components. There are many different scenarios, depending on if the failed component is non-repairable (Models C1-C4) or repairable (Models C5-C8), and the type of repair or replaced component.

5.5.3 Model C1 (Sensor-Embedded Component, Non-Repairable, Replace by New)

In this model, the remanufactured component's RL is known due to sensors. However, since the failed components are non-repairable, they are replaced by new components. In this model, only CM is performed to rectify any warranty claims during the warranty period. Therefore, there is no effect on the remanufactured product's failure rate (Figure 5.7).

5.5.3.1 First Failure of Non-Repairable Sensor-Embedded Component

Let the failure distribution for a failed component be given by a distribution function $F_i(x)$ and failure density function $f_i(x)$. For a new component, with remaining life, RL_i, the distribution function $F_{i1}(x)$ for the time to first failure subsequent to the sale is given by:

$$F_{i1}(x) = \left[F_i(RL_i) - F_i(RL_i - x)\right] / \left[1 - F_i(RL_i)\right] \tag{5.20}$$

For example, if the failure distribution of a remanufactured component follows a Weibull distribution with shape parameter β and scale parameter (1/λ), it can be represented as follows:

$$F_i(x) = \begin{cases} 1 - e^{-(\lambda x)^{\beta}} & \text{for } x \geq 0 \\ 0 & \text{for } x < 0 \end{cases} \tag{5.21}$$

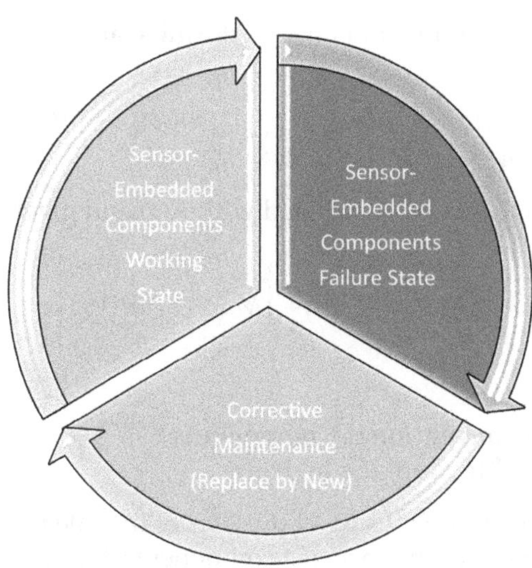

FIGURE 5.7
Model C1 for SEPs with non-repairable component replaced by new.

Then the function of the component remaining life is given as follows:

$$F_{i1}(x) = \begin{cases} \left[e^{-(\lambda RL_i)^{\beta}} - e^{-\{\lambda(RL_i - x)\}^{\beta}} \right] \Big/ e^{-(\lambda RL_i)^{\beta}} & \text{for } x \geq 0 \\ 0 & \text{for } x < 0 \end{cases} \tag{5.22}$$

5.5.3.2 *Succeeding Failures of Non-Repairable Sensor-Embedded Component*

Since remanufactured failed components are replaced by new ones due to the shortage in remanufactured components stock, the failure distribution of subsequent failures, $F_{i2}(x)$, is given by:

$$F_{i2}(x) = F_{i1}(x) \tag{5.23}$$

The number of failures during the warranty period is given by a modified renewal process with the distribution function for the first failure given by F_{i1} and for the succeeding failures given by F_{i2}, from Ross (1997), as follows:

$$P\{N_1(W, Rl_i) = n\} = F_{i1}(W) * \left[F_{i2}^{(n-1)}(W) - F_{i2}^{(n)}(W) \right] \tag{5.24}$$

where $F_{i2}^{(n)}(x)$ is given by:

$$F_{i2}^{(n)}(x) = F_{i2}^{(n-1)}(x) * F_{i2}(x) \tag{5.25}$$

The expected value of number of failures during warranty period is given by::

$$E\left[N_i(W; RL_i)\right] = [F_{i1}(W) + \int_0^W M_i(W - x)\, dF_{i1}(x) \tag{5.26}$$

where the renewal function associated with $F_i(x)$ and given by:

$$M_i(x) = \left[F_1(x) + \int_0^x M_i(x - y)\, dF_i(y) \right] \tag{5.27}$$

5.5.4 Model C2 (Conventional Components, Non-Repairable, Replace by New)

In this model, the component's RL at the time of the sale is unknown because of the lack of a sensor. In the case of a component's failure, a new component is used to replace it during the warranty period. As in Model C1, here, too, only CM is performed to rectify any warranty claims during the warranty period. Therefore, there is no effect on the remanufactured product's failure rate (Figure 5.8).

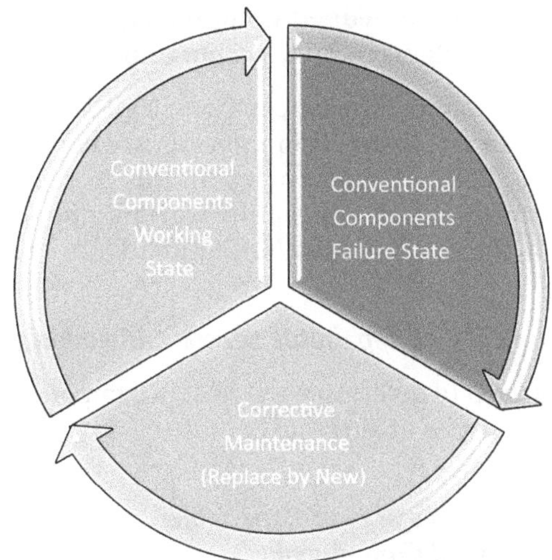

FIGURE 5.8
Model C2 for conventional products with non-repairable component replaced by new.

5.5.4.1 First Failure of Non-Repairable Conventional Component

The RL of new components used in the replacement is ranged and can vary from L_i to U_i according to a distribution function $H_i(v)$. As a result, the failure distribution of a new component is given by:

$$F_{iu}(x) = \int_{L_i}^{U_i} \left\{ \frac{\left[F(v) - F_i(v-x)\right]}{\left[1 - F(v)\right]} \right\} h_i(v)\,dv \tag{5.28}$$

The failure distribution for the first failure $F_{i1}(x)$, is given by:

$$F_{i1}(x) = F_i(x+v) - \int_{0}^{v} \left[1 - F_i(x+v-z)\right] dM_i(z) \tag{5.29}$$

where the renewal function given by (5.27).

5.5.4.2 Succeeding Failures of Non-Repairable Conventional Component

The failure distribution of succeeding failures, $F_{i2}(x)$, is given by (5.23). The expected number of failures over the warranty period is given by:

$$E\left[N_i(W)\right] = \left[F_{i1}(W) + \int_{0}^{W} M_i(W-x)\,dF_{i1}(x) \tag{5.30}$$

with $F_{i1}(x)$, $F_{i2}(x)$ and $M_i(x)$ given by (5.22), (5.23) and (5.27), respectively.

5.5.5 Model C3 (Sensor-Embedded Component, Non-Repairable, Replace by Remanufactured)

In this model, the remanufactured component's RL is known because of sensors. However, since the failed components are non-repairable, they are replaced by remanufactured components. In this model, CM is performed to rectify any warranty claims during the warranty period and PM is performed on all the working components. (Figure 5.9).

5.5.5.1 First Failure of Non-Repairable Sensor-Embedded Component

Since the sensor is used to determine the RL of a component, the distribution for the first failure, $F_{i1}(x)$, is given by (5.20).

5.5.5.2 Succeeding Failures of Non-Repairable Sensor-Embedded Component

A failed component is replaced by a remanufactured component with probability p that the remanufactured component is available or by a new one with probability (1-p). The distribution for succeeding failures, $F_{i2}(x)$, is given by:

$$F_{i2}(x) = p\,F_i(x) + (1-p)F_{iu}(x) \tag{5.31}$$

where F_{iu} (x) is given by (5.28).

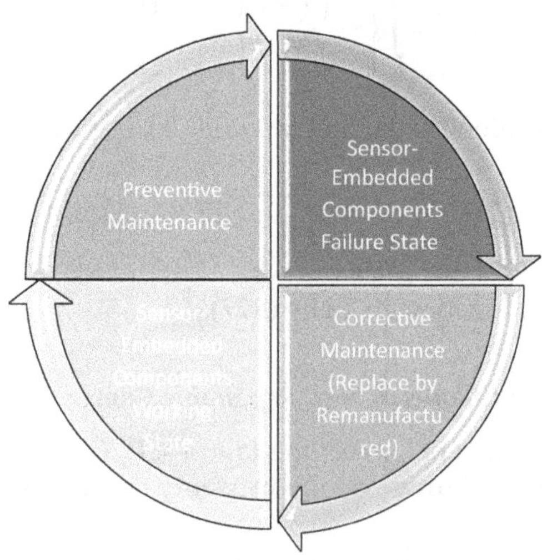

FIGURE 5.9
Model C3 for SEPs with non-repairable component replaced by remanufactured.

Accordingly, the expected number of failures over the warranty period is given by:

$$E\left[N_i\left(W;v_i\right)\right]=\left[F_{i1}\left(W\right)+\int_0^W M_{i2}\left(W-x\right)dF_{i1}\left(x\right) \tag{5.32}$$

where $M_{i2}(x)$ is the renewal function associated with $F_{i2}(x)$ given by (5.31). $F_{i1}(x)$ is given by (5.20).

5.5.6 Model C4 (Conventional Components, Non-Repairable, Replace by Remanufactured)

This model deals with a conventional product with no sensor embedded in the failed component. In this model, a CM is performed to rectify any warranty claims during the warranty period, and PM is performed on all the working components (Figure 5.10).

The RL of remanufactured components used in the replacement is ranged and can vary from L_i to U_i, according to a distribution function $H_i(v)$. As a result, the failure distribution of a remanufactured component is given by:

$$F_{iu}\left(x\right)=\int_{L_i}^{U_i}\left\{\frac{\left[F\left(v\right)-F_i\left(v-x\right)\right]}{\left[1-F\left(v\right)\right]}\right\}h_i\left(v\right)dv \tag{5.33}$$

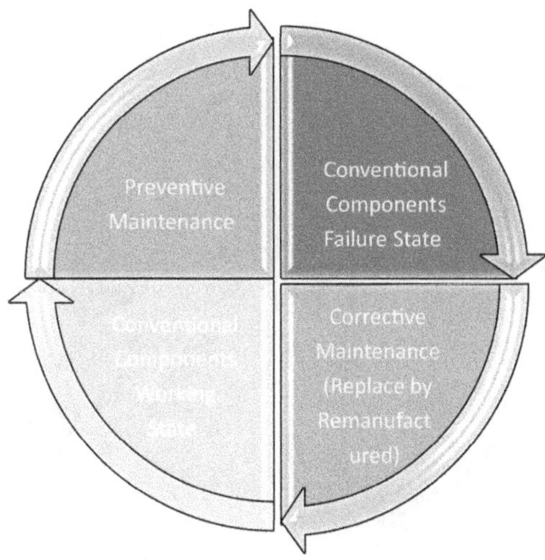

FIGURE 5.10
Model C4 for conventional product with non-repairable component replaced by remanufactured.

5.5.6.1 First Failure of Non-Repairable Conventional Component

The failure distribution for the first failure, $F_{i1}(x)$, is given by:

$$F_{i1}(x) = F_i(x+v) - \int_0^v [1 - F_i(x+v-z)] dM_i(z) \tag{5.34}$$

where the renewal function given by (5.27).

5.5.6.2 Succeeding Failures of Non-Repairable Conventional Component

In the meantime, a failed component is replaced by a remanufactured one with distribution for succeeding failures, $F_{i2}(x)$, given by (5.31):

$$F_{i2}(x) = pF_i(x) + (1-p)F_{iu}(x) \tag{5.35}$$

where $F_{iu}(x)$ is given by (5.28).

5.5.7 Model C5 (Sensor-Embedded Component, Repairable with Corrective Maintenance)

In this model, the sensor is used to determine the RL of a component. The remanufactured SEP is minimally repaired by performing CM during any warranty claim to ensure product functionality (Figure 5.11). This action restores the SEP to the same condition as before failure without changing the failure rate of the remanufactured SEP.

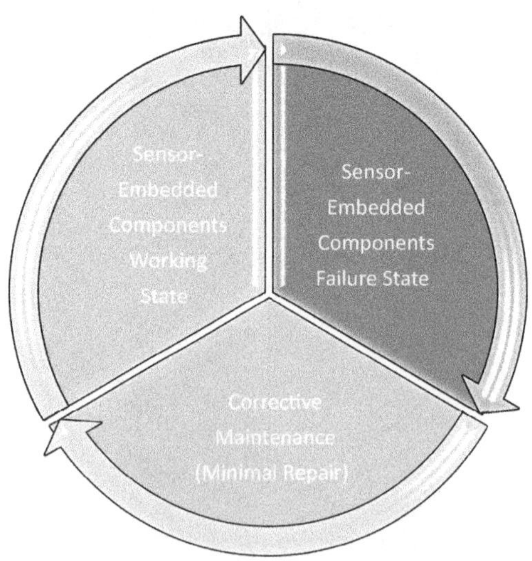

FIGURE 5.11
Model C5 for SEPs with repairable component repair using minimal repair.

The failures occur according to a non-stationary Poisson process with intensity function given by the failure rate:

$$r_i(x) = f_i(x)/[1 - F_i(x)] \tag{5.36}$$

The expected number of failures over the warranty period is given by:

$$E[N_i(W; A_i)] = \int_{A_i}^{A_i+W} r_i(x)dx \tag{5.37}$$

5.5.8 Model C6 (Conventional Components, Repairable with Corrective Maintenance)

In this model, the RL of a component is unknown because of the lack of a sensor. The component RL is modeled as a random variable with a distribution function $G_i(rl)$. All failures over the warranty period are minimally repaired by performing CM during any warranty claim to ensure product functionality (Figure 5.12). This action restores the conventional product to the same condition as before failure without changing the failure rate of the remanufactured product. The failures occur according to a non-stationary Poisson process with intensity function given by (5.36).

Then, conditioned on $RL_i = rl$, the expected number of failures over the warranty period is given by:

$$E[N_i(W \mid RL_i = rl)] = \int_{rl-W}^{rl} r_i(x)dx \tag{5.38}$$

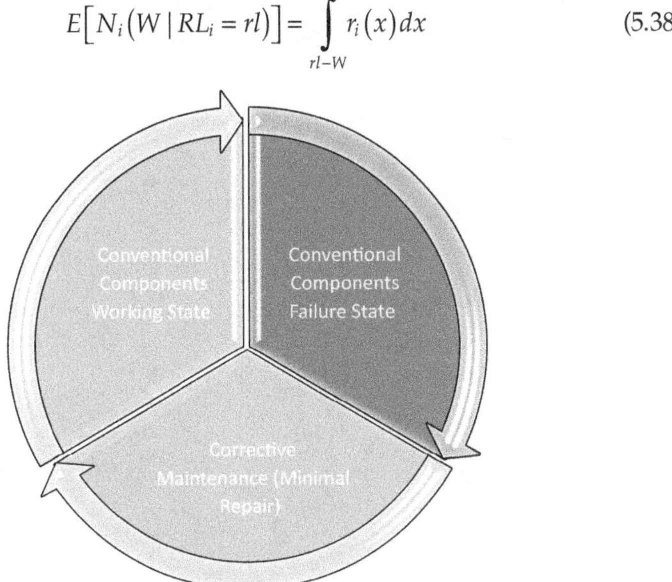

FIGURE 5.12
Model C6 for SEPs with repairable component repair using minimal repair.

On removing the condition, the expected number of failures over the warranty period is given by:

$$E\left[N_i(W)\right] = \int_0^{\infty} E\left[N_i(W \mid RL_i = rl)\right] dG_i(rl) \tag{5.39}$$

5.5.9 Model C7 (Sensor-Embedded Component, Repairable with Preventive Maintenance)

In this model, the failed components are repaired, and the failure distribution of a repaired component is given by $F_{ir}(x)$, which is different from $F_i(x)$, the failure distribution of a remanufactured component. All failures over the warranty period are imperfectly repaired by performing CM and PM during any warranty claim (Figure 5.13). This restores the remanufactured product functionality to a condition better than prior to failure but not as good as new, with a reduction in the failure rate of the remanufactured product.

As a result, the first and subsequent failures over the warranty period depend on RL_i, the remaining life of component of the SEP relative to the RL at which the component was subjected to the last repair.

5.5.9.1 *First Failure of Repairable Sensor-Embedded Component*

If the component never failed before, then the distribution for first failure is given by (5.20). If $RL_i < RL$, it implies that the sensor-embedded component

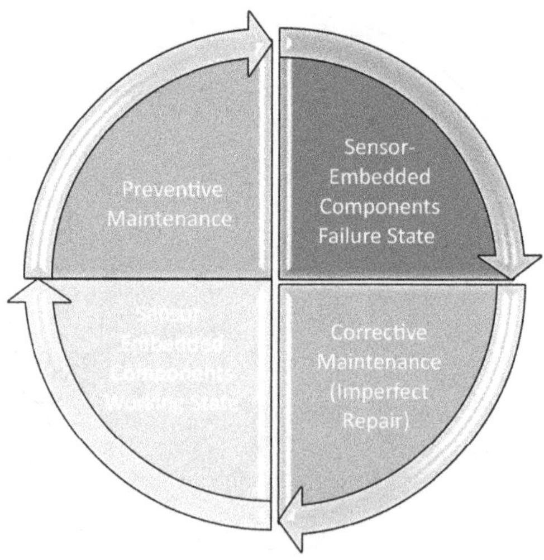

FIGURE 5.13
Model C7 for SEPs with repairable component replaced using imperfect repair.

has failed one or more times before and in that case the distribution for first failure is given by:

$$F_{i1}(x) = \left[F_{ir}(v_i + x) - F_{ir}(v_i)\right] / \left[1 - \left[F_{ir}(v)\right]\right] \quad (5.40)$$

5.5.9.2 Succeeding Failures of Repairable Sensor-Embedded Component

The failure distribution is given by:

$$F_{i2}(x) = F_{ir}(x) \quad (5.41)$$

The number of failures during the warranty period $N_i(W; v_i)$ is given by a modified renewal process with the distribution function for the first failure given by F_{i1} and for the subsequent failures given by F_{i2}.

As a result, the expected number of failures during the warranty period is given by (5.30), with F_{i1} given by either (5.20) or (5.40), and $M_{i2}(x)$ is the renewal function associated with $F_{i2}(x)$, given by (5.41).

5.5.10 Model C8 (Conventional Product, Repairable with Preventive Maintenance)

In this model, the RL of a component relative to the time at which the component was subjected to the last repair is unknown due to lack of a sensor. All failures over the warranty period are imperfectly repaired by performing CM and PM during any warranty claim (Figure 5.14). This restores the remanufactured product functionality to a condition better than prior to failure but

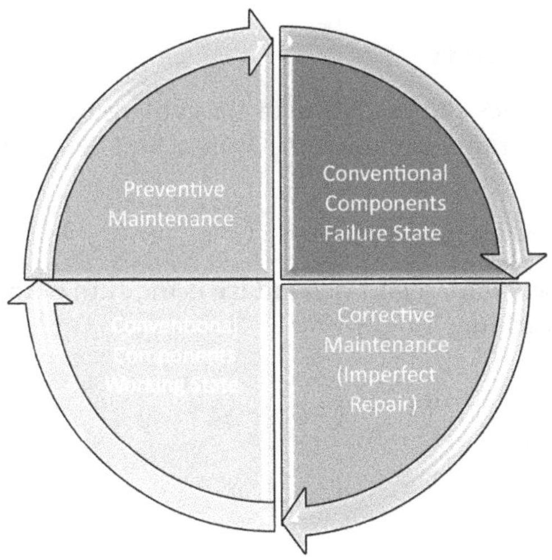

FIGURE 5.14
Model C8 for conventional product with repairable component replaced using imperfect repair

not as good as new, with a reduction in the failure rate of the remanufactured product. Therefore, RL_i is presented using a modified renewal process.

5.5.10.1 First Failure of Repairable Sensor-Embedded Component

$$F_{i1}(x) = F_i(x+v) - \int_0^v [1 - F_i(x+v-z)]\, dM_{id}(z) \tag{5.42}$$

where $M_{id}(x)$ is the modified renewal function, given by:

$$M_{id}(x) = \left[F_i(x) + \int_0^x M_{i2}(x-y)\, dF_i(y) \right] \tag{5.43}$$

where M_{i2} (x) is the renewal function associated with $F_{i2}(x)$ given by (5. 41).

5.5.10.2 Succeeding Failures of Repairable Sensor-Embedded Component

Succeeding failures are given by (5.41). The number of failures during the warranty period is given by a modified renewal process with the distribution function for the first failure given by F_{i1} and for the subsequent failures given by F_{i2}. Accordingly, the expected number of failures during the warranty period is given by (5.34) with F_{i1} given by (5.42), and M_{i2} (x) is the renewal function associated with F_{i2} (x) given by (5.41).

5.6 Costs of Warranty

This section discusses the modeling of the replacement/repair cost of each failure over the warranty period at the system and component levels.

5.6.1 Replacement/Repair Cost

The cost for replacement/repair of a failure is the sum of many different cost elements. These include:

1. Administrative Cost;
2. Material Cost;
3. Labor Cost;
4. Handling Cost;
5. Holding cost of products, components and materials;
6. Backorder cost of products, components and materials;

7. Disassembly cost;
8. Disposal cost of products, components and materials;
9. Testing cost;
10. Transportation cost;

5.6.2 Cost of Repair at System Level

The cost per repair, C_s, is a random variable that varies due to the failure of one or more components, and the cost of replacement fluctuates with the type of component involved. The replacement of failed components has negligible effect on the failure rate of the item when performing CM and minimal repair.

Therefore, the cost of each repair at the system level can be represented using a distribution function for costs of each minimal repair given by $G(c)$, that is:

$$G(c) = Prob\{C_r \leq c\} \tag{5.44}$$

Then the expected cost of each minimal repair is given by:

$$\bar{c} = \int_0^\infty cg(c)dc \tag{5.45}$$

If the distribution function for costs of each minimal repair follows an exponential distribution, as follows:

$$G(c) = 1 - e^{-\rho c} \tag{5.46}$$

Then the expected cost of each minimal repair is given by:

$$\bar{c} = [1/\rho] \tag{5.47}$$

Likewise, the cost of labor (C_L) and the cost of materials (C_M) for each repair is modeled by distribution functions $G_l(c)$ and $G_M(c)$, respectively, with means $\bar{c}_L$ for labor and $\bar{c}_M$ for materials. The cost of each repair for failures belong to the set E (C_E) and set I (C_I), and are modeled by distribution functions $G_E(c)$ and $G_I(c)$, respectively, with means $\bar{c}_E$ and $\bar{c}_I$. Expressions for these mean values are given by (5.45) using the appropriate distribution function.

5.6.3 Cost of Repair at Component Level

The action to repair\replace a failed remanufactured component depends on whether the component is repairable or not. Moreover, the variation in cost for each replacement/repair is very little, and therefore the cost of each replacement/repair can be modeled as a deterministic quantity.

Non-repairable failed components can be replaced by remanufactured components or new components (in case of shortage). Let c_{in} and c_{ir} be the cost of replacing a failed component by a new or remanufactured component, respectively.

Occasionally, a remanufactured component is not available when needed for replacement of a failed component. In such case, one needs to use a new component. Let (p_i) denote the probability that a remanufactured component is available when needed, and (1-p_i) is the probability that a new component is to be used due to the unavailability of a remanufactured component for replacement. Therefore, the expected cost of each replacement is given by:

$$c_c = p_i c_{\text{ir}} + \left(1 - p_i\right) c_{\text{in}} \tag{5.48}$$

For repairable components, the cost of repair depends on the type of repair. Let, $c_{\min}$ be the cost of each minimal repair and c_{imp} be the cost of each imperfect repair. Normally, $c_{\text{imp}} > c_{\min}$.

5.7 Costs of Maintenance

The cost of each maintenance action depends on the RL of the remanufactured item, the degree or level of maintenance effort and the improvement resulting from the maintenance action. The maintenance cost increases with these variables. This follows, since for a given level of improvement, the less remaining life the remanufactured item has, the greater the number of worn-out components that need to be replaced. This section investigates the system maintenance cost. Two maintenance strategies are used in this book: PM and CM. The cost of each maintenance strategy is presented next.

5.7.1 Cost of Each Preventive Maintenance

In PM, the improvement is given by v, and the RL increment factor results from performing PM with effort m. The cost of an improvement action on an item with remaining life, RL, which increases its remaining life by δ, is given by:

$$C_{\text{PM}}\left(RL; v\right) = c\tau^{\Psi} RL^{\xi} \tag{5.49}$$

for $0 \leq v >$ RL and the parameters c, Ω, δ> 0.

5.7.2 Cost of Each Corrective Maintenance

The cost per repair is, in general, a random variable because the CM is due to the failure of one or more components, and the cost of repairing/replacing varies with the type of component involved. When CM action is performed, there is no improvement to the overall remanufactured item's performance. CM is used to rectify the warranty claim by replacing or repairing the failed remanufactured components. Therefore, failures over the warranty period occur according a point process with intensity function Λ (t). After CM, the failures occur according to a point process with intensity function given by Λ (t). Here, the cost for a CM action is a function of the remaining life and it is given by:

$$C_{CM}\left(RL;\theta\right) = c\tau^{\psi} RL^{\xi} \tag{5.50}$$

5.8 Conclusions

This chapter presented mathematical models to analyze warranty costs with PM for remanufactured products when failures occur at the system and component levels. These models will be used to compute the expected warranty costs to the remanufacturer and the buyer for different warranty policies in Chapters 7 through 11 of this book.

6

Representative Remanufacturing Facility Used for the Analysis of Warranty and Preventive Maintenance

6.1 Introduction

The increased rate of advancement in technology coupled with customers' passion for newer models has resulted in shorter product life cycles and premature disposal of products. The resulting decrease in available landfills and natural resources has forced many governments to mandate stricter environmental regulations on manufacturers. Some of these regulations require firms to take back their products at the end of their useful lives. Manufacturers try to comply with these regulations by setting up specific facilities for product recovery, which involves the minimization of the amount of waste sent to landfills by recovering materials and components from returned or end-of-life (EOL) products via recycling and remanufacturing. Moreover, the economic benefits that can be gained by reusing products, subassemblies and components instead of disposing of them increase the importance of product recovery (Lambert & Gupta, 2008; Pochampally et al., 2009c; Ilgin and Gupta, 2010).

This chapter describes and analyzes a representative remanufacturing facility controlled by a superior pull-type methodology developed for disassembly and remanufacturing lines considering their stochastic behavior. The facility can process one of two types of products at a time, namely, one with sensors embedded in them (SEPs - Sensor-Embedded Products) and the other a conventional product with no sensors in them. The sensors are useful in the detection of failed or missing components in a product and are helpful in estimating the remaining life of a product before even disassembling it. In addition, SEPs provide the full maintenance history, which is very helpful in doing the warranty cost analysis.

The rest of the chapter is organized as follows. The next section (Section 6.2) describes the Advanced Remanufacture-To-Order (ARTO) system, which is considered as a representative system throughout the rest of this book. The Design-of-Experiments (DOE) study is presented in Section 6.3. Section 6.4

presents the parameter values for warranty analysis which will be used to illustrate numerical examples in the rest of this book. The conclusions are presented in Section 6.5.

6.2 System Description

This section introduces the representative remanufacturing facility called the Advanced Remanufacture-To-Order (ARTO) system, which is considered throughout this book. Also presented is the information about the characteristics and precedence relationships of the components disassembled and remanufactured at different stations of the remanufacturing line.

6.2.1 Advanced Remanufacture-to-Order System

The ARTO system is a product recovery system. An EOL product, based on its condition, goes through a series of recovery operations. One or more of these recovery operations may require disassembly to retrieve reusable components to fulfill the demand of products and components.

Different types of arrivals occur at the ARTO system, for example, EOL products arrive for recovery process, remanufactured products arrive for PM or remanufactured products arrive for warranty processing by performing CM (see Figure 6.1). The arrival may be a SEP or a conventional product,

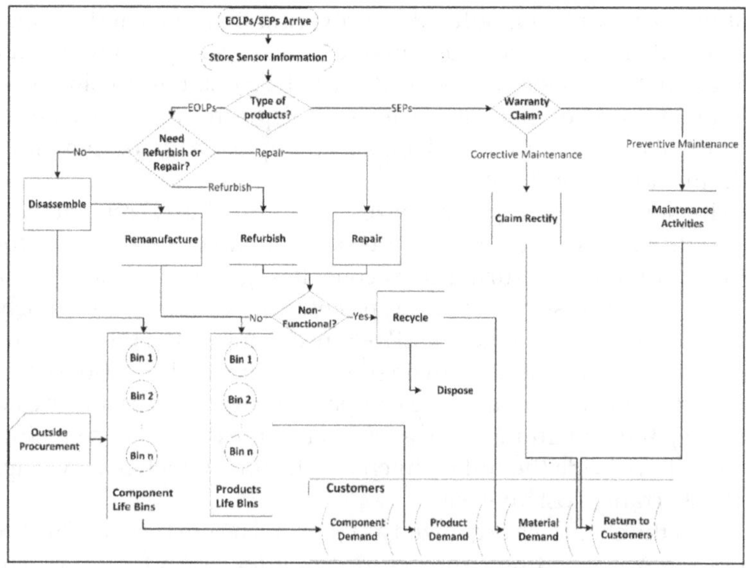

FIGURE 6.1
ARTO system components.

depending on the ARTO system. Each type of product goes through a different path in the ARTO system. This will be discussed separately in the following sections. This book considers an Air-Conditioner (AC) as an End-Of-Life Product (EOLP) example to exemplify the workings of the ARTO system.

6.2.1.1 Products Arrivals

Two types of EOL product arrivals occur at the ARTO system: SEPs and conventional products.

6.2.1.1.1 Sensor-Embedded EOL Product Arrival

EOL ACs arrive at the ARTO system, where information stored in their RFID is retrieved and kept in the facility's database. The AC then goes through various checkpoints and, if appropriate, a six-station disassembly line. Complete disassembly is performed to extract every single component. Table 6.1 shows all the AC components and the precedence relationships between them. There are nine components in the AC, namely, evaporator, control box, blower, air guide, motor, condenser, fan, protector and compressor, as shown in Figure 6.2. Note that the filter is disposed of. Exponential distribution is used to replicate disassembly times at each station, interarrival times of each components demand and interarrival times of EOL AC. The exponential distribution is used because of the randomness of these events, memoryless property and extreme nature of the distribution. (Marsaglia & Tubilla, 1975; Arnold & Huang, 1995). This allows the workings of the ARTO system to be tested in extreme situations.

After retrieving the information, the EOL AC is sent to station 1 for evaporator disassembly or to a different station, depending on which component is available (not missing) next based on the precedence relationship. One

TABLE 6.1

AC Components and Precedence Relationship

Component Name	Station	Code	Precedence relationship
Evaporator	1	A	-----
Control box	2	B	-----
Blower	3	C	A, B
Air guide	3	D	A, B, C
Motor	4	E	A, B, C, D
Condenser	5	F	-----
Fan	5	G	F
Protector	6	H	-----
Compressor	6	I	H

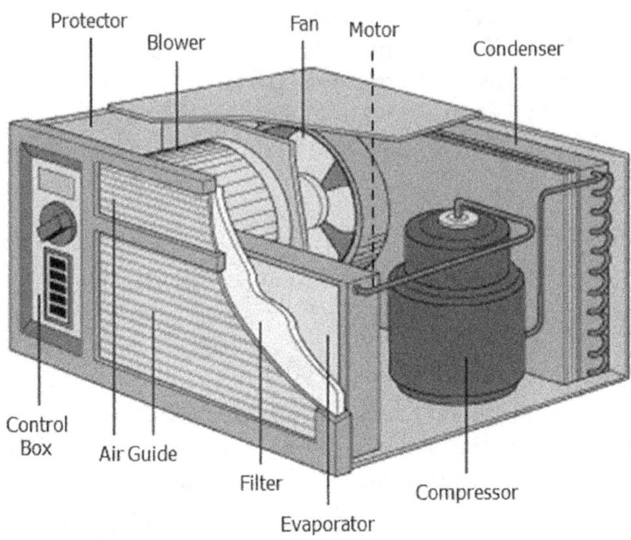

FIGURE 6.2
AC components.

of two different types of disassembly may be performed, namely, destructive or non-destructive, depending on the condition of the component. If the component is nonfunctional (or broken, or has zero remaining life), then destructive disassembly may be used such that other components are not damaged. Thus, the disassembly cost for a functional component is higher than for a nonfunctional component. After disassembly, no component testing is necessary because the information about the component's condition is available from sensors.

After complete disassembly, the disassembled components go through cleaning, repairing and/or refurbishing processes. Each component is stored in a life bin corresponding to its estimated remaining life. The components with less than one-year remaining life are either sent for recycling to fulfill the materials demand or disposed of if recycling is not possible (Figure 6.3).

Some of the EOLPs need refurbishing or repair action only. In that case, only partial disassembly might be required to perform the refurbishing or repair action. The product is then stored in one of the life bins corresponding to its estimated remaining life to fulfill the products' demand (Figure 6.4).

The remanufacturing process is also performed in the ARTO system. In order to produce a remanufactured AC, the ARTO system uses the components from the life bins that came from the disassembly process. There are six assembly stations to assemble a remanufactured SEP using the precedence relationship in Table 6.1. Three different remaining life bins are available in the ARTO system for the remanufactured AC, namely, with 1-year,

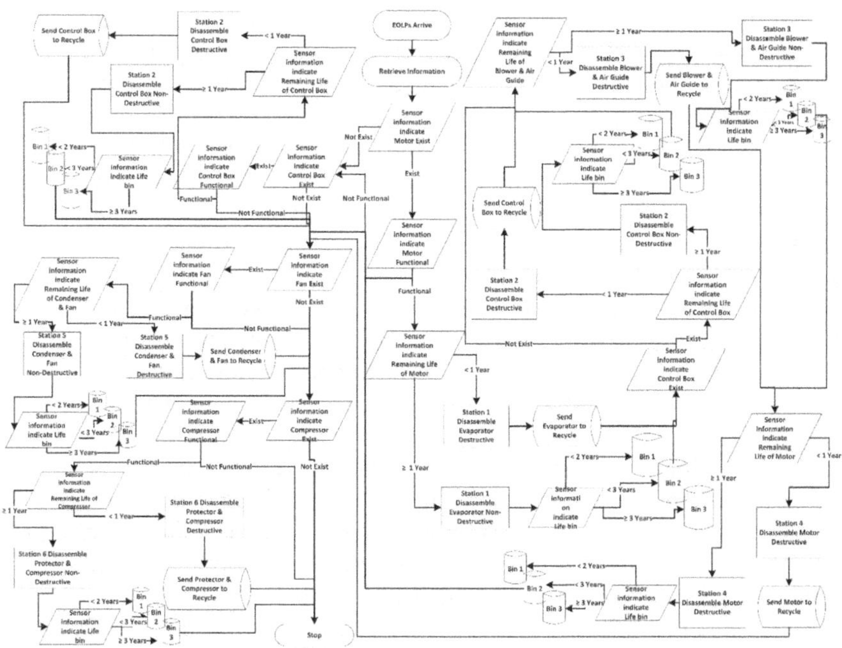

FIGURE 6.3
Disassembly process for SEPs in the ARTO system.

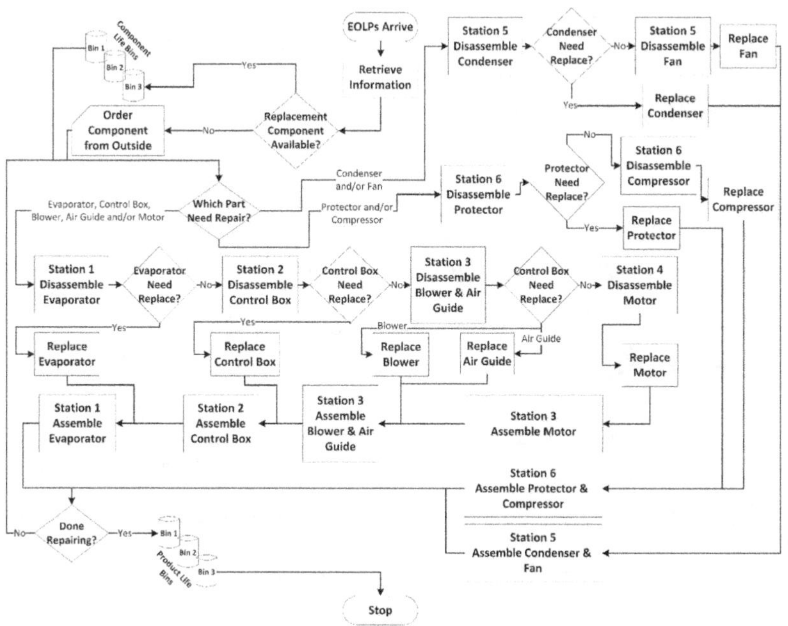

FIGURE 6.4
Refurbishing process for SEPs in the ARTO system.

2-years and 3-years of remaining life. For example, a 2-year- remaining-life sensor-embedded AC may not necessarily have all its components in it with exactly two years remaining life. Instead, every component needs to have at least two years remaining life. Sometime a 2-year-remaining-life component may not be available during the remanufacturing process. In that case, the ARTO system uses a component with a higher remaining life in order to satisfy this internal demand. If no component with higher remaining life is available, then the ARTO system procures the component from outside sources (Figure 6.5).

There are three types of demands in the ARTO system, namely, components, products and materials demands. Components demand could be internal (remanufactured products require specific remaining life components) or external. Both these demands are satisfied using the disassembled components available in the life bins. Products demand in the ARTO system is satisfied using the remanufactured products from the products life bins, depending on the required remaining life products needed. Finally, materials demand is satisfied using the materials revived from the recycling process (Figure 6.6). EOLP may have missing or nonfunctional (broken, zero remaining life) components that need to be replaced during the repairing process to meet certain remaining life requirements. In addition, EOLPs may consist of components that have less remaining life than what is desired, and for this reason have to be replaced.

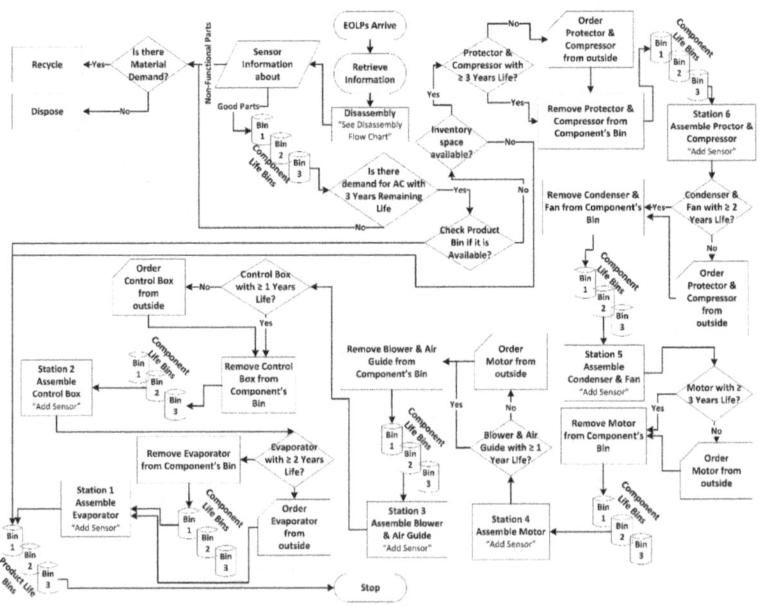

FIGURE 6.5
Remanufacturing process for SEPs in the ARTO system.

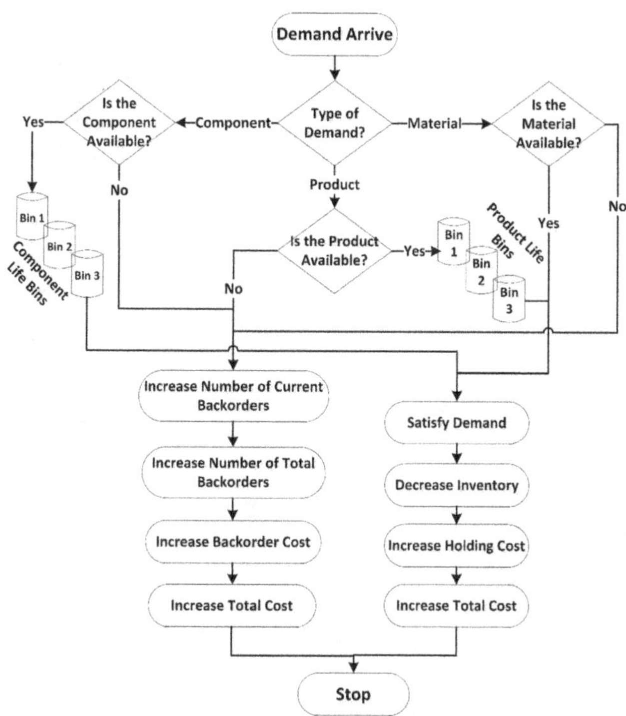

FIGURE 6.6
ARTO system's demand process.

6.2.1.1.2 Conventional EOL Product Arrival

When a conventional EOL AC arrives at the ARTO system, it is examined and tested to see which components are missing and nonfunctional. For the functional components, the remaining lives are estimated. Thus, every conventional EOLP goes through each and every station on the disassembly line. Complete and non-destructive disassembly is performed to extract every single component before examining and testing it. The components list and the precedence relationships between them is the same as the one given in Table 6.1. After retrieval, inspection, testing and determining the remaining life, components are placed in the appropriate life bins. The rest of the recovery operation is similar to that of the SEPs. The flow charts for the disassembly, refurbishing and remanufacturing processes for the conventional ACs in the ARTO system are shown in Figure 6.7, Figure 6.8 and Figure 6.9 respectively.

6.2.1.2 Preventive Maintenance Arrival

In addition to the EOL products arrival, there is a second type of arrival that can occur at the ARTO system. These are remanufactured products that

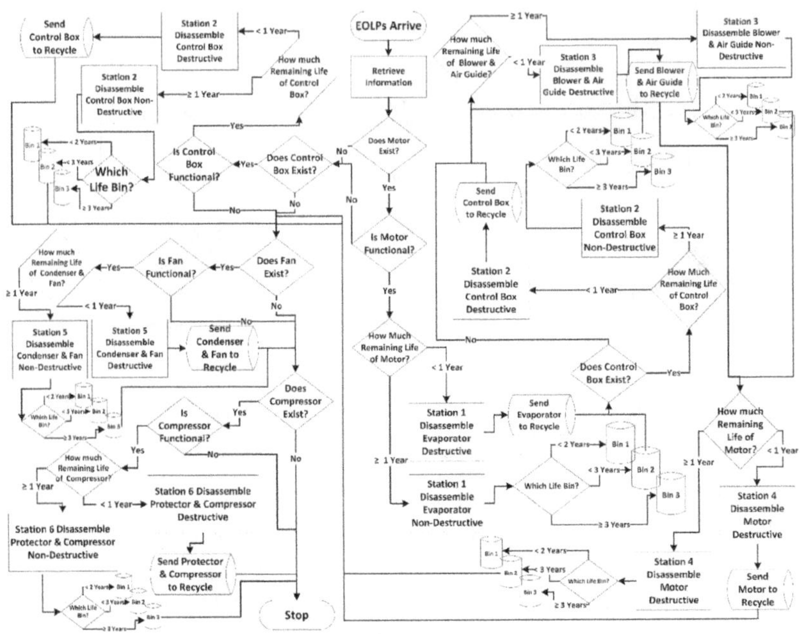

FIGURE 6.7
Disassembly process for conventional products in the ARTO system.

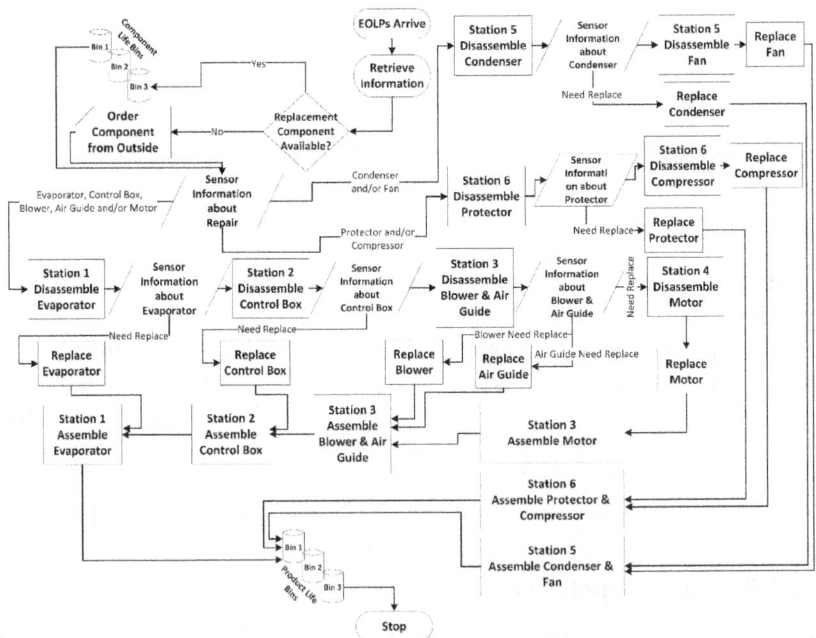

FIGURE 6.8
Refurbishing process for conventional products in the ARTO system.

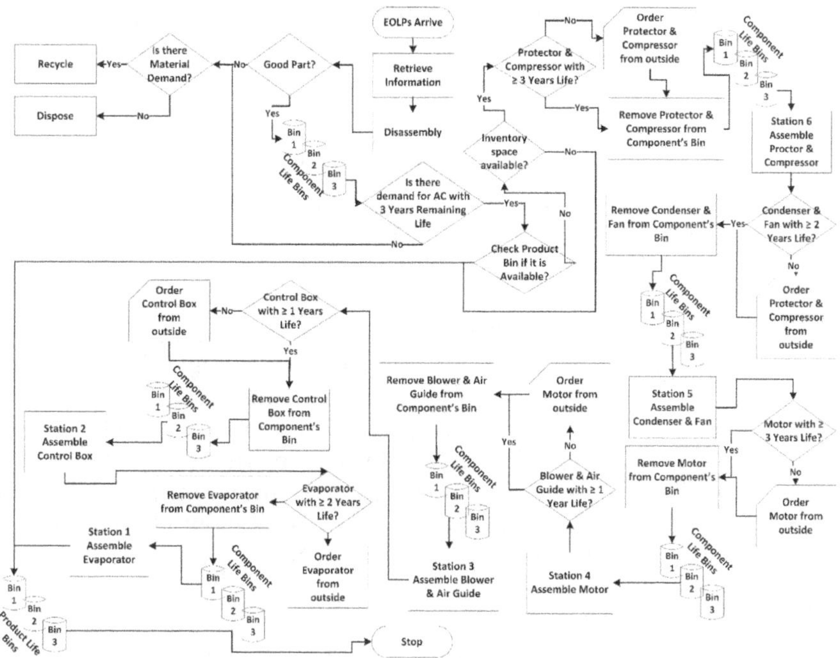

FIGURE 6.9
Remanufacturing process for conventional products in the ARTO system.

arrive for preventive maintenance (PM). Two types of products are considered here: SEPs and conventional products.

6.2.1.2.1 *Sensor-Embedded Products Preventive Maintenance*

When the remaining life of a remanufactured SEP reaches a pre-specified value, it arrives at the ARTO system, where its information is retrieved using a radio frequency data reader and stored in the facility's database. Then the SEP, based on the information retrieved from the sensors about its condition, goes through maintenance activities such as measurements, adjustments, parts replacements and cleaning (Figure 6.10). When PM is performed on a product with degree δ, its remaining life is revived and becomes δ time units more than before. It is then returned to the customer. Meanwhile, any failures between two successive PM actions during the warranty period is rectified at no cost to the customer.

6.2.1.2.2 *Conventional Products Preventive Maintenance*

The remaining life of a conventional product cannot be easily determined because of the lack of sensor information availability. Therefore, in this case, the PM is scheduled based on a fixed elapsed duration, for example, every four months. The remanufactured conventional product arrives at the ARTO system, where it goes through inspection and testing before it goes through maintenance activities such as measurements, adjustments, parts replacements and cleaning (Figure 6.10).

6.2.1.3 Warranty Claims Arrival

A third type of arrival that can occur at the ARTO system is a remanufactured product that arrives for warranty processing using corrective maintenance (CM). Two types of products are considered here: SEPs and conventional products.

6.2.1.3.1 SEP EOL Warranty Claims

When a remanufactured SEP fails during the warranty period, the customer returns the product for corrective maintenance under the warranty claim. The product then arrives at the ARTO system for information retrieval using a radio frequency data reader, and the information is then stored in the facility's database. Then the SEP goes through corrective maintenance activities based on the information retrieved from the sensor about its condition and warranty policy type (Figure 6.11).

6.2.1.3.2 Conventional EOL Warranty Claims

Since the remaining life of a conventional product is not known, a failure could occur at any time during the warranty period. Thus, the remanufactured conventional product arrives at the ARTO system, where it goes

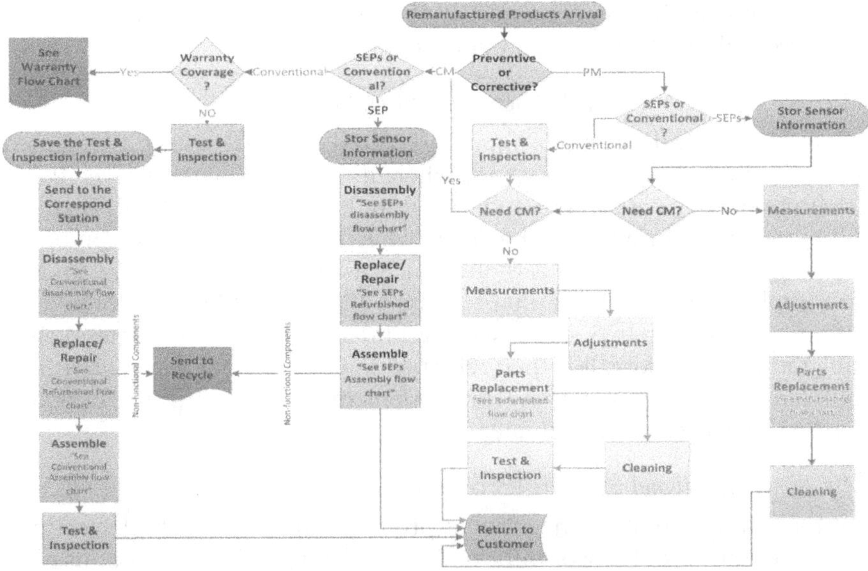

FIGURE 6.10
Maintenance process for SEPs and conventional products in the ARTO system.

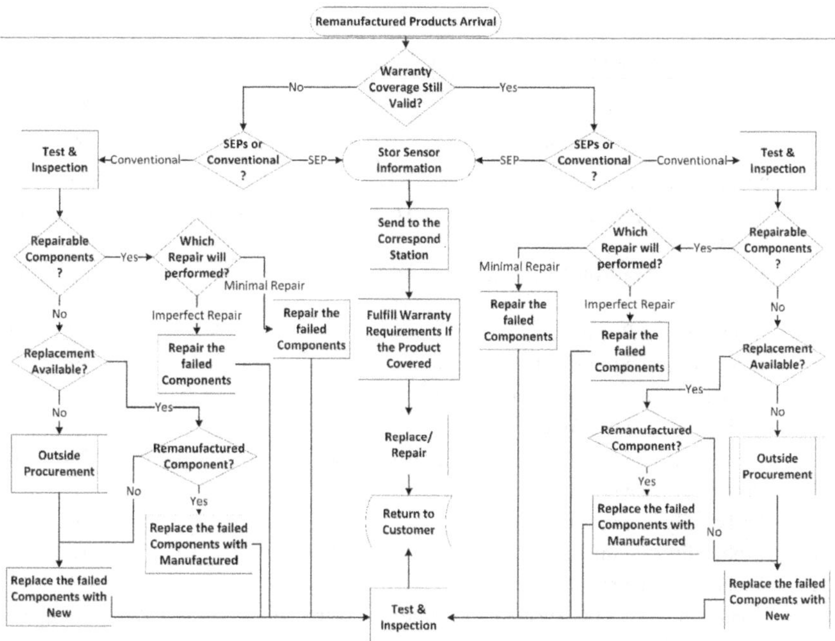

FIGURE 6.11
Warranty claim process for SEPs and conventional products in the ARTO system.

through inspection and testing before it is sent for corrective maintenance based on the information gleaned from inspection and testing about its condition and warranty policy type (Figure 6.11).

6.3 Design-of-Experiments Study

Design-of-Experiments (DOE) is a systematic methodology to determine the relationship between factors affecting a process and the output of that process. In other words, it is used to find cause-and-effect relationships. This information is needed to manage process inputs in order to optimize the output (Montgomery, 2008)

A comprehensive study about the quantitative evaluation of SEPs on the performance of a disassembly line conducted by Ilgin & Gupta (2011) showed that SEPs are much better at handling remanufacturing uncertainties. To test this claim on the performance of the ARTO system, a simulation model was built to represent the full recovery system, and its behavior was observed under different experimental conditions. Arena version 14.5 was used to build the discrete-event simulation model. Three-level factorial

TABLE 6.2

Factors and Factor Levels (1 to 48) Used in Design-Of-Experiments Study

No	Factor	Unit	Levels 1	2	3
1	Mean arrival rate of EOL ACs	Products/hour	10	20	30
2	Mean arrival rate of Remanufactured ACs for CM	Products/hour	10	20	30
3	Mean arrival rate of Remanufactured ACs for PM	Products/hour	10	20	30
4	Probability of Repair EOLPs	%	5	10	15
5	Probability of a nonfunctional control box	%	10	20	30
6	Probability of a nonfunctional motor	%	10	20	30
7	Probability of a nonfunctional fan	%	10	20	30
8	Probability of a nonfunctional compressor	%	10	20	30
9	Probability of a missing control box	%	5	10	15
10	Probability of a missing motor	%	5	10	15
11	Probability of a missing fan	%	5	10	15
12	Probability of a missing compressor	%	5	10	15
13	Mean non-distractive disassembly time for station 1	Minutes	0.8	1	1.3
14	Mean non-distractive disassembly time for station 2	Minutes	0.8	1	1.3
15	Mean non-distractive disassembly time for station 3	Minutes	0.8	1	1.3
16	Mean non-distractive disassembly time for station 4	Minutes	0.5	0.8	1
17	Mean non-distractive disassembly time for station 5	Minutes	0.8	1	1.3
18	Mean non-distractive disassembly time for station 6	Minutes	1	1.5	2
19	Mean distractive disassembly time for station 1	Minutes	0.4	0.5	0.7
20	Mean distractive disassembly time for station 2	Minutes	0.4	0.5	0.7
21	Mean distractive disassembly time for station 3	Minutes	0.4	0.5	0.7
22	Mean distractive disassembly time for station 4	Minutes	0.3	0.5	0.6
23	Mean distractive disassembly time for station 5	Minutes	0.4	0.5	0.7
24	Mean distractive disassembly time for station 6	Minutes	0.6	0.8	1
25	Mean Assembly time for station 1	Minutes	1	1.3	1.5
26	Mean Assembly time for station 2	Minutes	1	1.3	1.5

(*Continued*)

TABLE 6.2 (CONTINUED)

Factors and Factor Levels (1 to 48) Used in Design-Of-Experiments Study

No	Factor	Unit	Levels 1	2	3
27	Mean Assembly time for station 3	Minutes	1	1.3	1.5
28	Mean Assembly time for station 4	Minutes	0.8	1	1.3
29	Mean Assembly time for station 5	Minutes	1	1.3	1.5
30	Mean Assembly time for station 6	Minutes	1.3	1.5	1.8
31	Mean demand rate Evaporator	Parts/hour	10	15	20
32	Mean demand rate for Control Box	Parts/hour	10	15	20
33	Mean demand rate for Blower	Parts/hour	10	15	20
34	Mean demand rate for Air Guide	Parts/hour	10	15	20
35	Mean demand rate for Motor	Parts/hour	10	15	20
36	Mean demand rate for Condenser	Parts/hour	10	15	20
37	Mean demand rate for Fan	Parts/hour	10	15	20
38	Mean demand rate for Protector	Parts/hour	10	15	20
39	Mean demand rate for Compressor	Parts/hour	10	15	20
40	Mean demand rate for 1 Year AC	Products/hour	5	10	15
41	Mean demand rate for 2 Years AC	Products/hour	5	10	15
42	Mean demand rate for 3 Years AC	Products/hour	5	10	15
43	Mean demand rate for Refurbished AC	Products/hour	5	10	15
44	Mean demand rate for Material	Products/hour	5	10	15
45	Percentage of Good Parts to Recycling	%	95	0.9	0.8

design was used that included 90 factors, each at three levels: low, intermediate and high. The reason that the three-level design was proposed was to model the possibility of curvature in the response function and to handle the case of nominal factors at three levels. The factors, factor levels and parameters are given in Table 6.2, Table 6.3 and Table 6.4. A full factorial design with 90 factors at three levels requires an extensive number of experiments (namely, 8.728e+42). To reduce the number of experiments to a practical level, a small set of all the possible combinations is picked. The picked selection is called a fractional factorial design, which are experimental designs consisting of a carefully chosen sub-set (fraction) of the experimental runs of a full factorial design. The sub-set is chosen so as to exploit the Sparsity-of-Effects principle to expose information about the most important features of the problem studied while using a fraction of the effort of a full factorial design in terms of experimental runs and resources. This yields the maximum information possible of all the factors that affect the performance parameter with the minimum number of experiments possible (Montgomery, 2009). For these types of experiments, Taguchi made specific guidelines. The method of conducting the design of experiments, which uses a special set of arrays called the Orthogonal Arrays (OAs), was built by Taguchi. Construction of orthogonal arrays has been investigated by many researchers, including

TABLE 6.3

Factors and Factor Levels (49 to 90) Used in Design-Of-Experiments Study

			Levels		
No	**Factor**	**Unit**	**1**	**2**	**3**
46	Mean Metals Separation Process	Hour	1	1.3	1.5
47	Mean Copper Recycle Process	Minutes	1	1.3	1.5
48	Mean Steel Recycle Process	Minutes	1	1.3	1.5
49	Mean Fiberglass Recycle Process	Minutes	1	1.3	1.5
50	Mean Dispose Process	Minutes	0.5	0.8	1
51	Maximum inventory level for AC	Products/hour	10	15	20
52	Maximum inventory level for Refurbished AC	Products/hour	10	15	20
53	Maximum inventory level for AC Component	Products/hour	10	15	20
54	PM action effort level	number	0.2	0.5	0.6
55	Mean measurements time for Evaporator	Parts/hour	10	15	20
56	Mean measurements time for Control Box	Parts/hour	10	15	20
57	Mean measurements time for Blower	Parts/hour	10	15	20
58	Mean measurements time for Air Guide	Parts/hour	10	15	20
59	Mean measurements time for Motor	Parts/hour	10	15	20
60	Mean measurements time for Condenser	Parts/hour	10	15	20
61	Mean measurements time for Fan	Parts/hour	10	15	20
62	Mean measurements time for Protector	Parts/hour	10	15	20
63	Mean measurements time for Compressor	Parts/hour	10	15	20
64	Mean adjustments time for Evaporator	Parts/hour	10	15	20
65	Mean adjustments time for Control Box	Parts/hour	10	15	20
66	Mean adjustments time for Blower	Parts/hour	10	15	20
67	Mean adjustments time for Air Guide	Parts/hour	10	15	20
68	Mean adjustments time for Motor	Parts/hour	10	15	20
69	Mean adjustments time for Condenser	Parts/hour	10	15	20
70	Mean adjustments time for Fan	Parts/hour	10	15	20
71	Mean adjustments time for Protector	Parts/hour	10	15	20
72	Mean adjustments time for Compressor	Parts/hour	10	15	20
73	Mean part replacement time for Evaporator	Parts/hour	10	15	20
74	Mean part replacement time for Control Box	Parts/hour	10	15	20
75	Mean part replacement time for Blower	Parts/hour	10	15	20
76	Mean part replacement time for Air Guide	Parts/hour	10	15	20
77	Mean part replacement time for Motor	Parts/hour	10	15	20
78	Mean part replacement time for Condenser	Parts/hour	10	15	20
79	Mean part replacement time for Fan	Parts/hour	10	15	20
80	Mean part replacement time for Protector	Parts/hour	10	15	20
81	Mean part replacement time for Compressor	Parts/hour	10	15	20
82	Mean cleaning time for Evaporator	Parts/hour	10	15	20
83	Mean cleaning time for Control Box	Parts/hour	10	15	20

(*Continued*)

TABLE 6.3 (CONTINUED)

Factors and Factor Levels (49 to 90) Used in Design-Of-Experiments Study

No	Factor	Unit	Levels 1	2	3
84	Mean cleaning time for Blower	Parts/hour	10	15	20
85	Mean cleaning time for Air Guide	Parts/hour	10	15	20
86	Mean cleaning time for Motor	Parts/hour	10	15	20
87	Mean cleaning time for Condenser	Parts/hour	10	15	20
88	Mean cleaning time for Fan	Parts/hour	10	15	20
89	Mean cleaning time for Protector	Parts/hour	10	15	20
90	Mean cleaning time for Compressor	Parts/hour	10	15	20

Kempthorne (1979), Plackett & Burman (1946), Addelman (1962), Raghavarao (1971), Seiden (1954) and Taguchi (1987). Orthogonal arrays provide a way of conducting the minimal number of experiments. In most cases, orthogonal array is more efficient when compared to many other statistical designs. The minimum number of experiments that are required to conduct the Taguchi method can be calculated based on the degrees of freedom approach.

The first step in constructing an orthogonal array to fit a specific case study is to count the total degrees of freedom, which gives the minimum number of experiments that must be performed to study all the chosen control factors. In general, the number of degrees of freedom associated with a factor is equal to one less than the number of levels for that factor. In the ARTO system, there are 90 factors, each with three levels, which leads to 180 as the total degrees of freedom. Therefore, the minimum number of experiments that must be performed in the ARTO system is 180. Consequently, the number of experiments must be greater than or equal to the system degrees of freedom.

$$\text{Number of Experiments} = (\text{Number of Levels} - 1) \times \text{Number of Factors} + 1 \quad (6.1)$$

Precisely, $L_{181}(3^{90})$ Orthogonal Array was chosen using equation (6.1). This means that it requires 181 experiments to accommodate 90 factors at three levels each. The orthogonal array assumes that there is no interaction between any two factors.

Arena models calculate the profit using the following equation:

$$\text{Profit} = \text{SR} + \text{CR} + \text{SCR} - \text{HC} - \text{BC} - \text{DC} - \text{DPC} - \text{RPC} - \text{RMC} - \text{TPC} \quad (6.2)$$

where SR is the total revenue generated by the product, component and material sales during the simulated run time; CR is the total revenue generated by the collection of EOL ACs during the simulated run time; SCR is the total revenue generated by selling scrap components during the simulated

TABLE 6.4

Parameters Used in the ARTO System

No	Parameters	Unit	Value	No	Parameters	Unit	Value
1	Backorder cost rate	%	40	**40**	Weight for Compressor	lbs.	6
2	Holding cost rate	%	10	**41**	Unit copper scrap revenue	$/lbs	0.6
3	Remanufacturing cost/minute	$	1.5	**42**	Unit Fiberglass scrap revenue	$/lbs	0.9
4	Disassembly cost/minute	$	1	**43**	Unit steel scrap revenue	$/lbs	0.2
5	Price for 1 Year Evaporator	$	10	**44**	Unit disposal cost	$/lbs	0.3
6	Price for 1 Year Control Box	$	20	**45**	Unit copper scrap Cost	$/lbs	0.3
7	Price for 1 Year Blower	$	5	**46**	Unit Fiberglass scrap Cost	$/lbs	0.45
8	Price for 1 Year Air Guide	$	5	**47**	Unit steel scrap Cost	$/lbs	0.1
9	Price for 1 Year Motor	$	45	**48**	Price of 1 Year AC	$	180
10	Price for 1 Year Condenser	$	15	**49**	Price of 2 Years AC	$	240
11	Price for 1 Year Fan	$	15	**50**	Price of 3 Years AC	$	275
12	Price for 1 Year Protector	$	15	**51**	Price of Refurbished AC	$	220
13	Price for 1 Year Compressor	$	50	**52**	Assembly cost / minute	$	1.20
14	Price for 2 Years Evaporator	$	15	**53**	Measurements cost /minute	$	0.90
15	Price for 2 Years Control Box	$	30	**54**	Adjustments cost /minute	$	1.10
16	Price for 2 Years Blower	$	12	**55**	Replacements cost /minute	$	1.15
17	Price for 2 Years Air Guide	$	12	**56**	Cleaning cost / minute	$	1.00
18	Price for 2 Years Motor	$	55	**57**	Testing cost / minute	$	1.12
19	Price for 2 Years Condenser	$	18	**58**	Operation costs Evaporator	$/unit	4
20	Price for 2 Years Fan	$	18	**59**	Operation costs Control Box	$/unit	4
21	Price for 2 Years Protector	$	20	**60**	Operation costs Blower	$/unit	2.8
22	Price for 2 Years Compressor	$	60	**61**	Operation costs Air Guide	$/unit	1.2

(Continued)

TABLE 6.4 (CONTINUED)

Parameters Used in the ARTO System

No	Parameters	Unit	Value	No	Parameters	Unit	Value
23	Price for 3 Years Evaporator	$	20	**62**	Operation costs Motor	$/unit	4.
24	Price for 3 Years Control Box	$	35	**63**	Operation costs Condenser	$/unit	1.66
25	Price for 3 Years Blower	$	15	**64**	Operation costs Fan	$/unit	2.34
26	Price for 3 Years Air Guide	$	15	**65**	Operation costs Protector	$/unit	0.6
27	Price for 3 Years Motor	$	60	**66**	Operation costs Compressor	$/unit	3.4
28	Price for 3 Years Condenser	$	25	**67**	Operation costs AC	$/unit	55
29	Price for 3 Years Fan	$	20	**68**	Repair costs Evaporator	$/unit	8
30	Price for 3 Years Protector	$	20	**69**	Repair costs Control Box	$/unit	8
31	Price for 3 Years Compressor	$	65	**70**	Repair costs Blower	$/unit	5.6
32	Weight for Evaporator	lbs.	8	**71**	Repair costs Air Guide	$/unit	2.4
33	Weight for Control Box	lbs.	4	**72**	Repair costs Motor	$/unit	8
34	Weight for Blower	lbs.	2	**73**	Repair costs Condenser	$/unit	3.32
35	Weight for Air Guide	lbs.	2	**74**	Repair costs Fan	$/unit	4.68
36	Weight for Motor	lbs.	6	**75**	Repair costs Protector	$/unit	1.2
37	Weight for Condenser	lbs.	12	**76**	Repair costs Compressor	$/unit	6.8
38	Weight for Fan	lbs.	3	**77**	Repair costs AC	$/unit	85
39	Weight for Protector	lbs.	3				

run time; HC is the total holding cost of products, components, material and EOL ACs during the simulated run time; BC is the total backorder cost of products, components and material during the simulated run time; DC is the total disassembly cost during the simulated run time; DPC is the total disposal cost of components, material and EOL ACs during the simulated run time; RPC is the total repair cost during the simulated run time; RMC is the total remanufacturing cost of products during the simulated run time and TPC is the total transportation cost during the simulated run time.

In each AC, three types of scrap are recovered and sold. Evaporators and condensers are sold as copper scrap, chassis and metal covers are sold as steel scrap and blower, fan and air guide are sold as fiberglass. All the other components are considered as waste. Scrap revenue from steel, copper and fiberglass components is calculated by multiplying the weight in pounds by the unit scrap revenue of each metal type. The disposal cost is calculated by multiplying the waste weight by the unit disposal cost. The time of retrieving information from smart sensors is assumed to be 20 seconds per AC. The transportation cost is assumed to be $50 for each trip of the truck. There are different prices in the secondary market of recovering the product due to different levels of quality.

6.4 Parameter Values for Warranty Cost Analysis

Chapters 7 to 11 carry out the analysis to determine the expected warranty cost for different policies discussed in Chapter 4 with different models presented in Chapter 5. The numerical examples use the following two data sets.

6.4.1 Data Set I: (System Level Modeling)

Here the failures are modeled using equation (5.3) discussed in Chapter 5 with $\beta = 2$ and $\lambda = 0.443$. The mean time to first failure, μ, is two months. The expected cost of each repair is presented in Table 6.4. The remaining life distribution (when item remaining life is not known) is given by (5.7) with $\rho = 0.2$ with different values for lower (L) and upper (U) limit of the remaining life. For the case where components are grouped into including Set I and excluding Set E:

1. The modeling of failures for Set E is given by (5.8) with the following parameter values $\lambda_E = 0.441$ and $\beta_E = 2.31$; $\bar{C}_E = \$30$
2. The modeling of failures for Set I is given by (5.8) with the following parameter values $\lambda_I = 0.446$ and $\beta_I = 1.8$; $\bar{C}_I = \$70$

6.4.2 Data Set II: (Component Level Modeling)

1. Non-Repairable Component

   The failure distribution F_{i1} for a remanufactured component is given by Weibull distribution with parameter $\lambda_i = 0.443$ and $\beta_i = 2$. The cost of each replacement by a remanufactured component, $c_{in} = \$100$. The remaining life distribution, $H_i(a)$ (when component remaining life is not known) is given by (5.7) with $\rho = 0.2$, $L_i = 0$ and $U_i = 2$. The probability that a used component is not available and the remanufacturer uses a new component, $p = 0.4$. The cost of each replacement involving a used component, $c_{iu} = \$50$.

2. Repairable Component (Minimal Repair)
   The failure rate r_i (rl) is given by r_i (rl)=λ_i β_i $(\lambda_i\ rl)^{\beta i\text{-}1}$ and β_i = 1.3 and λ_i = 0.231. The expected cost of each minimal repair c_{ir} = \$25. The remaining life distribution function (when remaining life is unknown), $G_i(rl)$ is given by [1-e($^{-\rho_i rl}$)] with parameter ρ_i = 0.2.
3. Repairable Component
   The failures are given by a Weibull distribution with parameters λ_i = 0.283/year and β_i = 1.25. λ_i = 0.311/year The cost of each overhaul c_{io} = \$140.

6.5 Conclusions

This chapter illustrated how the ARTO system can be optimized when emerging information technologies are able to collect necessary life-cycle information. Also presented was the information about the characteristics and precedence relationships of the components disassembled and remanufactured at different stations of the remanufacturing line. Please note that the data presented in this chapter will be referred to in the examples considered in the subsequent chapters.

7

Cost Analysis of Simple Non-Renewing Warranties – Group 1

7.1 Introduction

In Chapter 4, several warranty policies with preventive maintenance for remanufactured products were introduced. This chapter presents the analysis of determining the expected cost of warranty, CM and PM (from both the buyer's and the remanufacturer's perspectives). Here, only two simple non-renewing policies, namely, Policy 1 (FRW) and Policy 2 (PRW) as defined in Chapter 4, are considered.

In Chapter 5, a variety of models were discussed at the system level (models S1 through S4) and at the component level (modes Cl through C8) for warranty failures of remanufactured products. The expected warranty cost for a given policy can be evaluated using one of those models. Here, analysis of the FRW policy based on the models at both the system and component levels are carried out. For the PRW policy, the analysis is very similar to that for the FRW policy. For that reason, for the PRW policy, only model C1 is discussed in this chapter as illustration. The warranty costs for the rest of the models can be carried out in a manner similar to that given for the FRW policy.

Section 7.2 presents some assumptions and notations used in this chapter. Section 7.3, deals with the analysis of the FRW policy and Sections 7.4 deals with the analysis of the PRW Policy. Finally, some conclusions are presented in Section 7.5.

7.2 Some Preliminaries

This section starts with some assumptions. Then the notations used in this chapter are presented.

7.2.1 Assumptions

1. Occurrence of failures are statistically independent.
2. Every failure results in warranty claims.
3. All claims are valid.
4. The time to service claim is negligible.
5. The cost to service warranty claim (for repair/replacement of failed components) is a random variable.

7.2.2 Notations

In addition to notations introduced in Chapter 4, the following added notations will be used.

B_j	Cost to buyer for replacement/repair jth failure, $j \geq 1$ [Note: $C_j = D_j + B_j$]
$C_b(W; RL)$	Total warranty cost to buyer for SEPs with CM
$C_b(W; v)$	Total warranty cost to buyer for SEPs with PM
$C_b(W)$	Total warranty cost to buyer for conventional product
$C_d(W; RL)$	Total warranty cost to remanufacturer for conventional product with CM
$C_d(W; v)$	Total warranty cost to remanufacturer for conventional product with PM
$C_d(W)$	Total warranty cost to remanufacturer for a conventional products
C_i	C_d (W: A) for the ith independent simulation run
$C_i(W; RL_i)$	Total warranty cost for sensor-embedded component I with CM
$C_i(W; v_i)$	Total warranty cost for sensor-embedded component i with PM
$C_i(W)$	Total warranty cost for conventional component i
C_j	Cost of replacement/repair jth failure, $j \geq 1$
$C_p(RL)$	Purchasing cost to remanufacturer for a remanufactured item of remaining life RL
$\bar{C}(n)$	Estimate of E [C_d (W; RL)] based on n independent simulation run
D_j	Cost to remanufacturer for replacement/repair jth failure, $j \geq 1$
$E[\,]$	Expected value
$G(c)$	Distribution function for C_j, $j \geq 1$
Q	Parameter for LCS Policy
Y_j	Binary random variable associated with jth failure for analysis of SPE Policy
$\bar{c}_b$	Expected cost to buyer per warranty claim in Cost Limit policies
$\bar{c}_d$	Expected cost to remanufacturer per warranty claim in Cost Limit policies (6, 7, 8 and 9)

7.2.3 Parameter Values for Numerical Examples

The data sets given in Section 6.4 are used to illustrate the numerical examples in this chapter.

7.3 Analysis of Free-Replacement Warranty Policy

This section presents the cost analysis of providing a Free-Replacement Warranty (FRW) Policy based on all the different models (models Sl through S4, and Cl through C8) for warranty failures of remanufactured products discussed in Chapter 5. The policy can be described as follows:
FRW POLICY: Under the free-replacement warranty policy, the remanufacturer resolves all failures over the warranty period at no cost to the buyer. The resolution can involve either repair or replacement of failed items or components. The warranty expires after time W from the time of sale.

If an item of remaining life, *RL*, fails at time (X_1) (where $X_1 < W$), then the replaced or repaired item is warranted for the remaining period, that is, (W-X_1) until the total operating time of the remanufactured item and its replacements/repaired items exceeds the warranty period, *W*. Under this policy, there is no cost to the buyer.

7.3.1 FRW for Model S1 (SEPs, Corrective Maintenance)

Since the cost is entirely borne by the remanufacturer, the cost to the remanufacturer for the replacement/repair of jth failure is:

$$D_j = C_j \tag{7.1}$$

The number of failures over the warranty period for a remanufactured SEPs is given by:

$$C_d(W;RL) = \sum_{j=1}^{N(W;RL)} D_j \tag{7.2}$$

$$E[C_d(w;A)|\,N(W;A) = n] = nE[D_j] \tag{7.3}$$

$$E\left[C_d(W;RL)\right] = E\left[N(W;RL)\right] \times E\left[D_j\right] = E\left[N(W;RL)\right] \times E\left[C_j\right] \tag{7.4}$$

Using (5.2) in (7.4) results in:

$$E\left[C_d\left(W;RL\right)\right]=\bar{c}\int_{RL-W}^{W}\Lambda\left(t\right)dt \tag{7.5}$$

Example 7.1

Using Data Set I (see Section 6.4), the expected warranty costs determined from (7.5) and the standard errors, along with confidence intervals of the simulation runs for different combinations of remaining lives and warranty periods, are shown in Table 7.1 and Table 7.2, respectively.

Table 7.1 presents the expected failure frequency and cost for remanufactured AC and components for the FRW policy. The expected failure frequency represents the expected number of failed items per unit of sale. In other words, it is the average number of free replacements that the remanufacturer would have to provide during the warranty period per unit sold. Expected cost to the remanufacturer includes the cost of supplying the original item, C_s. Thus, the expected cost of warranty is calculated by subtracting C_s from the expected cost to remanufacturer. For example, from Table 7.1, for $W = 0.5$ and $RL = 1$, the warranty cost for AC is $57.50–$C_s$ = $57.50–$55.00 = $2.50, which is ($2.50/$55.00 × 100) = 4.55% of the cost of the item, C_s, and is significantly less than C_s = $55.00. This cost might be acceptable, but the corresponding values for longer warranties are much higher. For example, for $W = 2$ years and $RL = 1$, the corresponding percentage is {[($70.50–$55.00)/$55.00] × 100} = 28.18%.

As shown in Table 7.1, the expected warranty cost decreases with increasing remaining life of the remanufactured item, as would be expected. The results were determined by carrying out k independent simulation run with $k = 2000$ for all simulation results. The mean and standard errors of these k independent runs are shown in Table 7.2. The confidence interval for the mean of k independent simulations is given by:

$$C\left(k\right)\mp t_{k-1,\left(1-\frac{\alpha}{2}\right)}\sqrt{\frac{S^2\left(k\right)}{k}} \tag{7.6}$$

$$\frac{S^2\left(k\right)}{k}=\sum\left[C_i-\bar{C}\left(k\right)\right]^2/\left(k-1\right) \tag{7.7}$$

For one-year remaining life remanufactured ACs sold with 0.5 year warranty, ARTO system can claim with 90% confidence that the expected warranty cost is in the interval [$57.20–$60.80]. The confidence interval for a one-year remaining life remanufactured AC sold with two years warranty is [$69.03–$71.97].

TABLE 7.1

The Expected Warranty Costs for FRW Policy, Model S1

		Expected Failures Frequency			Expected Warranty Cost to Remanufacturer		
Components	*W*	*RL* = 1	*RL* = 2	*RL* = 3	*RL* = 1	*RL* = 2	*RL* = 3
Evaporator	**0.5**	0.833	0.0054	0.0004	$4.50	$5.16	$4.12
	1.0	0.167	0.0217	0.0033	$5.00	$5.65	$4.20
	2.0	0.25	0.0483	0.0111	$7.50	$7.45	$4.33
Control Box	**0.5**	0.823	0.0051	0.0004	$4.42	$5.13	$4.11
	1.0	0.177	0.0213	0.0033	$5.21	$5.50	$4.17
	2.0	0.24	0.048	0.011	$7.41	$7.31	$4.30
Blower	**0.5**	0.813	0.005	0.0004	$2.21	$2.07	$2.11
	1.0	0.157	0.0218	0.0033	$2.91	$3.67	$2.16
	2.0	0.23	0.0488	0.011	$4.02	$4.52	$2.24
Air Guide	**0.5**	0.813	0.0022	0.0004	$1.22	$1.19	$1.02
	1.0	0.117	0.0221	0.0032	$1.76	$1.62	$1.12
	2.0	0.21	0.0423	0.0111	$2.33	$2.31	$1.19
Motor	**0.5**	0.789	0.0051	0.0004	$4.61	$4.42	$4.32
	1.0	0.171	0.0212	0.0033	$5.07	$4.73	$4.40
	2.0	0.241	0.0488	0.0111	$7.12	$6.12	$4.44
Condenser	**0.5**	0.822	0.0055	0.0005	$1.44	$1.23	$1.20
	1.0	0.16	0.0216	0.0033	$2.09	$1.76	$1.32
	2.0	0.252	0.0487	0.0112	$2.42	$2.03	$1.39
Fan	**0.5**	0.842	0.005	0.0004	$2.76	$2.33	$2.24
	1.0	0.184	0.0214	0.0033	$3.81	$2.73	$2.30
	2.0	0.242	0.0484	0.0111	$4.74	$3.79	$2.42
Protector	**0.5**	0.85	0.0054	0.0004	$0.73	$0.57	$0.41
	1.0	0.157	0.0215	0.0032	$1.13	$0.92	$0.49
	2.0	0.239	0.0488	0.0111	$1.98	$1.33	$0.53
Compressor	**0.5**	0.821	0.0054	0.0005	$3.20	$3.00	$2.87
	1.0	0.166	0.0216	0.0033	$4.12	$3.87	$3.11
	2.0	0.241	0.0485	0.0111	$5.61	$5.07	$3.21
AC	**0.5**	0.812	0.0054	0.0005	$57.50	$55.16	$54.64
	1.0	0.19	0.0218	0.0034	$60.00	$60.65	$57.20
	2.0	0.249	0.0485	0.011	$70.50	$69.45	$59.33

7.3.2 FRW for Model S2 (Conventional Product, Corrective Maintenance)

In this case, there is no sensor embedded in the remanufactured product. Therefore, the remaining life of the remanufactured item is considered a random variable (assuming values in the interval $[L, U]$) and is described by

TABLE 7.2

Standard Error and Confidence Interval for FRW Policy, Model S1

					Confidence Interval					
		Standard Error			*RL* = 1		*RL* = 2		*RL* = 3	
Components	***W***	***RL* = 1**	***RL* = 2**	***RL* = 3**	**Lower**	**Upper**	**Lower**	**Upper**	**Lower**	**Upper**
Evaporator	**0.5**	0.34	0.50	0.76	$4.30	$4.70	$4.87	$5.45	$3.68	$4.56
	1.0	0.87	1.28	1.34	$4.50	$5.50	$4.91	$6.39	$3.42	$4.98
	2.0	1.68	1.92	2.21	$6.53	$8.47	$6.34	$8.56	$3.05	$5.61
Control Box	**0.5**	0.38	0.56	0.85	$4.20	$4.64	$4.80	$5.46	$3.62	$4.60
	1.0	0.98	1.44	1.51	$4.64	$5.78	$4.67	$6.33	$3.30	$5.04
	2.0	1.89	2.16	2.48	$6.32	$8.50	$6.06	$8.56	$2.86	$5.74
Blower	**0.5**	0.43	0.63	0.96	$1.96	$2.46	$1.70	$2.44	$1.55	$2.67
	1.0	1.10	1.62	1.69	$2.27	$3.55	$2.73	$4.61	$1.18	$3.14
	2.0	2.12	2.42	2.79	$2.79	$5.25	$3.12	$5.92	$0.62	$3.86
Air Guide	**0.5**	0.54	0.80	1.22	$0.90	$1.54	$0.73	$1.65	$0.31	$1.73
	1.0	1.39	2.05	2.15	$0.95	$2.57	$0.43	$2.81	$0.61	$1.63
	2.0	2.69	3.08	3.54	$0.77	$3.89	$0.53	$4.09	$0.35	$2.03
Motor	**0.5**	0.48	0.71	1.08	$4.33	$4.89	$4.01	$4.83	$3.69	$4.95
	1.0	1.24	1.83	1.91	$4.35	$5.79	$3.67	$5.79	$3.29	$5.51
	2.0	2.40	2.74	3.15	$5.73	$8.51	$4.53	$7.71	$2.61	$6.27
Condenser	**0.5**	0.40	0.59	0.90	$1.21	$1.67	$0.89	$1.57	$0.68	$1.72
	1.0	1.03	1.51	1.58	$1.50	$2.68	$0.89	$2.63	$0.40	$2.24
	2.0	1.98	2.26	2.61	$1.27	$3.57	$0.72	$3.34	$0.77	$2.01
Fan	**0.5**	0.40	0.59	0.90	$2.53	$2.99	$1.99	$2.67	$1.72	$2.76
	1.0	1.03	1.51	1.58	$3.22	$4.40	$1.86	$3.60	$1.38	$3.22
	2.0	1.98	2.26	2.61	$3.59	$5.89	$2.48	$5.10	$0.91	$3.93
Protector	**0.5**	0.39	0.57	0.87	$0.51	$0.95	$0.24	$0.90	$0.20	$0.62
	1.0	0.99	1.46	1.53	$0.56	$1.70	$0.07	$1.77	$0.13	$0.85
	2.0	1.91	2.19	2.52	$0.87	$3.09	$0.06	$2.60	$0.11	$0.95
Compressor	**0.5**	0.39	0.57	0.87	$2.98	$3.42	$2.67	$3.33	$2.37	$3.37
	1.0	0.99	1.46	1.53	$3.55	$4.69	$3.02	$4.72	$2.23	$3.99
	2.0	1.91	2.19	2.52	$4.50	$6.72	$3.80	$6.34	$1.75	$4.67
AC	**0.5**	0.51	0.76	1.15	$57.20	$60.80	$54.72	$55.60	$53.97	$55.31
	1.0	1.32	1.28	2.03	$59.24	$60.76	$59.91	$61.39	$56.03	$58.37
	2.0	2.54	2.90	3.34	$69.03	$71.97	$67.77	$71.13	$57.39	$61.27

a density function $h(rl)$ conditioned on $RL = rl$. Following the approach used for the analysis of Model S1 (SEPs, Corrective Maintenance):

$$E\left[C_d\left(W \mid RL = rl\right)\right] = \bar{c} \int_{rl-W}^{rl} \Lambda(t)\,dt \tag{7.8}$$

On removing the condition, the result is:

$$E\left[C_d\left(W\right)\right] = \bar{c} \int_{L}^{U} \int_{rl-W}^{rl} \left\{\Lambda(t)\,dt\right\} h(rl)\,drl \tag{7.9}$$

TABLE 7.3

The Expected Warranty Costs for FRW Policy, Model S2

		Expected Warranty Cost to Remanufacturer								
		$L = 1$			$L = 2$			$L = 3$		
Components	W	$U = 1$	$U = 2$	$U = 3$	$U = 1$	$U = 2$	$U = 3$	$U = 1$	$U = 2$	$U = 3$
Evaporator	**0.5**	$6.52	$7.47	$5.97	$7.22	$8.28	$6.61	$7.47	$8.56	$6.83
	1.0	$7.23	$8.17	$6.07	$8.03	$9.06	$6.74	$8.30	$9.37	$6.96
	2.0	$10.86	$10.79	$6.27	$12.04	$11.96	$6.95	$12.44	$12.36	$7.19
Control Box	**0.5**	$5.18	$7.42	$5.94	$7.09	$8.23	$6.60	$7.09	$8.51	$6.82
	1.0	$6.11	$7.96	$6.04	$8.36	$8.83	$6.69	$8.36	$9.12	$6.92
	2.0	$8.69	$10.57	$6.23	$11.89	$11.74	$6.91	$11.89	$12.12	$7.13
Blower	**0.5**	$2.59	$3.00	$3.05	$3.55	$3.32	$3.39	$3.55	$3.43	$3.51
	1.0	$3.41	$5.31	$3.13	$4.67	$5.89	$3.47	$4.67	$6.08	$3.59
	2.0	$4.71	$6.54	$3.25	$6.45	$7.26	$3.60	$6.45	$7.50	$3.72
Air Guide	**0.5**	$1.43	$1.72	$1.48	$1.96	$1.91	$1.64	$1.96	$1.97	$1.69
	1.0	$2.06	$2.34	$1.62	$2.83	$2.60	$1.79	$2.83	$2.68	$1.85
	2.0	$2.73	$3.34	$1.72	$3.74	$3.70	$1.91	$3.74	$3.83	$1.97
Motor	**0.5**	$5.40	$6.40	$6.25	$7.40	$7.09	$6.93	$7.40	$7.33	$7.16
	1.0	$5.94	$6.85	$6.37	$8.14	$7.60	$7.06	$8.14	$7.84	$7.30
	2.0	$8.35	$8.86	$6.42	$11.43	$9.82	$7.13	$11.43	$10.15	$7.36
Condenser	**0.5**	$1.69	$1.78	$1.74	$2.31	$1.97	$1.92	$2.31	$2.04	$1.99
	1.0	$2.45	$2.54	$1.91	$3.35	$2.83	$2.12	$3.35	$2.92	$2.19
	2.0	$2.84	$2.94	$2.02	$3.88	$3.26	$2.23	$3.88	$3.36	$2.31
Fan	**0.5**	$3.24	$3.38	$3.25	$4.43	$3.74	$3.60	$4.43	$3.87	$3.72
	1.0	$4.47	$3.95	$3.33	$6.12	$4.38	$3.69	$6.12	$4.53	$3.81
	2.0	$5.56	$5.49	$3.51	$7.61	$6.08	$3.88	$7.61	$6.28	$4.01
Protector	**0.5**	$0.86	$0.82	$0.48	$1.17	$0.91	$0.66	$1.17	$0.95	$0.68
	1.0	$1.32	$1.34	$0.70	$1.82	$1.48	$0.79	$1.82	$1.52	$0.81
	2.0	$2.32	$1.92	$0.76	$3.18	$2.13	$0.86	$3.18	$2.20	$0.88
Compressor	**0.5**	$3.75	$4.34	$4.15	$5.13	$4.82	$4.61	$5.13	$4.98	$4.76
	1.0	$4.83	$5.60	$4.50	$6.61	$6.21	$4.99	$6.61	$6.42	$5.16
	2.0	$6.58	$7.34	$4.64	$9.00	$8.14	$5.15	$9.00	$8.41	$5.32
AC	**0.5**	$67.41	$79.84	$79.07	$92.29	$88.52	$87.69	$92.29	$91.50	$90.65
	1.0	$70.34	$87.77	$82.78	$96.30	$97.34	$91.81	$96.30	$100.61	$94.89
	2.0	$82.65	$100.52	$85.86	$113.14	$111.47	$95.22	$113.14	$115.21	$98.42

Example 7.2

Using Data Set I (see Section 6.4), the expected warranty costs determined from (7.9), and confidence intervals of the simulation runs for different combinations of lower and upper range of remaining lives and warranty periods, are shown in Table 7.3 and Table 7.4, respectively. In general, the expected warranty cost of a conventional remanufactured AC is significantly higher than that of the sensor-embedded remanufactured AC.

7.3.2.1 Pricing of Remanufactured Item

A remanufactured item with a small remaining life indicates a higher expected warranty cost, while a younger item with large remaining life implies a smaller expected warranty cost. Remanufacturers sell remanufactured items

TABLE 7.4

Confidence Interval for FRW Policy, Model S2

		L = 1						L = 2						L = 3					
Components	*W*	*U* = 1		*U* = 2		*U* = 3		*U* = 1		*U* = 2		*U* = 3		*U* = 1		*U* = 2		*U* = 3	
Evaporator	**0.5**	$6.28	$6.74	$7.23	$7.70	$6.95	$7.98	$6.99	$7.46	$7.94	$8.62	$6.10	$7.13	$7.23	$7.69	$7.13	$7.81	$6.95	$7.98
	1.0	$6.65	$7.83	$7.59	$8.77	$7.39	$9.20	$7.43	$8.62	$8.19	$9.94	$5.83	$7.66	$7.70	$8.89	$7.42	$9.17	$7.39	$9.20
	2.0	$9.71	$11.99	$9.64	$11.92	$10.94	$13.94	$10.89	$13.18	$10.66	$13.26	$5.45	$8.45	$11.30	$13.59	$11.14	$13.75	$10.94	$13.94
Control Box	**0.5**	$4.92	$5.44	$7.16	$7.68	$6.52	$7.68	$6.83	$7.35	$7.85	$8.62	$6.01	$7.17	$6.83	$7.35	$6.72	$7.48	$6.52	$7.68
	1.0	$5.44	$6.78	$7.29	$8.63	$7.34	$9.39	$7.70	$9.03	$7.85	$9.80	$5.67	$7.71	$7.70	$9.03	$7.39	$9.34	$7.34	$9.39
	2.0	$7.41	$9.96	$9.30	$11.86	$10.21	$13.58	$10.61	$13.18	$10.27	$13.20	$5.22	$8.59	$10.61	$13.18	$10.42	$13.35	$10.21	$13.58
Blower	**0.5**	$2.30	$2.88	$2.71	$3.28	$2.90	$4.20	$3.26	$3.83	$2.90	$3.75	$2.73	$4.03	$3.26	$3.83	$3.12	$3.97	$2.90	$4.20
	1.0	$2.66	$4.16	$4.56	$6.06	$3.52	$5.81	$3.93	$5.42	$4.79	$6.99	$2.32	$4.62	$3.93	$5.42	$3.58	$5.77	$3.52	$5.81
	2.0	$3.27	$6.15	$5.10	$7.98	$4.56	$8.35	$5.01	$7.89	$5.60	$8.90	$1.70	$5.49	$5.01	$7.89	$4.81	$8.10	$4.56	$8.35
Air Guide	**0.5**	$1.06	$1.81	$1.35	$2.09	$1.13	$2.79	$1.58	$2.33	$1.36	$2.45	$0.81	$2.46	$1.58	$2.33	$1.42	$2.50	$1.13	$2.79
	1.0	$1.11	$3.01	$1.40	$3.29	$1.37	$4.28	$1.88	$3.77	$1.21	$4.00	$0.34	$3.26	$1.88	$3.77	$1.43	$4.22	$1.37	$4.28
	2.0	$0.90	$4.56	$1.51	$5.17	$1.34	$6.14	$1.91	$5.57	$1.62	$5.80	$0.49	$4.31	$1.91	$5.57	$1.65	$5.83	$1.34	$6.14
Motor	**0.5**	$5.08	$5.73	$6.07	$6.73	$6.66	$8.14	$7.07	$7.73	$6.61	$7.57	$6.20	$7.67	$7.07	$7.73	$6.92	$7.88	$6.66	$8.14
	1.0	$5.10	$6.79	$6.00	$7.69	$6.83	$9.44	$7.29	$8.98	$6.35	$8.83	$5.77	$8.36	$7.29	$8.98	$6.89	$9.38	$6.83	$9.44
	2.0	$6.72	$9.98	$7.23	$10.48	$9.28	$13.56	$9.80	$13.06	$7.96	$11.69	$4.98	$9.27	$9.80	$13.06	$9.57	$13.28	$9.28	$13.56
Condenser	**0.5**	$1.42	$1.96	$1.51	$2.05	$1.70	$2.92	$2.04	$2.58	$1.57	$2.38	$1.31	$2.53	$2.04	$2.58	$1.91	$2.71	$1.70	$2.92
	1.0	$1.76	$3.14	$1.85	$3.25	$2.29	$4.43	$2.66	$4.06	$1.79	$3.85	$1.04	$3.19	$2.66	$4.06	$2.33	$4.38	$2.29	$4.43
	2.0	$1.49	$4.19	$1.59	$4.28	$2.11	$5.65	$2.53	$5.23	$1.72	$4.79	$0.46	$4.00	$2.53	$5.23	$2.34	$5.43	$2.11	$5.65
Fan	**0.5**	$2.97	$3.51	$3.09	$3.65	$3.82	$5.04	$4.16	$4.70	$3.34	$4.14	$2.99	$4.21	$4.16	$4.70	$4.03	$4.83	$3.82	$5.04
	1.0	$3.77	$5.16	$3.26	$4.64	$5.04	$7.19	$5.42	$6.81	$3.35	$5.40	$2.61	$4.76	$5.42	$6.81	$5.09	$7.14	$5.04	$7.19
	2.0	$4.21	$6.91	$4.14	$6.83	$5.84	$9.38	$6.26	$8.96	$4.55	$7.62	$2.11	$5.65	$6.26	$8.96	$6.07	$9.14	$5.84	$9.38
Protector	**0.5**	$0.60	$1.11	$0.56	$1.09	$0.59	$1.76	$0.90	$1.43	$0.53	$1.30	$0.07	$1.24	$0.90	$1.43	$0.79	$1.56	$0.59	$1.76
	1.0	$0.66	$1.99	$0.66	$2.00	$0.77	$2.85	$1.14	$2.49	$0.48	$2.46	$0.25	$1.83	$1.14	$2.49	$0.82	$2.80	$0.77	$2.85
	2.0	$1.02	$3.62	$0.62	$3.22	$1.47	$4.89	$1.88	$4.48	$0.64	$3.62	$0.86	$2.57	$1.88	$4.48	$1.69	$4.67	$1.47	$4.89
Compressor	**0.5**	$3.49	$4.01	$4.08	$4.61	$4.55	$5.72	$4.88	$5.40	$4.43	$5.21	$4.02	$5.19	$4.88	$5.40	$4.75	$5.52	$4.55	$5.72
	1.0	$4.16	$5.50	$4.92	$6.27	$5.58	$7.66	$5.94	$7.28	$5.22	$7.20	$3.95	$6.03	$5.94	$7.28	$5.62	$7.61	$5.58	$7.66
	2.0	$5.28	$7.88	$6.04	$8.64	$7.29	$10.72	$7.70	$10.30	$6.65	$9.62	$3.43	$6.86	$7.70	$10.30	$7.51	$10.49	$7.29	$10.72
AC	**0.5**	$64.47	$75.73	$76.35	$89.70	$75.62	$88.84	$88.25	$103.69	$84.66	$99.46	$83.86	$98.52	$88.25	$103.69	$87.50	$102.80	$86.68	$101.84
	1.0	$67.27	$79.03	$83.94	$98.62	$79.17	$93.00	$92.09	$108.20	$93.08	$109.37	$87.80	$103.14	$92.09	$108.20	$96.21	$113.04	$90.74	$106.61
	2.0	$79.04	$92.86	$96.12	$112.93	$82.11	$96.47	$108.2	$127.12	$106.6	$125.24	$91.06	$106.98	$108.2	$127.12	$110.1	$129.44	$94.12	$110.58

with different remaining lives. If a remanufacturer were to price each item so as to recover the warranty costs associated with the item, then the sale price, $C_S(RL)$, of a remanufactured item of remaining life RL needs to satisfy the inequality given below, and failure to do so would imply an expected loss (rather than expected profit):

$$C_S(A) > C_p(A) + C_d(W;A) \tag{7.10}$$

If the remanufacturer were to price an item based on a fixed expected warranty cost, then the warranty duration (*W*) must decrease as the remaining life (*RL*) decreases, as shown in Figure 7.1. This indicates a shorter warranty period for a remanufactured item with low remaining life. An alternative strategy for overcoming this problem is to determine the sale price based on a warranty cost averaged over the different remaining lives. That will make higher warranty costs for less remaining life. Remanufactured items are balanced by lower warranty costs for higher remaining life items. This lowers the sale price of lower remaining life items at the expense of higher sale price for higher remaining life items. From a marketing point of view, this is a more attractive and better strategy for the remanufacturer.

7.3.3 FRW for Model S3 (SEPs, Preventive Maintenance)

As the cost is totally carried by the remanufacturer, the costs of failures are:

$$C_d(W;v) = \sum_{j=1}^{N(W;v)} D_j \tag{7.11}$$

The number of failures over the warranty period for a remanufactured SEP with preventive maintenance is given by:

$$E\left[C_d(w;v) \mid N(W;v) = n\right] = nE\left[D_j\right] \tag{7.12}$$

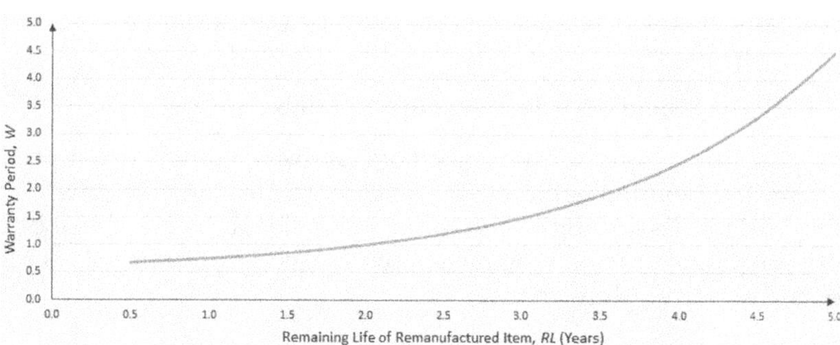

FIGURE 7.1
Remaining life vs. warranty period for same expected warranty cost

$$E\left[C_d(W;v)\right]=E\left[N(W;v)\right]\times E\left[D_j\right]=E\left[N(W;v)\right]\times E\left[C_j\right] \tag{7.13}$$

Using (5.2) in (7.13) the results in:

$$E\left[C_d(W;v)\right]=\bar{c}\int_{v-W}^{W}\Lambda(t)dt \tag{7.14}$$

Example 7.3

Using Data Set I (see Section 6.4), the expected warranty costs determined from (7.14), and the standard errors along with confidence intervals of the simulation runs for different combinations of remaining lives and warranty periods, are shown in Table 7.5 and Table 7.6, respectively.

Table 7.5 presents the expected failure frequency and cost for remanufactured AC and components for the FRW policy with PM. The expected failure frequency represents the expected number of failed items per unit of sale. In other words, it is the average number of free replacements that the remanufacturer would have to provide during the warranty period per unit sold. Expected cost to the remanufacturer includes the cost of supplying the original item, C_s. Thus, the expected cost of warranty is calculated by subtracting C_s from the expected cost to remanufacturer. For example, from Table 7.5, for $W = 0.5$ and $RL = 1$, the warranty cost for AC is \$45.43–C_s = \$57.50–\$55.00 = –\$9.57 which is (–\$9.57/\$55.00 × 100) = –17.40%, that is, 17.40% savings from the cost of the item, C_s. This is good, but the corresponding values for longer warranties may not provide any savings. For example, for $W = 2$ years and $RL = 1$, the corresponding percentage is {[(\$55.70–\$55.00)/\$55.00] × 100} = 1.27%. Here, instead of savings, there is an additional 1.27% cost associated with it.

As shown in Table 7.5, the expected warranty cost decreases with increasing remaining life of the remanufactured item, as would be expected. The results were determined by carrying out k independent simulation runs with $k = 2000$ for all simulation results. The mean and standard errors of these k independent runs are shown in Table 7.6. The confidence interval for the mean of k independent simulations are given by (7.6) and (7.7).

7.3.4 FRW for Model S4 (CPs, Preventive Maintenance)

In this case, there is no sensor embedded in the remanufactured product. Therefore, the remaining life of the remanufactured item is considered a random variable (assuming values in the interval $[L, U]$) and described by a density function $h(v)$. Following the approach used for the analysis of Model S3 (SEPs, Preventive Maintenance):

$$E\left[C_d(W)\right]=\bar{c}\int_{L}^{U}\int_{v-W}^{v}\left\{\Lambda(t)dt\right\}h(v)dv \tag{7.15}$$

TABLE 7.5

The Expected Warranty Costs for FRW Policy, Model S3

		Expected Failures Frequency			Expected Warranty Cost to Remanufacturer		
Components	*W*	*RL* = 1	*RL* = 2	*RL* = 3	*RL* = 1	*RL* = 2	*RL* = 3
Evaporator	**0.5**	0.6582	0.0043	0.0003	$3.56	$4.08	$3.26
	1.0	0.1320	0.0171	0.0026	$3.95	$4.46	$3.32
	2.0	0.1975	0.0382	0.0088	$5.93	$5.89	$3.42
Control Box	**0.5**	0.6503	0.0040	0.0003	$3.49	$4.05	$3.25
	1.0	0.1399	0.0168	0.0026	$4.12	$4.35	$3.29
	2.0	0.1896	0.0379	0.0087	$5.85	$5.78	$3.40
Blower	**0.5**	0.6424	0.0040	0.0003	$1.75	$1.64	$1.67
	1.0	0.1240	0.0172	0.0026	$2.30	$2.90	$1.71
	2.0	0.1817	0.0386	0.0087	$3.18	$3.57	$1.77
Air Guide	**0.5**	0.6424	0.0017	0.0003	$0.96	$0.94	$0.81
	1.0	0.0924	0.0175	0.0025	$1.39	$1.28	$0.88
	2.0	0.1659	0.0334	0.0088	$1.84	$1.83	$0.94
Motor	**0.5**	0.6234	0.0040	0.0003	$3.64	$3.49	$3.41
	1.0	0.1351	0.0168	0.0026	$4.01	$3.74	$3.48
	2.0	0.1904	0.0386	0.0088	$5.63	$4.84	$3.51
Condenser	**0.5**	0.6495	0.0043	0.0004	$1.14	$0.97	$0.95
	1.0	0.1264	0.0171	0.0026	$1.65	$1.39	$1.04
	2.0	0.1991	0.0385	0.0088	$1.91	$1.60	$1.10
Fan	**0.5**	0.6653	0.0040	0.0003	$2.18	$1.84	$1.77
	1.0	0.1454	0.0169	0.0026	$3.01	$2.16	$1.82
	2.0	0.1912	0.0382	0.0088	$3.75	$2.99	$1.91
Protector	**0.5**	0.6716	0.0043	0.0003	$0.58	$0.45	$0.32
	1.0	0.1240	0.0170	0.0025	$0.89	$0.73	$0.39
	2.0	0.1888	0.0386	0.0088	$1.56	$1.05	$0.42
Compressor	**0.5**	0.6487	0.0043	0.0004	$2.53	$2.37	$2.27
	1.0	0.1312	0.0171	0.0026	$3.26	$3.06	$2.46
	2.0	0.1904	0.0383	0.0088	$4.43	$4.01	$2.54
AC	**0.5**	0.6416	0.0043	0.0004	$45.43	$43.58	$43.17
	1.0	0.1501	0.0172	0.0027	$47.41	$47.92	$45.20
	2.0	0.1967	0.0383	0.0087	$55.70	$54.87	$46.88

Example 7.4

Based on Data Set I (see Section 6.4), the expected warranty costs determined using (7.15), and confidence intervals of the simulation runs for different combinations of lower and upper range of remaining lives and warranty periods, are shown in Table 7.7 and Table 7.8, respectively. In general, when comparing Model S3 and Model S4, here, too, it is clear that the expected warranty cost of conventional remanufactured AC is significantly higher than that of the sensor-embedded remanufactured AC.

Furthermore, when Model S1 and Model S3 are compared or Model S2 and Model S4 are compared, it is clear that the expected warranty costs of using preventive maintenance is much less than using corrective maintenance. Finally, when Model S2 and Model S3 are compared, the reduction in the expected warranty costs of using SEPs with preventive maintenance (S3) is more dramatic than using conventional products with corrective maintenance (S2)!

7.3.5 Model C1 (Sensor-Embedded Components, Non-Repairable, Corrective Maintenance, Replacement by New)

When a failed component arrives at the ARTO system, it is replaced by a new one due to the lack of availability of a remanufactured component in the life

TABLE 7.6

Standard Error and Confidence Interval for FRW Policy, Model S3

					Confidence Interval					
		Standard Error			*RL* = 1		*RL* = 2		*RL* = 3	
Components	*W*	*RL* = 1	*RL* = 2	*RL* = 3	Lower	Upper	Lower	Upper	Lower	Upper
Evaporator	**0.5**	0.27	0.40	0.60	$3.40	$3.71	$3.85	$4.31	$2.91	$3.60
	1.0	0.69	1.01	1.06	$3.56	$4.35	$3.88	$5.05	$2.70	$3.93
	2.0	1.33	1.52	1.75	$5.16	$6.69	$5.01	$6.76	$2.41	$4.43
Control Box	**0.5**	0.30	0.44	0.67	$3.32	$3.67	$3.79	$4.31	$2.86	$3.63
	1.0	0.77	1.14	1.19	$3.67	$4.57	$3.69	$5.00	$2.61	$3.98
	2.0	1.49	1.71	1.96	$4.99	$6.72	$4.79	$6.76	$2.26	$4.54
Blower	**0.5**	0.34	0.50	0.76	$1.55	$1.94	$1.34	$1.93	$1.22	$2.11
	1.0	0.87	1.28	1.34	$1.79	$2.80	$2.16	$3.64	$0.93	$2.48
	2.0	1.68	1.91	2.20	$2.20	$4.15	$2.47	$4.68	$0.49	$3.05
Air Guide	**0.5**	0.43	0.63	0.96	$0.71	$1.22	$0.58	$1.30	$0.24	$1.37
	1.0	1.10	1.62	1.70	$0.75	$2.03	$0.34	$2.22	$0.48	$1.29
	2.0	2.13	2.43	2.80	$0.61	$3.07	$0.42	$3.23	$0.28	$1.60
Motor	**0.5**	0.38	0.56	0.85	$3.42	$3.86	$3.17	$3.82	$2.92	$3.91
	1.0	0.98	1.45	1.51	$3.44	$4.57	$2.90	$4.57	$2.60	$4.35
	2.0	1.90	2.16	2.49	$4.53	$6.72	$3.58	$6.09	$2.06	$4.95
Condenser	**0.5**	0.32	0.47	0.71	$0.96	$1.32	$0.70	$1.24	$0.54	$1.36
	1.0	0.81	1.19	1.25	$1.19	$2.12	$0.70	$2.08	$0.32	$1.77
	2.0	1.56	1.79	2.06	$1.00	$2.82	$0.57	$2.64	$0.61	$1.59
Fan	**0.5**	0.32	0.47	0.71	$2.00	$2.36	$1.57	$2.11	$1.36	$2.18
	1.0	0.81	1.19	1.25	$2.54	$3.48	$1.47	$2.84	$1.09	$2.54
	2.0	1.56	1.79	2.06	$2.84	$4.65	$1.96	$4.03	$0.72	$3.11
Protector	**0.5**	0.31	0.45	0.69	$0.40	$0.75	$0.19	$0.71	$0.16	$0.49
	1.0	0.78	1.15	1.21	$0.44	$1.34	$0.06	$1.40	$0.10	$0.67
	2.0	1.51	1.73	1.99	$0.69	$2.44	$0.05	$2.05	$0.09	$0.75
Compressor	**0.5**	0.31	0.45	0.69	$2.35	$2.70	$2.11	$2.63	$1.87	$2.66
	1.0	0.78	1.15	1.21	$2.80	$3.71	$2.39	$3.73	$1.76	$3.15
	2.0	1.51	1.73	1.99	$3.56	$5.31	$3.00	$5.01	$1.38	$3.69
AC	**0.5**	0.40	0.60	0.91	$45.20	$48.04	$43.24	$43.93	$42.64	$43.70
	1.0	1.04	1.01	1.60	$46.81	$48.01	$47.34	$48.51	$44.27	$46.12
	2.0	2.01	2.29	2.64	$54.54	$56.87	$53.55	$56.20	$45.35	$48.41

bins. For the failure distribution is given in (5.21), the expected warranty cost associated with component i is given by:

$$E\left[C_i\left(W;RL_i\right)\right]=c_{\text{in}}\left[F_{i1}\left(W\right)+\int_{Rl}^{W}M_i\left(W-x\right)dF_{i1}\left(x\right)\right] \tag{7.16}$$

where $M_i(\ )$ is the renewal function associated with $F_i(\ )$ and is given by (5.27). $F_{i1}(x)$ is the distribution function for the first failure and is given by (5.22).

TABLE 7.7

The Expected Warranty Costs for FRW Policy, Model S4

		Expected Warranty Cost to Remanufacturer								
		$L = 1$			$L = 2$			$L = 3$		
Components	*W*	$U = 1$	$U = 2$	$U = 3$	$U = 1$	$U = 2$	$U = 3$	$U = 1$	$U = 2$	$U = 3$
Evaporator	**0.5**	$5.56	$6.37	$5.09	$6.16	$7.06	$5.64	$6.37	$7.30	$5.83
	1.0	$6.17	$6.97	$5.18	$6.85	$7.73	$5.75	$7.08	$7.99	$5.94
	2.0	$9.26	$9.20	$5.35	$10.27	$10.20	$5.93	$10.61	$10.54	$6.13
Control Box	**0.5**	$4.42	$6.33	$5.07	$6.05	$7.02	$5.63	$6.05	$7.26	$5.82
	1.0	$5.21	$6.79	$5.15	$7.13	$7.53	$5.71	$7.13	$7.78	$5.90
	2.0	$7.41	$9.02	$5.31	$10.14	$10.01	$5.89	$10.14	$10.34	$6.08
Blower	**0.5**	$2.21	$2.56	$2.60	$3.03	$2.83	$2.89	$3.03	$2.93	$2.99
	1.0	$2.91	$4.53	$2.67	$3.98	$5.02	$2.96	$3.98	$5.19	$3.06
	2.0	$4.02	$5.58	$2.77	$5.50	$6.19	$3.07	$5.50	$6.40	$3.17
Air Guide	**0.5**	$1.22	$1.47	$1.26	$1.67	$1.63	$1.40	$1.67	$1.68	$1.44
	1.0	$1.76	$2.00	$1.38	$2.41	$2.22	$1.53	$2.41	$2.29	$1.58
	2.0	$2.33	$2.85	$1.47	$3.19	$3.16	$1.63	$3.19	$3.27	$1.68
Motor	**0.5**	$4.61	$5.46	$5.33	$6.31	$6.05	$5.91	$6.31	$6.25	$6.11
	1.0	$5.07	$5.84	$5.43	$6.94	$6.48	$6.02	$6.94	$6.69	$6.23
	2.0	$7.12	$7.56	$5.48	$9.75	$8.38	$6.08	$9.75	$8.66	$6.28
Condenser	**0.5**	$1.44	$1.52	$1.48	$1.97	$1.68	$1.64	$1.97	$1.74	$1.70
	1.0	$2.09	$2.17	$1.63	$2.86	$2.41	$1.81	$2.86	$2.49	$1.87
	2.0	$2.42	$2.51	$1.72	$3.31	$2.78	$1.90	$3.31	$2.87	$1.97
Fan	**0.5**	$2.76	$2.88	$2.77	$3.78	$3.19	$3.07	$3.78	$3.30	$3.17
	1.0	$3.81	$3.37	$2.84	$5.22	$3.74	$3.15	$5.22	$3.86	$3.25
	2.0	$4.74	$4.68	$2.99	$6.49	$5.19	$3.31	$6.49	$5.36	$3.42
Protector	**0.5**	$0.73	$0.70	$0.41	$1.00	$0.78	$0.56	$1.00	$0.81	$0.58
	1.0	$1.13	$1.14	$0.60	$1.55	$1.26	$0.67	$1.55	$1.30	$0.69
	2.0	$1.98	$1.64	$0.65	$2.71	$1.82	$0.73	$2.71	$1.88	$0.75
Compressor	**0.5**	$3.20	$3.70	$3.54	$4.38	$4.11	$3.93	$4.38	$4.25	$4.06
	1.0	$4.12	$4.78	$3.84	$5.64	$5.30	$4.26	$5.64	$5.48	$4.40
	2.0	$5.61	$6.26	$3.96	$7.68	$6.94	$4.39	$7.68	$7.17	$4.54
AC	**0.5**	$57.5	$68.10	$67.45	$78.72	$75.51	$74.80	$78.72	$78.05	$77.32
	1.0	$60.0	$74.87	$70.61	$82.14	$83.03	$78.31	$82.14	$85.82	$80.94
	2.0	$70.5	$85.74	$73.24	$96.51	$95.08	$81.22	$96.51	$98.27	$83.95

TABLE 7.8

Confidence Interval for FRW Policy, Model S4

		L = 1						L = 2						L = 3					
Components	**W**	U = 1		U = 2		U = 3		U = 1		U = 2		U = 3		U = 1		U = 2		U = 3	
Evaporator	0.5	$5.36	$5.75	$6.17	$6.57	$5.93	$6.81	5.96	$6.36	$6.77	$7.35	$5.20	$6.08	6.17	$6.56	$6.08	$6.66	$5.93	$6.81
	1.0	$5.67	$6.68	$6.47	$7.48	$6.30	$7.85	6.34	$7.35	$6.99	$8.48	$4.97	$6.53	6.57	$7.58	$6.33	$7.82	$6.30	$7.85
	2.0	$8.28	$10.23	$8.22	$10.17	$9.33	$11.89	9.29	$11.24	$9.09	$11.31	$4.65	$7.21	9.64	$11.59	$9.50	$11.73	$9.33	$11.89
Control Box	0.5	$4.20	$4.64	$6.11	$6.55	$5.56	$6.55	$5.83	$6.27	$6.70	$7.35	$5.13	$6.12	$5.83	$6.27	$5.73	$6.38	$5.56	$6.55
	1.0	$4.64	$5.78	$6.22	$7.36	$6.26	$8.01	$6.57	$7.70	$6.70	$8.36	$4.84	$6.58	$6.57	$7.70	$6.30	$7.97	$6.26	$8.01
	2.0	$6.32	$8.50	$7.93	$10.12	$8.71	$11.58	$9.05	$11.24	$8.76	$11.26	$4.45	$7.33	$9.05	$11.24	$8.89	$11.39	$8.71	$11.58
Blower	0.5	$1.96	$2.46	$2.31	$2.80	$2.47	$3.58	2.78	$3.27	$2.47	$3.20	$2.33	$3.44	2.78	$3.27	$2.66	$3.39	$2.47	$3.58
	1.0	$2.27	$3.55	$3.89	$5.17	$3.00	$4.96	3.35	$4.62	$4.09	$5.96	$1.98	$3.94	3.35	$4.62	$3.05	$4.92	$3.00	$4.96
	2.0	$2.79	$5.25	$4.35	$6.81	$3.89	$7.12	4.27	$6.73	$4.78	$7.59	$1.45	$4.68	4.27	$6.73	$4.10	$6.91	$3.89	$7.12
Air Guide	0.5	$0.90	$1.54	$1.15	$1.78	$0.96	$2.38	$1.35	$1.99	$1.16	$2.09	$0.69	$2.10	$1.35	$1.99	$1.21	$2.13	$0.96	$2.38
	1.0	$0.95	$2.57	$1.19	$2.81	$1.17	$3.65	$1.60	$3.22	$1.03	$3.41	$0.29	$2.78	$1.60	$3.22	$1.22	$3.60	$1.17	$3.65
	2.0	$0.77	$3.89	$1.29	$4.41	$1.14	$5.24	$1.63	$4.75	$1.38	$4.95	$0.42	$3.68	$1.63	$4.75	$1.41	$4.97	$1.14	$5.24
Motor	0.5	$4.33	$4.89	$5.18	$5.74	$5.68	$6.94	6.03	$6.59	$5.64	$6.46	$5.29	$6.54	6.03	$6.59	$5.90	$6.72	$5.68	$6.94
	1.0	$4.35	$5.79	$5.12	$6.56	$5.83	$8.05	6.22	$7.66	$5.42	$7.53	$4.92	$7.13	6.22	$7.66	$5.88	$8.00	$5.83	$8.05
	2.0	$5.73	$8.51	$6.17	$8.94	$7.92	$11.57	8.36	$11.14	$6.79	$9.97	$4.25	$7.91	8.36	$11.14	$8.16	$11.33	$7.92	$11.57
Condenser	0.5	$1.21	$1.67	$1.29	$1.75	$1.45	$2.49	$1.74	$2.20	$1.34	$2.03	$1.12	$2.16	$1.74	$2.20	$1.63	$2.31	$1.45	$2.49
	1.0	$1.50	$2.68	$1.58	$2.77	$1.95	$3.78	$2.27	$3.46	$1.53	$3.28	$0.89	$2.72	$2.27	$3.46	$1.99	$3.74	$1.95	$3.78
	2.0	$1.27	$3.57	$1.36	$3.65	$1.80	$4.82	$2.16	$4.46	$1.47	$4.09	$0.39	$3.41	$2.16	$4.46	$2.00	$4.63	$1.80	$4.82
Fan	0.5	$2.53	$2.99	$2.64	$3.11	$3.26	$4.30	3.55	$4.01	$2.85	$3.53	$2.55	$3.59	3.55	$4.01	$3.44	$4.12	$3.26	$4.30
	1.0	$3.22	$4.40	$2.78	$3.96	$4.30	$6.13	4.62	$5.81	$2.86	$4.61	$2.23	$4.06	4.62	$5.81	$4.34	$6.09	$4.30	$6.13
	2.0	$3.59	$5.89	$3.53	$5.83	$4.98	$8.00	5.34	$7.64	$3.88	$6.50	$1.80	$4.82	5.34	$7.64	$5.18	$7.80	$4.98	$8.00
Protector	0.5	$0.51	$0.95	$0.48	$0.93	$0.50	$1.50	$0.77	$1.22	$0.45	$1.11	$0.06	$1.06	$0.77	$1.22	$0.67	$1.33	$0.50	$1.50
	1.0	$0.56	$1.70	$0.56	$1.71	$0.66	$2.43	$0.97	$2.12	$0.41	$2.10	$0.21	$1.56	$0.97	$2.12	$0.70	$2.39	$0.66	$2.43
	2.0	$0.87	$3.09	$0.53	$2.75	$1.25	$4.17	$1.60	$3.82	$0.55	$3.09	$0.73	$2.19	$1.60	$3.82	$1.44	$3.98	$1.25	$4.17
Compressor	0.5	$2.98	$3.42	$3.48	$3.93	$3.88	$4.88	$4.16	$4.61	$3.78	$4.44	$3.43	$4.43	4.16	$4.61	$4.05	$4.71	$3.88	$4.88
	1.0	$3.55	$4.69	$4.20	$5.35	$4.76	$6.53	$5.07	$6.21	$4.45	$6.14	$3.37	$5.14	5.07	$6.21	$4.79	$6.49	$4.76	$6.53
	2.0	$4.50	$6.72	$5.15	$7.37	$6.22	$9.14	$6.57	$8.79	$5.67	$8.21	$2.93	$5.85	6.57	$8.79	$6.41	$8.95	$6.22	$9.14
AC	0.5	$54.99	$64.60	$65.13	$76.51	$64.50	$75.78	$75.28	$88.45	$72.21	$84.84	$71.53	$84.04	$75.28	$88.45	$74.64	$87.69	$73.94	$86.87
	1.0	$57.38	$67.41	$71.60	$84.12	$67.53	$79.33	$78.55	$92.29	$79.40	$93.29	$74.89	$87.98	$78.55	$92.29	$82.07	$96.42	$77.40	$90.94
	2.0	$67.42	$79.21	$81.99	$96.33	$70.04	$82.29	$92.29	$108.43	$90.93	$106.83	$77.67	$91.25	$92.29	$108.43	$93.98	$110.41	$80.28	$94.32

Example 7.5

Based on Data Set II (i) (see Section 6.4), the expected warranty costs obtained from (7.16) for different combinations of RL_i and W are shown in Table 7.9, and the standard errors with the 90% confidence intervals are shown in Table 7.10. The failure distribution function for the excess remaining life [$F_{i1}(\ )$] is given by (5.23).

Table 7.9 presents the expected number of failures and cost for remanufactured AC components for FRW policy. In Table 7.9, the expected number of failures represents the expected number of failed items per unit of sale. The expected cost to the remanufacturer includes the cost of supplying the

TABLE 7.9

The Expected Warranty Costs for FRW Policy, Model C1

		Expected Failures Frequency			Expected Warranty Cost to Remanufacturer		
Components	*W*	$RL_i = 1$	$RL_i = 2$	$RL_i = 3$	$RL_i = 1$	$RL_i = 2$	$RL_i = 3$
Evaporator	**0.5**	0.2749	0.0018	0.0001	$4.10	$4.70	$3.75
	1.0	0.0551	0.0072	0.0011	$4.55	$5.14	$3.82
	2.0	0.0825	0.0159	0.0037	$6.83	$6.78	$3.94
Control Box	**0.5**	0.2716	0.0017	0.0001	$4.02	$4.67	$3.74
	1.0	0.0584	0.0070	0.0011	$4.74	$5.01	$3.79
	2.0	0.0792	0.0158	0.0036	$6.74	$6.65	$3.91
Blower	**0.5**	0.2683	0.0017	0.0001	$2.01	$1.88	$1.92
	1.0	0.0518	0.0072	0.0011	$2.65	$3.34	$1.97
	2.0	0.0759	0.0161	0.0036	$3.66	$4.11	$2.04
Air Guide	**0.5**	0.2683	0.0007	0.0001	$1.11	$1.08	$0.93
	1.0	0.0386	0.0073	0.0011	$1.60	$1.47	$1.02
	2.0	0.0693	0.0140	0.0037	$2.12	$2.10	$1.08
Motor	**0.5**	0.2604	0.0017	0.0001	$4.20	$4.02	$3.93
	1.0	0.0564	0.0070	0.0011	$4.61	$4.30	$4.00
	2.0	0.0795	0.0161	0.0037	$6.48	$5.57	$4.04
Condenser	**0.5**	0.2713	0.0018	0.0002	$1.31	$1.12	$1.09
	1.0	0.0528	0.0071	0.0011	$1.90	$1.60	$1.20
	2.0	0.0832	0.0161	0.0037	$2.20	$1.85	$1.26
Fan	**0.5**	0.2779	0.0017	0.0001	$2.51	$2.12	$2.04
	1.0	0.0607	0.0071	0.0011	$3.47	$2.48	$2.09
	2.0	0.0799	0.0160	0.0037	$4.31	$3.45	$2.20
Protector	**0.5**	0.2805	0.0018	0.0001	$0.66	$0.52	$0.37
	1.0	0.0518	0.0071	0.0011	$1.03	$0.84	$0.45
	2.0	0.0789	0.0161	0.0037	$1.80	$1.21	$0.48
Compressor	**0.5**	0.2709	0.0018	0.0002	$2.91	$2.73	$2.61
	1.0	0.0548	0.0071	0.0011	$3.75	$3.52	$2.83
	2.0	0.0795	0.0160	0.0037	$5.11	$4.61	$2.92

TABLE 7.10

Standard Error and Confidence Interval for FRW Policy, Model C1

		Standard Error			Confidence Interval					
					$RL_i = 1$		$RL_i = 2$		$RL_i = 3$	
Components	*W*	$RL_i = 1$	$RL_i = 2$	$RL_i = 3$	Lower	Upper	Lower	Upper	Lower	Upper
Evaporator	**0.5**	0.30	0.45	0.68	$3.96	$4.23	$4.49	$4.90	$3.44	$4.06
	1.0	0.77	1.14	1.19	$4.20	$4.90	$4.62	$5.66	$3.28	$4.36
	2.0	1.50	1.71	1.97	$6.15	$7.50	$6.00	$7.56	$3.05	$4.83
Control Box	**0.5**	0.34	0.50	0.76	$3.87	$4.18	$4.44	$4.90	$3.39	$4.09
	1.0	0.87	1.28	1.34	$4.35	$5.14	$4.42	$5.59	$3.19	$4.40
	2.0	1.68	1.92	2.21	$5.98	$7.51	$5.78	$7.53	$2.91	$4.92
Blower	**0.5**	0.38	0.56	0.85	$1.84	$2.18	$1.63	$2.14	$1.53	$2.31
	1.0	0.98	1.44	1.51	$2.20	$3.09	$2.69	$3.99	$1.28	$2.65
	2.0	1.89	2.16	2.48	$2.80	$4.52	$3.13	$5.09	$0.91	$3.17
Air Guide	**0.5**	0.48	0.71	1.08	$0.89	$1.33	$0.76	$1.41	$0.44	$1.42
	1.0	1.24	1.83	1.91	$1.04	$2.17	$0.64	$2.30	$0.15	$1.89
	2.0	2.40	2.74	3.15	$1.03	$3.21	$0.86	$3.35	$0.35	$2.52
Motor	**0.5**	0.43	0.63	0.96	$4.00	$4.39	$3.73	$4.31	$3.49	$4.37
	1.0	1.10	1.62	1.70	$4.11	$5.12	$3.57	$5.04	$3.23	$4.78
	2.0	2.13	2.44	2.80	$5.51	$7.45	$4.46	$6.68	$2.76	$5.32
Condenser	**0.5**	0.36	0.52	0.80	$1.15	$1.47	$0.88	$1.36	$0.73	$1.45
	1.0	0.91	1.34	1.41	$1.49	$2.32	$0.99	$2.21	$0.56	$1.84
	2.0	1.76	2.01	2.32	$1.40	$3.00	$0.93	$2.76	$0.21	$2.32
Fan	**0.5**	0.36	0.52	0.80	$2.35	$2.67	$1.88	$2.36	$1.68	$2.40
	1.0	0.91	1.34	1.41	$3.05	$3.88	$1.87	$3.10	$1.45	$2.73
	2.0	1.76	2.01	2.32	$3.51	$5.12	$2.53	$4.37	$1.15	$3.26
Protector	**0.5**	0.34	0.51	0.77	$0.51	$0.82	$0.29	$0.75	$0.02	$0.72
	1.0	0.88	1.30	1.36	$0.63	$1.43	$0.25	$1.43	$0.17	$1.06
	2.0	1.70	1.95	2.24	$1.03	$2.58	$0.32	$2.10	$0.54	$1.50
Compressor	**0.5**	0.34	0.51	0.77	$2.76	$3.07	$2.50	$2.96	$2.26	$2.96
	1.0	0.88	1.30	1.36	$3.35	$4.15	$2.93	$4.11	$2.21	$3.45
	2.0	1.70	1.95	2.24	$4.33	$5.88	$3.73	$5.50	$1.90	$3.94

original item, C_s. Thus, the expected cost of the warranty is calculated by subtracting C_s from the expected cost to the remanufacturer. For example, from Table 7.9, for $W = 0.5$ and $RL = 1$, the warranty cost for the sensor-embedded AC motor is $\$4.20 - C_s = |\$4.20 - \$4.00| = \$0.20$, which is $([\$0.20/\$4.00] \times 100) = 5\%$ of the cost of supplying the AC motor, C_s, which is significantly less than \$4.00, C_s. This cost might be acceptable, but the corresponding values for longer warranties are much higher. For example, for $W = 2$ years and $RL = 1$, the corresponding percentage is $([|\$6.48 - \$4.00|/\$4.00] \times 100) = 62\%$.

As shown in Table 7.10, for a one-year remaining-life remanufactured AC motor sold with a 0.5-year warranty, the ARTO system can claim with 90% confidence that the expected warranty cost is in the interval [\$4.00–\$4.39]. Similarly, the confidence interval for a one-year remaining-life remanufactured AC motor sold with two years of warranty is in the range [\$5.51–\$7.45].

7.3.6 Model C2 (Conventional Component, Non-Repairable, Corrective Maintenance, Replacement by New)

In this case, when a failed component arrives at the ARTO system, the component's remaining life is unknown because here there is no sensor embedded in the component. As a result, the expected number of failures is given by (5.30). Since failed components are replaced by remanufactured components, the expected warranty cost associated with the component is given by:

$$E\left[C_i(W)\right]=C_{in}[F_{i1}(W)+\int_0^W M_i(W-x)dF_{i1}(x) \tag{7.17}$$

with $F_{i1}(x)$, $F_{i2}(x)$ and $M_i\,(x)$ given by (5.29), (5.28) and (5.27), respectively.

Example 7.6

Based on Data Set II (i) (see Section 6.4), the expected warranty costs, determined from (7.17), and confidence intervals of the simulation runs for different combinations of lower and upper range of remaining lives and warranty periods, are shown in Table 7.11 and Table 7.12, respectively.

As shown in Table 7.11, when the warranty period is two years and the remanufactured conventional AC motor's remaining life varies from one to three years (i.e., $L = 1$ and $U = 3$), the expected warranty cost to the remanufacturer is \$9.10. As shown in Table 7.9, when the warranty period is two years, the expected cost of a sensor-embedded remanufactured AC motor with one year of remaining life is \$6.84, and the expected cost of a remanufactured AC motor with three years of remaining life is \$4.04. This shows that the expected warranty cost averaged over $L = 1$ to $U = 3$, is [(\$9.10 + \$8.15 + \$6.46)/3]=\$7.90, which is greater than $E\,[C_d\,(W;\,1)]$ by 15.49% and greater than $E\,[C_d\,(W;\,3)]$ by 95.54%.

7.3.7 Model C3 (Sensor-Embedded Component, Non-Repairable, Preventive Maintenance, Replace by Remanufactured)

When a failed component arrives at the ARTO system, it is replaced by a remanufactured component, assuming the remanufactured component is available. As a result, the expected number of failures is given by (5.32). As a result, the expected warranty cost is given by:

$$E\left[C_i(W;RL_i)\right]=C_i[F_{i1}(W)+\int_0^W M_{i2}(W-x)dF_{i1}(x) \tag{7.18}$$

where $M_{i2}(x)$ is the renewal function associated with $F_{i2}(x)$ given by (5.31) and $F_{iu}(x)$ is given by (5.28). $F_{i1}(.)$ is given by (5.20).

TABLE 7.11
The Expected Warranty Costs for FRW Policy, Model C2

		Expected Warranty Cost to Remanufacturer								
		$L = 1$			$L = 2$			$L = 3$		
Components	W	$U = 1$	$U = 2$	$U = 3$	$U = 1$	$U = 2$	$U = 3$	$U = 1$	$U = 2$	$U = 3$
Evaporator	**0.5**	$5.04	$5.12	$5.20	$5.78	$5.90	$6.02	$4.61	$4.79	$4.97
	1.0	$5.60	$5.81	$6.01	$6.33	$6.63	$6.93	$4.70	$5.02	$5.34
	2.0	$8.40	$8.80	$9.19	$8.34	$8.80	$9.25	$4.85	$5.37	$5.89
Control Box	**0.5**	$4.95	$5.04	$5.13	$5.75	$5.88	$6.01	$4.60	$4.81	$5.01
	1.0	$5.84	$6.07	$6.30	$6.16	$6.50	$6.84	$4.67	$5.03	$5.38
	2.0	$8.30	$8.75	$9.19	$8.19	$8.70	$9.20	$4.82	$5.41	$5.99
Blower	**0.5**	$2.48	$2.58	$2.68	$2.32	$2.47	$2.62	$2.36	$2.59	$2.82
	1.0	$3.26	$3.52	$3.78	$4.11	$4.49	$4.87	$2.42	$2.82	$3.22
	2.0	$4.50	$5.00	$5.50	$5.06	$5.64	$6.21	$2.51	$3.17	$3.82
Air Guide	**0.5**	$1.37	$1.50	$1.62	$1.33	$1.52	$1.71	$1.14	$1.43	$1.72
	1.0	$1.97	$2.30	$2.63	$1.81	$2.30	$2.78	$1.25	$1.76	$2.27
	2.0	$2.61	$3.25	$3.88	$2.59	$3.32	$4.04	$1.33	$2.17	$3.00
Motor	**0.5**	$5.16	$5.28	$5.39	$4.95	$5.12	$5.29	$4.84	$5.10	$5.35
	1.0	$5.68	$5.97	$6.26	$5.30	$5.73	$6.16	$4.93	$5.38	$5.83
	2.0	$7.97	$8.54	$9.10	$6.85	$7.50	$8.15	$4.97	$5.72	$6.46
Condenser	**0.5**	$1.61	$1.71	$1.80	$1.38	$1.52	$1.66	$1.34	$1.56	$1.77
	1.0	$2.34	$2.58	$2.82	$1.97	$2.33	$2.68	$1.48	$1.85	$2.22
	2.0	$2.71	$3.18	$3.64	$2.27	$2.81	$3.34	$1.56	$2.18	$2.79
Fan	**0.5**	$3.09	$3.19	$3.28	$2.61	$2.75	$2.89	$2.51	$2.72	$2.93
	1.0	$4.27	$4.51	$4.75	$3.06	$3.42	$3.77	$2.58	$2.95	$3.32
	2.0	$5.31	$5.78	$6.24	$4.24	$4.78	$5.31	$2.71	$3.33	$3.94
Protector	**0.5**	$0.82	$0.91	$1.00	$0.64	$0.78	$0.91	$0.46	$0.67	$0.87
	1.0	$1.27	$1.50	$1.73	$1.03	$1.38	$1.72	$0.55	$0.91	$1.27
	2.0	$2.22	$2.67	$3.12	$1.49	$2.01	$2.52	$0.59	$1.19	$1.78
Compressor	**0.5**	$3.58	$3.68	$3.77	$3.36	$3.50	$3.63	$3.21	$3.42	$3.62
	1.0	$4.61	$4.85	$5.08	$4.33	$4.68	$5.02	$3.48	$3.84	$4.20
	2.0	$6.28	$6.74	$7.19	$5.68	$6.20	$6.71	$3.60	$4.19	$4.78

Example 7.7

Based on Data Set II (i) (see Section 6.4), $F_{iu}(x)$ is given by:

$$F(x) = \int_0^2 \left\{ \frac{e^{-(\lambda_i r l)^{\beta_1}} - e^{-(\lambda_i (x+a))^{\beta_1}}}{e^{-(\lambda_i r l)^{\beta_1}}} \right\} \rho_i e^{-\rho_i r l} drl \tag{7.19}$$

and $F_{i2}(x)$ is given by $F(x) = 0.4\left(1 - e^{-(\lambda_i x)^{\beta_1}}\right) + 0.6F_{iu}(x)$.

Based on this and c_m = \$70, the expected warranty cost, and confidence intervals of the simulation runs for different combinations of lower and upper range of remaining lives and warranty periods, are shown in Table 7.13 and Table 7.14, respectively.

TABLE 7.12

Confidence Interval for FRW Policy, Model C2

		L = 1						*L* = 2						*L* = 3					
		U = 1		*U* = 2		*U* = 3		*U* = 1		*U* = 2		*U* = 3		*U* = 1		*U* = 2		*U* = 3	
Components	**W**	**Lower**	**Upper**	**Lower**	**Upper**	**Lower**	**Upper**	**Lower**	**Upper**	**Lower**	**Upper**	**Lower**	**Upper**	**Lower**	**Upper**	**Lower**	**Upper**	**Lower**	**Upper**
Evaporator	**0.5**	$4.60	$5.66	$4.67	$5.75	$4.74	$5.84	$5.27	$6.49	$5.38	$6.63	$5.49	$6.76	$4.21	$5.18	$4.37	$5.38	$4.53	$5.58
	1.0	$5.11	$6.29	$5.30	$6.52	$5.48	$6.75	$5.78	$7.11	$6.05	$7.45	$6.32	$7.79	$4.29	$5.28	$4.58	$5.64	$4.87	$6.00
	2.0	$7.66	$9.44	$8.02	$9.88	$8.38	$10.32	$7.61	$9.37	$8.02	$9.88	$8.44	$10.39	$4.42	$5.45	$4.90	$6.03	$5.37	$6.62
Control Box	**0.5**	$4.52	$5.56	$4.60	$5.66	$4.68	$5.76	$5.25	$6.46	$5.36	$6.61	$5.48	$6.75	$4.20	$5.17	$4.38	$5.40	$4.57	$5.63
	1.0	$5.33	$6.56	$5.54	$6.82	$5.75	$7.08	$5.62	$6.92	$5.93	$7.30	$6.24	$7.68	$4.26	$5.25	$4.58	$5.65	$4.91	$6.04
	2.0	$7.57	$9.32	$7.98	$9.82	$8.38	$10.32	$7.47	$9.20	$7.93	$9.77	$8.39	$10.34	$4.40	$5.42	$4.93	$6.07	$5.47	$6.73
Blower	**0.5**	$2.26	$2.79	$2.35	$2.90	$2.45	$3.01	$2.12	$2.61	$2.25	$2.77	$2.39	$2.94	$2.15	$2.65	$2.36	$2.91	$2.57	$3.17
	1.0	$2.97	$3.66	$3.21	$3.95	$3.45	$4.25	$3.75	$4.62	$4.10	$5.04	$4.44	$5.47	$2.21	$2.72	$2.57	$3.17	$2.94	$3.62
	2.0	$4.11	$5.06	$4.56	$5.62	$5.02	$6.18	$4.62	$5.68	$5.14	$6.33	$5.67	$6.98	$2.29	$2.82	$2.89	$3.56	$3.49	$4.29
Air Guide	**0.5**	$1.25	$1.54	$1.36	$1.68	$1.48	$1.82	$1.21	$1.49	$1.39	$1.71	$1.56	$1.92	$1.04	$1.28	$1.30	$1.61	$1.57	$1.93
	1.0	$1.80	$2.21	$2.10	$2.58	$2.40	$2.95	$1.65	$2.03	$2.09	$2.58	$2.54	$3.12	$1.14	$1.40	$1.61	$1.98	$2.07	$2.55
	2.0	$2.38	$2.93	$2.96	$3.65	$3.54	$4.36	$2.36	$2.91	$3.02	$3.72	$3.69	$4.54	$1.21	$1.49	$1.98	$2.43	$2.74	$3.37
Motor	**0.5**	$4.71	$5.80	$4.81	$5.93	$4.92	$6.06	$4.52	$5.56	$4.67	$5.75	$4.83	$5.94	$4.42	$5.44	$4.65	$5.72	$4.88	$6.01
	1.0	$5.18	$6.38	$5.45	$6.71	$5.71	$7.03	$4.84	$5.95	$5.23	$6.44	$5.62	$6.92	$4.50	$5.54	$4.91	$6.04	$5.32	$6.55
	2.0	$7.27	$8.95	$7.79	$9.59	$8.30	$10.22	$6.25	$7.70	$6.84	$8.43	$7.44	$9.16	$4.53	$5.58	$5.21	$6.42	$5.89	$7.26
Condenser	**0.5**	$1.47	$1.81	$1.56	$1.92	$1.64	$2.02	$1.26	$1.55	$1.39	$1.71	$1.51	$1.86	$1.22	$1.51	$1.42	$1.75	$1.61	$1.99
	1.0	$2.13	$2.63	$2.35	$2.90	$2.57	$3.17	$1.80	$2.21	$2.12	$2.61	$2.45	$3.01	$1.35	$1.66	$1.69	$2.08	$2.03	$2.49
	2.0	$2.47	$3.04	$2.90	$3.57	$3.32	$4.09	$2.07	$2.55	$2.56	$3.15	$3.05	$3.75	$1.42	$1.75	$1.98	$2.44	$2.55	$3.13
Fan	**0.5**	$2.82	$3.47	$2.91	$3.58	$2.99	$3.68	$2.38	$2.93	$2.51	$3.09	$2.64	$3.25	$2.29	$2.82	$2.48	$3.06	$2.67	$3.29
	1.0	$3.90	$4.80	$4.11	$5.07	$4.33	$5.34	$2.79	$3.44	$3.12	$3.84	$3.44	$4.24	$2.35	$2.90	$2.69	$3.31	$3.03	$3.73
	2.0	$4.84	$5.97	$5.27	$6.49	$5.69	$7.01	$3.87	$4.76	$4.36	$5.36	$4.84	$5.97	$2.47	$3.04	$3.03	$3.74	$3.59	$4.43
Protector	**0.5**	$0.75	$0.92	$0.83	$1.02	$0.91	$1.12	$0.58	$0.72	$0.71	$0.87	$0.83	$1.02	$0.42	$0.52	$0.61	$0.75	$0.79	$0.98
	1.0	$1.16	$1.43	$1.37	$1.69	$1.58	$1.94	$0.94	$1.16	$1.25	$1.54	$1.57	$1.93	$0.50	$0.62	$0.83	$1.02	$1.16	$1.43
	2.0	$2.03	$2.49	$2.44	$3.00	$2.85	$3.51	$1.36	$1.67	$1.83	$2.25	$2.30	$2.83	$0.54	$0.66	$1.08	$1.33	$1.62	$2.00
Compressor	**0.5**	$3.27	$4.02	$3.35	$4.13	$3.44	$4.24	$3.07	$3.77	$3.19	$3.93	$3.31	$4.08	$2.93	$3.61	$3.12	$3.84	$3.30	$4.07
	1.0	$4.21	$5.18	$4.42	$5.44	$4.63	$5.71	$3.95	$4.86	$4.27	$5.25	$4.58	$5.64	$3.18	$3.91	$3.50	$4.31	$3.83	$4.72
	2.0	$5.73	$7.06	$6.14	$7.57	$6.56	$8.08	$5.18	$6.38	$5.65	$6.96	$6.12	$7.54	$3.28	$4.04	$3.82	$4.71	$4.36	$5.37

TABLE 7.13

The Expected Warranty Costs for FRW Policy, Model C3

		Expected Failures Frequency			Expected Warranty Cost to Remanufacturer		
Components	*W*	$RL_i = 1$	$RL_i = 2$	$RL_i = 3$	$RL_i = 1$	$RL_i = 2$	$RL_i = 3$
Evaporator	**0.5**	0.2203	0.0014	0.0001	$3.29	$3.77	$3.00
	1.0	0.0441	0.0058	0.0009	$3.65	$4.12	$3.06
	2.0	0.0661	0.0127	0.0030	$5.47	$5.43	$3.16
Control Box	**0.5**	0.2176	0.0014	0.0001	$3.22	$3.74	$3.00
	1.0	0.0468	0.0056	0.0009	$3.80	$4.01	$3.04
	2.0	0.0635	0.0127	0.0029	$5.40	$5.33	$3.13
Blower	**0.5**	0.2150	0.0014	0.0001	$1.61	$1.51	$1.54
	1.0	0.0415	0.0058	0.0009	$2.12	$2.68	$1.58
	2.0	0.0608	0.0129	0.0029	$2.93	$3.29	$1.63
Air Guide	**0.5**	0.2150	0.0006	0.0001	$0.89	$0.87	$0.75
	1.0	0.0309	0.0058	0.0009	$1.28	$1.18	$0.82
	2.0	0.0555	0.0112	0.0030	$1.70	$1.68	$0.87
Motor	**0.5**	0.2086	0.0014	0.0001	$3.37	$3.22	$3.15
	1.0	0.0452	0.0056	0.0009	$3.69	$3.45	$3.20
	2.0	0.0637	0.0129	0.0030	$5.19	$4.46	$3.24
Condenser	**0.5**	0.2174	0.0014	0.0002	$1.05	$0.90	$0.87
	1.0	0.0423	0.0057	0.0009	$1.52	$1.28	$0.96
	2.0	0.0667	0.0129	0.0030	$1.76	$1.48	$1.01
Fan	**0.5**	0.2227	0.0014	0.0001	$2.01	$1.70	$1.63
	1.0	0.0486	0.0057	0.0009	$2.78	$1.99	$1.67
	2.0	0.0640	0.0128	0.0030	$3.45	$2.76	$1.76
Protector	**0.5**	0.2247	0.0014	0.0001	$0.53	$0.42	$0.30
	1.0	0.0415	0.0057	0.0009	$0.83	$0.67	$0.36
	2.0	0.0632	0.0129	0.0030	$1.44	$0.97	$0.38
Compressor	**0.5**	0.2171	0.0014	0.0002	$2.33	$2.19	$2.09
	1.0	0.0439	0.0057	0.0009	$3.00	$2.82	$2.27
	2.0	0.0637	0.0128	0.0030	$4.09	$3.69	$2.34

Table 7.13 presents the expected number of failures and cost for remanufactured AC components for the FRW policy. In Table 7.13, the expected number of failures represents the expected number of failed items per unit of sale. The expected cost to the remanufacturer includes the cost of supplying the original item, C_s. Thus, the expected cost of the warranty is calculated by subtracting C_s from the expected cost to the remanufacturer. For example, from Table 7.13, for $W = 0.5$ and $RL = 1$, the warranty cost for AC's motor is \$3.37–*Cs* =|\$3.37–\$4.00| =\$0.63, which is ([\$0.63/\$4.00] × 100) = 15.75% savings in the cost of supplying the motor, *Cs*, which is significantly less than \$4.00, *Cs*. This cost is acceptable, but the corresponding values for longer warranties are much higher. For example, for $W = 2$ years and $RL = 1$, the corresponding percentage is ([|\$5.19–\$4.00|/\$4.00] × 100) = 29.75%.

TABLE 7.14

Standard Error and Confidence Interval for FRW Policy, Model C3

		Standard Error			Confidence Interval					
					RL = 1		*RL* = 2		*RL* = 3	
Components	*W*	*RL* = 1	*RL* = 2	*RL* = 3	Lower	Upper	Lower	Upper	Lower	Upper
Evaporator	**0.5**	0.24	0.36	0.54	$3.17	$3.39	$3.60	$3.93	$2.76	$3.25
	1.0	0.62	0.91	0.95	$3.37	$3.93	$3.70	$4.53	$2.63	$3.49
	2.0	1.20	1.37	1.58	$4.93	$6.01	$4.81	$6.06	$2.44	$3.87
Control Box	**0.5**	0.27	0.40	0.61	$3.10	$3.35	$3.56	$3.93	$2.72	$3.28
	1.0	0.70	1.03	1.07	$3.49	$4.12	$3.54	$4.48	$2.56	$3.53
	2.0	1.35	1.54	1.77	$4.79	$6.02	$4.63	$6.03	$2.33	$3.94
Blower	**0.5**	0.30	0.45	0.68	$1.47	$1.75	$1.31	$1.71	$1.23	$1.85
	1.0	0.79	1.15	1.21	$1.76	$2.48	$2.16	$3.20	$1.03	$2.12
	2.0	1.51	1.73	1.99	$2.24	$3.62	$2.51	$4.08	$0.73	$2.54
Air Guide	**0.5**	0.38	0.57	0.87	$0.71	$1.07	$0.61	$1.13	$0.35	$1.14
	1.0	0.99	1.47	1.53	$0.83	$1.74	$0.51	$1.84	$0.12	$1.51
	2.0	1.92	2.20	2.52	$0.83	$2.57	$0.69	$2.68	$0.28	$2.02
Motor	**0.5**	0.34	0.50	0.77	$3.20	$3.52	$2.99	$3.45	$2.80	$3.50
	1.0	0.88	1.30	1.36	$3.29	$4.10	$2.86	$4.04	$2.59	$3.83
	2.0	1.71	1.96	2.24	$4.41	$5.97	$3.57	$5.35	$2.21	$4.26
Condenser	**0.5**	0.29	0.42	0.64	$0.92	$1.18	$0.71	$1.09	$0.58	$1.16
	1.0	0.73	1.07	1.13	$1.19	$1.86	$0.79	$1.77	$0.45	$1.47
	2.0	1.41	1.61	1.86	$1.12	$2.40	$0.75	$2.21	$0.17	$1.86
Fan	**0.5**	0.29	0.42	0.64	$1.88	$2.14	$1.51	$1.89	$1.35	$1.92
	1.0	0.73	1.07	1.13	$2.44	$3.11	$1.50	$2.48	$1.16	$2.19
	2.0	1.41	1.61	1.86	$2.81	$4.10	$2.03	$3.50	$0.92	$2.61
Protector	**0.5**	0.27	0.41	0.62	$0.41	$0.66	$0.23	$0.60	$0.02	$0.58
	1.0	0.71	1.04	1.09	$0.50	$1.15	$0.20	$1.15	$0.14	$0.85
	2.0	1.36	1.56	1.79	$0.83	$2.07	$0.26	$1.68	$0.43	$1.20
Compressor	**0.5**	0.27	0.41	0.62	$2.21	$2.46	$2.00	$2.37	$1.81	$2.37
	1.0	0.71	1.04	1.09	$2.68	$3.33	$2.35	$3.29	$1.77	$2.76
	2.0	1.36	1.56	1.79	$3.47	$4.71	$2.99	$4.41	$1.52	$3.16

As shown in Table 7.14, for a one-year remaining-life remanufactured AC motor sold with a 0.5-year warranty, the ARTO system can claim with 90% confidence that the expected warranty cost is in the interval [$3.20–$3.52]. Similarly, the confidence interval for a one-year remaining-life remanufactured AC sold with two years of warranty is [$4.41–$5.97].

7.3.8 Model C4 (Conventional Component, Non-Repairable, Preventive Maintenance, Replacement by Remanufactured)

In this case, when a failed component arrives at the ARTO system, the component's remaining life is unknown because here there is no sensor embedded in the component. As a result, the expected number of failures is given by (5.32). Since failed components are replaced by remanufactured components, the expected warranty cost associated with the component is given by:

$$E\left[C_i(W)\right] = C_{CM}[F_{i1}(W) + \int_0^W M_{i2}(W-x)\,dF_{i1}(x) \tag{7.20}$$

where F_{i1} (x) is given by (5.34). M_{i2} (x) is the renewal function associated with $F_{i2}(x)$ given by (5.35), and $F_{iu}(x)$ is given by (5.28).

Example 7.8

Based on Data Set II(i) (see Section 6.4), for Model C4, the expected warranty costs for different combinations of warranty periods and remaining life are shown in Table 7.15. Table 7.16 shows the standard errors and the confidence intervals of the simulation runs.

As shown in Table 7.15, when the warranty period is two years and the remanufactured conventional AC's motor remaining life varies from one to three years (i.e., $L = 1$ and $U = 3$), the expected warranty cost to the remanufacturer is \$8.30. From Table 7.13, the expected cost of the sensor-embedded remanufactured AC's motor with one year of remaining life is \$5.19, and the expected cost of the remanufactured AC's motor with three years of remaining life is \$3.24. This shows that the expected warranty cost averaged over $L = 1$ to $U = 3$ is [(\$8.30 +\$7.44 +\$5.89)/3]=\$7.21, which is greater than $E\ [C_d\ (W;\ 1)]$ by 38.92% and greater than $E\ [C_d\ (W;\ 3)]$ by 122.53%.

It can be seen that the warranty cost of Model C1 (sensor-embedded non-repairable component, replaced by new with corrective maintenance) is less than Model C2 (conventional non-repairable component, replaced by new with corrective maintenance). The use of SEPs in Model C1 reduces the warranty cost by 34.93% compared to the conventional product in Model C2. Also, the warranty cost of Model C3 (sensor-embedded non-repairable component, replaced by remanufactured with preventive maintenance) is less than Model C4 (conventional non-repairable component, replaced by remanufactured with preventive maintenance) by 53.64%. In addition, preventive maintenance reduces the warranty cost in Model C3 by 24.81% compared to Model C1, and in Model C4 by 9.61% compared to Model C2. Moreover, when sensors are used along with preventive maintenance (Model C3), the warranty cost is reduced by 68.40% compared to the conventional product with corrective maintenance only (Model C2).

TABLE 7.15

The Expected Warranty Costs for FRW Policy, Model C4

		Expected Warranty Cost to Remanufacturer								
		L = 1			L = 2			L = 3		
Components	W	U = 1	U = 2	U = 3	U = 1	U = 2	U = 3	U = 1	U = 2	U = 3
Evaporator	**0.5**	$4.60	$4.67	$4.74	$5.27	$5.38	$5.49	$4.21	$4.37	$4.53
	1.0	$5.11	$5.30	$5.48	$5.78	$6.05	$6.32	$4.29	$4.58	$4.87
	2.0	$7.66	$8.03	$8.38	$7.61	$8.03	$8.44	$4.42	$4.90	$5.37
Control Box	**0.5**	$4.52	$4.60	$4.68	$5.25	$5.36	$5.48	$4.20	$4.39	$4.57
	1.0	$5.33	$5.54	$5.75	$5.62	$5.93	$6.24	$4.26	$4.59	$4.91
	2.0	$7.57	$7.98	$8.38	$7.47	$7.94	$8.39	$4.40	$4.94	$5.46
Blower	**0.5**	$2.26	$2.35	$2.45	$2.12	$2.25	$2.39	$2.15	$2.36	$2.57
	1.0	$2.97	$3.21	$3.45	$3.75	$4.10	$4.44	$2.21	$2.57	$2.94
	2.0	$4.11	$4.56	$5.02	$4.62	$5.15	$5.67	$2.29	$2.89	$3.49
Air Guide	**0.5**	$1.25	$1.37	$1.48	$1.21	$1.39	$1.56	$1.04	$1.30	$1.57
	1.0	$1.80	$2.10	$2.40	$1.65	$2.10	$2.54	$1.14	$1.61	$2.07
	2.0	$2.38	$2.97	$3.54	$2.36	$3.03	$3.69	$1.21	$1.98	$2.74
Motor	**0.5**	$4.71	$4.82	$4.92	$4.52	$4.67	$4.83	$4.42	$4.65	$4.88
	1.0	$5.18	$5.45	$5.71	$4.84	$5.23	$5.62	$4.50	$4.91	$5.32
	2.0	$7.27	$7.79	$8.30	$6.25	$6.84	$7.44	$4.53	$5.22	$5.89
Condenser	**0.5**	$1.47	$1.56	$1.64	$1.26	$1.39	$1.51	$1.22	$1.42	$1.61
	1.0	$2.13	$2.35	$2.57	$1.80	$2.13	$2.45	$1.35	$1.69	$2.03
	2.0	$2.47	$2.90	$3.32	$2.07	$2.56	$3.05	$1.42	$1.99	$2.55
Fan	**0.5**	$2.82	$2.91	$2.99	$2.38	$2.51	$2.64	$2.29	$2.48	$2.67
	1.0	$3.90	$4.11	$4.33	$2.79	$3.12	$3.44	$2.35	$2.69	$3.03
	2.0	$4.84	$5.27	$5.69	$3.87	$4.36	$4.84	$2.47	$3.04	$3.59
Protector	**0.5**	$0.75	$0.83	$0.91	$0.58	$0.71	$0.83	$0.42	$0.61	$0.79
	1.0	$1.16	$1.37	$1.58	$0.94	$1.26	$1.57	$0.50	$0.83	$1.16
	2.0	$2.03	$2.44	$2.85	$1.36	$1.83	$2.30	$0.54	$1.09	$1.62
Compressor	**0.5**	$3.27	$3.36	$3.44	$3.07	$3.19	$3.31	$2.93	$3.12	$3.30
	1.0	$4.21	$4.42	$4.63	$3.95	$4.27	$4.58	$3.17	$3.50	$3.83
	2.0	$5.73	$6.15	$6.56	$5.18	$5.66	$6.12	$3.28	$3.82	$4.36

7.3.9 Model C5 (Sensor-Embedded Component, Minimal Repair with Corrective Maintenance)

This case is similar to that in Section 7.3.1. The expected number of failures is given by (5.37), with $\Lambda(t)$ replaced by $r_i(t)$. As a result, the expected warranty cost associated with component is given by:

$$E\left[C_i\left(W;RL_i\right)\right]=C_{ir}\int_{RL_i-W}^{RL_i} r_i\left(t\right)dt \tag{7.21}$$

where $r_i(x)$ is given by (5.36).

TABLE 7.16

Confidence Interval for FRW Policy, Model C4

		$L = 1$						$L = 2$						$L = 3$					
		$U = 1$		$U = 2$		$U = 3$		$U = 1$		$U = 2$		$U = 3$		$U = 1$		$U = 2$		$U = 3$	
Components	W	Lower	Upper	Lower	Upper	Lower	Upper	Lower	Upper	Lower	Upper	Lower	Upper	Lower	Upper	Lower	Upper	Lower	Upper
Evaporator	**0.5**	$4.20	$5.16	$4.26	$5.25	$4.32	$5.33	$4.81	$5.92	$4.91	$6.05	$5.01	$6.17	$3.84	$4.73	$3.99	$4.91	$4.13	$5.09
	1.0	$4.66	$5.74	$4.84	$5.95	$5.00	$6.16	$5.27	$6.49	$5.52	$6.80	$5.77	$7.11	$3.91	$4.82	$4.18	$5.15	$4.44	$5.47
	2.0	$6.99	$8.61	$7.32	$9.01	$7.65	$9.42	$6.94	$8.55	$7.32	$9.01	$7.70	$9.48	$4.03	$4.97	$4.47	$5.50	$4.90	$6.04
Control Box	**0.5**	$4.12	$5.07	$4.20	$5.16	$4.27	$5.26	$4.79	$5.89	$4.89	$6.03	$5.00	$6.16	$3.83	$4.72	$4.00	$4.93	$4.17	$5.14
	1.0	$4.86	$5.98	$5.05	$6.22	$5.25	$6.46	$5.13	$6.31	$5.41	$6.66	$5.69	$7.01	$3.89	$4.79	$4.18	$5.15	$4.48	$5.51
	2.0	$6.91	$8.50	$7.28	$8.96	$7.65	$9.42	$6.82	$8.39	$7.23	$8.91	$7.65	$9.43	$4.01	$4.94	$4.50	$5.54	$4.99	$6.14
Blower	**0.5**	$2.06	$2.55	$2.14	$2.65	$2.24	$2.75	$1.93	$2.38	$2.05	$2.53	$2.18	$2.68	$1.96	$2.42	$2.15	$2.65	$2.34	$2.89
	1.0	$2.71	$3.34	$2.93	$3.60	$3.15	$3.88	$3.42	$4.22	$3.74	$4.60	$4.05	$4.99	$2.02	$2.48	$2.34	$2.89	$2.68	$3.30
	2.0	$3.75	$4.62	$4.16	$5.13	$4.58	$5.64	$4.22	$5.18	$4.69	$5.78	$5.17	$6.37	$2.09	$2.57	$2.64	$3.25	$3.18	$3.91
Air Guide	**0.5**	$1.14	$1.41	$1.24	$1.53	$1.35	$1.66	$1.10	$1.36	$1.27	$1.56	$1.42	$1.75	$0.95	$1.17	$1.19	$1.47	$1.43	$1.76
	1.0	$1.64	$2.02	$1.92	$2.35	$2.19	$2.69	$1.51	$1.85	$1.91	$2.35	$2.32	$2.85	$1.04	$1.28	$1.47	$1.81	$1.89	$2.33
	2.0	$2.17	$2.67	$2.70	$3.33	$3.23	$3.98	$2.15	$2.65	$2.76	$3.39	$3.37	$4.14	$1.10	$1.36	$1.81	$2.22	$2.50	$3.07
Motor	**0.5**	$4.30	$5.29	$4.39	$5.41	$4.49	$5.53	$4.12	$5.07	$4.26	$5.25	$4.41	$5.42	$4.03	$4.96	$4.24	$5.22	$4.45	$5.48
	1.0	$4.73	$5.82	$4.97	$6.12	$5.21	$6.41	$4.42	$5.43	$4.77	$5.88	$5.13	$6.31	$4.11	$5.05	$4.48	$5.51	$4.85	$5.98
	2.0	$6.63	$8.17	$7.11	$8.75	$7.57	$9.32	$5.70	$7.03	$6.24	$7.69	$6.79	$8.36	$4.13	$5.09	$4.75	$5.86	$5.37	$6.62
Condenser	**0.5**	$1.34	$1.65	$1.42	$1.75	$1.50	$1.84	$1.15	$1.41	$1.27	$1.56	$1.38	$1.70	$1.11	$1.38	$1.30	$1.60	$1.47	$1.82
	1.0	$1.94	$2.40	$2.14	$2.65	$2.34	$2.89	$1.64	$2.02	$1.93	$2.38	$2.24	$2.75	$1.23	$1.51	$1.54	$1.90	$1.85	$2.27
	2.0	$2.25	$2.77	$2.65	$3.26	$3.03	$3.73	$1.89	$2.33	$2.34	$2.87	$2.78	$3.42	$1.30	$1.60	$1.81	$2.23	$2.33	$2.86
Fan	**0.5**	$2.57	$3.17	$2.65	$3.27	$2.73	$3.36	$2.17	$2.67	$2.29	$2.82	$2.41	$2.97	$2.09	$2.57	$2.26	$2.79	$2.44	$3.00
	1.0	$3.56	$4.38	$3.75	$4.63	$3.95	$4.87	$2.55	$3.14	$2.85	$3.50	$3.14	$3.87	$2.14	$2.65	$2.45	$3.02	$2.76	$3.40
	2.0	$4.42	$5.45	$4.81	$5.92	$5.19	$6.40	$3.53	$4.34	$3.98	$4.89	$4.42	$5.45	$2.25	$2.77	$2.76	$3.41	$3.28	$4.04
Protector	**0.5**	$0.68	$0.84	$0.76	$0.93	$0.83	$1.02	$0.53	$0.66	$0.65	$0.79	$0.76	$0.93	$0.38	$0.47	$0.56	$0.68	$0.72	$0.89
	1.0	$1.06	$1.30	$1.25	$1.54	$1.44	$1.77	$0.86	$1.06	$1.14	$1.41	$1.43	$1.76	$0.46	$0.57	$0.76	$0.93	$1.06	$1.30
	2.0	$1.85	$2.27	$2.23	$2.74	$2.60	$3.20	$1.24	$1.52	$1.67	$2.05	$2.10	$2.58	$0.49	$0.60	$0.99	$1.21	$1.48	$1.82
Compressor	**0.5**	$2.98	$3.67	$3.06	$3.77	$3.14	$3.87	$2.80	$3.44	$2.91	$3.59	$3.02	$3.72	$2.67	$3.29	$2.85	$3.50	$3.01	$3.71
	1.0	$3.84	$4.73	$4.03	$4.96	$4.22	$5.21	$3.60	$4.43	$3.90	$4.79	$4.18	$5.15	$2.90	$3.57	$3.19	$3.93	$3.49	$4.31
	2.0	$5.23	$6.44	$5.60	$6.91	$5.98	$7.37	$4.73	$5.82	$5.15	$6.35	$5.58	$6.88	$2.99	$3.69	$3.49	$4.30	$3.98	$4.90

Example 7.9

Based on Data Set II (ii) (see Section 6.4), the expected warranty costs determined from (7.21), and the standard errors along with confidence intervals of the simulation runs for different combinations of remaining lives and warranty periods, are shown in Table 7.17 and Table 7.18, respectively.

Table 7.17 presents the expected failures frequency and cost for remanufactured AC and components for the FRW policy. The expected failures frequency represents the expected number of failed items per unit of sale. For example, from Table 7.17, for $W = 0.5$ and $RL = 1$, the warranty cost for a sensor-embedded AC's motor is $\$6.58 - C_s = |\$6.58 - \$4.00| = \$2.58$, which is $([\$2.58/\$4.00] \times 100) = 64.50\%$ of the cost of supplying

TABLE 7.17

The Expected Warranty Costs for FRW Policy, Model C5

		Expected Failures Frequency			Expected Warranty Cost to Remanufacturer		
Components	*W*	*RL* = 1	*RL* = 2	*RL* = 3	*RL* = 1	*RL* = 2	*RL* = 3
Evaporator	**0.5**	0.5124	0.0033	0.0002	$6.42	$7.36	$5.88
	1.0	0.1027	0.0133	0.0020	$7.13	$8.06	$5.99
	2.0	0.1538	0.0297	0.0068	$10.70	$10.63	$6.18
Control Box	**0.5**	0.5063	0.0031	0.0002	$6.31	$7.32	$5.86
	1.0	0.1089	0.0131	0.0020	$7.44	$7.85	$5.95
	2.0	0.1476	0.0295	0.0068	$10.57	$10.43	$6.13
Blower	**0.5**	0.5001	0.0031	0.0002	$3.15	$2.95	$3.01
	1.0	0.0966	0.0134	0.0020	$4.16	$5.24	$3.08
	2.0	0.1415	0.0300	0.0068	$5.74	$6.45	$3.20
Air Guide	**0.5**	0.5001	0.0014	0.0002	$1.74	$1.70	$1.46
	1.0	0.0720	0.0136	0.0020	$2.52	$2.31	$1.60
	2.0	0.1292	0.0260	0.0068	$3.32	$3.30	$1.70
Motor	**0.5**	0.4854	0.0031	0.0002	$6.58	$6.31	$6.17
	1.0	0.1052	0.0130	0.0020	$7.23	$6.75	$6.28
	2.0	0.1483	0.0300	0.0068	$10.16	$8.73	$6.33
Condenser	**0.5**	0.5057	0.0034	0.0003	$2.05	$1.76	$1.72
	1.0	0.0984	0.0133	0.0020	$2.99	$2.52	$1.88
	2.0	0.1550	0.0300	0.0069	$3.46	$2.89	$1.99
Fan	**0.5**	0.5180	0.0031	0.0002	$3.94	$3.32	$3.20
	1.0	0.1132	0.0132	0.0020	$5.43	$3.89	$3.28
	2.0	0.1489	0.0298	0.0068	$6.76	$5.41	$3.46
Protector	**0.5**	0.5229	0.0033	0.0002	$1.04	$0.82	$0.59
	1.0	0.0966	0.0132	0.0020	$1.62	$1.31	$0.70
	2.0	0.1470	0.0300	0.0068	$2.83	$1.90	$0.76
Compressor	**0.5**	0.5050	0.0033	0.0003	$4.57	$4.28	$4.10
	1.0	0.1021	0.0133	0.0020	$5.88	$5.52	$4.44
	2.0	0.1483	0.0298	0.0068	$8.01	$7.23	$4.58

the AC motor, C_s. This cost might be tolerable, but the corresponding values for longer warranties are much higher. For example, for W = 2 years and $RL = 1$, the corresponding percentage is ([|$10.16–$4.00|/ $4.00] × 100) = 154%.

For one-year remaining-life remanufactured AC motor sold with 0.5 year warranty, the ARTO system can claim with 90% confidence that the expected warranty cost is in the interval [$4.14–$4.57]. The confidence interval for a one-year remaining-life remanufactured AC motor sold with two years of warranty is [$5.67–$7.79].

TABLE 7.18

Standard Error and Confidence Interval for FRW Policy, Model C5

		Standard Error			Confidence Interval					
					$RL = 1$		$RL = 2$		$RL = 3$	
Components	W	$RL = 1$	$RL = 2$	$RL = 3$	Lower	Upper	Lower	Upper	Lower	Upper
Evaporator	**0.5**	0.49	0.72	1.09	$4.11	$4.40	$4.65	$5.10	$3.56	$4.23
	1.0	1.24	1.83	1.91	$4.34	$5.11	$4.77	$5.91	$3.37	$4.56
	2.0	2.40	2.73	3.15	$6.34	$7.83	$6.19	$7.89	$3.11	$5.07
Control Box	**0.5**	0.55	0.80	1.22	$4.00	$4.35	$4.60	$5.10	$3.51	$4.27
	1.0	1.40	2.05	2.15	$4.49	$5.36	$4.56	$5.83	$3.27	$4.61
	2.0	2.69	3.07	3.53	$6.17	$7.84	$5.96	$7.87	$2.97	$5.16
Blower	**0.5**	0.61	0.90	1.36	$1.90	$2.28	$1.67	$2.24	$1.57	$2.41
	1.0	1.56	2.30	2.41	$2.26	$3.24	$2.75	$4.18	$1.30	$2.79
	2.0	3.02	3.45	3.97	$2.86	$4.74	$3.20	$5.34	$0.88	$3.35
Air Guide	**0.5**	0.77	1.14	1.73	$0.91	$1.40	$0.77	$1.48	$0.43	$1.51
	1.0	1.99	2.92	3.06	$1.04	$2.28	$0.62	$2.44	$0.11	$2.01
	2.0	3.84	4.38	5.05	$1.01	$3.39	$0.82	$3.54	$0.29	$2.69
Motor	**0.5**	0.69	1.02	1.55	$4.14	$4.57	$3.86	$4.49	$3.60	$4.56
	1.0	1.77	2.60	2.73	$4.24	$5.34	$3.66	$5.27	$3.31	$5.01
	2.0	3.42	3.90	4.49	$5.67	$7.79	$4.58	$6.99	$2.80	$5.59
Condenser	**0.5**	0.57	0.84	1.28	$1.19	$1.54	$0.90	$1.42	$0.74	$1.53
	1.0	1.46	2.15	2.25	$1.52	$2.43	$0.99	$2.33	$0.55	$1.94
	2.0	2.82	3.22	3.71	$1.41	$3.16	$0.92	$2.92	$0.16	$2.46
Fan	**0.5**	0.57	0.84	1.28	$2.43	$2.78	$1.94	$2.46	$1.72	$2.52
	1.0	1.46	2.15	2.25	$3.15	$4.05	$1.91	$3.25	$1.47	$2.87
	2.0	2.82	3.22	3.71	$3.60	$5.36	$2.58	$4.58	$1.14	$3.44
Protector	**0.5**	0.56	0.81	1.24	$0.52	$0.86	$0.29	$0.79	$0.01	$0.77
	1.0	1.41	2.08	2.18	$0.63	$1.51	$0.23	$1.51	$0.14	$1.14
	2.0	2.73	3.11	3.58	$1.03	$2.72	$0.29	$2.22	$0.45	$1.62
Compressor	**0.5**	0.56	0.81	1.24	$2.85	$3.20	$2.58	$3.09	$2.33	$3.10
	1.0	1.41	2.08	2.18	$3.46	$4.33	$3.01	$4.30	$2.26	$3.62
	2.0	2.73	3.11	3.58	$4.46	$6.15	$3.83	$5.75	$1.92	$4.15

7.3.10 Model C6 (Conventional Component, Minimal Repair with Corrective Maintenance)

In this case, there is no sensor embedded in the remanufactured product. As a result, the expected number of failures is given by (5.38). The expected warranty cost associated with component *i* is given by:

$$E\left[C_i(W)\right]=C_{ir}\int_0^{\infty}E\left[N_i(W \mid RL_i = rl)\right]dG_i(rl) \tag{7.22}$$

Example 7.10

The expected warranty cost associated with component *i* is given by Gamma function as:

$$E\left[Ci(W)\right]=C_{ir}\left(\lambda_i/\rho_i\right)\beta_i\left[\left(x^2e^{\rho_i W}\right)\left\{\Gamma\left(\beta_i+1,\rho_i W\right)\right\}-\left\{\Gamma\left(\beta i+1\right)\right\}\right] \tag{7.23}$$

where

$$\Gamma(\beta i+1)=\int_0^{\infty}t^{\beta_i}e^{-t}dt \text{ and } \Gamma(\beta i+1,\rho_i W)=\int_{\rho_i W}^{\infty}t^{\beta_i}e^{-t}dt \tag{7.24}$$

Based on Data Set II (ii) (see Section 6.4), the expected warranty costs for different combinations of the warranty period are shown in Table 7.19 and Table 7.20.

In general, the values in Table 7.19 are always greater than the values for a remanufactured AC's components in Table 7.17.

7.3.11 Model C7 (Sensor-Embedded Component, Imperfect Repair with Preventive Maintenance)

Here, a repaired component has a failure distribution function $F_{i2}(x)$ given by (5.41). The remaining life of a component can be estimated from the information retrieved from the sensor embedded in the component. As a result, the expected number of failures is given by (5.39). Then, the expected warranty cost is given by:

$$E\left[C_i(W;v_i)\right]=C_{i0}[F_{i1}(W)+\int_0^{W}M_{i2}(W-x)dF_{i1}(x) \tag{7.25}$$

with F_{i1} given by (5.40). $M_{i2}(x)$ is the renewal function associated with $F_{i2}(x)$.

Example 7.11

Based on Data Set II (iii) (see Section 6.4), the expected warranty costs determined from (7.25) for different combinations of remaining life and warranty periods are shown in Table 7.21. Standard errors and confidence intervals of the ARTO simulation runs are shown in Table 7.22.

Table 7.21 presents the expected failures frequency and the warranty costs for remanufactured AC components for the FRW policy. For example, for $W = 0.5$ and $RL = 1$, the warranty cost for a sensor-embedded AC's motor is \$5.36–C_s =|\$5.36–\$4.00| =\$1.36, which is ([\$1.36/\$4.00] × 100) = 34.00% of the cost of supplying the AC motor, C_s, which is less than \$4.00, C_s. This cost might be acceptable, but the corresponding values for longer warranties are much higher. For example, for $W = 2$ years and $RL = 1$, the corresponding percentage is ([|\$8.27–\$4.00|/\$4.00] × 100) = 106.75%.

For one-year remaining-life remanufactured AC motor sold with 0.5 year warranty, the ARTO system can claim with 90% confidence that expected warranty cost is in the interval [\$5.13–\$5.58]. Similarly, the confidence interval for a one-year remaining-life remanufactured AC motor sold with two years warranty is [\$7.16–\$9.39].

7.3.12 Model C8 (Conventional Component, Imperfect Repair with Preventive Maintenance)

In this case, the remaining life of the component arriving at the ARTO system is unknown due to lack of sensor embedded in them. As a result, the expected number of failures is given by (5.37). The expected warranty cost is given by:

$$E\left[C_i(W)\right] = C_{i0}[F_{i1}(W) + \int_0^W M_{i2} dF_{i1}(x) \tag{7.26}$$

with F_{i1} given by (5. 42), and $M_{i2}(x)$ is the renewal function associated with $F_{i2}(x)$, given by: (5.34).

Example 7.12

Based on Data Set II (iii) (see Section 6.4), the expected warranty costs determined from (7.26) for different combinations of remaining lives and warranty periods are shown in Table 7.23. Table 7.24 shows the standard errors and the confidence intervals of the ARTO simulation runs.

As an example, from Table 7.23, when the warranty period is two years, the expected warranty cost to the remanufacturer for the remanufactured conventional AC's motor, with remaining life varying from one to three years (i.e., $L = 1$ and $U = 3$), is \$5.94.

It can be seen that the warranty cost of Model C5 (sensor-embedded repairable component, minimal repair with corrective maintenance) is less than Model C6 (Conventional repairable component, minimal repair with corrective maintenance). Using SEPs in Model C5 reduced the warranty cost by 18.87% compared to the conventional component in Model C6. Also, the warranty cost of Model C7 (sensor-embedded repairable component, imperfect repair with preventive maintenance) is less than Model C8 (conventional repairable component, imperfect with preventive maintenance) by 15.42%. Moreover, preventive maintenance reduced the warranty cost in Model C7 by 22.81% compared to Model C5 and in Model C8 by 26.48% compared to Model C6. When SEPs are used along with preventive maintenance (C7) the warranty cost is reduced by 45.98% compared to a conventional component with corrective maintenance only (C6).

7.3.13 FRW Summary Results

In order to assess the impact of PM on FRW cost, pairwise t tests were carried out for each performance measure. Table 7.25, Table 7.26 and Table 7.27

TABLE 7.19

The Expected Warranty Costs for FRW Policy, Model C6

		Expected Cost to Remanufacturer		
Components	*W*	$P_i = 0.2$	$P_i = 0.3$	$P_i = 0.4$
Evaporator	0.5	$7.63	$8.75	$6.99
	1.0	$8.48	$9.58	$7.12
	2.0	$12.72	$12.64	$7.35
Control Box	0.5	$7.50	$8.70	$6.97
	1.0	$8.84	$9.33	$7.07
	2.0	$12.57	$12.40	$7.29
Blower	0.5	$3.75	$3.51	$3.58
	1.0	$4.94	$6.23	$3.66
	2.0	$6.82	$7.67	$3.80
Air Guide	0.5	$2.07	$2.02	$1.73
	1.0	$2.99	$2.75	$1.90
	2.0	$3.95	$3.92	$2.02
Motor	0.5	$7.82	$7.50	$7.33
	1.0	$8.60	$8.02	$7.46
	2.0	$12.08	$10.38	$7.53
Condenser	0.5	$2.44	$2.09	$2.04
	1.0	$3.55	$2.99	$2.24
	2.0	$4.11	$3.44	$2.36
Fan	0.5	$4.68	$3.95	$3.80
	1.0	$6.46	$4.63	$3.90
	2.0	$8.04	$6.43	$4.11
Protector	0.5	$1.24	$0.97	$0.70
	1.0	$1.92	$1.56	$0.83
	2.0	$3.36	$2.26	$0.90
Compressor	0.5	$5.43	$5.09	$4.87
	1.0	$6.99	$6.56	$5.28
	2.0	$9.52	$8.60	$5.45
AC	0.5	$7.63	$8.75	$6.99
	1.0	$8.48	$9.58	$7.12
	2.0	$12.72	$12.64	$7.35

TABLE 7.20

Standard Error and Confidence Interval for FRW Policy, Model C6

		Standard Error			Confidence Interval					
					$P_i = 0.2$		$P_i = 0.3$		$P_i = 0.4$	
Components	*W*	$P_i = 0.2$	$P_i = 0.3$	$P_i = 0.4$	Lower	Upper	Lower	Upper	Lower	Upper
Evaporator	**0.5**	0.58	0.85	1.29	$6.83	$9.42	$7.83	$10.80	$6.25	$8.63
	1.0	1.47	2.17	2.27	$7.59	$10.47	$8.57	$11.83	$6.37	$8.79
	2.0	2.85	3.25	3.74	$11.38	$15.70	$11.31	$15.60	$6.58	$9.07
Control Box	**0.5**	0.65	0.95	1.45	$6.71	$9.26	$7.78	$10.74	$6.24	$8.60
	1.0	1.66	2.44	2.55	$7.91	$10.91	$8.35	$11.52	$6.32	$8.73
	2.0	3.20	3.65	4.20	$11.24	$15.52	$11.09	$15.31	$6.52	$9.00
Blower	**0.5**	0.73	1.07	1.62	$3.35	$4.63	$3.14	$4.33	$3.20	$4.42
	1.0	1.86	2.74	2.86	$4.42	$6.10	$5.57	$7.69	$3.27	$4.52
	2.0	3.59	4.10	4.72	$6.10	$8.42	$6.86	$9.47	$3.40	$4.69
Air Guide	**0.5**	0.92	1.36	2.06	$1.85	$2.56	$1.81	$2.49	$1.55	$2.14
	1.0	2.36	3.47	3.64	$2.67	$3.69	$2.46	$3.40	$1.70	$2.35
	2.0	4.56	5.21	6.00	$3.53	$4.88	$3.51	$4.84	$1.81	$2.49
Motor	**0.5**	0.82	1.21	1.84	$7.00	$9.65	$6.71	$9.26	$6.56	$9.05
	1.0	2.10	3.09	3.24	$7.69	$10.62	$7.17	$9.90	$6.67	$9.21
	2.0	4.06	4.64	5.34	$10.81	$14.91	$9.29	$12.81	$6.74	$9.30
Condenser	**0.5**	0.68	1.00	1.52	$2.18	$3.01	$1.87	$2.58	$1.82	$2.52
	1.0	1.74	2.56	2.68	$3.18	$4.38	$2.67	$3.69	$2.00	$2.77
	2.0	3.35	3.83	4.41	$3.68	$5.07	$3.08	$4.25	$2.11	$2.91
Fan	**0.5**	0.68	1.00	1.52	$4.19	$5.78	$3.53	$4.88	$3.40	$4.69
	1.0	1.74	2.56	2.68	$5.78	$7.98	$4.14	$5.72	$3.49	$4.81
	2.0	3.35	3.83	4.41	$7.19	$9.93	$5.75	$7.94	$3.68	$5.07
Protector	**0.5**	0.66	0.96	1.47	$1.11	$1.53	$0.87	$1.20	$0.63	$0.86
	1.0	1.68	2.47	2.59	$1.72	$2.37	$1.40	$1.93	$0.74	$1.02
	2.0	3.24	3.70	4.26	$3.01	$4.15	$2.02	$2.79	$0.81	$1.11
Compressor	**0.5**	0.66	0.96	1.47	$4.86	$6.70	$4.55	$6.28	$4.36	$6.01
	1.0	1.68	2.47	2.59	$6.25	$8.63	$5.87	$8.10	$4.72	$6.52
	2.0	3.24	3.70	4.26	$8.52	$11.75	$7.69	$10.62	$4.88	$6.73

present all warranty models with all costs. According to these tables, PM achieves significant savings in holding, backorder, disassembly, disposal, remanufacturing, transportation, warranty, PM costs and the number of warranty claims. In addition, SEPs provide significant improvements in total revenue and profit. According to these tables, offering PM along with sensor-embedded items helps remanufacturers achieve savings of 42.00%, 52.70% and 60.56% in total cost and an increase of 150.81%, 184.53% and 225.10% in profit for Models S3, C3 and C7, respectively.

For FRW policy, the lowest average value of warranty costs, the number of warranty claims and PM costs during the warranty period for remanufactured components and ACs across all models are $29,487.96, 13,960 claims

TABLE 7.21

The Expected Warranty Costs for FRW Policy, Model C7

		Expected Failures Frequency			Expected Warranty Cost to Remanufacturer		
Components	*W*	$RL_i = 1$	$RL_i = 2$	$RL_i = 3$	$RL_i = 1$	$RL_i = 2$	$RL_i = 3$
Evaporator	**0.5**	0.9679	0.0063	0.0005	\$5.23	\$6.00	\$4.79
	1.0	0.1941	0.0252	0.0038	\$5.81	\$6.57	\$4.88
	2.0	0.2905	0.0561	0.0129	\$8.72	\$8.66	\$5.03
Control Box	**0.5**	0.9563	0.0059	0.0005	\$5.14	\$5.96	\$4.78
	1.0	0.2057	0.0248	0.0038	\$6.05	\$6.39	\$4.85
	2.0	0.2789	0.0558	0.0128	\$8.61	\$8.49	\$5.00
Blower	**0.5**	0.9447	0.0058	0.0005	\$2.57	\$2.41	\$2.45
	1.0	0.1824	0.0253	0.0038	\$3.38	\$4.26	\$2.51
	2.0	0.2673	0.0567	0.0128	\$4.67	\$5.25	\$2.60
Air Guide	**0.5**	0.9447	0.0026	0.0005	\$1.42	\$1.38	\$1.19
	1.0	0.1360	0.0257	0.0037	\$2.05	\$1.88	\$1.30
	2.0	0.2440	0.0492	0.0129	\$2.71	\$2.68	\$1.38
Motor	**0.5**	0.9168	0.0059	0.0005	\$5.36	\$5.14	\$5.02
	1.0	0.1987	0.0246	0.0039	\$5.89	\$5.50	\$5.11
	2.0	0.2800	0.0567	0.0129	\$8.27	\$7.11	\$5.16
Condenser	**0.5**	0.9552	0.0064	0.0005	\$1.67	\$1.43	\$1.39
	1.0	0.1859	0.0251	0.0038	\$2.43	\$2.05	\$1.53
	2.0	0.2928	0.0566	0.0130	\$2.81	\$2.36	\$1.62
Fan	**0.5**	0.9784	0.0058	0.0005	\$3.21	\$2.71	\$2.60
	1.0	0.2138	0.0249	0.0038	\$4.43	\$3.17	\$2.67
	2.0	0.2812	0.0562	0.0129	\$5.51	\$4.40	\$2.81
Protector	**0.5**	0.9877	0.0063	0.0005	\$0.85	\$0.66	\$0.48
	1.0	0.1824	0.0250	0.0037	\$1.31	\$1.07	\$0.57
	2.0	0.2777	0.0567	0.0129	\$2.30	\$1.55	\$0.62
Compressor	**0.5**	0.9540	0.0063	0.0006	\$3.72	\$3.49	\$3.33
	1.0	0.1929	0.0251	0.0038	\$4.79	\$4.50	\$3.61
	2.0	0.2800	0.0564	0.0128	\$6.52	\$5.89	\$3.73

and \$1,413.84, respectively for Model C7 (Sensor-Embedded Component, Imperfect Repair with Preventive Maintenance). Model C6 (Component Conventional, Minimal Repair with Corrective Maintenance) has the worst values for the warranty cost and the number of warranty claims during the warranty period, with 167.65% and 255.10% increase in total cost and reduction in profit, respectively.

7.3.13.1 Effect of SEPs on FRW Warranty Policy

The MINITAB-17 program was used to carry out one-way analyses of variance (ANOVA) and Tukey pairwise comparisons for all the results in this

TABLE 7.22

Standard Error and Confidence Interval for FRW Policy, Model C7

		Standard Error			Confidence Interval					
					$RL_i = 1$		$RL_i = 2$		$RL_i = 3$	
Components	*W*	$RL_i = 1$	$RL_i = 2$	$RL_i = 3$	*L* Limit	*U* Limit	*L* Limit	*U* Limit	*L* Limit	*U* Limit
Evaporator	**0.5**	0.60	0.88	1.33	\$5.07	\$5.39	\$5.76	\$6.23	\$4.43	\$5.14
	1.0	1.52	2.24	2.35	\$5.40	\$6.22	\$5.97	\$7.16	\$4.26	\$5.51
	2.0	2.94	3.36	3.87	\$7.93	\$9.50	\$7.76	\$9.55	\$4.00	\$6.06
Control Box	**0.5**	0.67	0.98	1.50	\$4.96	\$5.31	\$5.70	\$6.22	\$4.38	\$5.17
	1.0	1.71	2.52	2.64	\$5.60	\$6.51	\$5.72	\$7.06	\$4.14	\$5.55
	2.0	3.31	3.78	4.35	\$7.73	\$9.49	\$7.49	\$9.50	\$3.84	\$6.16
Blower	**0.5**	0.75	1.11	1.68	\$2.37	\$2.77	\$2.11	\$2.70	\$2.00	\$2.90
	1.0	1.92	2.83	2.96	\$2.87	\$3.89	\$3.51	\$5.02	\$1.72	\$3.30
	2.0	3.71	4.24	4.89	\$3.68	\$5.66	\$4.12	\$6.38	\$1.30	\$3.90
Air Guide	**0.5**	0.95	1.40	2.13	\$1.16	\$1.67	\$1.01	\$1.76	\$0.62	\$1.75
	1.0	2.44	3.59	3.76	\$1.39	\$2.70	\$0.93	\$2.84	\$0.30	\$2.30
	2.0	4.71	5.39	6.20	\$1.45	\$3.96	\$1.25	\$4.12	\$0.35	\$3.03
Motor	**0.5**	0.85	1.25	1.90	\$5.13	\$5.58	\$4.80	\$5.47	\$4.51	\$5.53
	1.0	2.17	3.20	3.35	\$5.31	\$6.47	\$4.64	\$6.35	\$4.22	\$6.00
	2.0	4.20	4.80	5.52	\$7.16	\$9.39	\$5.83	\$8.39	\$3.69	\$6.63
Condenser	**0.5**	0.70	1.03	1.57	\$1.49	\$1.86	\$1.15	\$1.70	\$0.98	\$1.81
	1.0	1.80	2.64	2.77	\$1.95	\$2.91	\$1.34	\$2.75	\$0.80	\$2.27
	2.0	3.47	3.96	4.56	\$1.89	\$3.74	\$1.30	\$3.41	\$0.40	\$2.83
Fan	**0.5**	0.70	1.03	1.57	\$3.02	\$3.39	\$2.43	\$2.98	\$2.18	\$3.02
	1.0	1.80	2.64	2.77	\$3.95	\$4.91	\$2.47	\$3.88	\$1.94	\$3.41
	2.0	3.47	3.96	4.56	\$4.58	\$6.43	\$3.35	\$5.46	\$1.60	\$4.03
Protector	**0.5**	0.68	1.00	1.52	\$0.67	\$1.03	\$0.40	\$0.93	\$0.07	\$0.88
	1.0	1.74	2.55	2.67	\$0.85	\$1.78	\$0.39	\$1.75	\$0.17	\$1.28
	2.0	3.35	3.83	4.41	\$1.41	\$3.19	\$0.52	\$2.57	\$0.54	\$1.79
Compressor	**0.5**	0.68	1.00	1.52	\$3.54	\$3.90	\$3.22	\$3.75	\$2.93	\$3.74
	1.0	1.74	2.55	2.67	\$4.32	\$5.25	\$3.82	\$5.18	\$2.90	\$4.33
	2.0	3.35	3.83	4.41	\$5.63	\$7.41	\$4.87	\$6.91	\$2.56	\$4.90

section. ANOVA was used in order to determine whether there are any significant differences between the warranty costs, number of claims and PM costs for the 12 different models, namely, Model S1, Model S2, Model S3, Model S4, Model C1, Model C2, Model C3, Model C4, Model C5, Model C6, Model C7 and Model C8, while the Tukey pairwise comparisons were conducted to identify which models are similar and which models are not. Table 7.28 shows that there is a significant difference in warranty costs between different warranty policies. The Tukey test shows that all the models are different and that Model C7 (Sensor-Embedded Component, Imperfect Repair with Preventive Maintenance), with the FRW policy, has the lowest warranty cost,

TABLE 7.23

The Expected Warranty Costs for FRW Policy, Model C8

		Expected Warranty Cost to Remanufacturer								
		$L = 1$			$L = 2$			$L = 3$		
Components	*W*	$U = 1$	$U = 2$	$U = 3$	$U = 1$	$U = 2$	$U = 3$	$U = 1$	$U = 2$	$U = 3$
Evaporator	**0.5**	$6.02	$6.91	$5.52	$5.88	$6.18	$6.70	$7.13	$5.18	$5.85
	1.0	$6.70	$7.57	$5.63	$6.31	$7.08	$7.00	$8.13	$5.03	$6.21
	2.0	$10.04	$9.98	$5.80	$9.30	$10.79	$9.13	$10.82	$4.82	$6.77
Control Box	**0.5**	$5.92	$6.88	$5.50	$5.75	$6.09	$6.63	$7.12	$5.12	$5.88
	1.0	$6.98	$7.37	$5.58	$6.55	$7.40	$6.73	$8.00	$4.92	$6.25
	2.0	$9.92	$9.79	$5.76	$9.09	$10.75	$8.84	$10.74	$4.66	$6.85
Blower	**0.5**	$2.95	$2.77	$2.83	$2.77	$3.15	$2.49	$3.06	$2.40	$3.25
	1.0	$3.90	$4.92	$2.89	$3.42	$4.38	$4.20	$5.63	$2.15	$3.64
	2.0	$5.38	$6.06	$3.00	$4.45	$6.31	$4.99	$7.12	$1.78	$4.22
Air Guide	**0.5**	$1.63	$1.60	$1.37	$1.39	$1.88	$1.24	$1.94	$0.83	$1.90
	1.0	$2.36	$2.17	$1.51	$1.74	$2.97	$1.27	$3.08	$0.55	$2.45
	2.0	$3.12	$3.09	$1.60	$1.93	$4.30	$1.74	$4.45	$0.39	$3.16
Motor	**0.5**	$6.18	$5.92	$5.79	$5.97	$6.39	$5.61	$6.24	$5.30	$6.27
	1.0	$6.79	$6.34	$5.90	$6.25	$7.34	$5.53	$7.13	$5.06	$6.73
	2.0	$9.54	$8.20	$5.94	$8.48	$10.59	$6.99	$9.40	$4.56	$7.34
Condenser	**0.5**	$1.93	$1.65	$1.61	$1.75	$2.10	$1.39	$1.91	$1.21	$2.00
	1.0	$2.80	$2.36	$1.76	$2.35	$3.25	$1.70	$3.02	$1.07	$2.46
	2.0	$3.24	$2.72	$1.86	$2.37	$4.11	$1.72	$3.72	$0.71	$3.01
Fan	**0.5**	$3.70	$3.12	$3.00	$3.52	$3.88	$2.86	$3.38	$2.61	$3.39
	1.0	$5.10	$3.65	$3.08	$4.65	$5.55	$2.99	$4.33	$2.38	$3.77
	2.0	$6.35	$5.08	$3.24	$5.47	$7.22	$4.08	$6.08	$2.09	$4.39
Protector	**0.5**	$0.98	$0.76	$0.55	$0.81	$1.15	$0.52	$1.01	$0.17	$0.93
	1.0	$1.52	$1.24	$0.65	$1.08	$1.95	$0.58	$1.88	$0.19	$1.33
	2.0	$2.65	$1.79	$0.71	$1.81	$3.49	$0.82	$2.74	$0.61	$1.82
Compressor	**0.5**	$4.28	$4.02	$3.84	$4.11	$4.46	$3.76	$4.27	$3.46	$4.22
	1.0	$5.52	$5.18	$4.17	$5.08	$5.95	$4.54	$5.83	$3.49	$4.84
	2.0	$7.52	$6.79	$4.30	$6.67	$8.36	$5.83	$7.75	$3.19	$5.40

$29,487.96. In addition, there is a significant difference in the number of warranty claims between different models for the FRW policy (see Table 7.29), except for Model C8 and Model C4 there is no significant difference in the number of claims. Model C7 with the FRW policy has the lowest number of claims, 13,960. Finally, Table 7.30 shows that there is a significant difference in PM costs between different warranty policies. The Tukey test shows that all models are different and Model C7 with the FRW policy has the lowest costs, $1,413.83. These results can be useful in determining the economical warranty policy associated with embedding sensors in ACs.

TABLE 7.24
Confidence Interval for FRW Policy, Model C8

		$L = 1$						$L = 2$						$L = 3$					
		$U = 1$		$U = 2$		$U = 3$		$U = 1$		$U = 2$		$U = 3$		$U = 1$		$U = 2$		$U = 3$	
Components	**W**	**Lower**	**Upper**	**Lower**	**Upper**	**Lower**	**Upper**	**Lower**	**Upper**	**Lower**	**Upper**	**Lower**	**Upper**	**Lower**	**Upper**	**Lower**	**Upper**	**Lower**	**Upper**
Evaporator	**0.5**	$5.49	$6.76	$6.30	$7.76	$5.03	$6.20	$5.36	$6.61	$5.64	$6.94	$6.11	$7.53	$6.52	$8.01	$4.73	$5.82	$5.35	$6.57
	1.0	$6.11	$7.53	$6.91	$8.50	$5.13	$6.33	$5.76	$7.09	$6.46	$7.95	$6.39	$7.86	$7.43	$9.13	$4.59	$5.65	$5.67	$6.98
	2.0	$9.17	$11.28	$9.11	$11.21	$5.29	$6.52	$8.49	$10.45	$9.84	$12.12	$8.34	$10.26	$9.88	$12.16	$4.40	$5.42	$6.18	$7.61
Control Box	**0.5**	$5.40	$6.65	$6.28	$7.73	$5.02	$6.18	$5.25	$6.46	$5.56	$6.84	$6.06	$7.45	$6.50	$8.00	$4.67	$5.75	$5.36	$6.61
	1.0	$6.37	$7.84	$6.73	$8.28	$5.10	$6.27	$5.98	$7.36	$6.76	$8.31	$6.15	$7.56	$7.30	$8.99	$4.49	$5.53	$5.71	$7.02
	2.0	$9.06	$11.14	$8.93	$11.00	$5.26	$6.47	$8.29	$10.21	$9.82	$12.08	$8.07	$9.93	$9.81	$12.07	$4.26	$5.24	$6.26	$7.70
Blower	**0.5**	$2.70	$3.31	$2.53	$3.11	$2.58	$3.18	$2.53	$3.11	$2.88	$3.54	$2.28	$2.80	$2.79	$3.44	$2.19	$2.70	$2.97	$3.65
	1.0	$3.56	$4.38	$4.49	$5.53	$2.64	$3.25	$3.12	$3.84	$4.00	$4.92	$3.83	$4.72	$5.13	$6.33	$1.95	$2.42	$3.33	$4.09
	2.0	$4.91	$6.04	$5.53	$6.81	$2.74	$3.37	$4.06	$5.00	$5.76	$7.09	$4.55	$5.61	$6.50	$8.00	$1.62	$2.00	$3.85	$4.74
Air Guide	**0.5**	$1.48	$1.83	$1.46	$1.80	$1.25	$1.54	$1.27	$1.56	$1.71	$2.11	$1.12	$1.39	$1.78	$2.18	$0.76	$0.93	$1.73	$2.13
	1.0	$2.16	$2.65	$1.98	$2.44	$1.37	$1.70	$1.58	$1.95	$2.71	$3.34	$1.16	$1.43	$2.81	$3.46	$0.51	$0.62	$2.24	$2.75
	2.0	$2.85	$3.51	$2.82	$3.47	$1.46	$1.80	$1.76	$2.17	$3.93	$4.83	$1.58	$1.95	$4.06	$5.00	$0.36	$0.44	$2.89	$3.55
Motor	**0.5**	$5.64	$6.94	$5.40	$6.65	$5.28	$6.50	$5.45	$6.71	$5.83	$7.18	$5.12	$6.30	$5.70	$7.01	$4.84	$5.95	$5.72	$7.04
	1.0	$6.19	$7.63	$5.79	$7.12	$5.38	$6.63	$5.71	$7.02	$6.70	$8.25	$5.04	$6.21	$6.52	$8.01	$4.62	$5.68	$6.15	$7.56
	2.0	$8.71	$10.72	$7.48	$9.21	$5.43	$6.67	$7.74	$9.53	$9.67	$11.90	$6.38	$7.85	$8.58	$10.56	$4.17	$5.12	$6.70	$8.25
Condenser	**0.5**	$1.76	$2.17	$1.51	$1.85	$1.47	$1.81	$1.60	$1.97	$1.92	$2.36	$1.27	$1.56	$1.74	$2.15	$1.11	$1.36	$1.82	$2.25
	1.0	$2.55	$3.15	$2.16	$2.65	$1.61	$1.98	$2.15	$2.64	$2.97	$3.65	$1.55	$1.91	$2.76	$3.39	$0.98	$1.20	$2.25	$2.76
	2.0	$2.95	$3.64	$2.48	$3.06	$1.71	$2.09	$2.17	$2.66	$3.75	$4.62	$1.57	$1.93	$3.39	$4.18	$0.65	$0.80	$2.75	$3.38
Fan	**0.5**	$3.37	$4.16	$2.85	$3.51	$2.74	$3.37	$3.21	$3.95	$3.54	$4.36	$2.62	$3.21	$3.09	$3.80	$2.38	$2.93	$3.10	$3.81
	1.0	$4.65	$5.73	$3.34	$4.10	$2.81	$3.46	$4.25	$5.22	$5.07	$6.24	$2.73	$3.36	$3.94	$4.86	$2.18	$2.67	$3.45	$4.24
	2.0	$5.80	$7.13	$4.64	$5.71	$2.95	$3.64	$5.00	$6.15	$6.59	$8.11	$3.72	$4.58	$5.55	$6.83	$1.91	$2.35	$4.01	$4.93
Protector	**0.5**	$0.89	$1.10	$0.70	$0.85	$0.51	$0.62	$0.74	$0.91	$1.04	$1.29	$0.47	$0.58	$0.92	$1.13	$0.16	$0.19	$0.85	$1.04
	1.0	$1.38	$1.71	$1.12	$1.39	$0.60	$0.73	$0.99	$1.21	$1.79	$2.19	$0.53	$0.65	$1.71	$2.11	$0.18	$0.21	$1.21	$1.49
	2.0	$2.42	$2.98	$1.63	$2.01	$0.65	$0.80	$1.65	$2.03	$3.19	$3.92	$0.75	$0.92	$2.51	$3.08	$0.55	$0.69	$1.66	$2.04
Compressor	**0.5**	$3.91	$4.81	$3.67	$4.52	$3.51	$4.31	$3.75	$4.62	$4.07	$5.01	$3.44	$4.22	$3.90	$4.80	$3.16	$3.89	$3.85	$4.74
	1.0	$5.03	$6.20	$4.73	$5.82	$3.81	$4.68	$4.64	$5.71	$5.44	$6.68	$4.15	$5.10	$5.33	$6.55	$3.19	$3.92	$4.42	$5.44
	2.0	$6.86	$8.45	$6.19	$7.63	$3.93	$4.83	$6.09	$7.49	$7.63	$9.39	$5.33	$6.55	$7.08	$8.71	$2.91	$3.58	$4.93	$6.07

TABLE 7.25

Results of Performance Measures for Different Models with System Level Failure

	Model			
Performance Measure	**S1**	**S2**	**S3**	**S4**
Holding Cost	$102,031.01	$133,573.05	$77,467.42	$121,864.80
Backorder Cost	$18,926.60	$24,777.60	$14,370.09	$22,605.74
Disassembly Cost	$220,315.58	$288,424.31	$167,275.40	$263,142.68
Disposal Cost	$35,689.95	$46,723.20	$27,097.72	$42,627.71
Testing Cost	N/A	$86,026.10	N/A	$78,485.54
Remanufacturing Cost	$757,446.06	$991,604.25	$575,093.67	$904,685.85
Transportation Cost	$19,112.37	$25,020.81	$14,511.14	$22,827.62
Warranty Cost	$47,988.76	$62,824.09	$36,435.64	$57,317.29
Number of Claims	22,718	29,741	17,249	27,134
Preventive Maintenance Cost	N/A	N/A	$1,746.95	$2,326.24
Total Cost	$1,224,228.54	$1,688,714.77	$931,246.91	$1,543,017.86
Total Revenue	$5,040,432.10	$3,642,805.95	$5,832,237.34	$4,110,260.16
Profit	$3,816,203.57	$1,954,091.18	$4,900,990.43	$2,567,242.29

TABLE 7.26

Results of Performance Measures for Different Models with Non-Repair Components

	Model			
Performance Measure	**C1**	**C2**	**C3**	**C4**
Holding Cost	$95,015.94	$148,174.63	$70,079.80	$115,922.01
Backorder Cost	$17,625.32	$27,486.17	$12,999.70	$21,503.36
Disassembly Cost	$205,167.93	$319,953.50	$151,323.33	$250,310.41
Disposal Cost	$33,236.11	$51,830.76	$24,513.57	$40,548.95
Testing Cost	N/A	$95,430.07	N/A	$74,658.16
Remanufacturing Cost	$705,368.37	$1,100,001.73	$520,250.37	$860,568.46
Transportation Cost	$17,798.32	$27,755.96	$13,127.30	$21,714.42
Warranty Cost	$44,689.33	$69,691.73	$32,960.99	$54,522.19
Number of Claims	21,156	32,993	15,604	25,811
Preventive Maintenance Cost	N/A	N/A	$1,580.35	$2,212.80
Total Cost	$1,140,057.54	$1,873,317.08	$842,439.37	$1,467,771.93
Total Revenue	$5,449,889.43	$3,736,600.14	$6,144,082.23	$4,617,699.68
Profit	$4,309,831.89	$1,863,283.06	$5,301,642.86	$3,149,927.75

TABLE 7.27

Results of Performance Measures for Different Models with Repair Components

	Model			
Performance Measure	**C5**	**C6**	**C7**	**C8**
Holding Cost	$85,631.65	$158,957.58	$62,695.64	$110,488.13
Backorder Cost	$15,884.54	$29,486.40	$11,629.95	$20,495.38
Disassembly Cost	$184,904.43	$343,237.13	$135,378.71	$238,577.03
Disposal Cost	$29,953.53	$55,602.59	$21,930.63	$38,648.21
Testing Cost	N/A	$102,374.70	N/A	$71,158.54
Remanufacturing Cost	$635,702.36	$1,180,050.99	$465,432.68	$820,229.03
Transportation Cost	$16,040.46	$29,775.82	$11,744.10	$20,696.55
Warranty Cost	$40,275.57	$74,763.33	$29,487.96	$51,966.44
Number of Claims	19,067	35,393	13,960	24,601
Preventive Maintenance Cost	N/A	N/A	$1,413.84	$2,109.07
Total Cost	$1,027,459.26	$2,009,641.99	$753,673.30	$1,398,969.65
Total Revenue	$5,518,383.06	$3,691,031.85	$6,219,935.10	$4,978,963.42
Profit	$4,490,923.80	$1,681,389.86	$5,466,261.80	$3,579,993.77

7.4 Analysis of Pro-Rata Warranty Policy

This section carries out an analysis of Pro-Rata Warranty (PRW) Policy to determine expected warranty costs. The PRW policy is as follows:

PRW POLICY: Under the pro-rata warranty policy the remanufacturer refunds a fraction of sale price if an item fails before the warranty period ends. The buyer is not constrained to buy a replacement item.

This book considers a linear refund function $S(x)$ given by (4.1). The 12 models discussed for the case of FRW in Section 7.3 can also be discussed for the case of PRW. However, the discussion is very similar. For that reason, only Model C1 is discussed in the next sub-section as an illustration. Other models for PRW policy follow the same pattern as was discussed in Section 7.3 for the FRW policy.

TABLE 7.28

ANOVA Table and Tukey Pairwise Comparisons for Warranty Cost

ANOVA: Warranty Cost

Null hypothesis All means are equal
Alternative hypothesis At least one mean is different
Significance level α = 0.05

SUMMARY

Models	Count	Sum	Average	StDev	95% CI
S1 Model FRW	2000	95,977,528.41	47,988.76	146.79	(47982, 47995)
S2 Model FRW	2000	125,648,187.81	62,824.09	184.71	(62816, 62832)
S3 Model FRW	2000	72,871,286.68	36,435.64	207.19	(36427, 36445)
S4 Model FRW	2000	114,634,581.21	57,317.29	164.66	(57310, 57325)
C1 Model FRW	2000	89,378,658.60	44,689.33	219.44	(44680, 44699)
C2 Model FRW	2000	139,383,453.26	69,691.73	260.71	(69680, 69703)
C3 Model FRW	2000	65,921,980.51	32,960.99	155.47	(32954, 32968)
C4 Model FRW	2000	109,044,376.32	54,522.19	195.63	(54514, 54531)
C5 Model FRW	2000	80,551,136.78	40,275.57	246.16	(40265, 40286)
C6 Model FRW	2000	149,526,657.00	74,763.33	174.40	(74756, 74771)
C7 Model FRW	2000	58,975,919.86	29,487.96	216.31	(29478, 29497)
C8 Model FRW	2000	103,932,886.07	51,966.44	276.13	(51954, 51979)

ANOVA

Source of Variation	SS	df	MS	F-Value	P-value
Model	5.37248E+12	11	1.79083E+12	3060975.56	0.000
Error	4678066569	23988	585051		
Total	5.37716E+12	23999			

Tukey Pairwise Comparisons

Grouping Information Using the Tukey Method and 95% Confidence

Model	N	Mean	Grouping
C7 Model FRW	2000	29,487.96	A
C3 Model FRW	2000	32,960.99	B
S3 Model FRW	2000	36,435.64	C
C5 Model FRW	2000	40,275.57	D
C1 Model FRW	2000	44,689.33	E
S1 Model FRW	2000	47,988.76	F
C8 Model FRW	2000	51,966.44	G
C4 Model FRW	2000	54,522.19	H
S4 Model FRW	2000	57,317.29	I
S2 Model FRW	2000	62,824.09	J
C2 Model FRW	2000	69,691.73	K
C6 Model FRW	2000	74,763.33	L

Means that do not share a letter are significantly different.

TABLE 7.29

ANOVA Table and Tukey Pairwise Comparisons for Number of Claims

ANOVA: Warranty Claims

Null hypothesis All means are equal
Alternative hypothesis At least one mean is different
Significance level α = 0.05

SUMMARY

Models	Count	Sum	Average	StDev	95% CI
S1 Model FRW	2000	45,436,404.20	22,718	292.4	(22705, 22731)
S2 Model FRW	2000	59,482,692.90	29,741	291.17	(29728, 29754)
S3 Model FRW	2000	34,497,754.74	17,249	288.32	(17236, 17262)
S4 Model FRW	2000	54,268,777.84	27,134	145.26	(27128, 27140)
C1 Model FRW	2000	42,312,455.07	21,156	338.27	(21141, 21171)
C2 Model FRW	2000	65,985,059.47	32,993	336.85	(32978, 33008)
C3 Model FRW	2000	31,207,906.70	15,604	333.55	(15589, 15619)
C4 Model FRW	2000	51,622,337.44	25,811	168.05	(25804, 25818)
C5 Model FRW	2000	38,133,447.17	19,067	391.34	(19050, 19084)
C6 Model FRW	2000	70,786,920.00	35,393	389.69	(35376, 35410)
C7 Model FRW	2000	27,919,595.11	13,960	385.88	(13943, 13977)
C8 Model FRW	2000	49,202,523.75	24,601	194.41	(24592, 24610)

ANOVA

Source of Variation	SS	df	MS	F-Value	P-value
Model	8.73274E+11	11	2.91091E+11	4241696.28	0.000
Error	548734919	23988	68626		
Total	8.73823E+11	23999			

Tukey Pairwise Comparisons

Grouping Information Using the Tukey Method and 95% Confidence

Model	N	Mean	Grouping
C7 Model FRW	2000	13,960	A
C3 Model FRW	2000	15,604	A
S3 Model FRW	2000	17,249	B
C5 Model FRW	2000	19,067	C
C1 Model FRW	2000	21,156	D
S1 Model FRW	2000	22,718	E
C8 Model FRW	2000	24,601	F
C4 Model FRW	2000	25,811	F
S4 Model FRW	2000	27,134	G
S2 Model FRW	2000	29,741	H
C2 Model FRW	2000	32,993	I
C6 Model FRW	2000	35,393	J

Means that do not share a letter are significantly different.

TABLE 7.30

ANOVA Table and Tukey Pairwise Comparisons for PM Cost

ANOVA: Preventive Maintenance

Null hypothesis All means are equal
Alternative hypothesis At least one mean is different
Significance level α = 0.05

SUMMARY

Models	Count	Sum	Average	StDev	95% CI
S3 Model FRW	2000	3,493,900.00	1746.95	40.93	(1745, 1749)
S4 Model FRW	2000	4,652,480.00	2326.24	29.24	(2325, 2328)
C3 Model FRW	2000	3,160,707.30	1580.35	32.41	(1579, 1582)
C4 Model FRW	2000	4,425,599.80	2212.80	36.42	(2211, 2214)
C7 Model FRW	2000	2,827,670.21	1413.84	32.86	(1412, 1415)
C8 Model FRW	2000	4,218,148.39	2109.07	28.84	(2108, 2110)

ANOVA

Source of Variation	SS	df	MS	F-Value	P-value
Model	1.37E+09	5	2.74E+08	2.41E+05	0.000
Error	1.36E+07	11,994	1136.43		
Total	1.38E+09	11,999			

Tukey Pairwise Comparisons

Grouping Information Using the Tukey Method and 95% Confidence

Model	N	Mean	Grouping					
C7 Model FRW	2000	1,413.84	A					
C3 Model FRW	2000	1,580.35		B				
S3 Model FRW	2000	1,746.95			C			
C8 Model FRW	2000	2,109.07				D		
C4 Model FRW	2000	2,212.80					E	
S4 Model FRW	2000	2,326.24						F

Means that do not share a letter are significantly different.

7.4.1 Model Cl (Sensor-Embedded Components, Non-Repairable, Corrective Maintenance, Replacement by New)

The time to failure, F_{i1}, is given by (5.2). As a result, the expected warranty cost to the remanufacturer is given by:

$$E\left[C_d(W;RL)\right]=\int_0^W S(x)\,dF_{i1}(x)$$
$$=c_S(RL)\left[F_{i1}(W)-\left(\frac{1}{W}\right)\int_0^W x\,dF_{i1}(x)\right] \tag{7.27}$$

TABLE 7.31

The Expected Warranty Costs for PRW Policy, Model C1

		Expected Failures Frequency			Expected Cost to Remanufacturer		
Components	*W*	*RL* = 1	*RL* = 2	*RL* = 3	*RL* = 1	*RL* = 2	*RL* = 3
Evaporator	**0.5**	0.9941	0.0064	0.0005	$5.37	$6.16	$4.92
	1.0	0.1993	0.0259	0.0039	$5.97	$6.74	$5.01
	2.0	0.2984	0.0576	0.0132	$8.95	$8.89	$5.17
Control Box	**0.5**	0.9822	0.0061	0.0005	$5.28	$6.12	$4.91
	1.0	0.2112	0.0254	0.0039	$6.22	$6.56	$4.98
	2.0	0.2864	0.0573	0.0132	$8.84	$8.72	$5.13
Blower	**0.5**	0.9703	0.0060	0.0005	$2.64	$2.47	$2.52
	1.0	0.1874	0.0260	0.0039	$3.47	$4.38	$2.58
	2.0	0.2745	0.0582	0.0132	$4.80	$5.39	$2.67
Air Guide	**0.5**	0.9703	0.0026	0.0005	$1.46	$1.42	$1.22
	1.0	0.1396	0.0264	0.0038	$2.10	$1.93	$1.34
	2.0	0.2506	0.0505	0.0132	$2.78	$2.76	$1.42
Motor	**0.5**	0.9416	0.0061	0.0005	$5.50	$5.28	$5.16
	1.0	0.2041	0.0253	0.0040	$6.05	$5.65	$5.25
	2.0	0.2876	0.0582	0.0132	$8.50	$7.30	$5.30
Condenser	**0.5**	0.9810	0.0066	0.0005	$1.72	$1.47	$1.43
	1.0	0.1910	0.0258	0.0040	$2.49	$2.10	$1.58
	2.0	0.3008	0.0581	0.0133	$2.89	$2.42	$1.66
Fan	**0.5**	1.0049	0.0060	0.0005	$3.29	$2.78	$2.67
	1.0	0.2196	0.0255	0.0039	$4.55	$3.26	$2.74
	2.0	0.2888	0.0578	0.0133	$5.66	$4.52	$2.89
Protector	**0.5**	1.0144	0.0064	0.0005	$0.87	$0.68	$0.49
	1.0	0.1874	0.0257	0.0038	$1.35	$1.10	$0.58
	2.0	0.2852	0.0582	0.0132	$2.36	$1.59	$0.63
Compressor	**0.5**	0.9798	0.0064	0.0006	$3.82	$3.58	$3.43
	1.0	0.1981	0.0258	0.0039	$4.92	$4.62	$3.71
	2.0	0.2876	0.0579	0.0132	$6.70	$6.05	$3.83

Example 7.13

Based on Data Set II (i) (see Section 6.4), the expected warranty cost for different combinations of the warranty period and remaining life are shown in Table 7.31. Table 7.32 shows the standard errors and the confidence intervals of the ARTO simulation runs.

7.4.2 PRW Summary Results

In order to assess the impact of PM on PRW policy cost, pairwise t tests were carried out for each performance measure. Table 7.33, Table 7.34 and Table 7.35 present all models' costs for warranty models. According to these

TABLE 7.32

Standard Error and Confidence Intervals on PRW Policy, Model C1

					Confidence Interval					
		Standard Error			$RL_i = 1$		$RL_i = 2$		$RL_i = 3$	
Components	*W*	$RL_i = 1$	$RL_i = 2$	$RL_i = 3$	*L* Limit	*U* Limit	*L* Limit	*U* Limit	*L* Limit	*U* Limit
Evaporator	**0.5**	0.66	0.97	1.48	$4.26	$6.49	$4.52	$7.80	$2.42	$7.41
	1.0	1.69	2.49	2.61	$3.11	$8.82	$2.54	$10.94	$0.62	$9.41
	2.0	3.27	3.74	4.30	$3.44	$14.46	$2.59	$15.19	$2.08	$12.42
Control Box	**0.5**	0.74	1.09	1.66	$4.02	$6.53	$4.28	$7.96	$2.10	$7.71
	1.0	1.90	2.80	2.93	$3.01	$9.42	$1.85	$11.28	$0.04	$9.91
	2.0	3.67	4.20	4.83	$2.65	$15.03	$1.65	$15.80	$3.01	$13.28
Blower	**0.5**	0.83	1.23	1.87	$1.23	$4.05	$0.40	$4.54	$0.63	$5.66
	1.0	2.14	3.14	3.29	$0.13	$7.07	$0.92	$9.68	$2.97	$8.13
	2.0	4.13	4.72	5.43	$2.16	$11.75	$2.55	$13.34	$6.48	$11.82
Air Guide	**0.5**	1.06	1.56	2.37	$0.33	$3.24	$1.21	$4.05	$2.78	$5.21
	1.0	2.71	3.99	4.18	$2.47	$6.67	$4.79	$8.66	$5.70	$8.38
	2.0	5.24	5.98	6.89	$6.05	$11.61	$7.37	$12.85	$10.19	$13.03
Motor	**0.5**	0.94	1.39	2.11	$3.91	$7.09	$2.94	$7.61	$1.60	$8.71
	1.0	2.41	3.55	3.72	$1.98	$10.12	$0.34	$11.63	$1.02	$11.52
	2.0	4.66	5.33	6.13	$0.64	$16.36	$1.68	$16.28	$5.04	$15.64
Condenser	**0.5**	0.78	1.15	1.74	$0.40	$3.03	$0.47	$3.40	$1.51	$4.37
	1.0	2.00	2.94	3.07	$0.87	$5.86	$2.85	$7.05	$3.61	$6.76
	2.0	3.85	4.40	5.07	$3.61	$9.38	$5.00	$9.85	$6.89	$10.20
Fan	**0.5**	0.78	1.15	1.74	$1.98	$4.61	$0.85	$4.71	$0.27	$5.61
	1.0	2.00	2.94	3.07	$1.18	$7.91	$1.69	$8.21	$2.44	$7.93
	2.0	3.85	4.40	5.07	$0.84	$12.15	$2.90	$11.95	$5.66	$11.43
Protector	**0.5**	0.75	1.11	1.68	$0.40	$2.14	$1.19	$2.55	$2.35	$3.33
	1.0	1.93	2.84	2.97	$1.90	$4.60	$3.39	$5.88	$4.42	$5.59
	2.0	3.72	4.26	4.90	$3.92	$8.64	$5.59	$8.76	$7.63	$8.89
Compressor	**0.5**	0.75	1.11	1.68	$2.55	$5.09	$1.71	$5.45	$0.59	$6.27
	1.0	1.93	2.84	2.97	$1.67	$8.17	$0.16	$9.40	$1.30	$8.72
	2.0	3.72	4.26	4.90	$0.42	$12.97	$1.12	$13.23	$4.43	$12.09

tables, PM achieves significant savings in holding, backorder, disassembly, disposal, remanufacturing, transportation, warranty, PM costs and number of warranty claims. In addition, SEPs provide significant improvements in total revenue and profit. According to these tables, offering PM along with an embedded sensor helps the remanufacturer achieve saving 45.34%, 55.42%, and 61.82% in total cost and increase 148.61%, 182.06% and 230.96% in profit for S3, C3, and C7, respectively.

For PRW policy, the lowest average value of the warranty, the number of warranty claims and PM costs during the warranty period for remanufactured components and ACs across all models are $33,321.36, 15,775 claims

TABLE 7.33

Results of Performance Measures for Different Models with System Level Failure

	Model			
Performance Measure	**S1**	**S2**	**S3**	**S4**
Holding Cost	$117,335.66	$152,273.28	$87,538.18	$136,488.57
Backorder Cost	$21,765.59	$28,246.47	$16,238.20	$25,318.43
Disassembly Cost	$253,362.91	$328,803.72	$189,021.20	$294,719.80
Disposal Cost	$41,043.44	$53,264.45	$30,620.43	$47,743.04
Testing Cost	N/A	$98,069.76	N/A	$87,903.81
Remanufacturing Cost	$871,062.97	$1,130,428.84	$649,855.85	$1,013,248.15
Transportation Cost	$21,979.23	$28,523.72	$16,397.59	$25,566.94
Warranty Cost	$55,187.08	$71,619.47	$41,172.28	$64,195.37
Number of Claims	$26,125.93	$33,905.13	$19,491.23	$30,390.52
Preventive Maintenance Cost	N/A	N/A	$1,974.05	$2,605.39
Total Cost	$1,407,862.82	$1,925,134.84	$1,052,309.01	$1,728,180.01
Total Revenue	$5,796,496.92	$4,152,798.79	$6,590,428.19	$4,603,491.38
Profit	$4,388,634.10	$2,227,663.95	$5,538,119.19	$2,875,311.37

TABLE 7.34

Results of Performance Measures for Different Models with Non-Repair Components

	Model			
Performance Measure	**C1**	**C2**	**C3**	**C4**
Holding Cost	$105,467.69	$170,400.82	$79,890.98	$130,991.87
Backorder Cost	$19,564.10	$31,609.10	$14,819.66	$24,298.80
Disassembly Cost	$227,736.40	$367,946.52	$172,508.59	$282,850.76
Disposal Cost	$36,892.08	$59,605.38	$27,945.47	$45,820.32
Testing Cost	N/A	$109,744.58	N/A	$84,363.72
Remanufacturing Cost	$782,958.89	$1,265,001.99	$593,085.42	$972,442.35
Transportation Cost	$19,756.13	$31,919.36	$14,965.12	$24,537.30
Warranty Cost	$49,605.16	$80,145.49	$37,575.53	$61,610.07
Number of Claims	$23,483.41	$37,941.41	$17,788.51	$29,166.62
Preventive Maintenance Cost	N/A	N/A	$1,801.60	$2,500.46
Total Cost	$1,265,463.86	$2,154,314.64	$960,380.88	$1,658,582.28
Total Revenue	$6,049,377.26	$4,297,090.17	$7,004,253.74	$5,218,000.64
Profit	$4,783,913.40	$2,142,775.52	$6,043,872.86	$3,559,418.36

TABLE 7.35

Results of Performance Measures for Different Models with Repair Components

	Model			
Performance Measure	**C5**	**C6**	**C7**	**C8**
Holding Cost	$95,907.45	$176,442.92	$70,846.07	$125,404.03
Backorder Cost	$17,790.69	$32,729.90	$13,141.84	$23,262.26
Disassembly Cost	$207,092.96	$380,993.21	$152,977.94	$270,784.93
Disposal Cost	$33,547.96	$61,718.87	$24,781.61	$43,865.72
Testing Cost	N/A	$113,635.92	N/A	$80,764.94
Remanufacturing Cost	$711,986.64	$1,309,856.60	$525,938.93	$930,959.95
Transportation Cost	$17,965.31	$33,051.16	$13,270.83	$23,490.59
Warranty Cost	$45,108.64	$82,987.29	$33,321.39	$58,981.91
Number of Claims	$21,354.73	$39,286.74	$15,774.57	$27,922.43
Preventive Maintenance Cost	N/A	N/A	$1,597.63	$2,393.80
Total Cost	$1,150,754.37	$2,230,702.61	$851,650.83	$1,587,830.55
Total Revenue	$6,180,589.03	$4,097,045.35	$7,028,526.66	$5,651,123.48
Profit	$5,029,834.65	$1,866,342.74	$6,176,875.83	$4,063,292.93

and $1,597.63, respectively, for the Model C7 (Sensor-Embedded Component, Imperfect Repair with Preventive Maintenance). Model C6 (Component Conventional, Minimal Repair with Corrective Maintenance) has the worst values for the warranty and the number of warranty claims during the warranty period, with a 161.93% and a 230.96% increase in total cost and reduction in profit, respectively.

7.4.2.1 Effect of SEPs on PRW Warranty Policy

The MINITAB-17 program was used to carry out one-way analyses of variance (ANOVA) and Tukey pairwise comparisons for all the results of PRW warranty policy. ANOVA was used in order to determine whether there are any significant differences between the warranty costs, number of claims and PM costs for the 12 different models, namely, Model S1, Model S2, Model S3, Model S4, Model C1, Model C2, Model C3, Model C4, Model C5, Model C6, Model C7 and Model C8. The Tukey pairwise comparisons were conducted to identify which models are similar and which models are not. ANOVA showed that there was a significant difference in warranty costs between different warranty policies. The Tukey test showed that all the models were different and that Model C7 (Sensor-Embedded Component, Imperfect Repair with Preventive Maintenance) with PRW policy had the lowest warranty cost, $33,321.39. In addition, there was a significant difference in the number of warranty claims between different models for PRW warranty policy, except for

Model C4 and Model S4, for which there was no significant difference in the number of claims. The Model C7 with PRW policy had the lowest number of claims, 15,775.

7.5 Conclusions

In this chapter, two simple non-renewing warranty policies, namely, Free-Replacement Warranty (FRW) and Pro-Rata Warranty (PRW), were discussed. In order to assess the impact of these two policies in terms of warranty cost, pairwise t tests were carried out for different performance measures, namely, Holding Cost, Backorder Cost, Disassembly Cost, Disposal Cost, Testing Cost, Remanufacturing Cost, Transportation Cost, Warranty Cost, Number of Claims and Preventive Maintenance Cost.

8

Cost Analysis of Simple Non-Renewing Warranties – Group 2

8.1 Introduction

In Chapter 4, several warranty policies with preventive maintenance for remanufactured products were introduced. This chapter presents the analysis of determining the expected cost of warranty, CM and PM (from both the buyer's and remanufacturer's perspectives). Chapter 7 considered two such policies, namely, Policy 1 (FRW) and Policy 2 (PRW). Here, the remaining simple non-renewing policies, namely, Policy 3 (SPE), Policy 4 (LCS), Policy 5 (LMS), Policy 6 (LIC), Policy 7 (ICD), Policy 8 (LTC), Policy 9 (TCD) and Policy 10 (MBG), as defined in Chapter 4, are considered.

In Chapter 5, a variety of models were discussed at the system level (Models S1 through S4) and at the component level (Models Cl through C8) for warranty failures of remanufacturing products. The expected warranty cost for a given policy can be evaluated using one of those models. In Chapter 7, analysis of FRW policy based on the models at both the system and component levels were carried out. For the policies considered in this chapter, the analysis is very similar to that for the FRW policy. For that reason, for the policies considered in this chapter, only selected models at the system level are discussed as illustrations. The warranty costs for the rest of the models can be carried out in a manner similar to these and the ones given for the FRW policy in Chapter 7.

Section 8.2 presents some assumptions and notations used in this chapter. Sections 8.3 through 8.10 deal with the analyses of Specified Parts Excluded (SPE), Lump-Sum Cost-Sharing (LCS), Labor or Material Cost-Shared (LMS), Limit on Individual Cost (LIC), Individual Cost Deductible (ICD), Limit on Total Cost (LTC), Total Cost Deductible (TCD) and Money-Back Guarantee (MBG), respectively. Finally, some conclusions are presented in Section 8.11.

8.2 Some Preliminaries

All the assumptions, notations and the parameter values for the numerical examples given in Section 7.2 are also valid here.

8.3 Analysis of Specified Parts Excluded Policy

This section presents the cost analysis of providing the Specified Parts Excluded (SPE) Policy based on Model S3 (SEPs - Sensor-Embedded Products, Preventive Maintenance) and Model S4 (Conventional Product, Preventive Maintenance) for warranty failures of remanufactured products discussed in Chapter 5. The policy can be described as follows:

POLICY SPE: Under the Specified Parts Excluded policy, the remanufacturer resolves all failures from set I over the warranty period at no cost to the buyer. Buyer pays for any replacement/repair of failure resulting from set *E*, specified as parts excluded.

8.3.1 Model S3 (SEPs, Preventive Maintenance)

Here, two different methods are used to analyze the warranty cost, as follows.

8.3.1.1 Method 1: Binary Random Variable

In this method, each failure of an item is marked whether it is covered by warranty (Set Included) or not (Set Excluded). Let Y_{ji} be a binary random variable for the jth failure where i is the component which has failed. Then Y_{ji} is given by:

$$Y_{ji} = \begin{cases} 1 & \text{for } i \in Set\, I \\ 0 & \text{for } i \in Set\, E \end{cases} \tag{8.1}$$

Because the cost in this model is shared by the remanufacturer and the buyer, then:

$$D_j = Y_{ji} C_j \tag{8.2}$$

$$B_j = \left(1 - Y_{ji}\right) C_j \tag{8.3}$$

The cost to the remanufacturer is given by (7.2), with D_j given by (8.2). The cost to the buyer is given by:

$$C_b(W;v) = \sum_{j=1}^{N(W;v)} B_j \tag{8.4}$$

where B_j is given by (8.3).

Let p denote the probability that an item failure is due to the failure of a component from Set E. Then E $[Y_{ji}]$ = $[1\text{-}p]$. As a result, the expected number of failures covered by warranty is given by (5.12) and not covered by warranty is given by (5.13). Then, the expected warranty cost to the remanufacturer is given by:

$$E\left[C_d(W;v)\right] = E\left[Y_{ji}C_j\right]E\left[N(W;v)\right] = \bar{c}(1-p)\int_{v-W}^{v}\Lambda(t)dt \tag{8.5}$$

The expected cost to the buyer over the warranty period is given by:

$$E\left[C_d(W;v)\right] = \bar{c}\,p + \int_{v-W}^{v}\Lambda(t)dt \tag{8.6}$$

Note that the sum of the expected warranty cost to the remanufacturer given by (8.5) and the expected cost to the buyer given by (8.6) equals E $[C_d\ (W;\ RL)]$, given by (7.5).

Example 8.1

Based on Data Set I (see Section 6.4), and p = 0.4, the expected warranty costs determined from (8.5) and (8.6) for different combinations of remaining lives and warranty periods are shown in Table 8.1. Table 8.2 shows the confidence intervals of the ARTO simulation runs.

TABLE 8.1

The Expected Warranty Costs for SPE Policy, Model S3-Method 1

		Expected Cost to Remanufacturer			**Expected Cost to Buyer**		
Item	*W*	*RL* = 1	*RL* = 2	*RL* = 3	*RL* = 1	*RL* = 2	*RL* = 3
AC	**0.50**	\$34.50	\$33.10	\$32.78	\$23.00	\$22.06	\$21.86
	1.00	\$36.00	\$36.39	\$34.32	\$24.00	\$24.26	\$22.88
	2.00	\$42.30	\$41.67	\$35.60	\$28.20	\$27.78	\$23.73

TABLE 8.2

Confidence Intervals for SPE Policy, Model S3, Method 1

	Confidence Interval on Expected Cost to Remanufacturer						**Confidence Interval on Expected Cost to Buyer**					
	$RL = 1$		**$RL = 2$**		**$RL = 3$**		**$RL = 1$**		**$RL = 2$**		**$RL = 3$**	
W	***L* limit**	***U* limit**	***L* limit**	***U* limit**	***L* limit**	***U* limit**	***L* limit**	***U* limit**	***L* limit**	***U* limit**	***L* limit**	***U* limit**
0.5	$34.38	$34.62	$32.92	$32.96	$32.51	$33.06	$22.88	$23.12	$21.88	$22.24	$21.58	$22.13
1.0	$35.69	$36.31	$35.93	$34.78	$33.84	$34.80	$23.69	$24.31	$23.80	$24.72	$22.40	$23.36
2.0	$41.70	$42.90	$40.98	$36.29	$34.80	$36.39	$27.60	$28.80	$27.09	$28.47	$22.94	$24.53

The expected warranty cost to the remanufacturer is reduced by 32.69% compared to that of the FRW policy for a remanufactured AC with one-year remaining life sold with a 0.5-year warranty. And this is reduced by 31.68% for a three-year remaining life AC sold with a two-year warranty.

8.3.1.2 Method 2: Different Intensity Function

In this method, the failures of Set I and E are modeled by intensity functions Λ_i and Λ_E, respectively. Thus, the expected number of failures of Set I is given by (5.14) and that of Set E is given by (5.15). Then, the expected warranty cost to the remanufacturer is given by:

$$E\left[C_d\left(W;v\right)\right]=\overline{c_I}+\int_{v-W}^{w}\Lambda_I\left(t\right)dt \tag{8.7}$$

The expected cost to the buyer over the warranty period is given by:

$$E\left[C_b\left(W;A\right)\right]=\overline{c_E}+\int_{A}^{A+W}\Lambda_E\left(t\right)dt \tag{8.8}$$

Example 8.2

Based on Data Set I (see Section 6.4), the expected costs over the warranty period are shown in Table 8.3. Table 8.4 shows the confidence intervals of the ARTO simulation runs.

The expected warranty cost to the remanufacturer is reduced by 30.36% compared to that of the FRW policy for a remanufactured AC with one-year remaining life sold with a 0.5-year warranty. And this is reduced by 26.40% for a three-year remaining life AC sold with a two-year warranty.

8.3.2 Model S4 (CPs, Preventive Maintenance)

In this model, there is no sensor embedded in the item. Therefore, the remaining life of an item at arrival to the ARTO system is unknown and is given by a distribution function $H(v)$. There are two methods to analyze the warranty cost, as follows.

TABLE 8.3

The Expected Warranty Costs for SPE Policy, Model S3-Method 2

		Expected Cost to Remanufacturer			Expected Cost to Buyer		
Item	*W*	*RL* = 1	*RL* = 2	*RL* = 3	*RL* = 1	*RL* = 2	*RL* = 3
AC	0.5	$34.85	$33.43	$33.11	$23.23	$22.28	$22.07
	1.0	$36.36	$36.75	$34.66	$24.24	$24.50	$23.11
	2.0	$42.72	$42.09	$36.95	$28.48	$28.06	$23.97

TABLE 8.4

Confidence Intervals for SPE Policy, Model S3, Method 2

	Confidence Interval on Expected Cost to Remanufacturer						Confidence Interval on Expected Cost to Buyer					
	RL = 1		*RL* = 2		*RL* = 3		*RL* = 1		*RL* = 2		*RL* = 3	
W	*L* limit	*U* limit	*L* limit	*U* limit	*L* limit	*U* limit	*L* limit	*U* limit	*L* limit	*U* limit	*L* limit	*U* limit
0.5	$34.72	$34.97	$33.25	$33.29	$32.84	$33.39	$23.11	$23.35	$22.10	$22.46	$21.80	$22.35
1.0	$36.05	$36.67	$36.29	$35.12	$34.18	$35.14	$23.93	$24.55	$24.04	$24.96	$22.63	$23.59
2.0	$42.12	$43.33	$41.40	$36.64	$35.16	$36.75	$27.88	$29.09	$27.37	$28.75	$23.17	$24.76

8.3.2.1 Method 1: Binary Random Variable

In this approach, the expected number of failures covered by the warranty is given by (5.16), and the failures not covered by the warranty are given by (5.17). Let p denote the probability that the item failure is due to the failure of a component from set E. Then, the expected warranty cost to the remanufacturer is given by:

$$E\left[C_d(W;v)\right]=\overline{c_I}+\int_L^U\int_{v-W}^{v}\Lambda_I(t)dt\}h(v)dv \tag{8.9}$$

The expected cost to the buyer over the warranty period is given by:

$$E\left[C_b(W;v)\right]=\overline{c_E}+\int_L^U\int_{v-W}^{v}\Lambda_E(t)dt\}h(v)dv \tag{8.10}$$

Example 8.3

Based on Data Set I (see Section 6.4), and p = 0.4, the expected costs determined from (8.9) and (8.10), for different combinations of *L*, *U* and *W*, are shown in Table 8.5 and Table 8.6, respectively. Confidence intervals are shown in Table 8.7 and Table 8.8, respectively.

TABLE 8.5

The Expected Warranty Costs for SPE Policy, Model S4-Method 1

		Expected Cost to Remanufacturer								
		L = 1			*L* = 2			*L* = 3		
Item	*W*	*U* = 1	*U* = 2	*U* = 3	*U* = 1	*U* = 2	*U* = 3	*U* = 1	*U* = 2	*U* = 3
AC	**0.5**	$58.19	$68.91	$68.26	$79.66	$76.42	$75.70	$79.66	$78.99	$78.24
	1.0	$60.72	$75.77	$71.46	$83.13	$84.03	$79.25	$83.13	$86.85	$81.91
	2.0	$71.35	$86.76	$74.12	$97.67	$96.22	$82.20	$97.67	$99.45	$84.96

TABLE 8.6

The Expected Warranty Costs for SPE Policy, Model S4-Method 1

		Expected Cost to Buyer								
		L = 1			*L* = 2			*L* = 3		
Item	*W*	*U* = 1	*U* = 2	*U* = 3	*U* = 1	*U* = 2	*U* = 3	*U* = 1	*U* = 2	*U* = 3
AC	**0.5**	$33.35	$39.50	$39.12	$45.66	$43.80	$43.39	$45.66	$45.27	$44.84
	1.0	$34.80	$43.43	$40.96	$47.64	$48.16	$45.42	$47.64	$49.78	$46.94
	2.0	$40.89	$49.73	$42.48	$55.98	$55.14	$47.11	$55.98	$57.00	$48.69

TABLE 8.7
Confidence Intervals for SPE Policy, Model S4, Method 1

		Standard Error			**Confidence Interval on the Expected Cost to Remanufacturer**											
					$L = 1$						**$L = 2$**					
					$U = 1$		**$U = 2$**		**$U = 3$**		**$U = 1$**		**$U = 2$**		**$U = 3$**	
Item	***W***	***RL* = 1**	***RL* = 2**	***RL* = 3**	***L* limit**	***U* limit**	***L* limit**	***U* limit**	***L* limit**	***U* limit**	***L* limit**	***U* limit**	***L* limit**	***U* limit**	***L* limit**	***U* limit**
AC	**0.5**	0.68	0.99	1.51	\$57.80	\$58.58	\$68.34	\$69.49	\$67.39	\$69.14	\$79.27	\$80.05	\$75.84	\$77.00	\$74.82	\$76.58
	1.0	1.73	2.54	2.66	\$59.72	\$61.72	\$74.77	\$76.77	\$69.92	\$73.00	\$82.12	\$84.13	\$82.55	\$85.50	\$77.70	\$80.79
	2.0	3.34	3.82	4.39	\$69.41	\$73.28	\$84.83	\$88.70	\$71.58	\$76.67	\$95.74	\$99.61	\$94.01	\$98.43	\$79.65	\$84.74
					$L = 3$											
					$U = 1$		**$U = 2$**		**$U = 3$**							
					L limit		***L* limit**		***L* limit**							
					\$79.27	\$80.05	\$78.41	\$79.56	\$77.37	\$79.12						
					\$82.12	\$84.13	\$85.37	\$88.32	\$80.37	\$83.45						
					\$95.74	\$99.61	\$97.24	\$101.66	\$82.41	\$87.51						

TABLE 8.8

Confidence Intervals for SPE Policy, Model S4, Method 1

					Confidence Interval on the Expected Cost to Buyer											
		Standard Error			$L = 1$						$L = 2$					
					$U = 1$		$U = 2$		$U = 3$		$U = 1$		$U = 2$		$U = 3$	
Item	*W*	$RL = 1$	$RL = 2$	$RL = 3$	L limit	U limit	L limit	U limit	L limit	U limit	L limit	U limit	L limit	U limit	L limit	U limit
AC	**0.5**	0.68	0.99	1.51	$32.96	$33.74	$38.92	$40.07	$38.25	$40.00	$45.26	$46.05	$43.22	$44.37	$42.51	$44.26
	1.0	1.73	2.54	2.66	$33.80	$35.80	$42.42	$44.43	$39.41	$42.50	$46.64	$48.64	$46.68	$49.63	$43.87	$46.96
	2.0	3.34	3.82	4.39	$38.95	$42.83	$47.79	$51.66	$39.93	$45.03	$54.04	$57.91	$52.93	$57.36	$44.56	$49.66
							$L = 3$									
					$U = 1$		$U = 2$		$U = 3$							
					L limit		L limit		L limit							
					$45.26	$46.05	$44.69	$45.85	$43.97	$45.72						
					$46.64	$48.64	$48.30	$51.25	$45.40	$48.49						
					$54.04	$57.91	$54.79	$59.21	$46.15	$51.24						

The expected warranty cost to the remanufacturer is reduced by 1.18% compared to that of the FRW policy when a remanufactured AC remaining life varies from one to three years (i.e., $L = 1$ and $U = 3$) and items are sold with a 0.5-year warranty. It is reduced by 2.43% when the remaining life varies from one to three years (i.e., $L = 1$ and $U = 3$) and the warranty period is two years.

8.3.2.2 Method 2: Different Intensity Function

In this method, the expected number of failures of Set I is given by (5.18) and that of Set E is given by (5.19). Then, the expected warranty cost to the remanufacturer is given by:

$$E\left[C_d(W;v)\right] = \bar{c}_I + \int_L^U \int_{v-W}^{v} \Lambda_I(t)dt\}h(v)dv \tag{8.11}$$

The expected cost to the buyer over the warranty period is given by:

$$E\left[C_b(W;v)\right] = \bar{c}_E + \int_L^U \int_{v-W}^{v} \Lambda_E(t)dt\}h(v)dv \tag{8.12}$$

Example 8.4

The expected cost to the remanufacturer is given by:

$$E\left[C_d(W)\right] = \bar{c}_I\left(\frac{\lambda_I}{\rho}\right)^{\beta_I}\begin{bmatrix}\{\exp(\rho W)\} \\ \{\Gamma(\beta_I+1,p(L+W)) - \Gamma(\beta_I+1,\rho(U+W)\} \\ -\{\Gamma(\beta_I+1,\rho L) - \Gamma(\beta_I+1,\rho U)\}\end{bmatrix} \tag{8.13}$$
$$/\left[\exp(-\rho L) - \exp(-\rho U)\right]$$

The expected cost to the buyer is given by:

$$E\left[C_d(W)\right] = \bar{c}_E\left(\frac{\lambda_E}{\rho}\right)^{\beta_E}\begin{bmatrix}\{\exp(\rho W)\} \\ \{\Gamma(\beta_E+1,p(L+W)) - \Gamma(\beta_E+1,\rho(U+W)\} \\ -\{\Gamma(\beta_E+1,\rho L) - \Gamma(\beta_E+1,\rho U)\}\end{bmatrix} \tag{8.14}$$
$$/\left[\exp(-\rho L) - \exp(-\rho U)\right]$$

Expressions for the incomplete Gamma functions are the same as in Example 7.10. Based on Data Set I (see Section 6.4), the expected warranty costs are shown in Table 8.9 and Table 8.10.

TABLE 8.9

The Expected Warranty Costs for SPE Policy, Model S4-Method 2

		Expected Cost to Remanufacturer								
		$L = 1$			$L = 2$			$L = 3$		
Item	W	$U = 1$	$U = 2$	$U = 3$	$U = 1$	$U = 2$	$U = 3$	$U = 1$	$U = 2$	$U = 3$
AC	**0.5**	$65.17	$77.18	$76.45	$89.22	$85.59	$84.78	$89.22	$88.47	$87.63
	1.0	$68.01	$84.86	$80.04	$93.10	$94.11	$88.76	$93.10	$97.27	$91.74
	2.0	$79.91	$97.18	$83.02	$109.39	$107.76	$92.06	$109.39	$111.39	$95.15

TABLE 8.10

The Expected Warranty Costs for SPE Policy, Model S4-Method 2

		Expected Cost to Buyer								
		$L = 1$			$L = 2$			$L = 3$		
Item	W	$U = 1$	$U = 2$	$U = 3$	$U = 1$	$U = 2$	$U = 3$	$U = 1$	$U = 2$	$U = 3$
AC	**0.5**	$37.35	$44.23	$43.82	$51.13	$49.05	$48.59	$51.13	$50.70	$50.22
	1.0	$38.98	$48.64	$45.87	$53.36	$53.94	$50.87	$53.36	$55.75	$52.58
	2.0	$45.80	$55.69	$47.58	$62.70	$61.76	$52.76	$62.70	$63.84	$54.54

The expected warranty cost to the remanufacturer is reduced by 53.94% compared to that of the FRW policy when a remanufactured AC remaining life varies from one to three years (i.e., $L = 1$ and $U = 3$) and items are sold with a 0.5-year warranty. It is reduced by 50.20% when the remaining life varies from one to three years (i.e., $L = 1$ and $U = 3$) and the warranty period is two years.

8.4 Analysis of Lump-Sum Cost-Sharing Policy

This section presents the cost analysis of providing the LCS Policy based on models S1 through S4 for warranty failures of remanufactured products discussed in Chapter 5. The policy can be described as follows:

LCS POLICY: Under the lump-sum cost-sharing policy, the remanufacturer resolves all failures over the warranty period. The costs of replacement/repair are shared, with the buyer paying (1-α) portion and the remanufacturer also paying α portion of the repair costs.

8.4.1 Model S1 (Sensor-Embedded, Corrective Maintenance)

Here, for the jth failure:

$$D_j = \alpha C_j \tag{8.15}$$

$$B_j = (1-\alpha)C_j \tag{8.16}$$

The cost to the remanufacturer is given by (5.16), where D_j is given by (8.15). The cost to the buyer is given by (5.17), where β_j is given by (8.16) and where α. (0 < α. < 1) is the fraction of cost shared by the remanufacturer. In this case, the expected number of failures is given by (5.30). Then, the expected warranty cost to the remanufacturer is given by:

$$E\left[C_d(W;RL)\right] = (\alpha)\bar{c} + \int_{RL-W}^{RL} \Lambda(t)dt \tag{8.17}$$

The expected cost to the buyer over the warranty period is given by:

$$E\left[C_b(W;RL)\right] = (1-\alpha)\bar{c} + \int_{RL-W}^{RL} \Lambda(t)dt \tag{8.18}$$

Example 8.5

Based on Data Set I (see Section 6.4) with α= 0.75, the expected costs determined from (8.17) and (8.18), for different combinations of remaining life and warranty period are shown in Table 8.11. Table 8.12 shows the confidence intervals of the ARTO simulation runs.

TABLE 8.11

The Expected Warranty Costs for LCS Policy, Model S1

		Expected Cost to Remanufacturer			**Expected Cost to Buyer**		
Item	*W*	*RL* = 1	*RL* = 2	*RL* = 3	*RL* = 1	*RL* = 2	*RL* = 3
AC	**0.5**	$38.68	$37.10	$36.75	$25.79	$24.74	$24.50
	1.0	$40.36	$40.80	$38.48	$26.91	$27.20	$25.65
	2.0	$47.42	$46.72	$39.91	$31.62	$31.14	$26.61

TABLE 8.12

Confidence Intervals for LCS Policy, Model S1

	Confidence Interval on Expected Cost to Remanufacturer						**Confidence Interval on Expected Cost to Buyer**					
	RL = 1		*RL* = 2		*RL* = 3		*RL* = 1		*RL* = 2		*RL* = 3	
W	*L* **limit**	*U* **limit**	*L* **limit**	*U* **limit**	*L* **limit**	*U* **limit**	*L* **limit**	*U* **limit**	*L* **limit**	*U* **limit**	*L* **limit**	*U* **limit**
0.5	$38.52	$38.84	$36.86	$36.99	$36.39	$37.12	$25.62	$25.95	$24.50	$24.98	$24.14	$24.87
1.0	$39.94	$40.78	$40.18	$39.09	$37.84	$39.12	$26.49	$27.32	$26.59	$27.81	$25.01	$26.29
2.0	$46.62	$48.23	$45.80	$40.83	$38.85	$40.97	$30.81	$32.42	$30.23	$32.06	$25.55	$27.66

The expected warranty cost to the remanufacturer is reduced by 17.46 % compared to that of the FRW policy for a remanufactured AC with one year of remaining life sold with a 0.5-year warranty. This is reduced by 14.86% for a 3-year remaining-life AC sold with a two-year warranty.

8.4.2 Model S2 (Conventional Product, Corrective Maintenance)

In this model, the expected number of failures is given by (5.10). Then, the expected warranty cost to the remanufacturer is given by:

$$E\left[C_d\left(W;RL\right)\right]=\left(\alpha\right)\bar{c}+\int_{L}^{U}\int_{rl-W}^{rl}\left\{\Lambda\left(t\right)dt\right\}h\left(rl\right)drl \tag{8.19}$$

The expected cost to the buyer over the warranty period is given by:

$$E\left[C_b\left(W;RL\right)\right]=\left(1-\alpha\right)\bar{c}+\int_{L}^{U}\int_{rl-W}^{rl}\left\{\Lambda\left(t\right)dt\right\}h\left(rl\right)drl \tag{8.20}$$

Example 8.6

Based on Data Set I (see Section 6.4) and α = 0.75, the expected costs determined from (8.19) and (8.20), for different combinations of L, U and W, are shown in Tables 8.13 and Table 8.14.

TABLE 8.13

The Expected Warranty Costs for LCS Policy, Model S2

		Expected Cost to Remanufacturer								
		$L = 1$			$L = 2$			$L = 3$		
Item	*W*	$U = 1$	$U = 2$	$U = 3$	$U = 1$	$U = 2$	$U = 3$	$U = 1$	$U = 2$	$U = 3$
AC	**0.5**	$73.19	$86.67	$85.86	$100.20	$96.12	$95.21	$100.20	$99.35	$98.41
	1.0	$76.37	$95.30	$89.88	$104.55	$105.68	$99.67	$104.55	$109.24	$103.02
	2.0	$89.74	$109.13	$93.23	$122.85	$121.02	$103.38	$122.85	$125.09	$106.86

TABLE 8.14

The Expected Warranty Costs for LCS Policy, Model S2

		Expected Cost to Buyer								
		$L = 1$			$L = 2$			$L = 3$		
Item	*W*	$U = 1$	$U = 2$	$U = 3$	$U = 1$	$U = 2$	$U = 3$	$U = 1$	$U = 2$	$U = 3$
AC	**0.5**	$41.95	$49.68	$49.21	$57.42	$55.09	$54.57	$57.42	$56.94	$56.40
	1.0	$43.77	$54.62	$51.51	$59.92	$60.57	$57.12	$59.92	$62.61	$59.04
	2.0	$51.43	$62.54	$53.43	$70.41	$69.36	$59.25	$70.41	$71.69	$61.24

The expected warranty cost to the remanufacturer is reduced by 37.08% compared to that of the FRW policy when a remanufactured AC remaining life varies from one to three years (i.e., $L = 1$ and $U = 3$) and items are sold with a 0.5-year warranty. It is reduced by 29.14% when the remaining life varies from one to three years (i.e., $L = 1$ and $U = 3$) and the warranty period is two years.

8.4.3 Model S3 (SEPs, Preventive Maintenance)

In this case, for the jth failure:

$$D_j = C_j - Q \tag{8.21}$$

$$B_j = Q \tag{8.22}$$

The expected cost to the remanufacturer over the warranty period is given by (7.2), using D_j from (8.21). The expected cost to the buyer over the warranty period is given by (7.11), using B_j from (8.22). The expected warranty cost to the remanufacturer is given by:

$$E\left[C_d(W;RL)\right] = (\bar{c} - Q) + \int_{RL-W}^{RL} \Lambda(t)dt \tag{8.23}$$

The expected cost to the buyer over the warranty period is given by:

$$E\left[C_b(W;RL)\right] = (\bar{c} - Q) + \int_{RL-W}^{RL} \Lambda(t)dt \tag{8.24}$$

Example 8.7

Based on Data Set I (see Section 6.4) with Q = $25, the expected warranty costs determined from (8.23) and (8.24) for different combinations of remaining life and warranty period are shown in Table 8.15 and the confidence interval is presented in Table 8.16.

The expected warranty cost to the remanufacturer is reduced by 41.53% compared to that of the FRW policy for a remanufactured AC with one-year remaining life sold with a 0.5-year warranty. This is reduced by 41.54% for a three-year remaining-life AC sold with a two-year warranty.

TABLE 8.15

The Expected Warranty Costs for LCS Policy, Model S3

		Expected Cost to Remanufacturer			Expected Cost to Buyer		
Item	*W*	*RL* = 1	*RL* = 2	*RL* = 3	*RL* = 1	*RL* = 2	*RL* = 3
AC	**0.5**	$32.10	$30.80	$30.51	$28.88	$27.70	$27.44
	1.0	$33.50	$33.86	$31.94	$30.14	$30.46	$28.73
	2.0	$39.36	$38.77	$33.12	$35.41	$34.88	$29.80

TABLE 8.16

Confidence Intervals for LCS Policy, Model S3

	Confidence Interval on Expected Cost to Remanufacturer						Confidence Interval on Expected Cost to Buyer					
	$RL = 1$		$RL = 2$		$RL = 3$		$RL = 1$		$RL = 2$		$RL = 3$	
W	L limit	U limit	L limit	U limit	L limit	U limit	L limit	U limit	L limit	U limit	L limit	U limit
0.5	$31.18	$33.03	$29.43	$31.87	$28.44	$32.58	$27.95	$29.81	$26.34	$29.07	$25.37	$29.51
1.0	$31.13	$35.87	$30.37	$35.42	$28.29	$35.59	$27.77	$32.50	$26.98	$33.95	$25.08	$32.38
2.0	$36.17	$42.55	$35.12	$36.77	$28.92	$37.33	$32.21	$38.60	$31.23	$38.53	$25.60	$34.00

8.4.4 Model S4 (Conventional Product, Preventive Maintenance)

The expected warranty cost to the remanufacturer is given by:

$$E\left[C_d\left(W;RL\right)\right]=\left(\bar{c}-Q\right)\int_{L}^{U}\int_{rl-W}^{rl}\left\{\Lambda\left(t\right)dt\right\}h\left(rl\right)drl \tag{8.25}$$

The expected cost to the buyer over the warranty period is given by:

$$E\left[C_b\left(W;RL\right)\right]=Q\int_{L}^{U}\int_{rl-W}^{rl}\left\{\Lambda\left(t\right)dt\right\}h\left(rl\right)drl \tag{8.26}$$

Example 8.8

Based on Data Set I (see Section 6.4) and Q =$45, the expected warranty costs determined from (8.25) and (8.26), for different combinations of L, U and W, are shown in Table 8.17 and Table 8.18, respectively.

The expected warranty cost to the remanufacturer is reduced by 1.18% compared to that of the FRW policy when a remanufactured AC remaining life varies from one to three years (i.e., L = 1 and U = 3) and items are sold

TABLE 8.17

The Expected Warranty Costs for LCS Policy, Model S4

		Expected Cost to Remanufacturer								
		$L = 1$			$L = 2$			$L = 3$		
Item	W	$U = 1$	$U = 2$	$U = 3$	$U = 1$	$U = 2$	$U = 3$	$U = 1$	$U = 2$	$U = 3$
AC	**0.5**	$65.69	$77.80	$77.07	$89.94	$86.28	$85.46	$89.94	$89.17	$88.33
	1.0	$68.55	$85.54	$80.68	$93.85	$94.86	$89.47	$93.85	$98.05	$92.47
	2.0	$80.55	$97.95	$83.68	$110.27	$108.63	$92.80	$110.27	$112.28	$95.92

TABLE 8.18

The Expected Warranty Costs for LCS Policy, Model S4

		Expected Cost to Buyer								
		$L = 1$			$L = 2$			$L = 3$		
Item	*W*	$U = 1$	$U = 2$	$U = 3$	$U = 1$	$U = 2$	$U = 3$	$U = 1$	$U = 2$	$U = 3$
AC	**0.5**	$37.65	$44.59	$44.17	$51.54	$49.45	$48.98	$51.54	$51.11	$50.63
	1.0	$39.29	$49.03	$46.24	$53.79	$54.37	$51.28	$53.79	$56.19	$53.00
	2.0	$46.16	$56.14	$47.96	$63.20	$62.26	$53.18	$63.20	$64.35	$54.97

with a 0.5-year warranty. It is reduced by 9.20% when the remaining life varies from one to three years (i.e., $L = 1$ and $U = 3$) and the warranty period is two years.

8.5 Analysis of Labor/Material Cost-Sharing Policy

This section presents the cost analysis of providing the Labor/Material Cost-Sharing (LMS) Policy based on Model S3 (SEPs, Preventive Maintenance) and Model S4 (Conventional Product, Preventive Maintenance) for warranty failures of remanufactured products discussed in Chapter 5. The policy can be described as follows:

LMS POLICY: Under the labor or material cost-sharing policy, the buyer and the remanufacturer share labor/material cost for repairs during the warranty period.

Since the cost is shared by the remanufacturer and the buyer, we have for the jth failure,

$$D_j = C_{ji} \tag{8.27}$$

$$B_j = C_{jm} \tag{8.28}$$

The expected warranty cost to the remanufacturer is given by (7.2), where D_j is given by (8.27). The expected warranty cost to the buyer is given by (7.11), where B_j is given by (8.28).

8.5.1 Model S3 (SEPs, Preventive Maintenance)

Here, the expected number of failures is given by (5.3). Then, the expected warranty cost to the remanufacturer is given by:

$$E\left[C_d(W;RL)\right] = \bar{c}_L \int_{RL-W}^{Rl} \Lambda(t)\,dt \tag{8.29}$$

The expected cost to the buyer over the warranty period is given by:

$$E\left[C_b(W;RL)\right]=\bar{c}_M\int_{RL-W}^{RL}\Lambda(t)dt \tag{8.30}$$

Note $\bar{c}$ for the FRW policy is the sum of $\bar{c}_L$ and $\bar{c}_M$. Hence, the reduction of the warranty cost to the remanufacturer is $\bar{c}_M/(\bar{c}_L+\bar{c}_M)$.

Example 8.9

Based on Data Set I (see Section 6.4) and $\bar{c}_L$=\$65; $\bar{c}_M$=\$35, the expected warranty costs for the remanufacturer and the buyer are determined from (8.29) and (8.30), respectively. The different combinations of remaining life and warranty period are shown in Table 8.19, and the confidence interval is presented in Table 8.20.

The expected warranty cost to the remanufacturer is reduced by 54.90% compared to that of the FRW policy for a remanufactured AC with one-year remaining life sold with a 0.5-year warranty. This is reduced by 54.87% for a three-year remaining-life AC sold with a two-year warranty.

8.5.2 Model S4 (CPs, Preventive Maintenance)

Here, the expected number of failures is given by (5.16). Then, the expected warranty cost to the remanufacturer is given by:

$$E\left[C_d(W;RL)\right]=\bar{c}_L\int_{L}^{U}\int_{rl-W}^{rl}\left\{\Lambda(t)dt\right\}h(rl)drl \tag{8.31}$$

The expected cost to the buyer over the warranty period is given by:

$$E\left[C_b(W;RL)\right]=\bar{c}_M\int_{L}^{U}\int_{rl-W}^{rl}\left\{\Lambda(t)dt\right\}h(rl)drl \tag{8.32}$$

TABLE 8.19

The Expected Warranty Costs for LMS Policy, Model S1

		Expected Cost to Remanufacturer			Expected Cost to Buyer		
Item	*W*	*RL* = 1	*RL* = 2	*RL* = 3	*RL* = 1	*RL* = 2	*RL* = 3
AC	**0.5**	\$29.33	\$28.14	\$27.87	\$26.39	\$25.31	\$25.08
	1.0	\$30.61	\$30.94	\$29.18	\$27.54	\$27.83	\$26.25
	2.0	\$35.96	\$35.43	\$30.27	\$32.35	\$31.87	\$27.23

TABLE 8.20

Confidence Intervals on LMS Policy, Model S1

	Confidence Interval Expected Cost to Remanufacturer						Confidence Interval Expected Cost to Buyer					
	RL = 1		*RL* = 2		*RL* = 3		*RL* = 1		*RL* = 2		*RL* = 3	
W	*L* limit	*U* limit	*L* limit	*U* limit	*L* limit	*U* limit	*L* limit	*U* limit	*L* limit	*U* limit	*L* limit	*U* limit
0.5	$28.57	$30.09	$27.02	$28.99	$26.17	$29.57	$25.63	$27.15	$24.20	$26.43	$23.38	$26.77
1.0	$28.66	$32.55	$28.08	$32.04	$26.18	$32.18	$25.59	$29.48	$24.97	$30.70	$23.25	$29.25
2.0	$32.21	$39.72	$31.14	$34.56	$25.32	$35.21	$28.60	$36.11	$27.58	$36.17	$22.29	$32.17

Example 8.10

Based on Data Set I (see Section 6.4) and $\overline{c}_L$=$65; $\overline{c}_M$=$35, the expected warranty costs, determined from (8.31) and (8.32) for different combinations of *L*, *U* and *W*, are shown in Table 8.21 and Table 8.22, respectively.

The expected warranty cost to the remanufacturer is reduced by 5.46% compared to that of the FRW policy when the item's remaining life varies from one to three years (i.e., $L = 1$ and $U = 3$) and items are sold with a 0.5-year warranty. It is reduced by 13.97% when the remaining life varies from one to three years (i.e., $L = 1$ and $U = 3$) and the warranty period is two years.

TABLE 8.21

The Expected Warranty Costs to Remanufacturer for LMS Policy, Model S2

		Expected Cost to Remanufacturer								
		L = 1			*L* = 2			*L* = 3		
Item	*W*	*U* = 1	*U* = 2	*U* = 3	*U* = 1	*U* = 2	*U* = 3	*U* = 1	*U* = 2	*U* = 3
AC	**0.5**	$54.53	$64.57	$63.96	$74.65	$71.61	$70.93	$74.65	$74.02	$73.32
	1.0	$56.90	$71.00	$66.96	$77.89	$78.74	$74.26	$77.89	$81.38	$76.75
	2.0	$66.85	$81.30	$69.46	$91.52	$90.16	$77.02	$91.52	$93.19	$79.61

TABLE 8.22

The Expected Warranty Costs to Buyer for LMS Policy, Model S2

		Expected Cost to Buyer								
		L = 1			*L* = 2			*L* = 3		
Item	*W*	*U* = 1	*U* = 2	*U* = 3	*U* = 1	*U* = 2	*U* = 3	*U* = 1	*U* = 2	*U* = 3
AC	**0.5**	$31.25	$37.01	$36.66	$42.78	$41.04	$40.65	$42.78	$42.42	$42.02
	1.0	$32.61	$40.69	$38.38	$44.64	$45.13	$42.56	$44.64	$46.64	$43.99
	2.0	$38.32	$46.60	$39.81	$52.45	$51.67	$44.14	$52.45	$53.41	$45.63

8.6 Analysis of Limit on Individual Cost Policy

This section presents the cost analysis of providing the Limit on Individual Cost (LIC) Policy based on Model S3 (SEPs, Preventive Maintenance) and Model S4 (Conventional Product, Preventive Maintenance) for warranty failures of remanufactured products discussed in Chapter 5. The policy can be described as follows:

LIC POLICY: Under the Limit on Individual Cost Policy, the remanufacturer repairs all failures at no cost to the buyer as long as the cost of any repair during the warranty period is less than a specified limit c_I. The buyer pays the excess if the cost of any repair during the warranty period exceeds c_I.

Since the cost of individual claims to the remanufacturer is limited to c_I, we have for the jth:

$$D_j = \min\{C_j, c_i\} \tag{8.33}$$

$$B_j = \min\{0, C_j - c_i)\} \tag{8.34}$$

The cost to the remanufacturer is determined from (7.2), with D_j given by (8.33). The cost to the buyer is determined from (7.11), with B_j given by (8.34). Let the individual cost of replacement/repair, C_j, be given by a distribution function $G(c)$. Then, the expected cost of a claim to the remanufacturer, $\bar{c}_d$, is given by:

$$\bar{c}_d = \int_0^{c_I} cg(c)\,dc + c_I \bar{G}(c_I) \tag{8.35}$$

The expected cost to the buyer for a repair during the warranty period, $\bar{c}_b$, is given by:

$$\bar{c}_b = \int_{c_I}^{\infty} (c - c_I)\,g(c)\,dc \tag{8.36}$$

8.6.1 Model S3 (SEPs, Preventive Maintenance)

Here, the expected number of failures is given by (5.16). Then, the expected warranty cost to the remanufacturer is given by:

$$E\left[C_d(W;RL)\right] = \bar{c}_d + \int_{RL-W}^{RL} \Lambda(t)\,dt \tag{8.37}$$

The expected cost to the buyer over the warranty period, E [C_b (W; A)], is given by:

$$E\left[C_b\left(W;RL\right)\right]=\bar{c}_b+\int_{RL-W}^{RL}\Lambda\left(t\right)dt \tag{8.38}$$

Example 8.11

Based on Data Set I (see Section 6.4) and c_I =$125, the expected warranty costs for various combinations of remaining life and warranty periods are shown in Table 8.23, and the confidence interval is presented in Table 8.24.

The expected warranty cost to the remanufacturer is reduced by 72.0925% compared to that of the FRW policy for a remanufactured AC with one-year remaining life sold with a 0.5-year warranty. This is reduced by 66.00% for a three-year remaining-life AC sold with a two-year warranty.

8.6.2 Model S4 (CPs, Preventive Maintenance)

In this model, the expected number of failures is given by (5.18). Then, the expected warranty cost to the remanufacturer is given by:

$$E\left[C_d\left(W;RL\right)\right]=\bar{c}_d\int_{L}^{U}\int_{rl-W}^{rl}\left\{\Lambda\left(t\right)dt\right\}h\left(rl\right)drl \tag{8.39}$$

TABLE 8.23

The Expected Warranty Costs for LIC Policy, Model S1

		Expected Cost to Remanufacturer			Expected Cost to Buyer		
Item	*W*	*RL* = 1	*RL* = 2	*RL* = 3	*RL* = 1	*RL* = 2	*RL* = 3
AC	**0.5**	$26.40	$25.33	$25.09	$23.75	$22.78	$22.57
	1.0	$27.55	$27.85	$26.26	$24.78	$25.05	$23.63
	2.0	$32.37	$31.89	$28.24	$29.12	$28.68	$24.50

TABLE 8.24

Confidence Intervals on LIC Policy, Model S1

	Confidence Interval Expected Cost to Remanufacturer						Confidence Interval Expected Cost to Buyer					
	RL = 1		*RL* = 2		*RL* = 3		*RL* = 1		*RL* = 2		*RL* = 3	
W	*L* limit	*U* limit	*L* limit	*U* limit	*L* limit	*U* limit	*L* limit	*U* limit	*L* limit	*U* limit	*L* limit	*U* limit
0.5	$25.64	$27.16	$24.21	$26.20	$23.39	$26.79	$22.99	$24.51	$21.66	$23.90	$20.87	$24.27
1.0	$25.60	$29.49	$24.98	$29.12	$23.27	$29.26	$22.84	$26.73	$22.19	$27.91	$20.63	$26.62
2.0	$28.61	$36.13	$27.59	$31.53	$22.30	$32.18	$25.36	$32.88	$24.39	$32.98	$19.56	$29.45

The expected cost to the buyer over the warranty period is given by:

$$E\left[C_b\left(W;RL\right)\right]=\bar{c}_b\int_{L}^{U}\int_{rl-W}^{rl}\left\{\Lambda\left(t\right)dt\right\}h\left(rl\right)drl \tag{8.40}$$

Example 8.12

Based on Data Set I (see Section 6.4) and c_l =$125, the expected warranty costs for various combinations of W and [L, U] are shown in Table 8.25 and Table 8.26, respectively.

The expected warranty cost to the remanufacturer is reduced by 6.13% compared to that of the FRW policy when item remaining life varies from one to three years (i.e., L = 1 and U = 3) and items are sold with a 0.5-year warranty. It is reduced by 23.97% when the remaining life varies from one to three years (i.e., L = 1 and U = 3) and the warranty period is two years.

8.7 Analysis of Individual Cost Deductible Policy

This section presents the cost analysis of providing the Individual Cost Deductible (ICD) Policy based on Model S3 (SEPs, Preventive Maintenance)

TABLE 8.25

The Expected Warranty Costs to Remanufacturer for LIC Policy, Model S2

		Expected Cost to Remanufacturer								
		L = 1			*L* = 2			*L* = 3		
Item	*W*	*U* = 1	*U* = 2	*U* = 3	*U* = 1	*U* = 2	*U* = 3	*U* = 1	*U* = 2	*U* = 3
AC	**0.5**	$61.26	$72.55	$71.86	$83.86	$80.45	$79.69	$83.86	$83.15	$82.37
	1.0	$63.92	$79.77	$75.23	$87.51	$88.46	$83.42	$87.51	$91.43	$86.23
	2.0	$75.11	$91.34	$78.03	$102.82	$101.29	$86.53	$102.82	$104.69	$89.44

TABLE 8.26

The Expected Warranty Costs to Buyer for LIC Policy, Model S2

		Expected Cost to Buyer								
		L = 1			*L* = 2			*L* = 3		
Item	*W*	*U* = 1	*U* = 2	*U* = 3	*U* = 1	*U* = 2	*U* = 3	*U* = 1	*U* = 2	*U* = 3
AC	**0.5**	$35.11	$41.58	$41.19	$48.06	$46.11	$45.67	$48.06	$47.66	$47.21
	1.0	$36.63	$45.72	$43.12	$50.15	$50.70	$47.81	$50.15	$52.40	$49.42
	2.0	$43.05	$52.35	$44.72	$58.93	$58.05	$49.59	$58.93	$60.00	$51.26

and Model S4 (Conventional Product, Preventive Maintenance) for warranty failures of remanufactured products discussed in Chapter 5. The policy can be described as follows:

ICD POLICY: Under the Individual Cost Deductible Policy, the remanufacturer charges the full cost of repair to the buyer as long as the cost of any replacement/repair during the warranty period is less than a specified limit c_E. If the cost of any repair exceeds c_E, the remanufacturer pays the excess.

Since the cost of individual claims to the buyer is limited to c_E, we have for the jth failure,

$$D_j = \text{Max}\{0,(C_j,-c_E)\} \tag{8.41}$$

$$B_j = \min\{C_j, c_E\} \tag{8.42}$$

The warranty cost to the remanufacturer is determined from (7.2) with D_j given by (8.41). The warranty cost to the buyer is determined from (7.11), with B_j given by (8.42). The expected cost of a claim to the remanufacturer, $\bar{c}_d$, is given by:

$$\bar{c}_d = \int_{c_E}^{\infty} (c - c_E) g(c) dc \tag{8.43}$$

The expected cost to the buyer for a repair during the warranty period, $\bar{c}_b$, is given by:

$$\bar{c}_b = \int_0^{c_E} c g(c) dc + \bar{c}_E \bar{G}(c_E) \tag{8.44}$$

8.7.1 Model S3 (SEPs, Preventive Maintenance)

Here, the expected warranty cost to the remanufacturer is given by (8.35), with $\bar{c}_d$ given by (8.43). The expected cost to the buyer during the warranty period is given by (8.36), with $\bar{c}_b$ given by (8.44).

Example 8.13

Based on Data Set I (see Section 6.4) and c_E =\$25, the expected warranty costs for various combinations of remaining life and warranty periods are shown in Table 8.27, and the confidence interval is presented in Table 8.28.

The expected warranty cost to the remanufacturer is reduced by 93.33% compared to that of the FRW policy for a remanufactured AC with one-year remaining life sold with a 0.5-year warranty. This is reduced by 85.73% for a three-year remaining-life AC sold with a two-year warranty.

TABLE 8.27

The Expected Warranty Costs for ICD Policy, Model S1

		Expected Cost to Remanufacturer			Expected Cost to Buyer		
Item	*W*	*RL* = 1	*RL* = 2	*RL* = 3	*RL* = 1	*RL* = 2	*RL* = 3
AC	0.5	$23.50	$22.54	$22.33	$21.14	$20.28	$20.09
	1.0	$24.52	$24.78	$23.37	$22.06	$22.29	$21.03
	2.0	$28.81	$28.38	$25.24	$25.92	$25.53	$21.81

TABLE 8.28

Confidence Intervals on ICD Policy, Model S1

	Confidence Interval Expected Cost to Remanufacturer						Confidence Interval Expected Cost to Buyer					
	RL = 1		*RL* = 2		*RL* = 3		*RL* = 1		*RL* = 2		*RL* = 3	
W	*L* limit	*U* limit	*L* limit	*U* limit	*L* limit	*U* limit	*L* limit	*U* limit	*L* limit	*U* limit	*L* limit	*U* limit
0.5	$22.74	$24.26	$21.42	$23.45	$20.63	$24.03	$20.38	$21.90	$19.16	$21.39	$18.39	$21.78
1.0	$22.57	$26.46	$21.92	$26.24	$20.38	$26.37	$20.11	$24.00	$19.43	$25.16	$18.03	$24.02
2.0	$25.05	$32.56	$24.08	$28.54	$19.30	$29.19	$22.16	$29.67	$21.24	$29.82	$16.87	$26.75

8.7.2 Model S4 (CPs, Preventive Maintenance)

In this model, the expected warranty cost to the remanufacturer is given by (8.35), with $\bar{c}_d$ given by (8.43). The expected cost to the buyer over the warranty period is given by (8.36), with $\bar{c}_b$ given by (8.44).

Example 8.14

Based on Data Set I (see Section 6.4) and c_E =$25, the expected warranty costs, E [C_d (W)] and E [C_b (W)], for various combinations of remaining life and *L*, *U* are shown in Table 8.29 and Table 8.30, respectively (Table 8.31).

The expected warranty cost to the remanufacturer is reduced by 9.01% compared to that of the FRW policy when item remaining life varies from

TABLE 8.29

The Expected Warranty Costs to Remanufacturer for ICD Policy, Model S2

		Expected Cost to Remanufacturer								
		L = 1			*L* = 2			*L* = 3		
Item	*W*	*U* = 1	*U* = 2	*U* = 3	*U* = 1	*U* = 2	*U* = 3	*U* = 1	*U* = 2	*U* = 3
AC	0.5	$63.20	$74.84	$74.14	$86.52	$82.99	$82.21	$86.52	$85.78	$84.97
	1.0	$65.94	$82.29	$77.61	$90.28	$91.26	$86.06	$90.28	$94.32	$88.96
	2.0	$77.48	$94.23	$80.50	$106.08	$104.50	$89.27	$106.08	$108.01	$92.27

TABLE 8.30

The Expected Warranty Costs to Buyer for ICD Policy, Model S2

		Expected Cost to Buyer								
		$L = 1$			$L = 2$			$L = 3$		
Item	*W*	$U = 1$	$U = 2$	$U = 3$	$U = 1$	$U = 2$	$U = 3$	$U = 1$	$U = 2$	$U = 3$
AC	**0.5**	$36.22	$42.89	$42.49	$49.58	$47.57	$47.12	$49.58	$49.16	$48.70
	1.0	$37.79	$47.16	$44.48	$51.74	$52.30	$49.33	$51.74	$54.06	$50.98
	2.0	$44.41	$54.00	$46.14	$60.79	$59.89	$51.16	$60.79	$61.90	$52.88

TABLE 8.31

The Expected Warranty Costs for LTC Policy, Model S1

		Expected Cost to Remanufacturer			Expected Cost to Buyer		
Item	*W*	$RL = 1$	$RL = 2$	$RL = 3$	$RL = 1$	$RL = 2$	$RL = 3$
AC	**0.5**	$21.85	$20.96	$20.76	$19.66	$18.86	$18.68
	1.0	$22.80	$23.05	$21.74	$20.51	$20.73	$19.55
	2.0	$26.79	$26.39	$23.55	$24.10	$23.74	$20.28

one to three years (i.e., $L = 1$ and $U = 3$), and items are sold with a 0.5-year warranty. It is reduced by 10.35% when the remaining life varies from one to three years (i.e., $L = 1$ and $U = 3$) and the warranty period is two years.

8.8 Analysis of Limit on Total Cost Policy

This section presents the cost analysis of providing the Limit on Total Cost (LTC) Policy based on Model S3 (SEPs, Preventive Maintenance) and Model S4 (Conventional Product, Preventive Maintenance) for warranty failures of remanufactured products discussed in Chapter 5. The policy can be described as follows:

LTC POLICY: Under this policy, the remanufacturer's obligation ceases when the total repair cost over the warranty period exceeds c_T. As a result, the warranty ceases at W or earlier if the total repair cost, at any time during the warranty period, exceeds c_T.

Let TC_j be the cost of replacement/repair for the first jth failures, as follows:

$$TC_j = \sum_{i=1}^{j} C_i \quad (j = 1,2,\ldots) \tag{8.45}$$

Since the total cost (of claims) to the remanufacturer over the warranty period is limited to c_T, we have for the ith failure,

$$D_i = \text{Min}\left\{C_i, \left(c_T - TC_{(i-1)}\right)\right\} \tag{8.46}$$

$$B_i = \text{Max}\left\{0, TC_i - c_T\right\} \tag{8.47}$$

Let TD_j be the cost to the remanufacturer of replacement/repair first j failures and is given by

$$TD_j = \sum_{i=1}^{j} D_i \quad (j = 1, 2, \ldots) \tag{8.48}$$

Let TB_j be the cost to the buyer of replacement/repair first j failures and is given by:

$$TB_j = \sum_{i=1}^{j} B_i \quad (j = 1, 2, \ldots) \tag{8.49}$$

with D_i and B_i given by (8.46) and (8.47), respectively $TD_0 = TB_0 = 0$.

The warranty ceases at W or earlier at the jth failure if $TD_{j\text{-}i} < c_T$ and $TD_j \geq c_T$. The total cost to the remanufacturer is a random variable as follows:

Let Z_w be the cost of replacement/repair of all the failures over the period [0, W) and let V (z) be the distribution function for Z. Then we have:

$$V(z) = \sum_{r=0}^{\infty} \text{Prob.}\left\{Z_W \leq z \mid N(W;RL) = r\right\} \text{Prob.}\left\{N(W;RL) = r\right\} \tag{8.50}$$

Let Z_W, conditioned on N (W; RL) = r, be the sum of r random independent variables with distribution $G(z)$. Since N (W, RL) is Poisson distributed, then:

$$V(z) = \sum_{r=0}^{\infty} \left[G^{(r)}(z)\left\{\int_{RL-W}^{RL} \Lambda(t)\,dt\right\}\left\{\frac{e^{-\int_{RL-W}^{RL}\Lambda(t)dt}}{r!}\right\}\right] \tag{8.51}$$

where $G^{(r)}(z)$ is the r-fold convolution of $G(z)$ with itself.

8.8.1 Model S3 (SEPs, Preventive Maintenance)

The cost to the remanufacturer = Z_w if $Z_w \leq c_T$ and = c_T if $Z_w > c_T$. The expected warranty cost to the remanufacturer is given by:

$$E\left[C_d(W;RL)\right] = \int_{0}^{c_T} z\,v(z)\,dz + c_T\bar{V}(c_T) \tag{8.52}$$

where v (z) is the density function (= $dV(z)/dz$) for $V(z)$.

The cost to the buyer over the period [0, W) is max {0, Z_w-c_T}. The expected cost to the buyer over the warranty period is given by:

$$E\left[C_b(W;A)\right]=\int_{c_T}^{\infty}(z-c_T)v(z)dz \tag{8.53}$$

If $G(z)$ is exponentially distributed and $\Lambda(t)=\lambda$ (failures occur according to stationary Poisson process), then v (z) can be determined analytically (Cox, 1962). For a general $\Lambda(t)$, it is not possible to determine v (z) analytically, and one needs to use the simulation approach. The numerical results presented below were determined using the simulation approach.

Example 8.15

Based on Data Set I (see Section 6.4) and c_T =$450, the expected costs for various combinations of remaining life and warranty periods are shown in Table 8.32, and the confidence interval is presented in Table 8.33.

The expected warranty cost to the remanufacturer is reduced by 107.93 % compared to that of the FRW policy for a remanufactured AC with one-year remaining life sold with a 0.5-year warranty. This is reduced by 99.06% for a three-year remaining life AC sold with a two-year warranty.

8.8.2 Model S4 (CPs, Preventive Maintenance)

Using $V(z)$ given by (8.50) and the approach used in Model S4, the expected warranty cost to the remanufacturer is given by:

$$E\left[C_d(W;RL)\right]=\int_{L}^{U}\int_{0}^{c_T} zv(z\,|\,rl)dz+c_T\bar{V}(c_T\,|\,rl)\}h(rl)drl \tag{8.54}$$

TABLE 8.32

Confidence Intervals on LTC Policy, Model S1

	Confidence Interval Expected Cost to Remanufacturer						Confidence Interval Expected Cost to Buyer					
	RL = 1		*RL* = 2		*RL* = 3		*RL* = 1		*RL* = 2		*RL* = 3	
W	*L* limit	*U* limit	*L* limit	*U* limit	*L* limit	*U* limit	*L* limit	*U* limit	*L* limit	*U* limit	*L* limit	*U* limit
0.5	$21.03	$22.68	$19.75	$21.98	$18.92	$22.61	$18.83	$20.48	$17.64	$20.07	$16.83	$20.52
1.0	$20.69	$24.91	$19.94	$24.84	$18.48	$24.99	$18.40	$22.62	$17.63	$23.84	$16.30	$22.81
2.0	$22.71	$30.87	$21.73	$27.21	$17.18	$27.91	$20.02	$28.18	$19.08	$28.40	$14.92	$25.65

The expected cost to the buyer over the warranty period is given by:

$$E\left[C_b\left(W;RL\right)\right]=\int_L^U\left\{\int_{CT}^{\infty}\left(z-c_T\right)v\left(z\mid rl\right)\right\}h\left(rl\right)drl \tag{8.55}$$

Example 8.16

Based on Data Set I (see Section 6.4) and c_T =\$450, the expected costs for various combinations of remaining life, *L*, *U* are shown in Table 8.33, and the confidence interval is presented in Table 8.34.

The expected warranty cost to the remanufacturer is reduced by 1.85% compared to that of the FRW policy when the item's remaining life varies from one to three years (i.e., $L = 1$ and $U = 3$) and items are sold with a 0.5-year warranty. It is reduced by 0.97% when the remaining life varies from one to three years (i.e., $L = 1$ and $U = 3$) and the warranty period is two years.

8.9 Analysis of Total Cost Deductibles Policy

This section presents the cost analysis of providing the Total Cost Deductibles (TCD) Policy based on Model S3 (SEPs, Preventive Maintenance) and Model S4 (Conventional Product, Preventive Maintenance) for warranty

TABLE 8.33

The Expected Warranty Costs to Remanufacturer for LTC Policy, Model S2

		Expected Cost to Remanufacturer								
		L = 1			L = 2			L = 3		
Item	W	U = 1	U = 2	U = 3	U = 1	U = 2	U = 3	U = 1	U = 2	U = 3
AC	**0.5**	\$57.03	\$67.54	\$66.91	\$78.08	\$74.90	\$74.20	\$78.08	\$77.42	\$76.69
	1.0	\$59.51	\$74.27	\$70.04	\$81.48	\$82.36	\$77.67	\$81.48	\$85.12	\$80.28
	2.0	\$69.93	\$85.04	\$72.65	\$95.73	\$94.31	\$80.57	\$95.73	\$97.48	\$83.27

TABLE 8.34

The Expected Warranty Costs to Buyer for LTC Policy, Model S2

		Expected Cost to Buyer								
		L = 1			L = 2			L = 3		
Item	W	U = 1	U = 2	U = 3	U = 1	U = 2	U = 3	U = 1	U = 2	U = 3
AC	**0.5**	\$36.22	\$42.89	\$42.49	\$49.58	\$47.57	\$47.12	\$49.58	\$49.16	\$48.70
	1.0	\$37.79	\$47.16	\$44.48	\$51.74	\$52.30	\$49.33	\$51.74	\$54.06	\$50.98
	2.0	\$44.41	\$54.00	\$46.14	\$60.79	\$59.89	\$51.16	\$60.79	\$61.90	\$52.88

failures of remanufactured products discussed in Chapter 5. The policy can be described as follows:

TCD POLICY: Under this policy, the remanufacturer's obligation starts when the total repair cost over the warranty period exceeds c_x. As a result, the remanufacturer charges the full cost of repair to the buyer if the total cost of repair during the warranty period is less than c_x. If the total repair cost in the warranty period exceeds c_x, then the remanufacturer pays the excess until the warranty expires.

Since the total cost to the buyer is limited to c_x, we have for the ith failure,

$$D_j = \begin{cases} \max\{0, (TC_i - c_x)\} & \text{if } TC_{(i-1)} < c_x \\ C_i & \text{if } TC_{(i-1)} > c_x \end{cases} \tag{8.56}$$

$$B_j = \begin{cases} \min\{C_i, c_x - TC_{(i-1)}\} & \text{if } TC_{(i-1)} < c_x \\ 0 & \text{if } TC_{(i-1)} > c_x \end{cases} \tag{8.57}$$

The warranty cost to the remanufacturer is determined from TD_j given by (8.48) with D_i given by (8.56). The warranty cost to the buyer is determined from TB_j given by (8.49) and B_i given by (8.57).

8.9.1 Model S3 (SEPs, Preventive Maintenance)

Using $V(z)$ given by (8.50), the expected warranty cost to the remanufacturer is given by:

$$E\left[C_d(W;RL)\right] = \int_{c_x}^{\infty} (z - c_x) v(z) dz \tag{8.58}$$

The expected cost to the buyer over the warranty period is given by:

$$E\left[C_b(W;RL)\right] = \int_{0}^{c_x} z v(z) dz + c_x \bar{V}(c_x) \tag{8.59}$$

Example 8.17

Based on Data Set I (see Section 6.4) and c_x =\$50, the expected costs for various combinations of remaining life and warranty periods are shown in Table 8.35, and the confidence interval is presented in Table 8.36.

The expected warranty cost to the remanufacturer is reduced by 82.38 % compared to that of the FRW policy for a remanufactured AC with one-year remaining life sold with a 0.5-year warranty. This is reduced by 69.23% for a three-year remaining life AC sold with a two-year warranty.

TABLE 8.35

The Expected Warranty Costs for TCD Policy, Model S1

		Expected Cost to Remanufacturer			Expected Cost to Buyer		
Item	*W*	*RL* = 1	*RL* = 2	*RL* = 3	*RL* = 1	*RL* = 2	*RL* = 3
AC	0.5	$24.91	$23.90	$23.67	$22.41	$21.50	$21.29
	1.0	$25.99	$26.27	$24.78	$23.38	$23.64	$22.29
	2.0	$30.54	$30.09	$27.70	$27.48	$27.07	$23.12

TABLE 8.36

Confidence Intervals on TCD Policy, Model S1

	Confidence Interval Expected Cost to Remanufacturer						Confidence Interval Expected Cost to Buyer					
	RL = 1		*RL* = 2		*RL* = 3		*RL* = 1		*RL* = 2		*RL* = 3	
W	*L* limit	*U* limit	*L* limit	*U* limit	*L* limit	*U* limit	*L* limit	*U* limit	*L* limit	*U* limit	*L* limit	*U* limit
0.5	$24.08	$25.74	$22.68	$24.89	$21.82	$25.52	$21.58	$23.24	$20.28	$22.71	$19.45	$23.14
1.0	$23.88	$28.11	$23.16	$27.89	$21.52	$28.04	$21.27	$25.50	$20.52	$26.75	$19.03	$25.55
2.0	$26.46	$34.63	$25.43	$30.36	$20.33	$31.08	$23.39	$31.56	$22.41	$31.73	$17.75	$28.50

8.9.2 Model S4 (CPs, Preventive Maintenance)

Using $V(z)$ given by (8.50), the expected warranty cost to the remanufacturer is given by:

$$E\left[C_d(W;RL)\right]=\int_L^U\left\{\int_{c_x}^{\infty}(z-c_x)v(z)dz\right\}h(rl)drl \tag{8.60}$$

The expected cost to the buyer over the warranty period is given by:

$$E\left[C_b(W;RL)\right]=\int_L^U\left\{\int_0^{c_x}zv(z)dz+c_x\bar{V}(c_x)\right\}h(rl)drl \tag{8.61}$$

Example 8.18

Based on Data Set I (see Section 6.4) and c_x =$50, the expected costs for various combinations of L, U and W are shown in Table 8.37, and the confidence interval is presented in Table 8.38.

TABLE 8.37

The Expected Warranty Costs to Remanufacturer for TCD Policy, Model S2

		Expected Cost to Remanufacturer								
		$L = 1$			$L = 2$			$L = 3$		
Item	W	$U = 1$	$U = 2$	$U = 3$	$U = 1$	$U = 2$	$U = 3$	$U = 1$	$U = 2$	$U = 3$
AC	**0.5**	$59.01	$69.88	$69.22	$80.78	$77.49	$76.76	$80.78	$80.10	$79.34
	1.0	$61.57	$76.83	$72.46	$84.29	$85.20	$80.36	$84.29	$88.07	$83.06
	2.0	$72.35	$87.98	$75.16	$99.04	$97.57	$83.35	$99.04	$100.84	$86.15

TABLE 8.38

The Expected Warranty Costs to Buyer for TCD Policy, Model S2

		Expected Cost to Buyer								
		$L = 1$			$L = 2$			$L = 3$		
Item	W	$U = 1$	$U = 2$	$U = 3$	$U = 1$	$U = 2$	$U = 3$	$U = 1$	$U = 2$	$U = 3$
AC	**0.5**	$37.47	$44.38	$43.96	$51.30	$49.21	$48.75	$51.30	$50.86	$50.38
	1.0	$39.10	$48.79	$46.02	$53.53	$54.11	$51.03	$53.53	$55.93	$52.74
	2.0	$45.94	$55.87	$47.73	$62.90	$61.96	$52.93	$62.90	$64.04	$54.71

The expected warranty cost to the remanufacturer is reduced by 2.55% compared to that of the FRW policy when the item's remaining life varies from one to three years (i.e., $L = 1$ and $U = 3$) and items are sold with a 0.5-year warranty. It is reduced by 5.71% when the remaining life varies from one to three years (i.e., $L = 1$ and $U = 3$) and the warranty period is two years.

8.10 Analysis of Money-Back Guarantee Policy

This section presents the cost analysis of providing the Money-Back Guarantee (MBG) Policy based on Model S1 (Sensor-Embedded, Minimal Repair) for warranty failures of remanufactured products discussed in Chapter 5. The policy can be described as follows:

MBG POLICY: Under the MBG Policy, all failures over the warranty period $[0, W)$ are replaced/repaired at no cost to the buyer. If the number of failures over $[0, W)$ exceeds a specified value k ($k > 1$), then at the $(k+l)$st failure, the buyer has the option of returning the item for 100% money-back. The warranty ceases when the buyer exercises this option. If the number of failures over $[0, W)$ is either k or the buyer does not exercise the buyback option when the $(k+l)$st failure occurs, then the item is covered for all failures until W.

8.10.1 Model S1 (SEPs, Minimal Repair, Corrective Maintenance)

In this model, the buyer has the option of returning the item at the (k+l)st failure, should this occur within the warranty period. The warranty can cease before the item reaches a remaining life (RL-W).

Let N be the number of item failures over [RL-W, RL). Since failures are replaced/repaired minimally, then:

$$P_n(RL-W,RL)=\text{Prob}\{N=n\}=\frac{\int_{RL-W}^{RL}\Lambda(t)dt\}^n e^{-\left\{\int_{RL-W}^{RL}\Lambda(t)\,dt\right\}}}{n!} \quad (8.62)$$

The expected warranty cost to the remanufacturer can be determined using a conditional approach. Let $E\,[J_d(W;RL)\mid N=n]$ be the expected cost conditional on $N=n$. We need to consider two cases:

Case (i): $n \le k$, in which case $E\,[J_d\,(W;RL)\mid N=n]=n\,\bar{c}$

Case (ii): when $n > k$, the cost is $k\,\bar{c}+\bar{c}_{dd}$ if the buyer exercises the buyback option. If not, it is $n\,\bar{c}$ since the buyer does not exercise the buyback option. These occur with probability γ and (l-γ) respectively. As a result, the conditional expected cost to the remanufacturer is given by:

$$E\left[J_d(W;RL)\mid N=n\right]=(k\bar{c}+\bar{c}_{dd})\gamma+n\bar{c}\,(1-\gamma) \quad (8.63)$$

On removing the conditioning, the expected warranty cost to the remanufacturer is given by:

$$E\left[J_d(W;RL)=\sum_{n=0}^{k}n\bar{c}P_n(RL-W,RL)+\sum_{n=k+1}^{\infty}\{(k\bar{c}+\bar{c}_{dd})\gamma+\quad+n\bar{c}(1-\gamma)\}P_n(RL-W,) \quad (8.64)$$

Example 8.19

Based on Data Set I (see Section 6.4) and γ = 0.7; $\bar{c}$ =\$100; $\bar{c}_{dd}$ =\$1000; k = 3, the expected costs for different combinations of remaining life and warranty periods are shown in Table 8.39, and the confidence interval is presented in Table 8.40.

TABLE 8.39

The Expected Warranty Costs for MBG Policy, Model S1

		Expected After Sales Cost to Remanufacturer		
Item	*W*	*RL* = 1	*RL* = 2	*RL* = 3
AC	0.5	\$57.92	\$55.56	\$55.04
	1.0	\$60.44	\$61.09	\$57.62
	2.0	\$71.01	\$69.96	\$59.76

TABLE 8.40

Standard Error and Confidence Intervals on MBG Policy, Model S1

					Confidence Interval					
		Standard Error			*RL* = 1		*RL* = 2		*RL* = 3	
Item	W	*RL* = 1	*RL* = 2	*RL* = 3	*L* Limit	*U* Limit	*L* Limit	*U* Limit	*L* Limit	*U* Limit
AC	**0.5**	0.82	1.21	1.83	$57.64	$58.20	$55.15	$55.97	$54.41	$55.67
	1.0	2.10	3.09	3.23	$59.72	$61.15	$60.04	$62.15	$56.51	$58.72
	2.0	4.05	4.63	5.33	$69.63	$72.40	$68.37	$71.54	$57.94	$61.5

The expected warranty cost to the remanufacturer is increased by 21.56 % compared to that of the FRW policy for a remanufactured AC with one-year remaining life sold with a 0.5-year warranty. This is increased by 18.84% for a three-year remaining life AC sold with a two-year warranty.

8.11 Conclusions

In this chapter, eight simple non-renewing warranty policies,, namely, SPE, LCS, LMS, LIC, ICD, LTC, TCD and MBG, were discussed. In order to assess the impact of these eight policies in terms of warranty cost, pair-wise t tests were carried out for different performance measures, namely, Holding Cost, Backorder Cost, Disassembly Cost, Disposal Cost, Testing Cost, Remanufacturing Cost, Transportation Cost, Warranty Cost, Number of Claims and Preventive Maintenance Cost.

9

Cost Analysis of Combination Warranties

9.1 Introduction

In Chapter 4, several warranty policies with preventive maintenance for remanufactured products were introduced. This chapter presents the analysis of determining the expected cost of warranty, CM and PM (from both the buyer's and remanufacturer's perspectives). Chapter 7 and Chapter 8 considered ten of these policies. Here, non-renewing combination policies, namely, Policy 11 (LITC), Policy 12 (FRW-PRW), Policy 13 (FRW-LIC), Policy 14 (FRW-LCS), Policy 15 (FRW-LMS), Policy 16 (MBG-FRW), Policy 17 (MBG-PRW), Policy 18 (MBG-LIC) and Policy 19 (MBG-LITC), as defined in Chapter 4, are considered.

In Chapter 5, a variety of models were discussed at a system level (Models S1 through S4) and at a component level (Models Cl through C8) for warranty failures of remanufacturing products. The expected warranty cost for a given policy can be evaluated using one of those models. In Chapter 7, analysis of the FRW policy based on the models at both the system and component levels was carried out. For the policies considered in this chapter, the analysis is very similar to that for the FRW policy. For that reason, for the policies considered in this chapter, only selected models are discussed as illustrations. The warranty costs for the rest of the models can be carried out in a manner similar to these and the ones given for the FRW policy in Chapter 7.

Section 9.2 presents some assumptions and notations used in this chapter. Section 9.3 deals with the analysis of the FRW-PRW Combination Policy, and Section 9.4 deals with the analysis of the LITC Policy. Section 9.5 deals with the analysis of the FRW-LIC Combination Policy, and Section 9.6 deals with the analysis of the FRW-LCS Combination Policy. Section 9.7 deals with the analysis of the FRW-LMS Combination Policy, and Section 9.8 deals with the analysis of the MBG-FRW Combination Policy. Section 9.9 deals with the analysis of the MBG-PRW Combination Policy, and Sections 9.10 and 9.11 deal with the analyses of the MGB-LIC Combination Policy and the MBG-LITC Combination Policy, respectively. Finally, some conclusions are presented in Section 9.12.

9.2 Some Preliminaries

All the assumptions, notations and parameter values for the numerical examples given in section 7.2 are also applicable here, along with some new notations and parameter values given below.

9.2.1 Notations

$C_d(W_1; RL)$	Warranty cost to the remanufacturer in the period $[0, W_1)$ for an item with sensor embedded and corrective maintenance.
$C_b(W - W_1; v)$	Cost to the buyer in the period $[W_1, W)$ for an item of excess remaining life v
$C_d(W - W_1; v)$	Warranty cost to the remanufacturer in the period $[W_1, W)$ for an item of excess remaining life v
$C_b(W_1, W; RL)$	Cost to the buyer for an item of remaining life RL with sensor embedded
$C_d(W_1, W; RL)$	Total warranty cost to the remanufacturer for item of remaining life RL with sensor embedded
$C_b(W_1, W)$	Cost to the buyer for an item of remaining life RL unknown due to lack of sensor embedded used
$C_d(W_1, W)$	Total warranty cost to the remanufacturer for item of remaining life RL unknown due to lack of sensor embedded used
$F_w(x)$	Distribution function for the first failure in the period (W_1, W) given by the excess remaining life of renewal process associated with failures in the period $[0, W_1)$ with first failure given by $F_{i1}(x)$ for remaining life known [or $F_{iu}(x)$ for remaining life unknown] and succeeding failures given by $F_{iu}(x)$
v	Excess remaining life of renewal process associated with failures in the period $[0, W_1)$ with first failure given by $F_{i1}(x)$ for remaining life known [or $F_{iu}(x)$ for remaining life unknown] and subsequent failures given by $F_{iu}(x)$
$J_d(W; RL)$	Total after sale cost to remanufacturer for an item with sensor embedded sold with warranty (W).
$J_d(W_1, W; RL)$	Total after sale cost to remanufacturer for an item with sensor embedded sold with combination warranty (W_1, W).
$J_b(W_1, W; RL)$	Total after sale cost to buyer for an item with sensor embedded sold with combination warranty (W_1, W).
n	Number of failures
k	Parameter of policy
$\bar{c}_{bb}$	Expected cost of buyback to remanufacturer (may be full sale price if the item has to be scrapped and the difference between sale price and salvage value otherwise)
$P_n(RL, RL+W)$	Probability of n failures over $[0, W)$ given the remaining life of the item is RL
γ	Probability that buyer will execute money-back option

9.2.2 Parameter Values for Numerical Examples

The data sets of Section 6.4 and W_1 = 0.5W are used to illustrate numerical examples. The probability of buyback option γ ($0 < \gamma \leq 1$) is known to the remanufacturer.

9.3 Analysis of the FRW-PRW Combination Policy

This section presents the cost analysis of providing the FRW-PRW Policy based on Model C3 (Sensor-Embedded Component, Non-Repairable, Replacement by Remanufactured, Preventive Maintenance) and Model C4 (Conventional Component, Non-Repairable, Replacement by Remanufactured, Preventive Maintenance) for warranty failures of remanufactured products discussed in Chapter 5. The policy can be described as follows:

FRW-PRW POLICY: Under this policy, the remanufacturer replaces failed items at no cost to the buyer up to W1 (W1 < W). If a failure occurs in the interval [W1, W), the remanufacturer refunds a fraction of the sale price and the warranty terminates.

9.3.1 Model C3 (Sensor-Embedded Component, Non-Repairable, Replacement by Remanufactured)

Since the component has a sensor embedded in it, all the data needed is retrieved and the remaining life, *RL*, is estimated. The failures over the first sub-interval, $[0, W_1)$, are given by a modified renewal process. In this case, the first failure is given by (5.20) and subsequent failures are given by (5.31). The expected number of failures in $[0, W_1)$ is given by (5.32) and is rewritten as

$$E\left[N_i(W_1;RL)\right] = \left[F_{i1}(W_1) + \int_0^{W_1} M_{iu}(W_1 - x)\,dF_{i1}(x)\right. \tag{9.1}$$

Therefore, the expected warranty cost to the remanufacturer for failures in $[0, W_1)$ is given by:

$$E\left[C_d(W_1;RL)\right] = c_b\left[F_{i1}(W_1) + \int_0^{W_1} M_{iu}(W_1 - x)\,dF_{i1}(x)\right. \tag{9.2}$$

where $M_{iu}(x)$ is the renewal function associated with $F_{iu}(x)$ and c_b is the purchasing cost per item to remanufacturer. For failures over the interval $[W_1, W)$, we have the remaining life, v, and the warranty term changes from FRW to PRW. Thus $F_W(v)$ is as follows:

$$F_W(v) = F_{i1}(v - W_1) - \int_0^{W_1} \left[1 - F_{i1}(v - W_1 - z)\right] dM_{iu}(z) \tag{9.3}$$

Let $S(Y)$ denote the linear refund function and is given by:

$$S(Y) = \begin{cases} C_S(RL)\left\{1 - \dfrac{W_1 + Y}{W}\right\} & \text{for } 0 \le v \le (W - W_1) \\ 0 & \text{for } v > (W - W_1) \end{cases} \tag{9.4}$$

where $C_s(RL)$ is the sale price.

Then the expected warranty cost to the remanufacturer resulting from a failure in the second sub-interval $[W_1, W)$ is given by:

$$E\left[C_d(W - W_1); v)\right] = c_S(RL)\left[\left\{\frac{W - W_1}{W}\right\} F_W(W - W_1) - \left(\frac{1}{W}\right) \int_0^{(W-W_1)} v dF_W(v)\right] \tag{9.5}$$

Combining the costs over the two intervals, the result is given by:

$$\begin{aligned} E\left[C_d(W_1, W; RL)\right] = C_b &\left[F_{i1}(W_1) + \int_0^{W_1} M_{iu}(W_1 - x) dF_{i1}(x)\right] \\ &+ c_S(RL)\left[\left\{\frac{W - W_1}{W}\right\} F_W(W - W_1) - \left(\frac{1}{W}\right) \int_0^{(W-W_1)} v dF_W(v)\right] \end{aligned} \tag{9.6}$$

Example 9.1

Based on Data Set II (i) (see Section 6.4) with c_b = \$10 and $C_S(RL)$ = \$20, the expected warranty costs determined from (9.6), for different combinations of remaining life and warranty periods, are shown in Table 9.1. Table 9.2 shows the standard errors and confidence intervals of the ARTO simulation runs.

Table 9.1 presents the expected number of failures and cost for remanufactured AC components for the FRW-PRW policy. In Table 9.1, the expected failures frequency represents the expected number of failed items per unit of sale. The expected cost to the remanufacturer includes the cost of supplying the original item, C_s. Thus, the expected cost of the warranty is calculated by

TABLE 9.1

The Expected Warranty Costs for FRW-PRW Policy, Model C3

		Expected Failures Frequency			Expected Warranty Cost to Remanufacturer		
Components	*W*	*RL* = 1	*RL* = 2	*RL* = 3	*RL* = 1	*RL* = 2	*RL* = 3
Evaporator	**0.5**	0.4853	0.0031	0.0007	$4.10	$4.70	$3.75
	1.0	0.0973	0.0126	0.0058	$4.55	$5.14	$3.82
	2.0	0.1456	0.0281	0.0196	$6.83	$6.78	$3.94
Control Box	**0.5**	0.4795	0.0030	0.0038	$4.02	$4.67	$3.74
	1.0	0.1031	0.0124	0.0311	$4.74	$5.01	$3.79
	2.0	0.1398	0.0280	0.1047	$6.74	$6.65	$3.91
Blower	**0.5**	0.4736	0.0029	0.0202	$2.01	$1.88	$1.92
	1.0	0.0915	0.0127	0.1664	$2.65	$3.34	$1.97
	2.0	0.1340	0.0284	0.5596	$3.66	$4.11	$2.04
Air Guide	**0.5**	0.4736	0.0013	0.1078	$1.11	$1.08	$0.93
	1.0	0.0682	0.0129	0.8893	$1.60	$1.47	$1.02
	2.0	0.1223	0.0246	0.3644	$2.12	$2.10	$1.08
Motor	**0.5**	0.4597	0.0030	0.5762	$4.20	$4.02	$3.93
	1.0	0.0996	0.0124	0.7474	$4.61	$4.30	$4.00
	2.0	0.1404	0.0284	0.0156	$6.48	$5.57	$4.04
Condenser	**0.5**	0.4789	0.0032	0.7163	$1.31	$1.12	$1.09
	1.0	0.0932	0.0126	0.7537	$1.90	$1.60	$1.20
	2.0	0.1468	0.0284	0.0832	$2.20	$1.85	$1.26
Fan	**0.5**	0.4905	0.0029	0.7474	$2.51	$2.12	$2.04
	1.0	0.1072	0.0125	0.1520	$3.47	$2.48	$2.09
	2.0	0.1410	0.0282	0.4450	$4.31	$3.45	$2.20
Protector	**0.5**	0.4952	0.0031	0.5325	$0.66	$0.52	$0.37
	1.0	0.0915	0.0125	0.8124	$1.03	$0.84	$0.45
	2.0	0.1392	0.0284	0.7505	$1.80	$1.21	$0.48
Compressor	**0.5**	0.4783	0.0031	0.0159	$2.91	$2.73	$2.61
	1.0	0.0967	0.0126	0.0832	$3.75	$3.52	$2.83
	2.0	0.1404	0.0283	0.7537	$5.11	$4.61	$2.92

subtracting C_s from the expected cost to the remanufacturer. For example, from Table 9.1, for $W = 0.5$ and $RL = 1$, the warranty cost for the AC's motor is $4.20–$C_s$ = $4.20–$4.00 = $0.20, which is ([$0.20/$4.00] × 100) = 5.00% of the cost of supplying the motor, C_s, which is significantly less than $4.00, C_s. This cost might be acceptable, but the corresponding values for longer warranties are much higher. For example, for $W = 2$ years and $RL = 1$, the corresponding percentage is ([($6.48–$4.00)/$4.00] × 100) = 62.00%.

For a one-year remaining-life remanufactured AC motor sold with a 0.5-year warranty, the ARTO system can claim with 90% confidence that the expected warranty cost is in the interval [$3.97–$4.42]. As shown in Table 9.2,

TABLE 9.2
Standard Error and Confidence Interval on FRW-PRW Policy, Model C3

					Confidence Interval					
		Standard Error			*RL* = 1		*RL* = 2		*RL* = 3	
Components	*W*	*RL* = 1	*RL* = 2	*RL* = 3	*L* Limit	*U* Limit	*L* Limit	*U* Limit	*L* Limit	*U* Limit
Evaporator	**0.5**	0.46	0.67	1.02	$3.94	$4.25	$4.47	$4.92	$3.40	$4.10
	1.0	1.17	1.71	1.80	$4.15	$4.95	$4.55	$5.73	$3.21	$4.44
	2.0	2.25	2.57	2.96	$6.05	$7.60	$5.90	$7.66	$2.93	$4.95
Control Box	**0.5**	0.51	0.75	1.14	$3.85	$4.20	$4.41	$4.93	$3.35	$4.13
	1.0	1.31	1.93	2.02	$4.29	$5.19	$4.35	$5.66	$3.10	$4.48
	2.0	2.53	2.89	3.33	$5.88	$7.61	$5.66	$7.64	$2.77	$5.05
Blower	**0.5**	0.57	0.85	1.29	$1.81	$2.21	$1.59	$2.17	$1.48	$2.36
	1.0	1.47	2.16	2.27	$2.14	$3.15	$2.60	$4.08	$1.19	$2.74
	2.0	2.84	3.25	3.74	$2.69	$4.63	$3.00	$5.22	$0.76	$3.32
Air Guide	**0.5**	0.73	1.07	1.63	$0.86	$1.36	$0.72	$1.45	$0.37	$1.49
	1.0	1.87	2.75	2.88	$0.96	$2.24	$0.53	$2.41	$0.04	$2.00
	2.0	3.61	4.12	4.74	$0.89	$3.35	$0.69	$3.51	$0.35	$2.71
Motor	**0.5**	0.65	0.96	1.45	$3.97	$4.42	$3.70	$4.35	$3.43	$4.43
	1.0	1.66	2.45	2.56	$4.04	$5.18	$3.47	$5.14	$3.13	$4.88
	2.0	3.21	3.67	4.22	$5.38	$7.58	$4.31	$6.82	$2.60	$5.49
Condenser	**0.5**	0.54	0.79	1.20	$1.13	$1.49	$0.85	$1.39	$0.68	$1.50
	1.0	1.37	2.02	2.12	$1.43	$2.37	$0.91	$2.29	$0.48	$1.93
	2.0	2.65	3.03	3.49	$1.29	$3.11	$0.81	$2.89	$0.07	$2.46
Fan	**0.5**	0.54	0.79	1.20	$2.33	$2.70	$1.85	$2.39	$1.63	$2.45
	1.0	1.37	2.02	2.12	$3.00	$3.94	$1.79	$3.18	$1.37	$2.82
	2.0	2.65	3.03	3.49	$3.41	$5.22	$2.41	$4.49	$1.01	$3.40
Protector	**0.5**	0.52	0.76	1.16	$0.49	$0.84	$0.26	$0.78	$0.02	$0.77
	1.0	1.33	1.95	2.05	$0.57	$1.48	$0.17	$1.51	$0.17	$1.15
	2.0	2.56	2.93	3.37	$0.92	$2.68	$0.21	$2.21	$0.54	$1.64
Compressor	**0.5**	0.52	0.76	1.16	$2.73	$3.09	$2.47	$2.99	$2.21	$3.01
	1.0	1.33	1.95	2.05	$3.29	$4.20	$2.85	$4.19	$2.13	$3.53
	2.0	2.56	2.93	3.37	$4.23	$5.98	$3.61	$5.62	$1.77	$4.08

the confidence interval for a one-year remaining-life remanufactured AC motor sold with a two-year warranty is [$5.38 -$7.58].

The expected warranty cost to the remanufacturer is reduced by 19.88% compared to that of the FRW policy for a remanufactured AC motor. The expected warranty cost to the remanufacturer is reduced by 31.18% compared to that of the PRW policy for a remanufactured AC motor.

9.3.2 Model C4 (Conventional Component, Replacement by Remanufactured)

In this model, the failure distribution of the component i, at the time of arrival to the ARTO system, is given by F_{iu}. Then, failures over $[0, W_1)$ are given by an ordinary renewal process. The cost over $[W_1, W)$ is given by:

$$E\left[C_d\left(W_1,W;RL\right)\right]=C_b\left[F_{i1}\left(W_1\right)+\int_0^{W_1} M_{iu}\left(W_1-x\right)dF_{i1}\left(x\right)\right] + c_S\left[\left\{\frac{W-W_1}{W}\right\}F_W\left(W-W_1\right)-\left(\frac{1}{W}\right)\int_0^{(W-W_1)} v\,dF_W\left(v\right)\right] \tag{9.7}$$

Example 9.2

Based on Data Set II (i) (see Section 6.4) with c_b = \$10 and c_S = \$20, the expected warranty costs determined from (9.7) for different warranty periods are shown in Table 9.3. Table 9.4 shows the confidence intervals of the ARTO simulation runs.

TABLE 9.3

The Expected Warranty Costs for FRW-PRW Policy, Model C4

		Expected Warranty Cost to Remanufacturer								
		L = 1			L = 2			L = 3		
Components	W	U = 1	U = 2	U = 3	U = 1	U = 2	U = 3	U = 1	U = 2	U = 3
Evaporator	0.5	\$5.01	\$5.09	\$5.17	\$5.75	\$5.86	\$5.98	\$4.58	\$4.76	\$4.94
	1	\$5.57	\$5.78	\$5.97	\$6.29	\$6.59	\$6.89	\$4.67	\$4.99	\$5.31
	2	\$8.35	\$8.75	\$9.14	\$8.29	\$8.75	\$9.20	\$4.82	\$5.34	\$5.85
Control Box	0.5	\$4.92	\$5.01	\$5.10	\$5.72	\$5.85	\$5.97	\$4.57	\$4.78	\$4.98
	1	\$5.81	\$6.03	\$6.26	\$6.12	\$6.46	\$6.80	\$4.64	\$5.00	\$5.35
	2	\$8.25	\$8.70	\$9.14	\$8.14	\$8.65	\$9.15	\$4.79	\$5.38	\$5.95
Blower	0.5	\$2.47	\$2.56	\$2.66	\$2.31	\$2.46	\$2.60	\$2.35	\$2.57	\$2.80
	1	\$3.24	\$3.50	\$3.76	\$4.09	\$4.46	\$4.84	\$2.41	\$2.80	\$3.20
	2	\$4.47	\$4.97	\$5.47	\$5.03	\$5.61	\$6.17	\$2.50	\$3.15	\$3.80
Air Guide	0.5	\$1.36	\$1.49	\$1.61	\$1.32	\$1.51	\$1.70	\$1.13	\$1.42	\$1.71
	1	\$1.96	\$2.29	\$2.61	\$1.80	\$2.29	\$2.76	\$1.24	\$1.75	\$2.26
	2	\$2.59	\$3.23	\$3.86	\$2.57	\$3.30	\$4.02	\$1.32	\$2.16	\$2.98
Motor	0.5	\$5.13	\$5.25	\$5.36	\$4.92	\$5.09	\$5.26	\$4.81	\$5.07	\$5.32
	1	\$5.65	\$5.93	\$6.22	\$5.27	\$5.70	\$6.12	\$4.90	\$5.35	\$5.80
	2	\$7.92	\$8.49	\$9.05	\$6.81	\$7.46	\$8.10	\$4.94	\$5.69	\$6.42
Condenser	0.5	\$1.60	\$1.70	\$1.79	\$1.37	\$1.51	\$1.65	\$1.33	\$1.55	\$1.76
	1	\$2.33	\$2.56	\$2.80	\$1.96	\$2.32	\$2.66	\$1.47	\$1.84	\$2.21
	2	\$2.69	\$3.16	\$3.62	\$2.26	\$2.79	\$3.32	\$1.55	\$2.17	\$2.77
Fan	0.5	\$3.07	\$3.17	\$3.26	\$2.59	\$2.73	\$2.87	\$2.50	\$2.70	\$2.91
	1	\$4.24	\$4.48	\$4.72	\$3.04	\$3.40	\$3.75	\$2.56	\$2.93	\$3.30
	2	\$5.28	\$5.75	\$6.20	\$4.21	\$4.75	\$5.28	\$2.69	\$3.31	\$3.92
Protector	0.5	\$0.82	\$0.90	\$0.99	\$0.64	\$0.78	\$0.90	\$0.46	\$0.67	\$0.86
	1	\$1.26	\$1.49	\$1.72	\$1.02	\$1.37	\$1.71	\$0.55	\$0.90	\$1.26
	2	\$2.21	\$2.65	\$3.10	\$1.48	\$2.00	\$2.51	\$0.59	\$1.18	\$1.77
Compressor	0.5	\$3.56	\$3.66	\$3.75	\$3.34	\$3.48	\$3.61	\$3.19	\$3.40	\$3.60
	1	\$4.58	\$4.82	\$5.05	\$4.30	\$4.65	\$4.99	\$3.46	\$3.82	\$4.18
	2	\$6.24	\$6.70	\$7.15	\$5.65	\$6.16	\$6.67	\$3.58	\$4.17	\$4.75

TABLE 9.4

Confidence Interval for FRW-PRW Policy, Model C4

		$L = 1$						$L = 2$						$L = 3$					
		$U = 1$		$U = 2$		$U = 3$		$U = 1$		$U = 2$		$U = 3$		$U = 1$		$U = 2$		$U = 3$	
Components	**W**	**Lower**	**Upper**	**Lower**	**Upper**	**Lower**	**Upper**	**Lower**	**Upper**	**Lower**	**Upper**	**Lower**	**Upper**	**Lower**	**Upper**	**Lower**	**Upper**	**Lower**	**Upper**
Evaporator	**0.5**	$4.57	$5.63	$4.64	$5.72	$4.71	$5.81	$5.24	$6.45	$5.35	$6.59	$5.46	$6.72	$4.18	$5.15	$4.34	$5.35	$4.50	$5.55
	1.0	$5.08	$6.25	$5.27	$6.48	$5.45	$6.71	$5.75	$7.07	$6.01	$7.41	$6.28	$7.74	$4.26	$5.25	$4.55	$5.61	$4.84	$5.96
	2.0	$7.61	$9.38	$7.97	$9.82	$8.33	$10.26	$7.56	$9.31	$7.97	$9.82	$8.39	$10.33	$4.39	$5.42	$4.87	$5.99	$5.34	$6.58
Control Box	**0.5**	$4.49	$5.53	$4.57	$5.63	$4.65	$5.73	$5.22	$6.42	$5.33	$6.57	$5.45	$6.71	$4.18	$5.14	$4.35	$5.37	$4.54	$5.60
	1.0	$5.30	$6.52	$5.51	$6.78	$5.72	$7.04	$5.59	$6.88	$5.89	$7.26	$6.20	$7.63	$4.23	$5.22	$4.55	$5.62	$4.88	$6.00
	2.0	$7.53	$9.26	$7.93	$9.76	$8.33	$10.26	$7.43	$9.15	$7.88	$9.71	$8.34	$10.28	$4.37	$5.39	$4.90	$6.03	$5.44	$6.69
Blower	**0.5**	$2.25	$2.77	$2.34	$2.88	$2.44	$2.99	$2.11	$2.59	$2.24	$2.75	$2.38	$2.92	$2.14	$2.63	$2.35	$2.89	$2.55	$3.15
	1.0	$2.95	$3.64	$3.19	$3.93	$3.43	$4.22	$3.73	$4.59	$4.08	$5.01	$4.41	$5.44	$2.20	$2.70	$2.55	$3.15	$2.92	$3.60
	2.0	$4.09	$5.03	$4.53	$5.59	$4.99	$6.14	$4.59	$5.65	$5.11	$6.29	$5.64	$6.94	$2.28	$2.80	$2.87	$3.54	$3.47	$4.26
Air Guide	**0.5**	$1.24	$1.53	$1.35	$1.67	$1.47	$1.81	$1.20	$1.48	$1.38	$1.70	$1.55	$1.91	$1.03	$1.27	$1.29	$1.60	$1.56	$1.92
	1.0	$1.79	$2.20	$2.09	$2.56	$2.39	$2.93	$1.64	$2.02	$2.08	$2.56	$2.52	$3.10	$1.13	$1.39	$1.60	$1.97	$2.06	$2.53
	2.0	$2.37	$2.91	$2.94	$3.63	$3.52	$4.33	$2.35	$2.89	$3.00	$3.70	$3.67	$4.51	$1.20	$1.48	$1.97	$2.42	$2.72	$3.35
Motor	**0.5**	$4.68	$5.77	$4.78	$5.89	$4.89	$6.02	$4.49	$5.53	$4.64	$5.72	$4.80	$5.90	$4.39	$5.41	$4.62	$5.69	$4.85	$5.97
	1.0	$5.15	$6.34	$5.42	$6.67	$5.68	$6.99	$4.81	$5.91	$5.20	$6.40	$5.59	$6.88	$4.47	$5.51	$4.88	$6.00	$5.29	$6.51
	2.0	$7.23	$8.90	$7.74	$9.53	$8.25	$10.16	$6.21	$7.65	$6.80	$8.38	$7.40	$9.11	$4.50	$5.55	$5.18	$6.38	$5.85	$7.22
Condenser	**0.5**	$1.46	$1.80	$1.55	$1.91	$1.63	$2.01	$1.25	$1.54	$1.38	$1.70	$1.50	$1.85	$1.21	$1.50	$1.41	$1.74	$1.60	$1.98
	1.0	$2.12	$2.61	$2.34	$2.88	$2.55	$3.15	$1.79	$2.20	$2.11	$2.59	$2.44	$2.99	$1.34	$1.65	$1.68	$2.07	$2.02	$2.48
	2.0	$2.46	$3.02	$2.88	$3.55	$3.30	$4.07	$2.06	$2.53	$2.54	$3.13	$3.03	$3.73	$1.41	$1.74	$1.97	$2.43	$2.53	$3.11

(Continued)

TABLE 9.4 (CONTINUED)

Confidence Interval for FRW-PRW Policy, Model C4

		$L = 1$						$L = 2$						$L = 3$					
		$U = 1$		$U = 2$		$U = 3$		$U = 1$		$U = 2$		$U = 3$		$U = 1$		$U = 2$		$U = 3$	
Components	*W*	Lower	Upper	Lower	Upper	Lower	Upper	Lower	Upper	Lower	Upper	Lower	Upper	Lower	Upper	Lower	Upper	Lower	Upper
Fan	**0.5**	$2.80	$3.45	$2.89	$3.56	$2.97	$3.66	$2.37	$2.91	$2.50	$3.07	$2.62	$3.23	$2.28	$2.80	$2.47	$3.04	$2.65	$3.27
	1.0	$3.88	$4.77	$4.09	$5.04	$4.30	$5.31	$2.77	$3.42	$3.10	$3.82	$3.42	$4.21	$2.34	$2.88	$2.67	$3.29	$3.01	$3.71
	2.0	$4.81	$5.93	$5.24	$6.45	$5.66	$6.97	$3.85	$4.73	$4.33	$5.33	$4.81	$5.93	$2.46	$3.02	$3.01	$3.72	$3.57	$4.40
Protector	**0.5**	$0.75	$0.91	$0.83	$1.01	$0.90	$1.11	$0.58	$0.72	$0.71	$0.86	$0.83	$1.01	$0.42	$0.52	$0.61	$0.75	$0.79	$0.97
	1.0	$1.15	$1.42	$1.36	$1.68	$1.57	$1.93	$0.93	$1.15	$1.24	$1.53	$1.56	$1.92	$0.50	$0.62	$0.83	$1.01	$1.15	$1.42
	2.0	$2.02	$2.48	$2.43	$2.98	$2.83	$3.49	$1.35	$1.66	$1.82	$2.24	$2.29	$2.81	$0.54	$0.66	$1.07	$1.32	$1.61	$1.99
Compressor	**0.5**	$3.25	$4.00	$3.33	$4.11	$3.42	$4.21	$3.05	$3.75	$3.17	$3.91	$3.29	$4.06	$2.91	$3.59	$3.10	$3.82	$3.28	$4.05
	1.0	$4.18	$5.15	$4.39	$5.41	$4.60	$5.68	$3.93	$4.83	$4.24	$5.22	$4.55	$5.61	$3.16	$3.89	$3.48	$4.28	$3.81	$4.69
	2.0	$5.70	$7.02	$6.10	$7.53	$6.52	$8.03	$5.15	$6.34	$5.62	$6.92	$6.08	$7.50	$3.26	$4.02	$3.80	$4.68	$4.33	$5.34

It can be seen that the warranty cost of the Model C3 (sensor-embedded non-repairable component, replace by remanufactured with preventive maintenance) is less than the Model C4 (Conventional non-repairable component, replace by remanufactured with preventive maintenance) for the AC motor. Using SEPs in Model C3 reduced the warranty cost by 26.78%, 31.53% and 34.41% for 0.5 years, one year and two years' warranty period, respectively, compared to the conventional product in Model C4.

The expected warranty cost to the remanufacturer is reduced by 8.95% compared to that of the FRW policy for a remanufactured AC motor. The expected warranty cost to the remanufacturer is reduced by 2.24% compared to that of the PRW policy for a remanufactured AC motor.

9.4 Analysis of the Limits on Individual and Total Cost Policy

This section presents the cost analysis of providing the Limits on Individual and Total Cost (LITC) Policy based on Model S3 (SEPs, Preventive Maintenance) and Model S4 (Conventional Product, Preventive Maintenance) for warranty failures of remanufactured products discussed in Chapter 5. The policy can be described as follows:

LITC POLICY: Under this policy, the cost to the remanufacturer has an upper limit (c_I) for each replacement/repair, and the warranty ceases when the total cost to the remanufacturer exceeds c_T or at time W, whichever occurs first. The difference in the actual cost of replacement/repair and the cost carried by the remanufacturer is paid by the buyer.

Since the total cost of claims to the remanufacturer is limited to c_T and the cost of individual claims are limited by c_I, we have for the ith failure:

$$D_j = \begin{cases} \text{Min}\left\{C_i, c_I, \left(c_T - TD_{(i-1)}\right)\right\} & \text{for } TD_{(i-1)} \le c_T \\ 0 & \text{for } TD_{(i-1)} > c_T \end{cases} \tag{9.8}$$

$$B_j = \begin{cases} \text{Max}\left\{0, (C_i - c_I), (TD_i - c_T)\right\} & \text{for } TD_{(i-1)} < c_T \\ C_i & \text{for } TD_{(i-1)} > c_T \end{cases} \tag{9.9}$$

$$TD_j = \begin{cases} \sum_{i=1}^{j} D_i & \text{for } i \ge 1 \\ 0 & \text{for no failure} \end{cases} \tag{9.10}$$

and

$$TB_j = \begin{cases} \sum_{i=1}^{j} B_i & \text{for } i \geq 1 \\ 0 & \text{for no failure} \end{cases} \tag{9.11}$$

The warranty can expire before W if the total cost to the remanufacturer exceeds c_T. Let T_b denote the time at which the warranty expires. It is given by the total cost to the remanufacturer:

$$T_b > t \quad \text{iff} \quad Z_t < c_1 \tag{9.12}$$

Let $V_d(z; t)$ denote the distribution for the total cost to the remanufacturer by time t. Then $V_d\,(z; t)$ is given by:

$$V_d(z;t) = \sum_{r=0}^{\infty} G_d^{\,r}(z)\left[\text{prob.}\{N(t) = r\}\right] \tag{9.13}$$

where $G_d\,(c)$ is given by:

$$G_d(c) = \begin{cases} G(c) & \text{for } c \leq c_I \\ 1 & \text{for } c > c_I \end{cases} \tag{9.14}$$

Since the cost of a single repair to the remanufacturer is constrained to be less than c_I:

$$\text{Prob}\{N(t) = r\} = \frac{\left[\int_{v-W}^{v} \Lambda(x)dx]^r e^{-\int_{v-W}^{v}\Lambda(x)dx}\right]}{r!} \tag{9.15}$$

Let $Q\,(t;\, c_T)$ and $q\,(t;\, c_T)$ denote the distribution and density function for T_b, respectively. Then, from (8.12):

$$\int_t^{\infty} q(x;c_T)dx = \int_0^{c_T} v_d(z;t)dz \tag{9.16}$$

9.4.1 Model S3 (SEPs, Preventive Maintenance)

The expected warranty cost to the remanufacturer can be determined in a manner similar to that for the LTC policy, except that $G(c)$ is replaced by $G_d\,(c)$. Then, expected total cost to the remanufacturer is given by:

$$E\left[C_d(W;RL)\right] = \int_0^{c_T} z v_d(z)dz + \bar{c}_T V_d(c_T) \tag{9.17}$$

where $V_d(z)$ is the density function associated with $V_d(z)$ given by (8.51) with $G^{(r)}(c)$ replaced by $G_d^{(r)}(c)$. The expected cost to the buyer until the warranty expires (when Z_t first time crosses c_T at T_b) is given by:

$$E\left[C_b(W;RL)\right] = E\left[N(T_b)\right]\int_0^{\infty}(c-c_I)g(c)dc \tag{9.18}$$

where expected number of failures over $[0, T_b)$ is given by:

$$E\left[N(T_b)\right] = \int_0^{W}\int_{RL-t}^{RL}\Lambda(x)dx\,]q(t;c_T)dt \tag{9.19}$$

As can be seen, it is not possible to evaluate the costs analytically, and one needs to use a simulation approach.

Example 9.3

Based on Data Set I (see Section 6.4) and $c_I = \$125$; $c_T = \$450$, the expected warranty costs for different combinations of remaining life and warranty periods are shown in Table 9.5. Table 9.6 shows the confidence interval of the ARTO simulation runs.

The expected warranty cost to the remanufacturer is reduced by 21.44% compared to that of the FRW-PRW policy for a remanufactured AC with one-year remaining life sold with a 0.5-year warranty. This is reduced by 19.00% for a three-year remaining life AC sold with a two-year warranty.

9.4.2 Model S4 (CPs, Preventive Maintenance)

The expected costs can be determined from the results of Model S3 (SEPs, Corrective Maintenance) by carrying out the expectation over *RL* using the distribution function *H(rl)*. The expected warranty cost to the remanufacturer is given by:

TABLE 9.5

The Expected Warranty Costs for LITC Policy. Model S3

		Expected Cost to Remanufacturer			Expected Cost to Buyer		
Item	*W*	*RL* = 1	*RL* = 2	*RL* = 3	*RL* = 1	*RL* = 2	*RL* = 3
AC	**0.5**	$70.99	$68.10	$67.46	$25.41	$24.37	$24.14
	1.0	$74.07	$74.88	$70.62	$26.51	$26.80	$25.27
	2.0	$87.04	$85.74	$73.25	$31.15	$30.69	$26.21

TABLE 9.6

Standard Error and Confidence Interval on LITC Policy, Model S3

		Confidence Interval on Expected Cost to Remanufacturer						Confidence Interval on Expected Cost to Buyer					
		RL = 1		*RL* = 2		*RL* = 3		*RL* = 1		*RL* = 2		*RL* = 3	
Item	*W*	*L* Limit	*U* Limit	*L* Limit	*U* Limit	*L* Limit	*U* Limit	*L* Limit	*U* Limit	*L* Limit	*U* Limit	*L* Limit	*U* Limit
AC	**0.5**	$70.38	$71.59	$67.21	$68.99	$66.10	$68.81	$24.80	$26.01	$23.48	$25.26	$22.79	$25.49
	1.0	$72.53	$75.62	$73.37	$76.38	$68.23	$73.00	$24.96	$28.06	$25.29	$28.30	$22.89	$27.66
	2.0	$84.05	$90.03	$82.32	$89.16	$69.31	$77.18	$28.16	$34.14	$27.27	$34.10	$22.28	$30.15

$$E\left[C_d(W;RL)\right]=\int_{L}^{U}\int_{0}^{c_T} zv_d(z\mid rl)dz+\bar{c}_T V_d(c_T\mid a)\}h(rl)drl \tag{9.20}$$

The expected cost to the buyer during the warranty period is given by:

$$E\left[C_b(W;RL)\right]=\int_{L}^{U}E\left[N(t_b\mid rl)\right]\int_{c_I}^{\infty}(c-c_I)g(c)dc\}h(rl)drl \tag{9.21}$$

Example 9.4

Based on Data Set I (see Section 6.4) and c_I = \$125; c_T = \$450 the expected warranty costs for different combinations of L, U and W are shown in Table 9.7 and Table 9.8, respectively.

The expected warranty cost to the remanufacturer is reduced by 16.78% compared to that of the FRW-PRW policy when the item's remaining life varies from one to three years (i.e., $L = 1$ and $U = 3$) and items are sold with a 0.5-year warranty. It is reduced by 28.02% when the remaining life varies from one to three years (i.e., $L = 1$ and $U = 3$) and the warranty period is two years.

TABLE 9.7

The Expected Warranty Costs to Remanufacturer for LITC Policy, Model S4

		Expected Cost to Remanufacturer								
		$L = 1$			$L = 2$			$L = 3$		
Item	W	$U = 1$	$U = 2$	$U = 3$	$U = 1$	$U = 2$	$U = 3$	$U = 1$	$U = 2$	$U = 3$
AC	**0.5**	\$57.50	\$68.10	\$67.45	\$78.72	\$75.51	\$74.80	\$78.72	\$78.05	\$77.32
	1.0	\$60.00	\$74.87	\$70.61	\$82.14	\$83.03	\$78.31	\$82.14	\$85.82	\$80.94
	2.0	\$70.50	\$85.74	\$73.24	\$96.51	\$95.08	\$81.22	\$96.51	\$98.27	\$83.95

TABLE 9.8

The Expected Warranty Costs to Buyer for LITC Policy, Model S4

		Expected Cost to Buyer								
		$L = 1$			$L = 2$			$L = 3$		
Item	W	$U = 1$	$U = 2$	$U = 3$	$U = 1$	$U = 2$	U = 3	$U = 1$	$U = 2$	$U = 3$
AC	**0.5**	\$21.28	\$25.20	\$24.96	\$29.13	\$27.94	\$27.68	\$29.13	\$28.88	\$28.61
	1.0	\$22.20	\$27.70	\$26.13	\$30.39	\$30.72	\$28.97	\$30.39	\$31.75	\$29.95
	2.0	\$26.09	\$31.72	\$27.10	\$35.71	\$35.18	\$30.05	\$35.71	\$36.36	\$31.06

9.5 Analysis of the FRW-LIC Combination Policy

This section presents the cost analysis of providing the FRW-LIC Combination Policy based on Model S3 (SEPs, Preventive Maintenance) and Model S4 (Conventional Product, Preventive Maintenance) for warranty failures of remanufactured products discussed in Chapter 5. The policy can be described as follows:

FRW-LIC POLICY: Under this policy, the remanufacturer repairs all failures in the interval $[0, W_1)$ at no cost to the buyer. The replacement/repair of a failure in the interval $[W_1, W)$ results in no cost to the buyer if it is below c_I and an amount which is the excess if it exceeds c_I.

9.5.1 Model S3 (SEPs, Preventive Maintenance)

In this model, the expected number of failures during the warranty period is given by (5.3) The expected cost of a claim to the remanufacturer in $[W_1, W)$, $\overline{c}_d$, is given by (8.29), and the expected cost to the buyer for a repair, $\overline{c}_b$, is given by (8.30). Then, the expected warranty cost to the remanufacturer is given by:

$$E\left[C_d\left(W_1, W; RL\right)\right] = \overline{c} + \int_{RL-W_1}^{RL} \Lambda(t)dt + \overline{c_d} + \int_{RL-W}^{RL-W_1} \Lambda(t)dt \tag{9.22}$$

The expected cost to the buyer over the warranty period is given by:

$$E\left[C_b\left(W_1, W; RL\right)\right] = \overline{c_b} + \int_{RL-W}^{RL} \Lambda(t)dt \tag{9.23}$$

Example 9.5

Based on Data Set I (see Section 6.4) and $\overline{c}$= \$100; c_I = \$125, the expected warranty costs determined from (9.22) and (9.23), for different combinations of remaining life and warranty periods, are shown in Table 9.9. Table 9.10 shows the confidence intervals for the ARTO simulation runs.

TABLE 9.9

The Expected Warranty Costs for FRW-LIC Policy, Model S3

		Expected Cost to Remanufacturer			Expected Cost to Buyer		
Item	*W*	*RL* = 1	*RL* = 2	*RL* = 3	*RL* = 1	*RL* = 2	*RL* = 3
AC	**0.5**	\$62.22	\$59.69	\$59.13	\$62.22	\$59.69	\$59.13
	1.0	\$64.93	\$65.63	\$61.90	\$64.93	\$65.63	\$61.90
	2.0	\$76.29	\$75.16	\$64.20	\$76.29	\$75.16	\$64.20

TABLE 9.10

Standard Error and Confidence Interval on FRW-LIC Policy, Model S3

	Confidence Interval on Expected Cost to Remanufacturer						Confidence Interval on Expected Cost to Buyer					
	RL = 1		*RL* = 2		*RL* = 3		*RL* = 1		*RL* = 2		*RL* = 3	
W	*L* Limit	*U* Limit	*L* Limit	*U* Limit	*L* Limit	*U* Limit	*L* Limit	*U* Limit	*L* Limit	*U* Limit	*L* Limit	*U* Limit
0.5	$56.53	$56.77	$54.16	$54.52	$53.56	$54.10	$24.35	$24.59	$23.30	$23.66	$22.98	$23.53
1.0	$58.80	$59.42	$59.29	$60.21	$55.87	$56.83	$25.22	$25.85	$25.35	$26.27	$23.86	$24.83
2.0	$68.85	$70.06	$67.73	$69.11	$57.66	$59.25	$29.40	$30.61	$28.87	$30.25	$24.46	$26.05

The expected warranty cost to the remanufacturer is reduced by 8.21 % compared to that of the FRW-PRW policy for a remanufactured AC with one-year remaining life sold with a 0.5-year warranty. This is reduced by 7.59% for a three-year remaining life AC sold with a two-year warranty.

9.5.2 Model S4 (CPs, Preventive Maintenance)

Using the results of Model S3 (SEPs, Corrective Maintenance) and carrying out the expectation over the remaining life of the item at sale, return or fail, the expected warranty cost to the remanufacturer is given by:

$$E\left[C_d\left(W_1,W\right)\right]=\bar{c}\int_{L}^{U}\int_{rl-W_1}^{rl}\left\{\Lambda(t)dt\right\}h(rl)drl+\bar{c}_d\int_{L}^{U}\int_{rl-W}^{rl-W_1}\left\{\Lambda(t)dt\right\}h(rl)drl \qquad (9.24)$$

The expected cost to the buyer over the warranty period is given by:

$$E\left[C_d\left(W_1,W\right)\right]=\bar{c}_b\int_{L}^{U}\int_{rl-W}^{rl-W_1}\left\{\Lambda(t)dt\right\}h(rl)drl \qquad (9.25)$$

where $\bar{c}_d$ and $\bar{c}_b$ are given by (8.31) and (8.32), respectively.

Example 9.6

Based on Data Set I (see Section 6.4) and c = \$100; $\bar{c_l}$ = \$125, the expected warranty cost determined from (9.24) and (9.25), for different combinations of L, U and W, are shown in Table 9.11. Table 9.12 shows the confidence intervals for the ARTO simulation runs.

The expected warranty cost to the remanufacturer is reduced by 3.95% compared to that of the FRW policy when the item's remaining life varies from one to three years (i.e., L = 1 and U = 3) and items are sold with a 0.5-year warranty. It is reduced by 13.97% when the remaining life varies from one to three years (i.e., L = 1 and U = 3) and the warranty period is two years.

TABLE 9.11

The Expected Warranty Costs to Remanufacturer for FRW-LIC Policy, Model S4

		Expected Cost to Remanufacturer								
		L = 1			L = 2			L = 3		
Item	*W*	U = 1	U = 2	U = 3	U = 1	U = 2	U = 3	U = 1	U = 2	U = 3
AC	**0.5**	\$64.60	\$76.50	\$75.78	\$88.44	\$84.84	\$84.04	\$88.44	\$87.69	\$86.86
	1.0	\$67.41	\$84.12	\$79.33	\$92.28	\$93.28	\$87.97	\$92.28	\$96.41	\$90.93
	2.0	\$79.20	\$96.32	\$82.28	\$108.43	\$106.81	\$91.25	\$108.43	\$110.40	\$94.32

TABLE 9.12

The Expected Warranty Costs to Buyer for FRW-LIC Policy, Model S4

		Expected Cost to Buyer								
		$L = 1$			$L = 2$			$L = 3$		
Item	*W*	$U = 1$	$U = 2$	$U = 3$	$U = 1$	$U = 2$	$U = 3$	$U = 1$	$U = 2$	$U = 3$
AC	**0.5**	$26.85	$31.80	$31.50	$36.76	$35.26	$34.93	$36.76	$36.45	$36.11
	1.0	$28.02	$34.96	$32.98	$38.36	$38.77	$36.57	$38.36	$40.08	$37.80
	2.0	$32.92	$40.04	$34.20	$45.07	$44.40	$37.93	$45.07	$45.89	$39.20

9.6 Analysis of the FRW-LCS Combination Policy

This section presents the cost analysis of providing the FRW-LCS Combination Policy based on Model S3 (SEPs, Preventive Maintenance) and Model S4 (Conventional Product, Preventive Maintenance) for warranty failures of remanufactured products discussed in Chapter 5. The policy can be described as follows:

FRW-LCS POLICY: Under this policy, the remanufacturer repairs failures in the interval $[0, W_1]$ at no cost to the buyer. The replacement/repair cost of each failure in the interval $[W_1, W)$ is shared by both the remanufacturer and the buyer. For failures in the interval $[W1, W)$, the buyer pays $(1-\alpha)$ $(0 \le \alpha < 1)$, and the remanufacturer pays a portion of the replacement/repair cost.

9.6.1 Model S3 (SEPs, Preventive Maintenance)

The expected warranty cost to the remanufacturer is given by:

$$E\left[C_d\left(W_1, W; RL\right)\right] = \bar{c}\left[\int_{RL-W}^{RL} \Lambda(t)dt + (\alpha)\int_{RL-W}^{RL-W_1} \Lambda(t)dt\right. \tag{9.26}$$

The expected cost to the buyer over the warranty period is given by:

$$E\left[C_b\left(W_1, W; RL\right)\right] = \bar{c}\left[(1-\alpha)\int_{RL-W}^{RL-W_1} \Lambda(t)dt\right. \tag{9.27}$$

Example 9.7

Based on Data Set I (see Section 6.4) with $\bar{c} = \$100$ and $\alpha = 0.75$, the expected warranty costs determined from (9.26) and (9.27) for different combinations of remaining life and warranty periods are shown in

TABLE 9.13

The Expected Warranty Costs for FRW-LCS Policy, Model S3

		Expected Cost to Remanufacturer			Expected Cost to Buyer		
Item	*W*	*RL* = 1	*RL* = 2	*RL* = 3	*RL* = 1	*RL* = 2	*RL* = 3
AC	**0.5**	\$56.65	\$54.34	\$53.83	\$24.47	\$23.48	\$23.25
	1.0	\$59.11	\$59.75	\$56.35	\$25.54	\$25.81	\$24.34
	2.0	\$69.46	\$68.42	\$58.45	\$30.00	\$29.56	\$25.25

Table 9.13. Table 9.14 shows the confidence intervals for the ARTO simulation runs.

The expected warranty cost to the remanufacturer is increased by 1.48 % compared to that of the FRW-PRW policy for a remanufactured AC with one-year remaining life sold with a 0.5-year warranty. This is increased by 1.51% for a three-year remaining life AC sold with a two-year warranty.

9.6.2 Model S4 (CPs, Preventive Maintenance)

The expected warranty cost to the remanufacturer is given by:

$$E\left[C_d\left(W_1,W\right)\right]=\bar{c}\left[\int_{L}^{U}\int_{rl-W_1}^{rl}\left\{\Lambda\left(t\right)dt\right\}h\left(rl\right)drl+\left(\alpha\right)\int_{L}^{U}\int_{rl-W}^{rl-W_1}\left\{\Lambda\left(t\right)dt\right\}h\left(rl\right)drl\right] \tag{9.28}$$

The expected cost to the buyer over the warranty period is given by:

$$E\left[C_d\left(W_1,W\right)\right]=\left(1-\alpha\right)\bar{c}\int_{L}^{U}\int_{rl-W}^{rl-W_1}\left\{\Lambda\left(t\right)dt\right\}h\left(rl\right)drl \tag{9.29}$$

Example 9.8

Based on Data Set I (see Section 6.4) with $\bar{c}$ = \$100 and α = 0.75, the expected warranty costs determined from (9.28) and (9.29), for different combinations of L, U and W, are shown in Table 9.15. Table 9.16 shows the confidence intervals for the ARTO simulation runs.

The expected warranty cost to the remanufacturer is reduced by 22.76% compared to that of the FRW policy when the item's remaining life varies from one to three years (i.e., $L = 1$ and $U = 3$) and items are sold with a 0.5-year warranty. It is reduced by 15.32% when the remaining life varies from one to three years (i.e., $L = 1$ and $U = 3$) and the warranty period is two years.

TABLE 9.14

Confidence Intervals on FRW-LCS Policy, Model S3

	Confidence Interval Expected Cost to Remanufacturer						Confidence Interval Expected Cost to Buyer					
	$RL = 1$		$RL = 2$		$RL = 3$		$RL = 1$		$RL = 2$		$RL = 3$	
W	L Limit	U Limit	L Limit	U Limit	L Limit	U Limit	L Limit	U Limit	L Limit	U Limit	L Limit	U Limit
0.5	$56.53	$56.77	$54.16	$54.52	$53.56	$54.10	$24.35	$24.59	$23.30	$23.66	$22.98	$23.53
1.0	$58.80	$59.42	$59.29	$60.21	$55.87	$56.83	$25.22	$25.85	$25.35	$26.27	$23.86	$24.83
2.0	$68.85	$70.06	$67.73	$69.11	$57.66	$59.25	$29.40	$30.61	$28.87	$30.25	$24.46	$26.05

TABLE 9.15

The Expected Warranty Costs to Remanufacturer for FRW-LCS Policy, Model S4

		Expected Cost to Remanufacturer								
		$L = 1$			$L = 2$			$L = 3$		
Item	*W*	$U = 1$	$U = 2$	$U = 3$	$U = 1$	$U = 2$	$U = 3$	$U = 1$	$U = 2$	$U = 3$
AC	**0.5**	$86.93	$102.95	$101.98	$119.00	$114.16	$113.09	$119.00	$118.00	$116.89
	1.0	$90.71	$113.19	$106.75	$124.18	$125.52	$118.38	$124.18	$129.74	$122.36
	2.0	$106.58	$129.62	$110.73	$145.91	$143.74	$122.79	$145.91	$148.57	$126.92

TABLE 9.16

The Expected Warranty Costs to Buyer for FRW-LCS Policy, Model S4

		Expected Cost to Buyer								
		$L = 1$			$L = 2$			$L = 3$		
Item	*W*	$U = 1$	$U = 2$	$U = 3$	$U = 1$	$U = 2$	$U = 3$	$U = 1$	$U = 2$	$U = 3$
AC	**0.5**	$36.13	$42.79	$42.39	$49.47	$47.45	$47.01	$49.47	$49.05	$48.59
	1.0	$37.71	$47.05	$44.37	$51.62	$52.18	$49.21	$51.62	$53.93	$50.86
	2.0	$44.30	$53.88	$46.03	$60.65	$59.75	$51.04	$60.65	$61.76	$52.76

9.7 Analysis of the FRW-LMS Combination Policy

This section presents the cost analysis of providing the FRW-LMS Combination Policy based on Model S3 (SEPs, Preventive Maintenance) and Model S4 (Conventional Product, Preventive Maintenance) for warranty failures of remanufactured products discussed in Chapter 5. The policy can be described as follows:

FRW-LMS POLICY: Under this policy, the remanufacturer repairs all failures in the interval $[0, W_1)$ at no cost to the buyer. For failures occurring in the interval $[W_1, W)$, the replacement/repair costs are shared. The buyer pays for the labor cost, and the remanufacturer pays for the material cost of each replacement/repair in $[W_1, W)$.

9.7.1 Model S3 (SEPs, Preventive Maintenance)

The expected warranty cost to the remanufacturer is given by:

$$E\left[C_d\left(W_1, W; RL\right)\right] = \bar{c} \int_{RL-W}^{RL} \Lambda(t)\,dt + \bar{c}_l \int_{RL-W}^{RL-W_1} \Lambda(t)\,dt \tag{9.30}$$

The expected cost to the buyer over the warranty period is given by:

$$E\left[C_b\left(W_1, W; RL\right)\right] = \bar{c}_m \int_{RL-W}^{RL} \Lambda(t)\,dt \tag{9.31}$$

Example 9.9

Based on Data Set I (see Section 6.4) with $\bar{c}_l = \$65$ and $\bar{c}_m = 35$, the expected warranty costs determined from (9.30) and (9.31), for different combinations of remaining life and warranty periods, are shown in Table 9.16. Table 9.17 shows the confidence intervals for the ARTO simulation runs.

The expected warranty cost to the remanufacturer is reduced by 0.96 % compared to that of the FRW-PRW policy for a remanufactured AC with one-year remaining life sold with a 0.5-year warranty. This is reduced by 2.65% for a three-years remaining life AC sold with a two-year warranty.

9.7.2 Model S4 (CPs, Preventive Maintenance)

The expected warranty cost to the remanufacturer is given by:

$$E\left[C_d\left(W_1, W\right)\right] = \bar{c}\int_{L}^{U}\int_{rl-W_1}^{rl} \left\{\Lambda(t)\,dt\right\} h(rl)\,drl + \bar{c}_l \int_{L}^{U}\int_{rl-W}^{rl-W_1} \left\{\Lambda(t)\,dt\right\} h(rl)\,drl \tag{9.32}$$

The expected cost to the buyer over the warranty period is given by:

$$E\left[C_b\left(W_1, W; RL\right)\right] = \bar{c}_m \int_{L}^{U}\int_{rl-W}^{rl-W_1} \left\{\Lambda(t)\,dt\right\} h(rl)\,drl \tag{9.33}$$

Example 9.10

Based on Data Set I (see Section 6.4) with $\bar{c}_l$ = \$65 and $\bar{c}_m$= \$35, the expected warranty costs determined from (9.32) and (9.33), for different combinations of *L*, *U* and *W* are shown in Table 9.18. Table 9.19 shows the confidence intervals for the ARTO simulation runs (Table 9.20).

TABLE 9.17

The Expected Warranty Costs for FRW-LMS Policy, Model S3

		Expected Cost to Remanufacturer			Expected Cost to Buyer		
Item	*W*	*RL* = 1	*RL* = 2	*RL* = 3	*RL* = 1	*RL* = 2	*RL* = 3
AC	**0.5**	\$58.06	\$55.69	\$55.17	\$24.77	\$23.77	\$23.54
	1.0	\$60.58	\$61.23	\$57.75	\$25.86	\$26.13	\$24.64
	2.0	\$71.19	\$70.12	\$60.90	\$30.37	\$29.92	\$25.56

TABLE 9.18

Confidence Interval on FRW-LMS Policy, Model S3

	Confidence Interval Expected Cost to Remanufacturer						Confidence Interval Expected Cost to Buyer					
	$RL = 1$		$RL = 2$		$RL = 3$		$RL = 1$		$RL = 2$		$RL = 3$	
W	L Limit	U Limit	L Limit	U Limit	L Limit	U Limit	L Limit	U Limit	L Limit	U Limit	L Limit	U Limit
0.5	$49.05	$50.25	$46.75	$48.51	$45.84	$48.52	$20.85	$22.05	$19.70	$21.46	$19.04	$21.72
1.0	$50.28	$53.34	$50.12	$54.63	$47.03	$51.75	$20.85	$23.92	$20.37	$24.88	$18.98	$23.70
2.0	$57.92	$63.84	$56.59	$63.35	$47.34	$55.13	$23.34	$29.26	$22.52	$29.29	$18.24	$26.03

TABLE 9.19

The Expected Warranty Costs to Remanufacturer for FRW-LMS Policy, Model S4

		Expected Cost to Remanufacturer								
		L = 1			L = 2			L = 3		
Item	*W*	*U* = 1	*U* = 2	*U* = 3	*U* = 1	*U* = 2	*U* = 3	*U* = 1	*U* = 2	*U* = 3
AC	**0.5**	$76.15	$90.18	$89.33	$104.25	$100.01	$99.06	$104.25	$103.37	$102.39
	1.0	$79.46	$99.16	$93.52	$108.78	$109.96	$103.70	$108.78	$113.65	$107.19
	2.0	$93.37	$113.54	$97.00	$127.82	$125.91	$107.57	$127.82	$130.14	$111.18

TABLE 9.20

The Expected Warranty Costs to Buyer for FRW-LMS Policy, Model S4

		Expected Cost to Buyer								
		L = 1			L = 2			L = 3		
Item	*W*	*U* = 1	*U* = 2	*U* = 3	*U* = 1	*U* = 2	*U* = 3	*U* = 1	*U* = 2	*U* = 3
AC	**0.5**	$31.65	$37.49	$37.13	$43.33	$41.57	$41.18	$43.33	$42.97	$42.56
	1.0	$33.03	$41.22	$38.87	$45.22	$45.71	$43.11	$45.22	$47.24	$44.56
	2.0	$38.81	$47.20	$40.32	$53.13	$52.34	$44.71	$53.13	$54.10	$46.21

9.8 Analysis of MBG-FRW Combination Policy

This section presents the cost analysis of providing the MBG-FRW Policy based on Model S3 (SEPs, Preventive Maintenance) for warranty failures of remanufactured products discussed in Chapter 5. The policy can be described as follows:

MBG-FRW POLICY: Under this policy, all failures over the warranty period [0, W) are replaced/repaired at no cost to the buyer. If the number of failures over [0, W1), for W1 ≤ W, exceeds a specified value k (k ≥ 1), then at the (k+l)st failure the buyer has the option of returning the item for 100% money-back, and the warranty ceases when the buyer exercises this option. If the number of failures over [0, W1) is either s k or the buyer does not exercise the buyback option when the (k+l)st failure occurs, the item is covered for all failures until W. This policy can be viewed as a combination policy. When W1 = W, the policy reduces to the MBG Policy.

9.8.1 Model S3 (SEPs, Preventive Maintenance)

Let N_1 denote the number of failures over $[RL, RL\text{-}W_1)$. Then, expected warranty cost is given by:

$$E\big[J_d(W_1,W;RL)\,|\,N_1=n\big]=n\bar{c}+\bar{c}\int_{RL-W}^{RL-W_1}\Lambda(t)dt \tag{9.34}$$

Case (i): $n \leq k$. In this case, the cost of repair over [RL, RL-W_1) is $n\,\bar{c}$, and since the buyer cannot exercise the buyback option, the expected warranty cost over [RL+W_1, RL+W) is given by $\bar{c}\int_{RL-W}^{RL-W_1}\Lambda(t)dt$. As a result, the conditional expected warranty cost is given by:

$$E\left[J_d(W_1,W;RL)\,|\,N_1=n\right]=n\bar{c}+\bar{c}\int_{RL-W}^{RL-W_1}\Lambda(t)dt \tag{9.35}$$

Case (ii): $n > k$. In this case, we need to consider two sub-cases. In the first, the buyer exercises the buyback option, in which case the cost to the remanufacturer is $k\bar{c}+\bar{c}_{dd}$. If the buyer does not exercise the buyback option, then the remanufacturer has to service all failures over [RL–W_1, RL–W) free of cost to the buyer. As a result, the conditional expected cost is $\bar{c}\int_{RL-W}^{RL-W_1}\Lambda(t)dt$. The remanufacturer incurs these costs with probability γ and (1–γ), respectively, so that the conditional expected warranty cost is given by:

$$E\left[J_d(W_1,W;RL)\,|\,N_1=n\right]=(k\bar{c}+\bar{c}_{dd})\gamma+\left\{n\bar{c}+\bar{c}\int_{RL-W}^{RL-W_1}\Lambda(t)dt\right\}(1-\gamma) \tag{9.36}$$

On removing the conditioning, the expected warranty cost to the remanufacturer is given by:

$$E\left[J_d(W;RL)=\sum_{n=0}^{k}\left\{n\bar{c}+\bar{c}\int_{RL-W}^{RL-W_1}\Lambda(t)dt\}\right\}P_n(RL,RL-W_1)\right.$$

$$+\sum_{n=k+1}^{\infty}\left[(k\bar{c}+\bar{c}_{dd})\gamma+\left\{n\bar{c}+\bar{c}\int_{RL-W}^{RL-W_1}\Lambda(t)dt\right\}\right. \tag{9.37}$$

$$\left.(1-\gamma)\right]P_n(RL,RL-W_1)$$

Example 9.11

Based on Data Set I (see Section 6.4), the expected total after sale costs for different combinations of remaining life and warranty periods are shown in Table 9.21. Table 9.22 shows standard errors and confidence intervals of the ARTO simulation system.

The expected warranty cost to the remanufacturer is reduced by 11.82 % compared to that of the FRW policy for a remanufactured AC with one-year remaining life sold with a 0.5-year warranty. This is reduced by 3.34% for a three-year remaining life AC sold with a two-year warranty.

TABLE 9.21

The Expected Warranty Costs for MBG-FRW Policy, Model S3

		Expected Cost to Remanufacturer		
Item	*W*	*RL* = 1	*RL* = 2	*RL* = 3
AC	**0.5**	\$74.05	\$71.04	\$70.37
	1.0	\$77.27	\$78.11	\$73.67
	2.0	\$90.79	\$89.44	\$76.41

TABLE 9.22

Standard Error and Confidence Intervals on MBG Policy, Model S3

					Confidence Interval					
		Standard Error			*RL* = 1		*RL* = 2		*RL* = 3	
Item	*W*	*RL* = 1	*RL* = 2	*RL* = 3	*L* Limit	*U* Limit	*L* Limit	*U* Limit	*L* Limit	*U* Limit
AC	**0.5**	0.75	1.10	1.67	\$73.80	\$74.31	\$70.66	\$71.41	\$69.80	\$70.94
	1.0	1.92	2.82	2.95	\$76.62	\$77.93	\$77.14	\$79.07	\$72.66	\$74.68
	2.0	3.70	4.23	4.87	\$89.53	\$92.06	\$87.99	\$90.89	\$74.74	\$78.07

9.9 Analysis of the MBG-PRW Combination Policy

This section presents the cost analysis of providing the MBG-PRW Policy based on Model C1 for warranty failures of remanufactured products discussed in Chapter 5. The policy can be described as follows:

MBG-PRW POLICY: Under this policy, a remanufactured item is covered for a period W subsequent to the sale. If the item fails over $[0, W_1)$, then the remanufacturer refunds the full sale price. If the item fails over $[W_1, W)$, then the remanufacturer refunds a fraction of the sale price. If the item does not fail over $[0, W)$, then the warranty ceases at W.

One can consider various forms for the fraction refunded. Let $S(x)$ denote the amount refunded should the item fail x units of time subsequent to the sale. Then, $S(x)$ is given by:

$$S(x) = \begin{cases} C_s & \text{for } 0 < x \leq W_1 \\ C_s.\dfrac{(W-x)}{W} & \text{for } W < x < W \end{cases} \tag{9.38}$$

The expected warranty cost to the remanufacturer is given by:

$$E[C_d(W_1,W;RL)] = \int_0^W S(x)dF(x)dx = C_s(RL)[F_{i1}(W)] - \left(\frac{1}{W}\right)\int_{W_1}^{W} xdF_{i1}(x) \quad (9.39)$$

where $F_{i1}(x)$ is given by (5.20).

Example 9.12

Based on Data Set II (i) (see Section 6.4) and c_s = \$20, the expected costs for different combinations of remaining life and warranty periods are shown in Table 9.23. Table 9.24 shows standard errors and confidence intervals of the ARTO simulation runs.

Table 9.23 presents the expected number of failures and cost for remanufactured AC components for the MBG-PRW Policy. In Table 9.23, the expected number of failures represents the expected number of failed items per unit of sale. The expected cost to the remanufacturer includes the cost of supplying the original item, C_s. Thus, the expected cost of the warranty is calculated by subtracting C_s from the expected cost to the remanufacturer. For example, from Table 9.23, for $W = 0.5$ and $RL = 1$, the warranty cost for the sensor-embedded AC motor is \$4.21–C_s = |\$4.21–\$4.00| = \$0.21, which is ([\$0.21/\$4.00] × 100) = 5.25% of the cost of supplying the AC motor, C_s, which is significantly less than \$4.00, C_s. This cost might be acceptable, but the corresponding values for longer warranties are much higher. For example, for W = 2 years and $RL = 1$, the corresponding percentage is ([|\$6.51–\$4.00|/\$4.00] × 100) = 62.75%.

For a one-year remaining life remanufactured AC motor sold with a 0.5-year warranty, the ARTO system can claim with 90% confidence that the expected warranty cost is in the interval [\$3.92–\$4.51]. As shown in Table 9.24, the confidence interval for a one-year remaining life remanufactured AC motor sold with two years of warranty is [\$5.04–\$7.97].

9.10 Analysis of the MBG-LIC Combination Policy

This section presents the cost analysis of providing the MBG-LIC Policy based on Model S3 (SEPs, Preventive Maintenance) for warranty failures of remanufactured products discussed in Chapter 5. The policy can be described as follows:

MBG-LIC POLICY: Under this policy, all failures are replaced/repaired at no cost to the buyer over $[0, W_1)$ for $W_1 \leq W$, and on a cost-sharing basis over

TABLE 9.23

The Expected Warranty Costs for MBG-PRW Policy, Model C1

Components	*W*	Expected Cost to Remanufacturer		
		$RL = 1$	$RL = 2$	$RL = 3$
Evaporator	**0.5**	$4.11	$4.71	$3.76
	1.0	$4.57	$5.16	$3.84
	2.0	$6.85	$6.81	$3.96
Control Box	**0.5**	$4.04	$4.69	$3.76
	1.0	$4.76	$5.03	$3.81
	2.0	$6.77	$6.68	$3.93
Blower	**0.5**	$2.02	$1.89	$1.93
	1.0	$2.66	$3.35	$1.97
	2.0	$3.67	$4.13	$2.05
Air Guide	**0.5**	$1.11	$1.09	$0.93
	1.0	$1.61	$1.48	$1.02
	2.0	$2.13	$2.11	$1.09
Motor	**0.5**	$4.21	$4.04	$3.95
	1.0	$4.63	$4.32	$4.02
	2.0	$6.51	$5.59	$4.06
Condenser	**0.5**	$1.32	$1.12	$1.10
	1.0	$1.91	$1.61	$1.21
	2.0	$2.21	$1.85	$1.27
Fan	**0.5**	$2.52	$2.13	$2.05
	1.0	$3.48	$2.49	$2.10
	2.0	$4.33	$3.46	$2.21
Protector	**0.5**	$0.67	$0.52	$0.37
	1.0	$1.03	$0.84	$0.45
	2.0	$1.81	$1.22	$0.48
Compressor	**0.5**	$2.92	$2.74	$2.62
	1.0	$3.76	$3.54	$2.84
	2.0	$5.13	$4.63	$2.93

$[W_1, W)$. If the number of failures over $[0, W_1)$ exceeds a specified value k ($k \geq 1$), then at the (k+1)st failure, the buyer has the option of returning the item for 100% money-back, and the warranty ceases when the buyer exercises this option. If the number of failures over [0, *W*1) is either: s k or the buyer does not exercise the buyback option when the (k+1)st failure occurs, then the item is covered with a cost limit on each individual claim over $[W_1, W)$, with the buyer paying the excess of any replacement/repair cost above cI per claim.

TABLE 9.24

Standard Error and Confidence Intervals on MBG-PRW Policy, Model C1

					Confidence Interval					
		Standard Error			*RL* = 1		*RL* = 2		*RL* = 3	
Components	*W*	*RL* = 1	*RL* = 2	*RL* = 3	*L* Limit	*U* Limit	*L* Limit	*U* Limit	*L* Limit	*U* Limit
Evaporator	**0.5**	0.73	1.07	1.63	$3.90	$4.32	$4.41	$5.02	$3.30	$4.23
	1.0	1.86	2.74	2.87	$4.04	$5.10	$4.38	$5.95	$3.02	$4.66
	2.0	3.60	4.11	4.74	$5.82	$7.88	$5.63	$7.98	$2.60	$5.31
Control Box	**0.5**	0.82	1.20	1.83	$3.80	$4.27	$4.34	$5.03	$3.23	$4.28
	1.0	2.09	3.08	3.23	$4.16	$5.36	$4.14	$5.91	$2.89	$4.73
	2.0	4.04	4.62	5.32	$5.61	$7.93	$5.36	$8.00	$2.41	$5.45
Blower	**0.5**	0.92	1.35	2.06	$1.76	$2.28	$1.50	$2.28	$1.34	$2.52
	1.0	2.35	3.46	3.62	$1.99	$3.33	$2.36	$4.34	$0.94	$3.01
	2.0	4.54	5.19	5.98	$2.37	$4.97	$2.65	$5.61	$0.34	$3.75
Air Guide	**0.5**	1.17	1.72	2.61	$0.78	$1.45	$0.60	$1.58	$0.19	$1.68
	1.0	2.99	4.39	4.60	$0.75	$2.46	$0.22	$2.74	$0.29	$2.34
	2.0	5.77	6.59	7.59	$0.48	$3.78	$0.23	$3.99	$0.35	$3.26
Motor	**0.5**	1.04	1.53	2.32	$3.92	$4.51	$3.60	$4.48	$3.28	$4.61
	1.0	2.66	3.91	4.09	$3.87	$5.39	$3.20	$5.44	$2.85	$5.19
	2.0	5.13	5.87	6.75	$5.04	$7.97	$3.92	$7.27	$2.13	$5.99
Condenser	**0.5**	0.86	1.26	1.92	$1.07	$1.56	$0.76	$1.48	$0.55	$1.65
	1.0	2.20	3.23	3.38	$1.28	$2.54	$0.68	$2.53	$0.24	$2.17
	2.0	4.24	4.85	5.58	$1.00	$3.42	$0.47	$3.24	$0.33	$2.87
Fan	**0.5**	0.86	1.26	1.92	$2.28	$2.77	$1.77	$2.49	$1.50	$2.60
	1.0	2.20	3.23	3.38	$2.85	$4.11	$1.57	$3.42	$1.13	$3.07
	2.0	4.24	4.85	5.58	$3.12	$5.54	$2.08	$4.85	$0.62	$3.81
Protector	**0.5**	0.83	1.22	1.86	$0.43	$0.90	$0.17	$0.87	$0.02	$0.90
	1.0	2.12	3.12	3.27	$0.43	$1.64	$0.05	$1.73	$0.17	$1.38
	2.0	4.10	4.69	5.39	$0.64	$2.98	$0.12	$2.55	$0.54	$2.03
Compressor	**0.5**	0.95	1.40	2.13	$2.65	$3.20	$2.34	$3.14	$2.01	$3.23
	1.0	2.44	3.59	3.76	$3.07	$4.46	$2.51	$4.56	$1.77	$3.92
	2.0	4.71	5.38	6.20	$3.78	$6.47	$3.09	$6.17	$1.16	$4.70

9.10.1 Model S3 (SEPs, Preventive Maintenance)

The analysis is similar to that in Section 9.9. Let N_1 denote the number of failures over $[RL, RL\text{-}W_1)$. The expected cost for both the remanufacturer and the buyer conditioned on N_1 is discussed below.

9.10.1.1 Remanufacturer's Expected Cost

Here, there are two possible scenarios:

Scenario (i) $n \leq k$. In this case, there is no buyback, and the costs of repairs over $[0, W_1)$ are carried by the remanufacturer, and this is given by $n\,\bar{c}$. The costs over $[W_1, W)$ are shared by both the remanufacturer and the buyer. The average cost per failure to the remanufacturer, $\bar{c}_d$, is given by (5.50). As a result, the expected warranty cost to the remanufacturer is given by:

$$E\left[J_d(W_1,W;RL) \mid N_1 = n\right] = n\bar{c} + \bar{c}_d \int_{A+W_1}^{A+W} \Lambda(t)dt \tag{9.40}$$

Scenario (ii): $n > k$. In this case, the buyer can exercise the buyback option at the $(k+1)$st failure. If the buyer exercises the option, then the conditional cost to the remanufacturer is given by $k\bar{c} + \bar{c}_{dd}$. If the buyer does not exercise the buyback option, then the costs of all replacement/repairs over $[W_1, W)$ are shared by the remanufacturer and the buyer. In this case, the expected cost of each failure is J_d. Note that if the buyer exercising the buyback option is uncertain, the expected cost to the remanufacturer is given by:

$$E\left[J_d(W_1,W;RL) \mid N_1 = n\right] = (k\bar{c} + \bar{c}_{dd})\gamma + \left\{n\bar{c} + \bar{c}_d \int_{RL-W}^{RL-W_1} \Lambda(t)dt\right\}(1-\gamma) \tag{9.41}$$

The expected warranty cost to the remanufacturer is given by:

$$\begin{aligned} E\left[J_d(W_1,W;RL)\right. &= \sum_{n=0}^{k}\left\{n\bar{c} + \bar{c}_d \int_{RL-W}^{RL-W_1} \Lambda(t)dt\right\} P_n(RL, RL-W_1) \\ &+ \sum_{n=k+1}^{\infty}\left[(k\bar{c} + \bar{c}_{dd})\gamma + \left\{n\bar{c} + \bar{c}_d \int_{RL-W}^{RL-W_1} \Lambda(t)dt\right\}(1-\gamma)\right] P_n(RL, RL-W_1) \end{aligned} \tag{9.42}$$

9.10.1.2 Buyer's Expected Cost

The buyer does not charge any cost if $n > k$ over $[0, W_1)$ and the buyer decides on the buyback option. Then the warranty ceases due to the buyback option. Here, to compute the cost, we need to consider (i) $n < k$ and (ii) $n > k$ and the buyback option not executed over $[0, W_1)$. Following an approach similar to the remanufacturer's case, the expected warranty cost to the buyer is given by:

$$\begin{aligned} E\left[J_b(W_1,W;RL)\right. &= \left\{\bar{c}_b \int_{RL-W}^{RL-W_1} \Lambda(t)dt\right\} P_n(RL, RL-W_1) \sum_{n=0}^{\infty} P_n(RL, RL-W_1) \\ &+ \left\{\bar{c}_b \int_{RL-W}^{RL-W_1} \Lambda(t)dt(1-\gamma)\right] P_n(RL, RL-W_1)\right\} \end{aligned} \tag{9.43}$$

where $\bar{c}_b$ is the expected cost of each repair to the buyer in $[W_1, W)$ and is given by (8.30).

Example 9.13

Based on Data Set I (see Section 6.4) and $c_l = \$125$; $\bar{c}_{bb} = \$1000$, the expected costs for different combinations of remaining life and warranty period are shown in Table 9.25. Table 9.26 shows standard errors and confidence intervals of the ARTO simulation runs.

The expected warranty cost to the remanufacturer is increased by 13.39% compared to that of the FRW policy for a remanufactured AC with one-year remaining life sold with a 0.5-year warranty. This is increase by 11.80% for a three-year remaining life AC sold with a two-year warranty.

9.11 Analysis of the MBG-LITC Combination Policy

This section presents the cost analysis of providing the MBG-LITC Policy based on Model S3 (SEPs, Preventive Maintenance) for warranty failures of remanufactured products discussed in Chapter 5. The policy can be described as follows:

TABLE 9.25

The Expected Warranty Costs for MBG-LIC Policy, Model S3

		Expected Cost to Remanufacturer		
Item	*W*	*RL* = 1	*RL* = 2	*RL* = 3
AC	**0.5**	\$50.71	\$48.65	\$48.19
	1.0	\$52.92	\$53.49	\$50.45
	2.0	\$62.18	\$61.25	\$52.33

TABLE 9.26

Standard Error and Confidence Intervals on MBG-LIC Policy, Model S3

					Confidence Interval					
		Standard Error			*RL* = 1		*RL* = 2		*RL* = 3	
Item	*W*	*RL* = 1	*RL* = 2	*RL* = 3	*L* Limit	*U* Limit	*L* Limit	*U* Limit	*L* Limit	*U* Limit
AC	**0.5**	1.01	1.49	2.26	\$50.37	\$51.06	\$48.14	\$49.16	\$47.42	\$48.97
	1.0	2.59	3.81	3.99	\$52.03	\$53.81	\$52.19	\$54.80	\$49.08	\$51.82
	2.0	5.01	5.72	6.58	\$60.47	\$63.89	\$59.30	\$63.21	\$50.07	\$54.58

MBG-LITC POLICY: Under this policy, all failures are replaced/repaired at no cost to the buyer over $[0, W_1)$, for $W_1 \leq W$, and on a cost-limiting basis over $[W_1, W)$. If the number of failures in the period $[0, W_1)$ exceeds a specified value k ($k \geq 1$), then at the $(k+1)$st failure, the buyer has the option of returning the item for 100% money-back, and the warranty ceases when the buyer exercises this option. If the number of failures over $[0, W_1)$ is either $\leq k$ or the buyer does not exercise the buyback option when the $(k+1)$st failure occurs, then the item is covered with a cost limit on each individual claim and also on the total repair cost over $[W_1, W)$. The buyer pays the excess of any replacement/repair cost above cI per claim, and the financial responsibility of the remanufacturer ends when the total repair cost to the remanufacturer over $[W_1, W)$ exceeds c_T or is at W, whichever occurs first.

9.11.1 Model S3 (SEPs, Preventive Maintenance)

The analysis is similar to that in Section 9.10, except that the warranty can cease during the period $[W_1, W)$ due to the total cost to the remanufacturer exceeding the cost limit c_T. The expected costs over $[W_1, W)$ can be determined using an approach used in Section 7.4. As before, we need to consider the expected costs to the remanufacturer and the buyer.

Let $N(t)$ be the number of failures over $[W_1, W_{1+t})$ and let $V_d(z; t)$ denote the distribution for the total cost to the remanufacturer up to t. Then $V_d(z; t)$ is given by:

$$V_d(z;t) = \sum_{r=0}^{\infty} G_d^r(z)\left[\text{prob.}\left\{N(t) = r\right\}\right] \tag{9.44}$$

$$G_d(c) = \begin{cases} G(c) & \text{for } c \leq c_I \\ 1 & \text{for } c > c_I \end{cases} \tag{9.45}$$

Since the cost of a single repair to the remanufacturer is constrained to be less than c_I:

$$\text{Prob}\left\{N(t) = r\right\} = \frac{\left[\int_A^{A+t} \Lambda(x)dx]^r e^{-\int_A^{A+t}\Lambda(x)dx}\right]}{r!} \tag{9.46}$$

Let $Q(t; c_T)$ and $q(t; c_T)$ denote the distribution and density function for T_b, respectively. Then (9.16) gives the result below:

$$\int_t^{\infty} q(t;c_T)dx = \int_0^{C_T} V_d(z;t)dz \tag{9.47}$$

9.11.1.1 Remanufacturer's Expected Cost

Let v_d (z) be the density function associated with distribution function $V_d(z)$ for total cost over $[W_1, W)$, $Z_{(w\text{-}w1)}$].
Scenario (i): $n \le k$. In this case, the cost to the remanufacturer is $n\bar{c}$ for failures over $[0, W_1)$. Then, all failures over $[W_1, W)$ are shared by the remanufacturer and the buyer. The buyer pays any excess over c_1 for individual replacement/repairs until the total cost to the remanufacturer over $[W_1, W)$ is $\le c_T$. In that case, the expected cost to the remanufacturer over $[W_1, W)$, using the approach used in Section 7.4, is given by:

$$\int_0^{c_T} z v_d(z) + c_T \bar{V}_d(c_T) \tag{9.48}$$

where $\bar{V}_d(c_T) = 1 - v_d(c_T)$. As a result, the expected warranty cost to the remanufacturer, E $[J_b (W_1, W; RL) \mid N_1 = n]$, is given below:

$$E\left[[J_b(W_1, W; RL) = \left\{ n\bar{c} + \int_0^{C_T} z v_d(z) dz + c_T \bar{V}_d(c_T) \right. \tag{9.49}$$

Scenario (ii): $n > k$. In this case, the buyer has the option of returning the item for 100% money-back at the $(k+l)^{st}$ failure. If the buyer exercises the option, then the conditional cost to the remanufacturer is given by $k\bar{c} + \bar{c}_{dd}$. If the buyer does not exercise the buyback option, then all failures over $[W_1$. $W)$ are shared by the remanufacturer and the buyer. The buyer pays any excess when the cost of any individual replacement/repair exceeds c_I until the total cost of replacement/repair to the remanufacturer over $[W_1, W)$ is $\le c_T$. In that case, the expected total cost is $n\bar{c} + \int_0^{C_T} z v_d(z) dz + c_T \bar{V}_d(c_T)$. As a result, the expected cost to the remanufacturer is given by:

$$\begin{aligned} E\left[J_b(W_1, W; RL) \mid N_1 = n\right] &= (k\bar{c} + \bar{c}_{dd})\gamma \\ &+ \left\{ n\bar{c} + \int_0^{c_T} z v_d(z) dz + c_T v_d(\bar{c}_T) \right\} (1 - \gamma) \end{aligned} \tag{9.50}$$

On removing the conditioning, the expected warranty cost to the remanufacturer is as given by:

$$E\left[J_d(W_1,W;A)\right]=\sum_{n=0}^{k}\left[\left\{n\bar{c}+\int_0^{c_T} zv_d(z)dz+c_T\bar{v}_d(\bar{c}_T)\right\}P_n(A,A+W_1)\right]$$

$$+\sum_{n=k+1}^{\infty}\left[(k\bar{c}+\bar{c}_{dd})\gamma+\left\{n\bar{c}+\int_0^{c_T} zv_d(z)dz+c_T\bar{v}_d(\bar{c}_T)\right\}(1-\gamma)\right]P_n(A,A+W_1) \tag{9.51}$$

9.11.1.2 Buyer's Expected Cost

The buyer's expected warranty cost is determined in a similar manner by conditioning on $N_1 = n$. If the number of failures over $[0, W_1)$ is $\leq k$ or the buyer does not exercise the buyback option at the $(K+1)$st when the number of failures over $[0, W_1)$ is $> k$, then warranty ceases when the total cost of replacement/repair to the remanufacturer over $[W_1, W)$ is $> c_T$ or at W, whichever occurs first. Let $N(t_b)$ be the number of failures at level crossing (the time when the total cost of replacement/repairs to the remanufacturer over $[W_1, W)$, z_t, is $> c_T$ for the first time at T_b). $N(t_b)$, is a random variable. The expected number of failures up to t_b. $E[N(t_b)]$, using the approach used in Section 9.4.1, is given by:

$$E\left[N(t_b)\right]=\int_0^{W-W_1}\left[\int_{RL-W_1}^{RL-W_1+t}\Lambda(t)dx\right]q(t;c_T)dt \tag{9.52}$$

Scenario (i): $n \leq k$, then there is no cost for failures over the period $[0, W_1)$ and the expected cost to the buyer until the warranty ceases at T_b, $E[J_d(W_1, W; RL) \mid N_1 = n]$, is given by:

$$E\left[J_b(W_1,W;RL)\mid N_1=n\right]=E\left[N(t_b)\right]\int_{c_I}^{\infty}(c-c_I)g(c)dc \tag{9.53}$$

TABLE 9.27

The Expected Warranty Costs for MBG-LITC Policy, Model S3

		Expected Cost to Remanufacturer			Expected Cost to Buyer		
Item	*W*	*RL* = 1	*RL* = 2	*RL* = 3	*RL* = 1	*RL* = 2	*RL* = 3
AC	**0.5**	\$62.94	\$60.38	\$59.81	\$22.53	\$21.61	\$21.41
	1.0	\$65.68	\$66.39	\$62.62	\$23.51	\$23.76	\$22.41
	2.0	\$77.18	\$76.03	\$64.95	\$27.62	\$27.21	\$23.24

TABLE 9.28

Standard Error and Confidence Interval on MBG-LITC Policy, Model S3

	Confidence Interval on Expected After Sales Cost to Remanufacturer						Confidence Interval on Expected After Sales Cost to Buyer					
	RL = 1		*RL* = 2		*RL* = 3		*RL* = 1		*RL* = 2		*RL* = 3	
W	*L* Limit	*U* Limit	*L* Limit	*U* Limit	*L* Limit	*U* Limit	*L* Limit	*U* Limit	*L* Limit	*U* Limit	*L* Limit	*U* Limit
0.5	$62.49	$63.40	$59.71	$61.05	$58.79	$60.83	$21.92	$23.13	$20.72	$22.50	$20.05	$22.76
1.0	$64.51	$66.85	$65.26	$67.53	$60.82	$64.41	$21.96	$25.05	$22.26	$25.27	$20.03	$24.79
2.0	$74.92	$79.43	$73.45	$78.60	$61.98	$67.91	$24.63	$30.61	$23.79	$30.63	$19.31	$27.18

Scenario (ii): $n > k$, then the cost is nil if the buyer exercises the buyback option at $(k+1)^{st}$ failure. If the buyer decides not to exercise the buyback option at the $(k+1)^{st}$ failure, then all costs over the period $[W_1, W)$ are shared. The buyer pays any amount beyond c_I for individual claims until the total cost of replacement/repair to the remanufacturer over $[W_1, W)$ is $\leq c_T$ and the expected cost is given by:

$$E[N(t_b)] = \int_0^\infty (c - c_I) g(c) dc \tag{9.54}$$

As a result, the expected cost to the buyer until the warranty expires over $[W_1, W)$ conditioned on $N_1 = n$, $E[J_b(W_1, W; A) \mid N_1 = n]$ is given by:

$$E[J_b(W_1, W; A) \mid N_1 = n] = \gamma + E[N(t_b)] \left\{ \int_{c_I}^\infty (c - c_I) g(c) dc \right\} \tag{9.55}$$

On removing the conditioning, the expected warranty cost to the buyer is given by:

$$E[J_d(W_1, W; RL)] = \sum_{n=0}^{k} E[N(t_b)] \left\{ \int_{c_I}^\infty (c - c_I) g(c) dc \right\} P_n(RL, RL - W_1)$$

$$+ \sum_{n=k+1}^{\infty} \left\{ E[N(t_b)] \int_{c_I}^{\infty} [(c - c_I) g(c) dc](1 - \gamma) \right\} \tag{9.56}$$

$$P_n(RL, RL - W_1)$$

Example 9.14

Based on Data Set I (see Section 6.4) and c_I = \$125; c_T = \$450; $\bar{c}_{bb}$ = \$1000, expected costs for different combinations of remaining life and warranty periods are shown in Table 9.27. Table 9.28 shows the standard errors and confidence intervals of the ARTO simulation runs.

The expected warranty cost to the remanufacturer is reduced by 8.64 % compared to that of the FRW policy for a remanufactured AC with one-year remaining life sold with a 0.5-year warranty. This is reduced by 9.47% for a three-year remaining life AC sold with a two-year warranty.

9.12 Conclusions

In this chapter, nine combination warranty policies were discussed. They were: Free-Replacement Warranty and Pro-Rata Warranty (FRW-PRW), Limits on Individual and Total Cost Policy (LITC), Combination of Free-Replacement Warranty & Limit on Individual Cost Warranty (FRW-LIC), Combination of Free-Replacement Warranty & Lump-Sum Cost-Sharing Warranty (FRW-LCS), Combination of Free-Replacement Warranty & Labor/Material Cost-Shared Warranty (FRW-LMS), Combination of Money-Back Guarantee & Free-Replacement Warranty (MBG-FRW), Combination of Money-Back Guarantee & Pro-Rata Warranty (MBG-PRW), Combination of Money-Back Guarantee & Limit on Individual Cost Warranty (MBG-LIC), Combination of Money-Back Guarantee & Limits on Total Cost Warranty (MBG-LITC), were discussed. In order to assess the impact of these nine policies in terms of warranty cost, pairwise t tests were carried out for different performance measure, namely, Holding Cost, Backorder Cost, Disassembly Cost, Disposal Cost, Testing Cost, Remanufacturing Cost, Transportation Cost, Warranty Cost, Number of Claims and Preventive Maintenance Cost.

10

Cost Analysis of Renewing Warranties

10.1 Introduction

In Chapter 4, several warranty policies with preventive maintenance for remanufactured products were introduced. This chapter presents the analysis of determining the expected cost of warranty, Corrective Maintenance (CM) and Preventive Maintenance (PM) (from both the buyer's and the remanufacturer's perspectives). Chapter 7, Chapter 8 and Chapter 9 together considered 19 of these policies. Here, two renewing policies, namely, Policy 20 (RFRW) and Policy 21 (RPRW), as defined in Chapter 4, are considered. Also, the combination of these two policies is considered.

In Chapter 5, a variety of models were discussed at the system level (Models S1 through S4) and at the component level (Models Cl through C8) for warranty failures of remanufacturing products. The expected warranty cost for a given policy can be evaluated using one of those models. In Chapter 7, analysis of the non-renewing FRW policy based on the models at both the system and component levels were carried out. For the policies considered in this chapter, the analysis is very similar to that for the non-renewing FRW policy. For that reason, for the policies considered in this chapter, only selected models are discussed as illustrations. The warranty costs for the rest of the models can be carried out in a manner similar to these and the ones given for the non-renewing FRW policy in Chapter 7.

Section 10.2 presents some assumptions and notations used in this chapter. Section 10.3 deals with the analysis of the RFRW policy and Section 10.4 deals with the analysis of the RPRW policy. Section 10.5 deals with the analysis of the combination RFRW and RPRW policy. Finally, some conclusions are presented in Section 10.6.

10.2 Preliminaries

The assumptions, notations and parameter values of Section 7.2, Section 8.2 and Section 9.2 are also applicable here, along with the following notations.

10.2.1 Notations

$N(\tilde{\theta})$ Number of failures under warranty

$N(\tilde{\theta} \mid r)$ Number of failures under warranty conditional on R = r.

10.3 Analysis of the Renewing Free-Replacement Warranty Policy

This section presents the cost analysis of providing the Renewing Free-Replacement Warranty (RFRW) Policy based on Model C3 (Sensor-Embedded Component, Non-Repairable, Replacement by Remanufactured, Preventive Maintenance) and Model C4 (Conventional Component, Non-Repairable, Replacement by Remanufactured, Preventive Maintenance) for warranty failures of remanufactured products discussed in Chapter 5. The policy can be described as follows:

RFRW POLICY: Under this policy, the remanufacturer resolves all failures in the interval $[0, W_1)$ at no cost to the buyer. The warranty period after replacement/repair is the remaining period of the original warranty. If a failure occurs in the interval $[W_1, W)$, then the item is replaced/repaired by the remanufacturer at no cost to the buyer and returned with a new warranty of duration $(W–W_1)$.

10.3.1 Model C3 (Sensor-Embedded Component, Non-Repairable, Replacement by Remanufactured)

Let K be the number of free replacements required under the renewing FRW. Then X_{k+1} is the first item lifetime in the sequence of replacements that is at least of length $(W\text{-}W_1)$. K is a random variable with:

$$P\{K=k\}=\begin{cases} \bar{F}_W(W-W_1) & k=0 \\ F_W(W-W_1)\bar{F}_{iu}(W-W_1)\left[\bar{F}_{iu}(W-W_1)\right]^{k-1} & k>0 \end{cases} \tag{10.1}$$

The expected number of renewals beyond W_1 is given by:

$$E[K]=F_W(W-W_1)/\bar{F}_{iu}(W-W_1) \tag{10.2}$$

where $F_{iu}(W\text{-}W_1)= 1\text{-}F_{iu}(W\text{-}W_1)$.

As a result, the expected warranty cost to the remanufacturer is given by:

$$\begin{aligned} \mathrm{E}\left[\mathrm{C}_d(\mathrm{W1},\mathrm{W};\mathrm{A})\right]= \mathrm{C}_b\Bigg[\Bigg\{F_{i1}(W_1)+\int_0^{W_1} M_{iu}(W_1-x)\,dF_{i1}(x)\Bigg\} \\ +F_W(W-W_1)/\bar{F}_{iu}(W-W_1)\Bigg] \end{aligned} \tag{10.3}$$

Example 10.1

Based on Data Set II (i) (see Section 6.4) and c_b = \$10, the expected warranty costs determined from (10.3), for different combinations of remaining life and warranty periods, are shown in Table 10.1. The standard error and 90% confidence interval are shown in Table 10.2.

Table 10.1 presents the expected failure frequency and cost for remanufactured AC components for the RFRW policy. The expected failure frequency represents the expected number of failed items per unit of sale. The expected cost to the remanufacturer includes the cost of supplying the original item, *Cs*. Thus, the expected cost of the warranty is calculated by subtracting *Cs*

TABLE 10.1

The Expected Warranty Costs for RFRW Policy, Model C3

		Expected Failures Frequency			Expected Cost to Remanufacturer		
Components	*W*	$RL_i = 1$	$RL_i = 2$	$RL_i = 3$	$RL_i = 1$	$RL_i = 2$	$RL_i = 3$
Evaporator	**0.5**	1.1754	0.0076	0.0006	\$6.35	\$7.28	\$5.82
	1	0.2356	0.0306	0.0046	\$7.06	\$7.97	\$5.92
	2	0.3528	0.0681	0.0156	\$10.58	\$10.51	\$6.11
Control Box	**0.5**	1.1613	0.0072	0.0006	\$6.24	\$7.24	\$5.81
	1	0.2497	0.03	0.0046	\$7.35	\$7.76	\$5.89
	2	0.3386	0.0677	0.0156	\$10.45	\$10.31	\$6.07
Blower	**0.5**	1.1472	0.0071	0.0006	\$3.12	\$2.92	\$2.98
	1	0.2216	0.0307	0.0046	\$4.10	\$5.18	\$3.05
	2	0.3246	0.0688	0.0156	\$5.68	\$6.37	\$3.16
Air Guide	**0.5**	1.1472	0.0031	0.0006	\$1.73	\$1.68	\$1.44
	1	0.1651	0.0312	0.0045	\$2.48	\$2.28	\$1.58
	2	0.2963	0.0597	0.0156	\$3.29	\$3.26	\$1.68
Motor	**0.5**	1.1133	0.0072	0.0006	\$6.50	\$6.24	\$6.10
	1	0.2413	0.0299	0.0047	\$7.15	\$6.68	\$6.21
	2	0.34	0.0688	0.0156	\$10.05	\$8.63	\$6.27
Condenser	**0.5**	1.1599	0.0078	0.0006	\$2.03	\$1.74	\$1.69
	1	0.2258	0.0305	0.0047	\$2.94	\$2.48	\$1.87
	2	0.3557	0.0687	0.0157	\$3.42	\$2.86	\$1.96
Fan	**0.5**	1.1882	0.0071	0.0006	\$3.89	\$3.29	\$3.16
	1	0.2596	0.0302	0.0046	\$5.38	\$3.85	\$3.24
	2	0.3415	0.0683	0.0157	\$6.69	\$5.34	\$3.42
Protector	**0.5**	1.1994	0.0076	0.0006	\$1.03	\$0.80	\$0.58
	1	0.2216	0.0304	0.0045	\$1.60	\$1.30	\$0.69
	2	0.3372	0.0688	0.0156	\$2.79	\$1.88	\$0.74
Compressor	**0.5**	1.1585	0.0076	0.0007	\$4.52	\$4.23	\$4.06
	1	0.2342	0.0305	0.0046	\$5.82	\$5.46	\$4.39
	2	0.34	0.0685	0.0156	\$7.92	\$7.15	\$4.53

TABLE 10.2

Standard Error and Confidence Interval on RFRW Policy, Model C3

					Confidence Interval					
		Standard Error			$RL_i = 1$		$RL_i = 2$		$RL_i = 3$	
Components	*W*	$RL_i = 1$	$RL_i = 2$	$RL_i = 3$	*L* Limit	*U* Limit	*L* Limit	*U* Limit	*L* Limit	*U* Limit
Evaporator	**0.5**	0.78	1.15	1.75	$5.04	$7.67	$5.34	$9.22	$2.86	$8.76
	1	2.00	2.94	3.09	$3.68	$10.43	$3.00	$12.94	$0.73	$11.13
	2	3.87	4.42	5.08	$4.07	$17.10	$3.06	$17.96	$2.46	$14.68
Control Box	**0.5**	0.87	1.29	1.96	$4.75	$7.72	$5.06	$9.41	$2.48	$9.12
	1	2.25	3.31	3.46	$3.56	$11.14	$2.19	$13.34	$0.05	$11.72
	2	4.34	4.97	5.71	$3.13	$17.77	$1.95	$18.68	$3.56	$15.70
Blower	**0.5**	0.98	1.45	2.21	$1.45	$4.79	$0.47	$5.37	$0.74	$6.69
	1	2.53	3.71	3.89	$0.15	$8.36	$1.09	$11.45	$3.51	$9.61
	2	4.88	5.58	6.42	$2.55	$13.89	$3.02	$15.77	$7.66	$13.98
Air Guide	**0.5**	1.25	1.84	2.80	$0.39	$3.83	$1.43	$4.79	$3.29	$6.16
	1	3.20	4.72	4.94	$2.92	$7.89	$5.66	$10.24	$6.74	$9.91
	2	6.20	7.07	8.15	$7.15	$13.73	$8.71	$15.19	$12.05	$15.41
Motor	**0.5**	1.11	1.64	2.49	$4.62	$8.38	$3.48	$9.00	$1.89	$10.30
	1	2.85	4.20	4.40	$2.34	$11.97	$0.40	$13.75	$1.21	$13.62
	2	5.51	6.30	7.25	$3.76	$19.34	$1.99	$19.25	$5.96	$18.49
Condenser	**0.5**	0.92	1.36	2.06	$0.47	$3.58	$0.56	$4.02	$1.79	$5.17
	1	2.36	3.48	3.63	$1.03	$6.93	$3.37	$8.34	$4.27	$7.99
	2	4.55	5.20	5.99	$4.27	$11.09	$5.91	$11.65	$8.15	$12.06
Fan	**0.5**	0.92	1.36	2.06	$2.34	$5.45	$1.01	$5.57	$0.32	$6.63
	1	2.36	3.48	3.63	$1.40	$9.35	$2.00	$9.71	$2.88	$9.38
	2	4.55	5.20	5.99	$0.99	$14.37	$3.43	$14.13	$6.69	$13.51
Protector	**0.5**	0.89	1.31	1.99	$0.47	$2.53	$1.41	$3.02	$2.78	$3.94
	1	2.28	3.36	3.51	$2.25	$5.44	$4.01	$6.95	$5.23	$6.61
	2	4.40	5.04	5.79	$4.63	$10.22	$6.61	$10.36	$9.02	$10.51
Compressor	**0.5**	0.89	1.31	1.99	$3.02	$6.02	$2.02	$6.44	$0.70	$7.41
	1	2.28	3.36	3.51	$1.97	$9.66	$0.19	$11.11	$1.54	$10.31
	2	4.40	5.04	5.79	$0.50	$15.34	$1.32	$15.64	$5.24	$14.29

from the expected cost to the remanufacturer. For example, from Table 10.1, for $W = 0.5$ and $RL = 1$, the warranty cost for AC's motor is \$6.50– Cs = |\$6.50–\$4.00| =\$2.50, which is ([\$2.50/\$4.00] x 100) = 62.50% of the cost of supplying the motor, C_s, which is significant compared to \$4.00, C_s. Even if this cost is acceptable, the corresponding values for longer warranties can be much higher. For example, for $W = 2$ years and $RL = 1$, the corresponding percentage is ([|\$10.05–\$4.00|/\$4.00] x 100) = 151.25%.

For a one-year remaining life remanufactured AC motor sold with 0.5-year warranty, the Advanced Remanufacturing-to-Order (ARTO) system can claim with 90% confidence that the expected warranty cost is in the interval [\$4.62–\$8.38]. As shown in Table 10.2, the confidence interval for a one-year remaining life remanufactured AC sold with two years of warranty is [$3.76–$19.34].

The expected warranty cost to the remanufacturer is increased by 18.24% compared to that of the non-renewable FRW policy for a remanufactured AC motor.

10.3.2 Model C4 (Conventional Component, Non-Repairable, Replacement by Remanufactured)

The expected warranty cost to the remanufacturer is given by:

$$E\left[C_d\left(W1,W;A\right)\right]=C_b\left[\left\{F_{iu}\left(W_1\right)+\int_0^{W_1} M_{iu}\left(W_1-x\right)dF_{iu}\left(x\right)\right\}\right.$$
$$\left.+F_W\left(W-W_1\right)/\bar{F}_{iu}\left(W-W_1\right)\right] \tag{10.4}$$

Example 10.2

Based on Data Set II (i) (see Section 6.4) and c_b = $10, the expected warranty costs for different warranty periods are shown in Table 10.3. Table 10.4 shows the confidence intervals for the ARTO simulation runs.

The expected warranty cost to the remanufacturer is increased by 14.95% compared to that of the FRW policy for a remanufactured AC component. The expected warranty cost to the remanufacturer is increase by 52.17% compared to that of the RFRW policy with a sensor-embedded remanufactured AC motor.

10.4 Analysis of the Renewing Pro-Rata Warranty Policy

This section presents the cost analysis of providing the Renewing Pro-Rata Warranty (RPRW) Policy based on Model C3 (Sensor-Embedded Component, Non-Repairable, Replacement by Remanufactured, Preventive Maintenance) for warranty failures of remanufactured products discussed in Chapter 5. The policy can be described as follows:

RPRW POLICY: Under this policy, the remanufacturer supplies a replacement item at a reduced price if an item fails before the warranty period W. This can be viewed as a conditional refund since the buyer is constrained to use the refund to buy a replacement item. The amount refunded is a function of the time period (X) elapsed subsequent to the sale. The replacement item comes with a new warranty identical to the original one.

TABLE 10.3

The Expected Warranty Costs for RFRW Policy, Model C4

		Expected Warranty Cost to Remanufacturer								
		$L = 1$			$L = 2$			$L = 3$		
Components	W	$U = 1$	$U = 2$	$U = 3$	$U = 1$	$U = 2$	$U = 3$	$U = 1$	$U = 2$	$U = 3$
Evaporator	0.5	$6.03	$6.13	$6.22	$6.92	$7.06	$7.20	$5.52	$5.73	$5.95
	1	$6.70	$6.95	$7.19	$7.57	$7.93	$8.29	$5.62	$6.01	$6.39
	2	$10.05	$10.53	$11.00	$9.98	$10.53	$11.07	$5.80	$6.43	$7.05
Control Box	0.5	$5.92	$6.03	$6.14	$6.88	$7.04	$7.19	$5.50	$5.76	$5.99
	1	$6.99	$7.26	$7.54	$7.37	$7.78	$8.18	$5.59	$6.02	$6.44
	2	$9.93	$10.47	$11.00	$9.80	$10.41	$11.01	$5.77	$6.47	$7.17
Blower	0.5	$2.97	$3.09	$3.21	$2.78	$2.96	$3.13	$2.82	$3.10	$3.37
	1	$3.90	$4.21	$4.52	$4.92	$5.37	$5.83	$2.90	$3.37	$3.85
	2	$5.38	$5.98	$6.58	$6.05	$6.75	$7.43	$3.00	$3.79	$4.57
Air Guide	0.5	$1.64	$1.79	$1.94	$1.59	$1.82	$2.05	$1.36	$1.71	$2.06
	1	$2.36	$2.75	$3.15	$2.17	$2.75	$3.33	$1.50	$2.11	$2.72
	2	$3.12	$3.89	$4.64	$3.10	$3.97	$4.83	$1.59	$2.60	$3.59
Motor	0.5	$6.17	$6.32	$6.45	$5.92	$6.13	$6.33	$5.79	$6.10	$6.40
	1	$6.80	$7.14	$7.49	$6.34	$6.86	$7.37	$5.90	$6.44	$6.98
	2	$9.54	$10.22	$10.89	$8.20	$8.97	$9.75	$5.95	$6.84	$7.73
Condenser	0.5	$1.93	$2.05	$2.15	$1.65	$1.82	$1.99	$1.60	$1.87	$2.12
	1	$2.80	$3.09	$3.37	$2.36	$2.79	$3.21	$1.77	$2.21	$2.66
	2	$3.24	$3.81	$4.36	$2.72	$3.36	$4.00	$1.87	$2.61	$3.34
Fan	0.5	$3.70	$3.82	$3.92	$3.12	$3.29	$3.46	$3.00	$3.25	$3.51
	1	$5.11	$5.40	$5.68	$3.66	$4.09	$4.51	$3.09	$3.53	$3.97
	2	$6.35	$6.92	$7.47	$5.07	$5.72	$6.35	$3.24	$3.98	$4.71
Protector	0.5	$0.98	$1.09	$1.20	$0.77	$0.93	$1.09	$0.55	$0.80	$1.04
	1	$1.52	$1.79	$2.07	$1.23	$1.65	$2.06	$0.66	$1.09	$1.52
	2	$2.66	$3.19	$3.73	$1.78	$2.41	$3.02	$0.71	$1.42	$2.13
Compressor	0.5	$4.28	$4.40	$4.51	$4.02	$4.19	$4.34	$3.84	$4.09	$4.33
	1	$5.52	$5.80	$6.08	$5.18	$5.60	$6.01	$4.16	$4.59	$5.03
	2	$7.51	$8.06	$8.60	$6.80	$7.42	$8.03	$4.31	$5.01	$5.72

10.4.1 Model C3 (Sensor-Embedded Component, Non-Repairable, Replacement by Remanufactured)

Let K be the number of renewals under the RPRW. K is a random variable with:

$$P\{K = k\} = \bar{F}_{iu}\left[F_{iu}(W)\right]^{k} \quad k = 1, 2, \ldots \tag{10.5}$$

The expected number of replacements is given by:

$$E[K] = F_{iu}(W)/\bar{F}_{iu}(W) \tag{10.6}$$

Then, the expected warranty cost to the remanufacturer is given by:

$$E\left[C_d(W)\right] = c_b\left[F_{iu}(W)/\bar{F}_{iu}(W)\right] \tag{10.7}$$

TABLE 10.4

Confidence Interval for RFRW Policy, Model C4

		$L=1$						$L=2$						$L=3$					
		$U=1$		$U=2$		$U=3$		$U=1$		$U=2$		$U=3$		$U=1$		$U=2$		$U=3$	
Components	W	lower	upper	lower	upper	lower	upper	lower	upper	lower	upper	lower	upper	lower	upper	lower	upper	lower	upper
Evaporator	0.5	$7.32	$9.01	$7.59	$9.33	$7.85	$9.66	$8.28	$10.18	$8.66	$10.67	$9.05	$11.15	$6.14	$7.56	$6.56	$8.07	$6.97	$8.59
	1.0	$10.97	$13.52	$11.48	$14.15	$12.00	$14.78	$10.90	$13.42	$11.48	$14.15	$12.08	$14.88	$6.33	$7.80	$7.02	$8.63	$7.69	$9.48
	2.0	$6.47	$7.96	$6.59	$8.10	$6.70	$8.25	$7.52	$9.25	$7.67	$9.46	$7.85	$9.66	$6.01	$7.40	$6.27	$7.73	$6.54	$8.06
Control Box	0.5	$7.63	$9.39	$7.93	$9.76	$8.23	$10.14	$8.05	$9.91	$8.49	$10.45	$8.93	$11.00	$6.10	$7.52	$6.56	$8.09	$7.03	$8.65
	1.0	$10.84	$13.34	$11.43	$14.06	$12.00	$14.78	$10.69	$13.17	$11.35	$13.99	$12.01	$14.80	$6.30	$7.76	$7.06	$8.69	$7.83	$9.64
	2.0	$3.24	$3.99	$3.36	$4.15	$3.51	$4.31	$3.04	$3.74	$3.22	$3.97	$3.42	$4.21	$3.08	$3.79	$3.38	$4.17	$3.68	$4.54
Blower	0.5	$4.25	$5.24	$4.60	$5.66	$4.94	$6.08	$5.37	$6.61	$5.87	$7.22	$6.36	$7.83	$3.16	$3.89	$3.68	$4.54	$4.21	$5.18
	1.0	$5.88	$7.24	$6.53	$8.05	$7.19	$8.85	$6.61	$8.13	$7.36	$9.06	$8.12	$9.99	$3.28	$4.04	$4.14	$5.10	$5.00	$6.14
	2.0	$1.79	$2.20	$1.95	$2.41	$2.12	$2.61	$1.73	$2.13	$1.99	$2.45	$2.23	$2.75	$1.49	$1.83	$1.86	$2.31	$2.25	$2.76
Air Guide	0.5	$2.58	$3.16	$3.01	$3.69	$3.44	$4.22	$2.36	$2.91	$2.99	$3.69	$3.64	$4.47	$1.63	$2.00	$2.31	$2.83	$2.96	$3.65
	1.0	$3.41	$4.19	$4.24	$5.23	$5.07	$6.24	$3.38	$4.17	$4.32	$5.33	$5.28	$6.50	$1.73	$2.13	$2.83	$3.48	$3.92	$4.82
	2.0	$6.74	$8.30	$6.89	$8.49	$7.04	$8.68	$6.47	$7.96	$6.69	$8.23	$6.92	$8.50	$6.33	$7.79	$6.66	$8.19	$6.99	$8.60
Motor	0.5	$7.42	$9.13	$7.80	$9.61	$8.18	$10.06	$6.93	$8.52	$7.49	$9.22	$8.05	$9.91	$6.44	$7.93	$7.03	$8.65	$7.62	$9.38
	1.0	$10.41	$12.81	$11.15	$13.73	$11.88	$14.63	$8.95	$11.02	$9.79	$12.07	$10.65	$13.11	$6.49	$7.99	$7.46	$9.19	$8.43	$10.39
	2.0	$2.10	$2.59	$2.23	$2.75	$2.35	$2.89	$1.80	$2.22	$1.99	$2.45	$2.16	$2.66	$1.75	$2.16	$2.03	$2.51	$2.31	$2.85
Condenser	0.5	$3.05	$3.77	$3.36	$4.15	$3.68	$4.54	$2.58	$3.16	$3.04	$3.74	$3.51	$4.31	$1.93	$2.38	$2.42	$2.98	$2.91	$3.56
	1.0	$3.54	$4.35	$4.15	$5.11	$4.75	$5.86	$2.96	$3.65	$3.67	$4.51	$4.37	$5.37	$2.03	$2.51	$2.83	$3.49	$3.65	$4.48
	2.0	$4.04	$4.97	$4.17	$5.13	$4.28	$5.27	$3.41	$4.19	$3.59	$4.42	$3.78	$4.65	$3.28	$4.04	$3.55	$4.38	$3.82	$4.71
Fan	0.5	$5.58	$6.87	$5.88	$7.26	$6.20	$7.65	$3.99	$4.93	$4.47	$5.50	$4.93	$6.07	$3.36	$4.15	$3.85	$4.74	$4.34	$5.34
	1.0	$6.93	$8.55	$7.55	$9.29	$8.15	$10.04	$5.54	$6.81	$6.24	$7.67	$6.93	$8.55	$3.54	$4.35	$4.34	$5.35	$5.14	$6.34
	2.0	$1.07	$1.32	$1.19	$1.46	$1.30	$1.60	$0.83	$1.03	$1.02	$1.25	$1.19	$1.46	$0.60	$0.74	$0.87	$1.07	$1.13	$1.40
Protector	0.5	$1.66	$2.05	$1.96	$2.42	$2.26	$2.78	$1.35	$1.66	$1.79	$2.20	$2.25	$2.76	$0.72	$0.89	$1.19	$1.46	$1.66	$2.05
	1.0	$2.91	$3.56	$3.49	$4.30	$4.08	$5.03	$1.95	$2.39	$2.62	$3.22	$3.29	$4.05	$0.77	$0.94	$1.55	$1.90	$2.32	$2.86
	2.0	$4.68	$5.76	$4.80	$5.91	$4.93	$6.07	$4.40	$5.40	$4.57	$5.63	$4.74	$5.84	$4.19	$5.17	$4.47	$5.50	$4.72	$5.83
Compressor	0.5	$6.03	$7.42	$6.33	$7.79	$6.63	$8.18	$5.66	$6.96	$6.11	$7.52	$6.56	$8.07	$4.55	$5.60	$5.01	$6.17	$5.48	$6.76
	1.0	$8.20	$10.11	$8.79	$10.84	$9.39	$11.57	$7.42	$9.13	$8.09	$9.96	$8.76	$10.80	$4.70	$5.78	$5.47	$6.74	$6.24	$7.69
	2.0	$6.86	$8.45	$7.35	$9.06	$7.85	$9.67	$6.20	$7.63	$6.76	$8.33	$7.32	$9.02	$3.92	$4.83	$4.57	$5.64	$5.22	$6.43

Example 10.3

Based on Data Set II (i) (see Section 6.4) and c_b = \$10, the expected warranty costs determined from (10.7) for different warranty periods are shown in Table 10.5. Table 10.6 shows the confidence intervals for the ARTO simulation runs.

The expected warranty cost to the remanufacturer is increased by 14.95% compared to that of the PRW policy for a remanufactured AC motor.

10.5 Analysis of the Renewing Combination RFRW-RPRW Warranty Policy

This section presents the cost analysis of providing the Renewing Free-Replacement Warranty combined with the Renewing Pro-Rata Warranty (RFRW-RPRW) Policy based on Model C3 (Sensor-Embedded Component, Non-Repairable, Replacement by Remanufactured, Preventive Maintenance) for warranty failures of remanufactured products discussed in Chapter 5. The policy can be described as follows:

RFRW-RPRW POLICY: Under this policy, if a failure occurs in $[0, W_1)$, the failed item is replaced with a remanufactured one at no cost to the buyer, and if it occurs in $[W_1, W)$, the buyer is provided with a remanufactured item at a cost less than the full price. The reduction in the price is given by a rebate function $S(x)$, as indicated earlier. All replacements come with a new warranty identical to the original.

Thus, this policy combines a renewing FRW policy (for failure in $[0, W_1)$) and a renewing PRW policy (for failures in $[W_1, W)$). Different forms for the rebate function $S(x)$ define a family of combination warranty policies:

$$S(x)=\begin{cases} C_s.\dfrac{(W-x)}{W-W_1} & \text{for } W_1 < x \le W \\ 0 & \text{otherwise} \end{cases} \tag{10.8}$$

The expected warranty cost per item is given by:

$$E\left[C_d(W)\right]=\frac{1}{\left[1-F(W)\right]}\times C_s/(W-W_1)\int_{W_1}^{W}F(x)dx \tag{10.9}$$

Example 10.4

Based on Data Set II (i) (see Section 6.4) and c_S = \$10, the expected warranty costs determined from (10.9) for different warranty periods are shown in Table 10.7. Table 10.8 shows the standard error and 90% confidence interval.

The expected warranty cost to the remanufacturer is increased by 23.35% compared to that of the RFRW policy for a remanufactured AC component.

TABLE 10.5

The Expected Warranty Costs for RPRW Policy, Model C3

		Expected Failures Frequency			Expected Cost to Remanufacturer		
Components	***W***	$RL_i = 1$	$RL_i = 2$	$RL_i = 3$	$RL_i = 1$	$RL_i = 2$	$RL_i = 3$
Evaporator	**0.5**	1.1953	0.0077	0.0006	$6.46	$7.41	$5.92
	1	0.2396	0.0311	0.0047	$7.18	$8.10	$6.02
	2	0.3588	0.0693	0.0159	$10.76	$10.69	$6.22
Control Box	**0.5**	1.181	0.0073	0.0006	$6.35	$7.36	$5.90
	1	0.2539	0.0305	0.0047	$7.48	$7.89	$5.99
	2	0.3444	0.0689	0.0159	$10.63	$10.48	$6.17
Blower	**0.5**	1.1667	0.0072	0.0006	$3.17	$2.97	$3.03
	1	0.2253	0.0313	0.0047	$4.17	$5.27	$3.10
	2	0.33	0.07	0.0159	$5.77	$6.48	$3.21
Air Guide	**0.5**	1.1667	0.0031	0.0006	$1.76	$1.71	$1.47
	1	0.1679	0.0317	0.0046	$2.52	$2.32	$1.61
	2	0.3013	0.0607	0.0159	$3.34	$3.32	$1.71
Motor	**0.5**	1.1321	0.0073	0.0006	$6.61	$6.35	$6.20
	1	0.2454	0.0304	0.0048	$7.27	$6.79	$6.31
	2	0.3458	0.07	0.0159	$10.22	$8.78	$6.37
Condenser	**0.5**	1.1795	0.0079	0.0006	$2.07	$1.77	$1.72
	1	0.2297	0.031	0.0048	$2.99	$2.52	$1.90
	2	0.3617	0.0699	0.016	$3.47	$2.91	$2.00
Fan	**0.5**	1.2083	0.0072	0.0006	$3.96	$3.34	$3.21
	1	0.264	0.0307	0.0047	$5.47	$3.92	$3.29
	2	0.3472	0.0695	0.016	$6.81	$5.43	$3.47
Protector	**0.5**	1.2197	0.0077	0.0006	$1.05	$0.82	$0.59
	1	0.2253	0.0309	0.0046	$1.62	$1.32	$0.70
	2	0.3429	0.07	0.0159	$2.84	$1.91	$0.76
Compressor	**0.5**	1.1781	0.0077	0.0007	$4.59	$4.30	$4.12
	1	0.2382	0.031	0.0047	$5.92	$5.55	$4.46
	2	0.3458	0.0696	0.0159	$8.06	$7.27	$4.61

The expected warranty cost to the remanufacturer is reduced by 12.98% compared to that of the RPRW policy for a remanufactured AC motor. The expected warranty cost to the remanufacturer is increased by 16.02% compared to that of the FRW-PRW policy for a remanufactured AC motor.

10.6 Summary Analysis of Renewing Warranty Policies

In this chapter, three different renewing warranty policies were discussed. In order to assess the impact of these three policies in terms of warranty costs, pairwise t tests were carried out for different performance measure,

TABLE 10.6

Standard Error and Confidence Interval on RPRW Policy, Model C3

		Standard Error			Confidence Interval					
					$RL_i = 1$		$RL_i = 2$		$RL_i = 3$	
Components	W	$RL_i = 1$	$RL_i = 2$	$RL_i = 3$	L limit	U limit	L limit	U limit	L limit	U limit
Evaporator	**0.5**	0.79	1.17	1.78	$5.12	$7.80	$5.43	$9.38	$2.91	$8.91
	1	2.03	2.99	3.14	$3.74	$10.60	$3.05	$13.15	$0.75	$11.31
	2	3.93	4.50	5.17	$4.14	$17.39	$3.11	$18.26	$2.50	$14.93
Control Box	**0.5**	0.89	1.31	2.00	$4.83	$7.85	$5.15	$9.57	$2.52	$9.27
	1	2.28	3.37	3.52	$3.62	$11.33	$2.22	$13.56	$0.05	$11.92
	2	4.41	5.05	5.81	$3.19	$18.07	$1.98	$19.00	$3.62	$15.97
Blower	**0.5**	1.00	1.48	2.25	$1.48	$4.87	$0.48	$5.46	$0.76	$6.81
	1	2.57	3.78	3.96	$0.16	$8.50	$1.11	$11.64	$3.57	$9.78
	2	4.97	5.68	6.53	$2.60	$14.13	$3.07	$16.04	$7.79	$14.21
Air Guide	**0.5**	1.27	1.88	2.85	$0.40	$3.90	$1.45	$4.87	$3.34	$6.26
	1	3.26	4.80	5.03	$2.97	$8.02	$5.76	$10.41	$6.85	$10.08
	2	6.30	7.19	8.28	$7.27	$13.96	$8.86	$15.45	$12.25	$15.67
Motor	**0.5**	1.13	1.67	2.54	$4.70	$8.52	$3.53	$9.15	$1.92	$10.47
	1	2.90	4.27	4.47	$2.38	$12.17	$0.41	$13.98	$1.23	$13.85
	2	5.60	6.41	7.37	$0.77	$19.67	$2.02	$19.57	$6.06	$18.80
Condenser	**0.5**	0.94	1.38	2.09	$0.48	$3.64	$0.57	$4.09	$1.82	$5.25
	1	2.40	3.53	3.69	$1.05	$7.05	$3.43	$8.48	$4.34	$8.13
	2	4.63	5.29	6.10	$4.34	$11.28	$6.01	$11.84	$8.28	$12.26
Fan	**0.5**	0.94	1.38	2.09	$2.38	$5.54	$1.02	$5.66	$0.32	$6.75
	1	2.40	3.53	3.69	$1.42	$9.51	$2.03	$9.87	$2.93	$9.53
	2	4.63	5.29	6.10	$1.01	$14.61	$3.49	$14.37	$6.81	$13.74
Protector	**0.5**	0.90	1.33	2.02	$0.48	$2.57	$1.43	$3.07	$2.83	$4.00
	1	2.32	3.41	3.57	$2.28	$5.53	$4.08	$7.07	$5.31	$6.72
	2	4.47	5.12	5.89	$4.71	$10.39	$6.72	$10.53	$9.17	$10.69
Compressor	**0.5**	0.90	1.33	2.02	$3.07	$6.12	$2.06	$6.55	$0.71	$7.54
	1	2.32	3.41	3.57	$2.01	$9.82	$0.19	$11.30	$1.56	$10.48
	2	4.47	5.12	5.89	$0.50	$15.59	$1.35	$15.91	$5.33	$14.54

namely, Holding Cost, Backorder Cost, Disassembly Cost, Disposal Cost, Remanufacturing Cost, Transportation Cost, Warranty Cost, Number of Claims and Preventive Maintenance Cost. Table 10.9 presents all policies' costs for the three warranty models. According to this table, the lowest average value of warranty cost, number of warranty claims and PM costs during the warranty period for remanufactured components and ACs across all policies are $94,260, 152,959 claims and $4,622 for the RFRW-RPRW policy, whereas the RPRW policy has the worst values, namely, $158,809, 261,479 claims and $12,395, respectively.

TABLE 10.7

The Expected Warranty Costs for RFRW-RPRW Policy, Model C3

		Expected Failures Frequency			Expected Cost to Remanufacturer		
Components	*W*	*RL* = 1	*RL* = 2	*RL* = 3	*RL* = 1	*RL* = 2	*RL* = 3
Evaporator	**0.5**	1.153	0.0074	0.0006	$6.23	$7.14	$5.71
	1.0	0.2312	0.03	0.0045	$6.92	$7.82	$5.81
	2.0	0.3461	0.0668	0.0153	$10.38	$10.31	$6.00
Control Box	**0.5**	1.1392	0.0071	0.0006	$6.12	$7.10	$5.69
	1.0	0.245	0.0295	0.0045	$7.21	$7.61	$5.78
	2.0	0.3322	0.0665	0.0153	$10.25	$10.11	$5.95
Blower	**0.5**	1.1254	0.007	0.0006	$3.06	$2.86	$2.92
	1.0	0.2174	0.0302	0.0045	$4.02	$5.08	$2.99
	2.0	0.3184	0.0675	0.0153	$5.57	$6.25	$3.10
Air Guide	**0.5**	1.1254	0.003	0.0006	$1.69	$1.65	$1.42
	1.0	0.1619	0.0306	0.0044	$2.44	$2.24	$1.55
	2.0	0.2907	0.0586	0.0153	$3.22	$3.20	$1.65
Motor	**0.5**	1.0921	0.0071	0.0006	$6.38	$6.12	$5.98
	1.0	0.2367	0.0293	0.0046	$7.02	$6.55	$6.09
	2.0	0.3336	0.0675	0.0153	$9.86	$8.47	$6.15
Condenser	**0.5**	1.1378	0.0077	0.0006	$1.99	$1.71	$1.66
	1.0	0.2215	0.0299	0.0046	$2.89	$2.44	$1.83
	2.0	0.3489	0.0674	0.0154	$3.35	$2.81	$1.93
Fan	**0.5**	1.1656	0.007	0.0006	$3.82	$3.22	$3.10
	1.0	0.2547	0.0296	0.0045	$5.28	$3.78	$3.18
	2.0	0.335	0.067	0.0154	$6.56	$5.24	$3.35
Protector	**0.5**	1.1766	0.0074	0.0006	$1.01	$0.79	$0.57
	1.0	0.2174	0.0298	0.0044	$1.57	$1.28	$0.67
	2.0	0.3308	0.0675	0.0153	$2.74	$1.84	$0.73
Compressor	**0.5**	1.1364	0.0074	0.0007	$4.43	$4.15	$3.98
	1.0	0.2298	0.0299	0.0045	$5.71	$5.36	$4.30
	2.0	0.3336	0.0672	0.0153	$7.77	$7.02	$4.44

The MINITAB-17 program was used to carry out a one-way analysis of variance (ANOVA) and Tukey pairwise comparisons for all the policies' results. ANOVA was used in order to determine whether there are any significant differences between the warranty costs, number of claims and PM costs for the three different renewing warranty policies, namely, RFRW, RPRW and RFRW-RPRW. The Tukey pairwise comparisons were conducted to identify which policies are similar and which policies are not.

Table 10.10 shows that there is a significant difference in warranty costs between different warranty policies. The Tukey test shows that all the policies are different in term of warranty cost except RFRW-RPRW and

TABLE 10.8

Standard Error and Confidence Interval on RFRW-RPRW Policy, Model C3

					Confidence Interval					
		Standard Error			$RL_i = 1$		$RL_i = 2$		$RL_i = 3$	
Components	*W*	$RL_i = 1$	$RL_i = 2$	$RL_i = 3$	*L* Limit	*U* Limit	*L* Limit	*U* Limit	*L* Limit	*U* Limit
Evaporator	**0.5**	0.77	1.13	1.72	$4.94	$7.53	$5.24	$9.05	$2.81	$8.59
	1	1.96	2.89	3.03	$3.61	$10.23	$2.95	$12.69	$0.72	$10.91
	2	3.79	4.34	4.99	$3.99	$16.77	$3.00	$17.62	$2.41	$14.41
Control Box	**0.5**	0.86	1.26	1.93	$4.66	$7.57	$4.96	$9.23	$2.44	$8.94
	1	2.20	3.25	3.40	$3.49	$10.93	$2.15	$13.08	$0.05	$11.49
	2	4.26	4.87	5.60	$3.07	$17.43	$1.91	$18.33	$3.49	$15.40
Blower	**0.5**	0.96	1.43	2.17	$1.43	$4.70	$0.46	$5.27	$0.73	$6.56
	1	2.48	3.64	3.82	$0.15	$8.20	$1.07	$11.23	$3.44	$9.43
	2	4.79	5.47	6.30	$2.51	$13.63	$2.96	$15.47	$7.52	$13.71
Air Guide	**0.5**	1.23	1.81	2.75	$0.38	$3.76	$1.40	$4.70	$3.22	$6.04
	1	3.14	4.63	4.85	$2.86	$7.74	$5.56	$10.04	$6.61	$9.72
	2	6.08	6.94	7.99	$7.02	$13.47	$8.55	$14.90	$11.82	$15.11
Motor	**0.5**	1.09	1.61	2.45	$4.54	$8.22	$3.41	$8.83	$1.86	$10.10
	1	2.80	4.12	4.31	$2.30	$11.74	$0.39	$13.49	$1.18	$13.36
	2	5.41	6.18	7.11	$0.74	$18.98	$1.95	$18.88	$5.85	$18.14
Condenser	**0.5**	0.90	1.33	2.02	$0.46	$3.51	$0.55	$3.94	$1.75	$5.07
	1	2.32	3.41	3.56	$1.01	$6.80	$3.31	$8.18	$4.19	$7.84
	2	4.47	5.10	5.88	$4.19	$10.88	$5.80	$11.42	$7.99	$11.83
Fan	**0.5**	0.90	1.33	2.02	$2.30	$5.35	$0.99	$5.46	$0.31	$6.51
	1	2.32	3.41	3.56	$1.37	$9.17	$1.96	$9.52	$2.83	$9.20
	2	4.47	5.10	5.88	$0.97	$14.09	$3.36	$13.86	$6.56	$13.26
Protector	**0.5**	0.87	1.29	1.95	$0.46	$2.48	$1.38	$2.96	$2.73	$3.86
	1	2.24	3.29	3.44	$2.20	$5.34	$3.93	$6.82	$5.13	$6.48
	2	4.31	4.94	5.68	$4.55	$10.02	$6.48	$10.16	$8.85	$10.31
Compressor	**0.5**	0.87	1.29	1.95	$2.96	$5.90	$1.98	$6.32	$0.68	$7.27
	1	2.24	3.29	3.44	$1.94	$9.48	$0.19	$10.90	$1.51	$10.11
	2	4.31	4.94	5.68	$0.49	$15.04	$1.30	$15.35	$5.14	$14.02

TABLE 10.9

Results of Performance Measures for Different Warranty Policies

	Warranty Policies		
Performance Measure	**RFRW**	**RPRW**	**RFRW-RPRW**
Holding Cost	$111,632.08	$159,523.15	$135,055.00
Backorder Cost	$17,727.09	$29,591.32	$25,052.51
Disassembly Cost	$206,352.58	$344,458.38	$291,624.29
Disposal Cost	$33,428.02	$55,800.42	$47,241.58
Remanufacturing Cost	$709,441.19	$1,184,249.63	$1,002,605.76
Transportation Cost	$17,901.08	$29,881.76	$25,298.39
Warranty Cost	$95,136.83	$158,809.15	$94,260.03
Number of Claims	156643	261479	152959
Preventive Maintenance Cost	$7,425.67	$12,395.46	$4,622.72
Total Cost	$1,199,044.53	$1,974,709.27	$1,625,760.28
Total Revenue	$4,027,674.87	$3,475,311.12	$3,899,230.60
Profit	$2,828,630.35	$1,500,601.86	$2,273,470.32

TABLE 10.10

ANOVA Table and Tukey Pairwise Comparisons for Warranty Cost

ANOVA: Warranty Cost

Null hypothesis All means are equal
Alternative hypothesis At least one mean is different
Significance level α = 0.05

SUMMARY

Models	*Count*	*Sum*	*Average*	*StDev*	*95% CI*
RFRW Policy	2000	97,476,255	48,738	92.89	(48734, 48742)
RPRW Policy	2000	162,714,291	81,357	116.88	(81352, 81362)
RFRW-RPRW Policy	2000	96,577,900	48,289	131.11	(48283, 48295)

ANOVA

Source of Variation	*SS*	*df*	*MS*	*F-Value*	*P-value*
Model	1.44E+12	2	7.19E+11	54653765	0.000
Error	7.89E+07	5997	13159.77		
Total	1.44E+12	5999			

Tukey Pairwise Comparisons

Grouping Information Using the Tukey Method and 95% Confidence

Model	**N**	**Mean**	**Grouping**
RFRW-RPRW Policy	2000	48,289	A
RFRW Policy	2000	48,738	A
RPRW Policy	2000	81,357	B

Means that do not share a letter are significantly different.

RFRW; there is no significant different between them. The RFRW-RPRW policy (Combination of Renewing Free-Replacement Warranty & Renewing Pro-Rata Warranty) has the lowest warranty cost, $94,260.03.

In addition, there is a significant difference in the number of warranty claims between different combination warranty policies (see Table 10.11). The RFRW-RPRW policy has the lowest number of claims, 152,958.

Finally, Table 10.12 shows that there is a significant difference in PM costs between different warranty policies. The Tukey test shows that all policies are different. The lowest PM cost was associated with the RFRW-RPRW policy (Combination of Renewing Free-Replacement Warranty & Renewing Pro-Rata Warranty), $4,622.72. These results can be useful in determining the economical warranty policy associated with embedding sensors in ACs.

TABLE 10.11

ANOVA Table and Tukey Pairwise Comparisons for Number of Claims

ANOVA: Warranty Claims

Null hypothesis All means are equal
Alternative hypothesis At least one mean is different
Significance level α = 0.05

SUMMARY

Models	*Count*	*Sum*	*Average*	*StDev*	*95% CI*
RFRW Policy	2000	73,074,072	36,537	213.96	(36528, 36546)
RPRW Policy	2000	121,980,433	60,990	190.05	(60982, 60998)
RFRW-RPRW Policy	2000	71,355,555	35,678	210.97	(35669, 35687)

ANOVA

Source of Variation	*SS*	*df*	*MS*	*F-Value*	*P-value*
Model	8.26E+11	2	4.13E+11	9804773.73	0.000
Error	2.53E+08	5997	42135.408		
Total	8.27E+11	5999			

Tukey Pairwise Comparisons

Grouping Information Using the Tukey Method and 95% Confidence

Model	**N**	**Mean**	**Grouping**
RFRW-RPRW Policy	2000	35,678	A
RFRW Policy	2000	36,537	B
RPRW Policy	2000	60,990	C

Means that do not share a letter are significantly different.

TABLE 10.12

ANOVA Table and Tukey Pairwise Comparisons for PM cost

ANOVA: Preventive Maintenance

Null hypothesis All means are equal

Alternative hypothesis At least one mean is different

Significance level α = 0.05

SUMMARY

Models	*Count*	*Sum*	*Average*	*StDev*	*95% CI*
RFRW Policy	2000	7,608,268.72	3,804.13	117.84	(3799, 3809)
RPRW Policy	2000	12,700,262.67	6,350.13	100.34	(6346, 6355)
RFRW-RPRW Policy	2000	4,736,395.02	2,368.20	99.19	(2364, 2373)

ANOVA

Source of Variation	*SS*	*df*	*MS*	*F-Value*	*P-value*
Model	1.63E+10	2	8.13E+09	592866.44	0
Error	8.23E+07	5997	13718.35		
Total	1.63E+10	5999			

Tukey Pairwise Comparisons

Grouping Information Using the Tukey Method and 95% Confidence

Model	*N*	*Mean*	*Grouping*
RFRW-RPRW Policy	2000	2,368.20	A
RFRW Policy	2000	3,804.13	B
RPRW Policy	2000	6,350.13	C

Means that do not share a letter are significantly different.

10.7 Conclusions

In this chapter, three renewing warranty policies, namely, Renewing Free-Replacement Warranty (RFRW), Renewing Pro-Rata Warranty (RPRW) and their combination, were discussed. In order to assess the impact of these two policies in terms of warranty cost, pairwise t tests were carried out for different performance measures, namely, Holding Cost, Backorder Cost, Disassembly Cost, Disposal Cost, Testing Cost, Remanufacturing Cost, Transportation Cost, Warranty Cost, Number of Claims and Preventive Maintenance Cost.

11

Cost Analysis of Two-Dimensional Warranties

11.1 Introduction

In Chapter 4, several warranty policies with preventive maintenance for remanufactured products were introduced. Chapter 7, Chapter 8, Chapter 9 and Chapter 10 together considered 21 of these policies. Here, six two-dimensional non-renewing, renewing and combination policies, namely, Policy 22 (2D FRW), Policy 23 (2D PRW), Policy 24 (2D RFRW), Policy 25 (2D RPRW), Policy 26 (2D FRW-PRW), and Policy 27 (2D RFRW-RPRW), as defined in Chapter 4, are considered.

Section 11.2 deals with the analyses of two-dimensional warranty policies. Some conclusions are presented in Section 11.3.

11.2 Two-Dimensional Warranty

This section presents the analysis of determining the expected cost of the warranty from the remanufacturer's perspective.

11.2.1 Analysis of Two-Dimensional FRW Policies

Here, the analysis of two-dimensional Free-Replacement Warranty (FRW) policies are considered. Remanufactured item failures are modeled through a conditional intensity function.

The warranty cost is of interest to the remanufacturer. This cost is a random variable since it depends on the number of failures under warranty. The expected value of this cost is important for the pricing of the remanufactured product that is sold with a warranty. Since the number of failures under warranty depends on the type of policy and its parameters, the expected warranty costs are a function of the parameter of the policy. Here, $\tilde{\theta}$ denotes a policy parameter. For a FRW policy characterized by:

1. a rectangle [0, W)×[0, U), as shown in Figure 11.1(a), or
2. two infinite dimensional strips, as shown in Figure 11.1(b), or
3. a triangle, as shown in Figure 11.1(d), $\tilde{\theta}$ is given by

$$\tilde{\theta} = \{W, U] \tag{11.1}$$

For the FRW policy characterized by:

4. a two-dimensional region as shown in Figure 11.1(c), $\tilde{\theta}$ is given by:

$$\tilde{\theta} = \{W_1, W_2, U_1, U_2\} \tag{11.2}$$

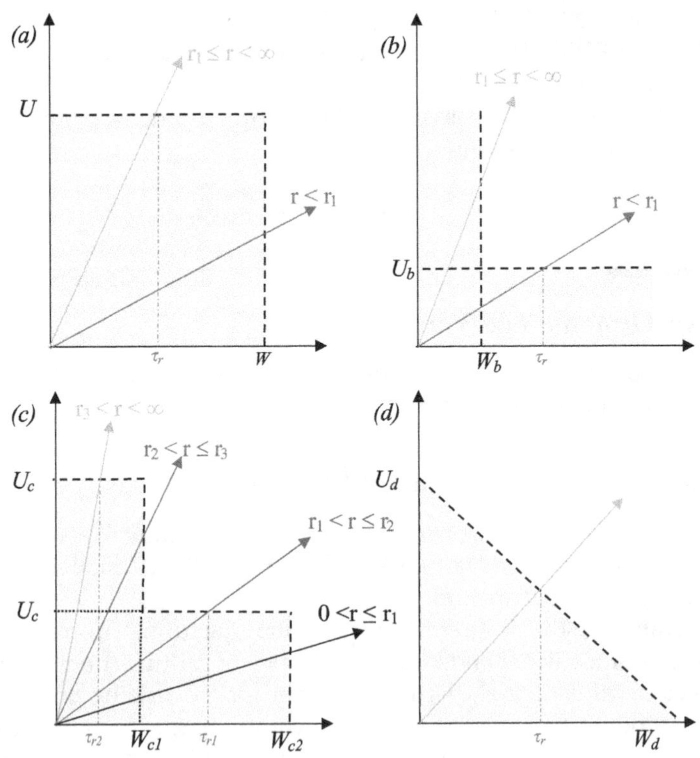

FIGURE 11.1
Warranty Regions for Policies 22(a)–22(d).

11.2.1.1 Analysis of Two-Dimensional Non-Renewing FRW Policies

POLICY 22 (NON-RENEWING FRW): Under this policy, whenever a remanufactured item fails in the warranty region Ω, the failed item is replaced by a new remanufactured one free of charge. The replacement comes with a new warranty identical to that of the original one.

Here, four possible warranty regions are considered and presented as follows:

Policy 22(a) Rectangular Two-Dimensional FRW Warranty Region: This policy is characterized by the rectangle [0, *W*) × [0, *U*) as shown in Figure 11.1.(a):

$$r_1 = U / W \tag{11.3}$$

$$\tau_r = U / r \tag{11.4}$$

The expected warranty cost is obtained by using the conditional approach. The time to first failure is given by:

$$F(t|r) = 1 - e^{-\int_0^t \lambda(x|r)dx} \tag{11.5}$$

where $\lambda(t|r)$ is the conditional intensity function given by:

$$\lambda(t|r) = \theta_0 + \theta_1 r + \theta_2 T_C + \theta_3 X_C(t) \tag{11.6}$$

where T_C (t) and X_C (t) represent the remaining life and usage of the item currently in use at time t. Since every failure results in replacement with a remanufactured one, $N(\tilde{\theta}|r)$ is a one-dimensional renewal process. As a result, the expected value of $N(\tilde{\theta}|r)$ is given by:

$$E\left[N(\tilde{\theta}|r)\right] = \begin{cases} M(K|r) & \text{if } r < r_1 \\ M(\tau_r|r) & \text{if } r \geq r_1 \end{cases} \tag{11.7}$$

where $M(t|r)$ is the renewal function associated with the distribution function F(t|r), given by:

$$M(t|r) = F(t|r) + \int_0^t M(t-u|r)dF(u|r) \tag{11.8}$$

On removing the conditioning, the result is given by:

$$E\left[N(\tilde{\theta})\right] = E\left[N(\tilde{\theta}|r)\right] = \int_0^\infty E\left[N(\tilde{\theta}|r)\right]dG(r) \tag{11.9}$$

which yields

$$E\left[N\left(\tilde{\theta}\right)\right]=\int_{0}^{r_1}M(K\mid r)dG(r)+\int_{r_1}^{\infty}M(\tau_r\mid r)dG(r) \tag{11.10}$$

where r_1 and τ_r are given by (11.3) and (11.4) respectively. The expected warranty cost, $EC\left(\tilde{\theta}\right)$, is given by:

$$EC\left(\tilde{\theta}\right)=cE\left[N\left(\tilde{\theta}\right)\right] \tag{11.11}$$

where c is the cost of each replacement and $E\left[N\left(\tilde{\theta}\right)\right]$ is given by (11.10).

Policy 22(b) Infinite Strips Two-Dimensional FRW Warranty Region: The warranty region Ω is given by two infinite dimensional strips, as shown in Figure 11.1 (b). Conditioned on usage rate $R=r$, the warranty ceases (see Figure 11.1 (b)) at time τ_r if $r < r_1$ and at time K if $r \geq r_1$. r_1 and τ_r are given by (11.3) and (11.4), respectively. The expected number of replacements under warranty is given by:

$$E\left[N\left(\tilde{\theta}\right)\right]=\int_{0}^{r_1}M(\tau_r\mid r)dG(r)+\int_{r_1}^{\infty}M(K\mid r)dG(r) \tag{11.12}$$

As a result, the expected warranty cost, $EC\left(\tilde{\theta}\right)$

$$EC\left(\tilde{\theta}\right)=cE\left[N\left(\tilde{\theta}\right)\right] \tag{11.13}$$

with $E\left[N\left(\tilde{\theta}\right)\right]$is given by (11.10).

Policy 22(c) Four Parameters Two-Dimensional FRW Warranty Region: The warranty region Ω is shown in Figure 11.1 (c). Define:

$$r_1=\frac{L_1}{K_2};r_2=\frac{L_1}{K_1};r_3=\frac{L_2}{K_1}; \tag{11.14}$$

Conditioned on usage rate $R=r$, the warranty ceases (see Figure 11.1 (c)) at time K_2 if $r \leq r_1$; at time τ_r, given by:

$$\tau_{r1}=\frac{L_1}{r} \tag{11.15}$$

if $r_1 < r \leq r_2$; at time K_1 if $r_2 < r \leq r_1$ and at time τ_{r2}, given by:

$$\tau_{r2}=\frac{L_2}{r} \tag{11.16}$$

if $r > r_3$.

The expected number of failures under warranty is given by:

$$E\left[N\left(\tilde{\theta}\right)\right] = \int_{0}^{r_1} M(K_2|r)dG(r) + \int_{r_1}^{r_2} M(\tau_{r1}|r)dG(r) + \int_{r_2}^{r_3} M(K_1|r)dG(r) + \int_{r_3}^{\infty} M(\tau_{r1}|r)dG(r) \tag{11.17}$$

where r_1, r_2 and r_3 are given by (11.14). The expected warranty cost, $EC\left(\tilde{\theta}\right)$ is given by:

$$EC\left(\tilde{\theta}\right) = cE\left[N\left(\tilde{\theta}\right)\right] \tag{11.18}$$

with $E\left[N\left(\tilde{\theta}\right)\right]$ given by (11.17).

Policy 22(d) Triangular Two-Dimensional FRW Warranty Region: The warranty region Ω is given by the triangular region, as shown in Figure 11.1 (d). Conditional on usage rate $R=r$, $0 < r < \infty$, the warranty ceases (see Figure 11.1 (d)) at time τ_r, is given by:

$$\tau_r = \frac{K \times L}{r \times K + L} \tag{11.19}$$

The expected number of failures under the warranty is given by:

$$E\left[N\left(\tilde{\theta}\right)\right] = \int_{0}^{r_1} M(\tau_r|r)dG(r) + \int_{r_1}^{\infty} M(K|r)dG(r) \tag{11.20}$$

As a result, the expected warranty cost per item, $EC\left(\tilde{\theta}\right)$ is given by:

$$EC\left(\tilde{\theta}\right) = cE\left[N\left(\tilde{\theta}\right)\right] \tag{11.21}$$

with $E\left[N\left(\tilde{\theta}\right)\right]$ given by (11.20).

Example 11.1

Based on Data Set II (i) (see Section 6.4) the expected warranty costs determined from the non-renewing FRW formulation for different warranty periods and usages are shown in Table 11.1. Table 11.2 shows the confidence intervals for the ARTO simulation runs. The example here considers a non-renewing two-dimensional FRW policy for the remanufactured AC with three different remaining lives (1 year, 2 years and 3 years) warranty periods (1 year, 2 years and 3 years) and usage

(100 hours, 200 hours and 300 hours). The warranty expires when either the age or usage limit is reached. We assume that $W = U$ and consider values of $W = U = 1, 2$ and 3. These correspond to warranties of 1 year/100 hours, 2 years/200 hours and 3 years/300 hours, respectively.

Table 11.1 presents the expected cost for the remanufactured ACs for the two-dimensional FRW policy. In Table 11.1, the expected cost to the remanufacturer includes the cost of supplying the original item, *Cs*. Thus, the expected cost of the warranty is calculated by subtracting *Cs* from the expected cost to the remanufacturer. For example, from Table 11.1, for $W = U = 1$ and $RL = 1$, the warranty cost for the remanufactured AC is \$70.58 – *Cs* = |\$70.58 –\$55.00| =\$15.58, which is ([\$15.58 /\$55.00] x 100) = 28.33% of the cost of supplying the AC, C_s, which is less than that \$55.00, C_s when the warranty area is Rectangular shape. The two-dimensional FRW warranty cost is \$3.15, \$11.51 and \$5.81 for Infinite Strips, Four Parameters and Triangular warranty shapes, respectively.

TABLE 11.1

The Expected Warranty Costs for 2D FRW Policy

				Expected Cost to Remanufacturer	
Two-Dimensional FRW					
Rectangular	*Item*	*W* = *U*	*RL* = 1	*RL* = 2	*RL* = 3
	AC	1.00	\$70.58	\$67.71	\$67.07
		2.00	\$73.65	\$74.45	\$70.21
		3.00	\$86.53	\$85.24	\$72.83
				Expected Cost to Remanufacturer	
Infinite Strips	*Item*	*W* = *U*	*RL* = 1	*RL* = 2	*RL* = 3
	AC	1.00	\$58.16	\$55.80	\$55.27
		2.00	\$60.69	\$61.35	\$57.86
		3.00	\$71.31	\$70.25	\$60.01
				Expected Cost to Remanufacturer	
Four Parameters	*Item*	*W* = *U*	*RL* = 1	*RL* = 2	*RL* = 3
	AC	1.00	\$64.51	\$61.89	\$61.31
		2.00	\$67.32	\$68.05	\$64.18
		3.00	\$711.10	\$77.92	\$66.57
				Expected Cost to Remanufacturer	
Triangular	*Item*	*W* = *U*	*RL* = 1	*RL* = 2	*RL* = 3
	AC	1.00	\$60.81	\$58.34	\$57.79
		2.00	\$63.45	\$64.14	\$60.49
		3.00	\$74.55	\$73.44	\$62.74

TABLE 11.2

Standard Error and Confidence Interval on 2D FRW Policy

							Confidence Interval					
				Standard Error			*RL* = 1		*RL* = 2		*RL* = 3	
Two-Dimensional FRW	Rectangular	*Item*	*W* = *U*	*RL* = 1	*RL* = 2	*RL* = 3	*L limit*	*U limit*	*L limit*	*U limit*	*L limit*	*U limit*
		AC	1.00	0.71	1.05	1.59	$70.34	$70.82	$67.35	$68.06	$66.53	$67.61
			2.00	1.83	2.69	2.81	$73.03	$74.27	$73.52	$75.36	$611.25	$71.18
			3.00	3.53	4.03	4.64	$85.33	$87.74	$83.86	$86.63	$71.23	$74.41
							Confidence Interval					
				Standard Error			*RL* = 1		*RL* = 2		*RL* = 3	
	Infinite Strips	*Item*	*W* = *U*	*RL* = 1	*RL* = 2	*RL* = 3	*L limit*	*U limit*	*L limit*	*U limit*	*L limit*	*U limit*
		AC	1.00	0.59	0.86	1.31	$57.96	$58.37	$55.50	$56.09	$54.82	$55.72
			2.00	1.51	2.21	2.32	$60.18	$61.21	$60.59	$62.10	$57.07	$58.66
			3.00	2.91	3.32	3.83	$70.32	$72.31	$611.11	$71.39	$58.70	$61.32
							Confidence Interval					
				Standard Error			*RL* = 1		*RL* = 2		*RL* = 3	
	Four Parameters	*Item*	*W* = *U*	*RL* = 1	*RL* = 2	*RL* = 3	*L limit*	*U limit*	*L limit*	*U limit*	*L limit*	*U limit*
		AC	1.00	0.65	0.96	1.45	$64.30	$64.74	$61.56	$62.21	$60.81	$61.80
			2.00	1.67	2.46	2.57	$66.75	$67.89	$67.21	$68.89	$63.30	$65.06
			3.00	3.22	3.69	4.24	$78.00	$80.21	$76.66	$711.19	$65.12	$68.02
							Confidence Interval					
				Standard Error			*RL* = 1		*RL* = 2		*RL* = 3	
	Triangular	*Item*	*W* = *U*	*RL* = 1	*RL* = 2	*RL* = 3	*L limit*	*U limit*	*L limit*	*U limit*	*L limit*	*U limit*
		AC	1.00	0.62	0.90	1.37	$60.60	$61.02	$58.02	$58.64	$57.32	$58.25
			2.00	1.58	2.32	2.42	$62.92	$63.99	$63.34	$64.93	$511.67	$61.32
			3.00	3.04	3.47	4.00	$73.52	$75.60	$72.25	$74.64	$61.37	$64.11

For a one-year remaining-life remanufactured AC sold with one year of warranty, the ARTO system can claim with 90% confidence that expected warranty cost is in the interval [$70.34–$70.82], [$57.96–$58.37], [$64.30–$64.74] and [$60.60–$61.02] for Rectangular, Infinite Strips, Four Parameters and Triangular warranty shapes, respectively, as shown in Table 11.2.

11.2.1.2 Analysis of Two-Dimensional Renewing FRW Policies

POLICY 24: (RENEWING FRW): Under this policy, whenever a remanufactured item fails in the warranty region Ω, the failed item is replaced by a new remanufactured one free of charge. The replacement comes with a new warranty identical to that of the original one. As with the non-renewing FRW policy, there are four different policies for the four different warranty regions.
Policy 24 (a) Rectangular Two-Dimensional RFRW Warranty Region: Whenever a remanufactured item fails under the warranty, it is replaced by another remanufactured one with a new warranty. Again use the conditional approach. Conditioned on $R = r$, the warranty ceases the first time an item survives for a period K when $r < r_1$ or the first time it survives for a period τ_r when $r \geq r_1$. r_1 and τ_r are given by (11.3) and (11.4), respectively. As a result, the number of replacements under the warranty $N(\tilde{\theta} \mid r)$, conditioned on $R = r$, is a random variable distributed according to a geometric distribution function. The expected value of $N(\tilde{\theta} \mid r)$, $E\left[N(\tilde{\theta} \mid r)\right]$, is given by:

$$E\left[N(\tilde{\theta} \mid r)\right] = \begin{cases} \dfrac{1}{1 - F(\tau_r \mid r)} & \text{if } r < r_1 \\ \dfrac{1}{1 - F(K \mid r)} & \text{if } r \geq r_1 \end{cases} \tag{11.22}$$

where $F(t \mid r)$ is given by (11.5). Hence, $E\left[N(\tilde{\theta})\right]$ is given by:

$$E\left[N(\tilde{\theta})\right] = \int_0^{r_1} \frac{1}{1 - F(K \mid r)} dG(r) + \int_{r_1}^{\infty} \frac{1}{1 - F(\tau_r \mid r)} dG(r) \tag{11.23}$$

The expected warranty cost per item, $E\left[N(\tilde{\theta} \mid r)\right]$, is given by:

$$EC(\tilde{\theta}) = cE\left[N(\tilde{\theta})\right] \tag{11.24}$$

Policy 24 (b) Infinite Strips Two-Dimensional RFRW Warranty Region: The expected number of replacements under the warranty, $E\left[N\left(\tilde{\theta} \mid r\right)\right]$, is given by:

$$E\left[N\left(\tilde{\theta}\right)\right] = \int_0^{r_1} \frac{1}{1-F(\tau_r|r)} dG(r) + \int_{r_1}^{\infty} \frac{1}{1-F(K|r)} dG(r) \tag{11.25}$$

As a result, the expected warranty cost per Item, $EC\left(\tilde{\theta}\right)$ is given by (11.24) with $E\left[N\left(\tilde{\theta}\right)\right]$ given by (11.25).

Policy 24 (c) Four Parameters Two-Dimensional RFRW Warranty Region: The expected number of replacements under warranty, $E\left[N\left(\tilde{\theta}\right)\right]$, is given by:

$$\begin{aligned} E\left[N\left(\tilde{\theta}\right)\right] &= \int_0^{r_1} \frac{1}{1-F(K|r)} dG(r) + \int_{r_1}^{r_2} \frac{1}{1-F(\tau_{r1}|r)} dG(r) \\ &+ \int_{r_2}^{r_3} \frac{1}{1-F(K_1|r)} dG(r) + \int_{r_3}^{\infty} \frac{1}{1-F(\tau_{r2}|r)} dG(r) \end{aligned} \tag{11.26}$$

As a result, the expected warranty cost, $EC\left(\tilde{\theta}\right)$is given by (11.24), with $E\left[N\left(\tilde{\theta}\right)\right]$, given by (11.26).

Policy 24 (d) Triangular Two-Dimensional RFRW Warranty Region: The expected number of failures under warranty is given by:

$$\int_0^{\infty} \frac{1}{1-F(\tau_r|r)} dG(r) \tag{11.27}$$

where τ_t is given by (11.19). As a result, the expected warranty cost, $EC\left(\tilde{\theta}\right)$ is given by (11.24) with $E\left[N\left(\tilde{\theta}\right)\right]$, given by (11.27).

Example 11.2

Based on Data Set II (i) (see Section 6.4), the expected warranty costs determined from the renewing FRW formulation for different warranty periods and usages are shown in Table 11.3. Table 11.4 shows the confidence intervals for the ARTO simulation system. The example here considers a two-dimensional RFRW policy for the remanufactured ACs with three different remaining lives (1 year, 2 years and 3 years) warranty periods (1 year, 2 years and 3 years) and usage (100 hours, 200 hours and 300 hours). The warranty expires when either the age or usage limit is reached. We assume that $W = U$ and consider values of $W = U = 1$, 2 and 3. These correspond to warranties of 1 year/100 hours, 2 years/200 hours and 3 years/300 hours, respectively.

TABLE 11.3

The Expected Warranty Costs for 2D RFRW Policy

		Item	W = U	Expected Cost to Remanufacturer		
				RL = 1	*RL* = 2	*RL* = 3
Two-Dimensional RFRW	Rectangular	AC	1.00	$711.29	$76.07	$75.35
			2.00	$82.74	$83.64	$78.88
			3.00	$97.21	$95.77	$81.82
	Infinite Strips	*Item*	*W* = *U*	Expected Cost to Manufacturer		
				RL = 1	*RL* = 2	*RL* = 3
		AC	1.00	$65.34	$62.69	$62.09
			2.00	$68.18	$68.92	$65.01
			3.00	$80.11	$78.92	$67.42
	Four Parameters	*Item*	*W* = *U*	Expected Cost to Remanufacturer		
				RL = 1	*RL* = 2	*RL* = 3
		AC	1.00	$72.48	$611.53	$68.88
			2.00	$75.63	$76.45	$72.11
			3.00	$88.86	$87.54	$74.79
	Triangular	*Item*	*W* = *U*	Expected Cost to Remanufacturer		
				RL = 1	*RL* = 2	*RL* = 3
		AC	1.00	$68.31	$65.54	$64.92
			2.00	$71.28	$72.06	$67.96
			3.00	$83.76	$82.51	$70.49

Table 11.3 presents the expected cost for remanufactured ACs for the two-dimensional RFRW policy. In Table 11.3, the expected cost to the remanufacturer includes the cost of supplying the original item, Cs. Thus, the expected cost of the warranty is calculated by subtracting Cs from the expected cost to the remanufacturer. For example, from Table 11.15, for $W = U = 1$ and $RL = 1$, the warranty cost for the remanufactured AC is $24.29, $10.34, $17.48 and $13.31 for Rectangular, Infinite Strips, Four Parameters and Triangular warranty shapes, respectively.

For a one-year remaining-life remanufactured AC sold with a one-year warranty, the ARTO system can claim with 90% confidence that the expected warranty cost is in the interval [$711.02–$711.57], [$65.12–$65.57], [$72.23–$72.73] and [$68.08–$68.55] for Rectangular, Infinite Strips, Four Parameters and Triangular warranty shapes, respectively, as shown in Table 11.4.

The expected warranty cost to the remanufacturer is increased by 12.35%, 10.99%, 13.57% and 12.86% compared to that of the FRW policy for Rectangular, Infinite Strips, Four Parameters and Triangular warranty shapes, respectively.

TABLE 11.4

Standard Error and Confidence Interval on 2D RFRW Policy

				Standard Error		Confidence Interval					
						RL = 1		RL = 2		RL = 3	
Two-Dimensional RFRW: Rectangular	Item	W = U	RL = 1	RL = 2	RL = 3	L limit	U limit	L limit	U limit	L limit	U limit
	AC	0.80	1.18	1.79	$711.02	$711.57	$75.66	$76.46	$74.74	$75.96	0.80
		2.06	3.02	3.16	$82.04	$83.44	$82.60	$84.66	$77.80	$711.96	2.06
		3.96	4.53	5.21	$95.86	$98.57	$94.22	$97.32	$80.03	$83.59	3.96
				Standard Error		Confidence Interval					
						RL = 1		RL = 2		RL = 3	
Infinite Strips	Item	W = U	RL = 1	RL = 2	RL = 3	L limit	U limit	L limit	U limit	L limit	U limit
	AC	1.00	0.66	0.97	1.47	$65.12	$65.57	$62.35	$63.01	$61.59	$62.60
		2.00	1.69	2.49	2.60	$67.61	$68.77	$68.07	$611.77	$64.12	$65.90
		3.00	3.26	3.73	4.30	$711.00	$81.23	$77.64	$80.20	$65.95	$68.89
				Standard Error		Confidence Interval					
						RL = 1		RL = 2		RL = 3	
Four Parameters	Item	W = U	RL = 1	RL = 2	RL = 3	L limit	U limit	L limit	U limit	L limit	U limit
	AC	1.00	0.73	1.08	1.63	$72.23	$72.73	$611.16	$611.90	$68.32	$611.44
		2.00	1.88	2.76	2.89	$74.99	$76.28	$75.50	$77.39	$71.12	$73.10
		3.00	3.62	4.14	4.77	$87.63	$90.11	$86.12	$88.96	$73.15	$76.41
				Standard Error		Confidence Interval					
						RL = 1		RL = 2		RL = 3	
Triangular	Item	W = U	RL = 1	RL = 2	RL = 3	L limit	U limit	L limit	U limit	L limit	U limit
	AC	1.00	0.69	1.01	1.54	$68.08	$68.55	$65.19	$65.88	$64.39	$65.44
		2.00	1.77	2.60	2.72	$70.68	$71.89	$71.16	$72.95	$67.03	$68.90
		3.00	3.41	3.90	4.49	$82.59	$84.93	$81.17	$83.85	$68.95	$72.02

11.2.2 Analysis of Two-Dimensional PRW Policies

This section deals with the analysis of two-dimensional Pro-Rata Warranty (PRW) policies as defined in Chapter 4 to obtain the expected warranty costs. The item failures are characterized through a conditional intensity function $\lambda(t|r)$. As a result, with the condition on $R = r$, the distribution function for the time to first failure is given by:

$$F(t|r) = 1 - e^{-\int_0^t \lambda(x|r)dx} \tag{11.28}$$

11.2.2.1 Analysis of Two-Dimensional Non-Renewing PRW Policies

POLICY 23 (NON-RENEWING PRW): Under this policy, the buyer is refunded a fraction of the original sale price when the failure occurs in the warranty region Ω. The amount of refund is a function of the remaining life and usage of the remanufactured item at failure. The refund is unconditional, as the buyer has no obligation to buy a replacement item.

As in Section 11.2.1, the conditional approach is used to obtain the expected warranty costs for the different PRW policies. The expected warranty costs, $EC(\tilde{\theta})$, for Policies 24(a)–24(b) is presented are follows:

Policy 23 (a): Rectangular Two-Dimensional PRW Warranty Region: The amount of refund, if the remaining life and usage at failure are t and x, $R(\text{t}, x|r)$ is given by:

$$R(t,x|r) = R(t,rt) = \begin{cases} \left(1-\frac{t}{k}\right)\left(1-\frac{rt}{L}\right)\times C_s & \text{if } (t,rt) \in \Omega \\ 0 & \text{otherwise} \end{cases} \tag{11.29}$$

where C_s is the sale price per unit. Hence, the expected refund per remanufactured item conditioned on $R = r$, $E[R(T,rT|r)]$, is given by:

$$E[R(T_1,rT_1|r) = \begin{cases} \int_0^K R(t_1,rt_1|r)dF(t_1|r) & \text{if } r < r_1 \\ \int_0^{\tau_r} R(t_1,rt_1)dF(t_1|r) & \text{if } r \geq r_1 \end{cases} \tag{11.30}$$

where $F(t|r)$ is given by (11.28). As a result, $EC(\tilde{\theta})$ is given by:

$$EC(\tilde{\theta}) = E[R(T_1, rT_1| r)$$

$$= C_S \times \int_0^{r_1}\int_0^{K} \left(1-\frac{t_1}{K}\right)\left(1-\frac{rt_1}{L}\right) dF(t_1| r)dG(r) \tag{11.31}$$

$$+\int_{r_1}^{\infty}\int_0^{\tau_r} \left(1-\frac{t_1}{K}\right)\left(1-\frac{rt_1}{L}\right) dF(t_1| r)dG(r)$$

Policy 23 (b): Infinite Strips Two-Dimensional PRW Warranty Region: Here, follow the approach used in Policy 23(a). Conditioned on $R = r$, the rebate function, $R(t, x|r)$, is given by:

$$R(t,x\,|\,r) = R(t,rt) = \begin{cases} \left[1\text{–Min}\left(\frac{t}{K},\frac{rt}{L}\right)\right]\times C_s & \text{if } (t,rt)\in\Omega \\ 0 & \text{otherwise} \end{cases} \tag{11.32}$$

The expected refund per item, conditional on $R = r$, $E[R(T,RT|R=r)]$, is given by:

$$E[R(T_1, rT_1\,|\,r) = \begin{cases} \int_0^{\tau_r} R(t_1, rt_1\,|\,r)dF(t_1\,|\,r) & \text{if } r < r_1 \\ \int_0^{K} R(t_1, rt_1)dF(t_1\,|\,r) & \text{if } r \geq r_1 \end{cases} \tag{11.33}$$

where $F(t|r)$ is given by (11.28). As a result, $EC(\tilde{\theta})$, is given by:

$$EC(\tilde{\theta}) = E[R(T_1, rT_1\,|\,r)$$

$$= C_S \times \int_0^{r_1}\int_0^{\tau_r} \left[1-\text{Min}\left(\frac{t_1}{K},\frac{rt_1}{L}\right)\right] dF(t_1\,|\,r)dG(r) \tag{11.34}$$

$$+\int_{r_1}^{\infty}\int_0^{K} \left[1-\text{Min}\left(\frac{t_1}{K},\frac{rt_1}{L}\right)\right] dF(t_1\,|\,r)dG(r)$$

Example 11.3

Based on Data Set II (i) (see Section 6.4), the expected warranty costs determined from a non-renewing PRW formulation for different warranty periods and usages are shown in Table 11.5. Table 11.6 shows the confidence intervals for the ARTO simulation runs. The example here considers a non-renewing two-dimensional PRW policy for the remanufactured ACs with three different remaining lives (1 year, 2 years and 3 years), warranty periods (1 year, 2 years and 3 years) and usage (100 hours, 200 hours and 300 hours). The warranty expires when either the age or usage limit is reached. We assume that $W = U$ and consider values of $W = U = 1, 2$ and 3. These correspond to warranties of 1 year/100 hours, 2 years/200 hours and 3 years/300 hours, respectively.

Table 11.5 presents the expected cost for remanufactured ACs for the two-dimensional PRW policy. In Table 11.5, the expected cost to the remanufacturer includes the cost of supplying the original item, *Cs*. Thus, the expected cost of the warranty is calculated by subtracting *Cs* ($55) from the expected cost to the remanufacturer. For example, from Table 11.5, for $W = U = 1$ and $RL = 1$, the warranty costs for the remanufactured AC are $18.41 and $16.29 for Rectangular and Infinite Strips warranty shapes, respectively.

For a one-year remaining-life remanufactured AC sold with a one-year warranty, the ARTO system can claim with 90% confidence that the expected warranty cost is in the interval [$73.02–$75.57] and [$72.15–$81.08] for Rectangular and Infinite Strips warranty shapes, respectively, as shown in Table 11.6.

The expected warranty cost to the remanufacturer is increased by 13.86% and 26.65% compared to that of the FRW Policy for Rectangular and Infinite Strips warranty shapes, respectively.

TABLE 11.5

The Expected Warranty Costs for 2D PRW Policy

				Expected Cost to Remanufacturer		
Two-Dimensional RFRW	**Rectangular**	*Item*	$W = U$	$RL = 1$	$RL = 2$	$RL = 3$
		AC	1.00	$73.41	$70.42	$611.76
			2.00	$76.60	$77.43	$73.03
			3.00	$90.00	$88.67	$75.75
				Expected Cost to Remanufacturer		
	Infinite Strips	*Item*	$W = U$	$RL = 1$	$RL = 2$	$RL = 3$
		AC	1.00	$71.29	$76.07	$75.35
			2.00	$82.74	$83.64	$78.88
			3.00	$97.21	$95.77	$81.82

TABLE 11.6

Standard Error and Confidence Interval on 2D PRW Policy

							Confidence Interval					
				Standard Error			*RL* = 1		*RL* = 2		*RL* = 3	
Two-Dimensional RFRW	**Rectangular**	*Item*	*W* = *U*	*RL* = 1	*RL* = 2	*RL* = 3	*L limit*	*U limit*	*L limit*	*U limit*	*L limit*	*U limit*
		AC	1.00	0.80	1.18	1.79	$73.02	$75.57	$64.09	$77.47	$65.99	$78.37
			2.00	2.06	3.02	3.16	$75.04	$78.44	$70.46	$85.18	$61.09	$82.05
			3.00	3.96	4.53	5.21	$81.86	$93.57	$80.69	$97.53	$71.66	$85.10
							Confidence Interval					
				Standard Error			*RL* = 1		*RL* = 2		*RL* = 3	
	Infinite Strips	*Item*	*W* = *U*	*RL* = 1	*RL* = 2	*RL* = 3	*L limit*	*U limit*	*L limit*	*U limit*	*L limit*	*U limit*
		AC	1.00	0.66	0.97	1.47	$72.15	$81.08	$61.22	$83.67	$71.28	$84.65
			2.00	1.69	2.49	2.60	$75.29	$92.95	$76.11	$92.00	$74.62	$88.62
			3.00	3.26	3.73	4.30	$88.46	$101.22	$87.15	$105.34	$77.40	$91.92

11.2.2.2 Analysis of Two-Dimensional RPRW Policies

POLICY 25 (RENEWING PRW): Under this policy, if the remanufactured item fails in the warranty region Ω, a replacement item is supplied at a reduced price. This can be viewed as a conditional refund since the refund is tied to a replacement purchase.
Here, expressions for the expected warranty costs for Policies 25(a) and 25(b) are presented.

Policy 25 (a): Rectangular Two-Dimensional RPRW Warranty Region: Let $N = \tilde{N}(\tilde{\theta})$ denote the number of replacements under the warranty plus one and let $N_r = \tilde{N}(\tilde{\theta} \mid r)$ denote N conditioned on $R = r$. N_r is a stopping time for the renewal (or replacement) process. Conditioned on $R = r$, the probability that the remanufactured item fails under warranty is given by:

$$H(\tilde{\theta} \mid r) = \begin{cases} F(K \mid r) & \text{if } r < r_1 \\ F(\tau_r \mid r) & \text{if } r \geq r_1 \end{cases} \tag{11.35}$$

The probability that an item does not fail under the warranty (conditioned on $R = r$) is given by:

$$\bar{H}(\tilde{\theta} \mid r) = 1 - H(\tilde{\theta} \mid r) \tag{11.36}$$

As a result, N_r is distributed according to a geometric distribution function with probability mass function given by:

$$\text{Prob.}\{N_r = n\} = H(\tilde{\theta} \mid r)^{n-1}\left[1 - H(\tilde{\theta} \mid r)\right] \tag{11.37}$$

Hence, the expected value of N_r is given by:

$$E[N_r] = 1\Big/\left[1 - H(\tilde{\theta} \mid r)\right] \tag{11.38}$$

Let $Q = Q(\tilde{\theta})$ denote the total refund per remanufactured item sold at full price. Q is equal to the total refund resulting from all replacement remanufactured items plus the original item. Conditioned on $R = r$, let $Q_r = Q(\tilde{\theta} \mid r)$ denote Q conditioned on R = r. Q_r is given by:

$$Q_r = \sum_{i=1}^{N_r} R(T_i, rT_i \mid r) \tag{11.39}$$

Since N_r is a stopping time, using Wald's theorem (Ross, 1970), we have the expected value of Q_r given by:

$$E[Q_r] = E[N_r] \times E\left[R(T_i, rT_i | r)\right] \tag{11.40}$$

where $E[N_r]$ and $E[R(T_i,RT_i|R=r)]$ are given by (11.38) and (11.34), respectively. As a result, the expected warranty cost (i.e. the expected total refund) per remanufactured item, $EC(\tilde{\theta})$, is given by:

$$\begin{aligned} EC\left[\tilde{\theta}\right] = C_s \times \int_0^{r_1} \left[\frac{1}{1-F(K|r)} \int_0^{k} \left(1-\frac{t_1}{K}\right)\left(1-\frac{rt_1}{L}\right) dF(t_1|r) \right] dG(r) \\ + \int_{r_1}^{\infty} \left[\frac{1}{1-F(\tau_r|r)} \int_0^{\tau_r} \left(1-\frac{t_1}{K}\right)\left(1-\frac{rt_1}{L}\right) dF(t_1|r) \right] dG(r) \end{aligned} \tag{11.41}$$

Policy 25 (b): Infinite Strips Two-Dimensional RPRW Warranty Region: The approach to obtaining the expected warranty cost is similar to that for Policy 25(a), except that $R(t, rt)$ is given by (11.32) and $H(\tilde{\theta}\,|r)$ is given by:

$$H\left(\tilde{\theta}\,|\,r\right) = \begin{cases} F(\tau_r|r) & \text{if } r < r_1 \\ F(\tau_r|r) & \text{if } r \geq r_1 \end{cases} \tag{11.42}$$

As a result, the expected warranty cost, $EC(\tilde{\theta})$, is given by:

$$\begin{aligned} EC\left[\tilde{\theta}\right] = C_s \times \int_0^{r_1} \frac{1}{1-F(\tau_r|r)} \int_0^{\tau_r} \left[1-\mathrm{Min}\left(\frac{t}{K}, \frac{rt_1}{L}\right) dF(t_1|r)\right] dG(r) \\ + \int_{r_1}^{\infty} \left[\frac{1}{1-F(K|r)} \int_0^{K} \left[1-\mathrm{Min}\left(\frac{t}{K}, \frac{rt}{L}\right) dF(t|r)\right] dG(r) \right] \end{aligned} \tag{11.43}$$

Example 11.4

Based on Data Set II (i) (see Section 6.4), the expected warranty costs determined from the renewing PRW formulation for different warranty periods and usages are shown in Table 11.7. Table 11.8 shows the confidence intervals for the ARTO simulation runs. The example here considers a two-dimensional RPRW policy for the remanufactured ACs with three different remaining lives (1 year, 2 years and 3 years), warranty periods (1 year, 2 years and 3 years) and usage (100 hours, 200 hours and 300 hours). The warranty expires when either the age or usage limit is reached. First, assume $W = U$ and consider values of $W = U = 1$, 2 and 3. These correspond to warranties of 1 year/100 hours, 2 years/200 hours and 3 years/300 hours.

TABLE 11.7

The Expected Warranty Costs for 2D RPRW Policy

				Expected Cost to Remanufacturer		
Two-Dimensional RFRW	**Rectangular**	*Item*	$W = U$	$RL = 1$	$RL = 2$	$RL = 3$
		AC	1.00	\$82.47	\$79.11	\$687.29
			2.00	\$86.06	\$86.99	\$82.05
			3.00	\$101.11	\$99.62	\$85.10
				Expected Cost to Remanufacturer		
	Infinite Strips	*Item*	$W = U$	$RL = 1$	$RL = 2$	$RL = 3$
		AC	1.00	\$80.09	\$85.46	\$84.65
			2.00	\$92.96	\$93.97	\$88.62
			3.00	\$109.21	\$107.59	\$91.92

Table 11.7 presents the expected cost for remanufactured ACs for the two-dimensional RPRW policy. In Table 11.7, the expected cost to the remanufacturer includes the cost of supplying the original item, *Cs*. Thus, the expected cost of the warranty is calculated by subtracting *Cs* from the expected cost to the remanufacturer. For example, from Table 11.7, for $W = U= 1$ and $RL = 1$, the warranty cost for the remanufactured AC is \$27.47.41 and \$25.09 for Rectangular and Infinite Strips warranty shapes, respectively.

For a one-year remaining-life remanufactured AC sold with a one-year warranty, the ARTO system can claim with 90% confidence that the expected warranty cost is in the interval [\$84.32–\$101.80] and [\$90.07–\$109.95] for Rectangular and Infinite Strips warranty shapes, respectively, as shown in Table 11.8.

The expected warranty cost to the remanufacturer is increased by 12.35% compared to that of the PRW policy for a remanufactured AC. The expected warranty cost to the remanufacturer is increased by 4.33% and 16.85% compared to that of the RFRW and FRW policies with Rectangular warranty region, respectively. The expected warranty cost to the remanufacturer is increased by 34.71% and 36.33% compared to that of the RFRW and FRW policies with Infinite Strips warranty region, respectively.

11.2.3 Analysis of Two-Dimensional Combination Warranties

This section considers two combinations of two-dimensional FRW policies and PRW policies. Under an FRW policy, rectification of all failed items occurring under the warranty is done at no cost to the consumer, even if failures occur just prior to the expiry of the warranty. Consequently, this policy favors the consumer at the expense of the remanufacturer. In contrast, under a PRW policy, rectification of a failed item is not free. The consumer pays a fraction of the selling price to get a replacement item even if an item

TABLE 11.8

Standard Error and Confidence Interval on 2D RPRW Policy

							Confidence Interval					
					Standard Error		RL = 1		RL = 2		RL = 3	
Two-Dimensional RFRW		*Item*	*W = U*	*RL = 1*	*RL = 2*	*RL = 3*	*L limit*	*U limit*	*L limit*	*U limit*	*L limit*	*U limit*
	Rectangular	AC	1.00	0.90	1.33	2.01	\$84.32	\$101.80	\$81.16	\$97.66	\$81.00	\$96.74
			2.00	2.31	3.39	3.55	\$87.98	\$106.23	\$80.24	\$107.38	\$84.80	\$101.28
			3.00	4.45	5.09	5.85	\$103.37	\$124.82	\$102.18	\$113.97	\$87.96	\$105.04
							Confidence Interval					
					Standard Error		RL = 1		RL = 2		RL = 3	
		Item	*W = U*	*RL = 1*	*RL = 2*	*RL = 3*	*L limit*	*U limit*	*L limit*	*U limit*	*L limit*	*U limit*
	Infinite Strips	AC	1.00	0.74	1.09	1.65	\$91.07	\$109.95	\$87.65	\$105.49	\$87.49	\$104.49
			2.00	1.90	2.80	2.92	\$95.03	\$114.74	\$96.38	\$115.99	\$91.60	\$109.39
			3.00	3.66	4.19	4.83	\$102.67	\$134.81	\$110.36	\$132.82	\$95.00	\$113.46

fails early under warranty. As a result, this policy favors the remanufacturer at the expense of the consumer.

In this section, we carry out the analysis of Policies 26 and 27 to obtain expected warranty costs. Failure under the warranty is modeled using the one-dimensional approach and it is characterized through the conditional intensity function, $\lambda(t|r)$. As a result, the distribution of the time to the first failure is given by $F(t|r)$.

Let $EC(\tilde{\theta})$ denote the expected warranty cost per item. $\tilde{\theta}$ represents the policy parameter and for Policies 26 and 27, it is given by:

$$\tilde{\theta} = \{K_1, K_2, L_1, L_2\} \tag{11.44}$$

First obtain $EC(\tilde{\theta})$ for Policy 26 and later on for Policy 27. As mentioned earlier, this book confines its attention to combination warranties where the warranty region Ω consists of two disjoint sub-regions Ω_1 and Ω_2.

11.2.3.1 Analysis of Two-Dimensional Non-Renewing FRW-PRW Policy

POLICY 26 (COMBINED NON-RENEWING FRW & NON-RENEWING PRW POLICY): Under this policy, the remanufacturer replaces a failed item with a remanufactured one at no cost should the failure occur in Ω_1. The replacement item comes with a reduced warranty which is tied to the remanufactured and usage at failure. If the failure occurs in Ω_2, the remanufacturer refunds a fraction of the selling price. The refund is unconditional, and the amount refunded depends on the remaining life and usage at failure and is given by the refund function *R(t, x)*.

Policy 26 (a): Rectangular Two-Dimensional FRW-PRW Warranty Region: The warranty region Ω is given by Figure 11.2 with Ω_1 and Ω_2 is given by:

$$\Omega_1 = [0, W_1) \times [0, U_1) \tag{11.45}$$

$$\Omega_2 = \frac{[0, W_1) \times [0, U_1)}{\Omega_1} \tag{11.46}$$

and the refund function is given by:

$$R(t,x) = \begin{cases} \left(1 - \dfrac{t}{W_2}\right)\left(1 - \dfrac{x - U_1}{U_2 - U_1}\right) \times C_s & \text{if } 0 < t \le W_1; U_1 < x \le U_2 \\ \left(1 - \dfrac{t - W_1}{W_2 - W_1}\right)\left(1 - \dfrac{x - U_1}{U_2 - U_1}\right) \times C_s & \text{if } W_1 < t \le W_2; U_1 < x \le U_2 \\ \left(1 - \dfrac{t - W_1}{W - W_1}\right)\left(1 - \dfrac{x}{U_2}\right) \times C_s & \text{if } W_1 < t \le W_2; U_1 < x \le U_2 \end{cases} \tag{11.47}$$

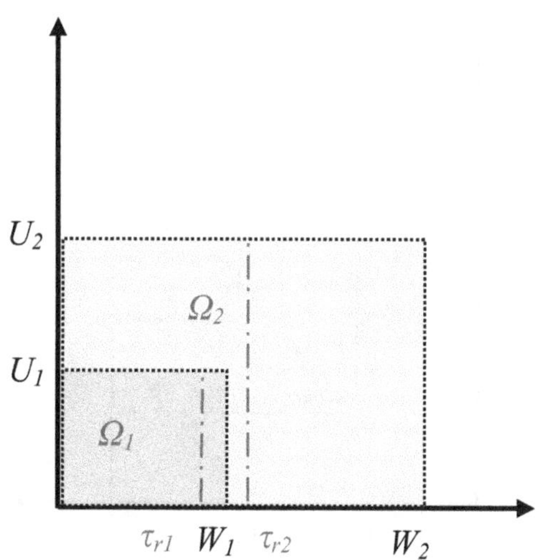

FIGURE 11.2
Warranty Regions for Policy 26(a) and Policy 27(a).

Using the condition $R = r$:

$$r_1 = \frac{U_1}{W_1} = \frac{U_2}{W_2} \tag{11.48}$$

The expected warranty cost $EC_r\,(\tilde{\theta})$ is given by:

$$EC\left[\tilde{\theta}\right] = \int_0^{r_1} EC_r\left(W_1, W\right)dG(r) + \int_{r_1}^{\infty} EC_r\left(\tau_{r1}, \tau_{r2}\right)dG(r) \tag{11.49}$$

Policy 26 (b): Infinite Strips Two-Dimensional FRW-PRW Warranty Region: The warranty region Ω is given by Figure 11.3 with Ω_1 and Ω_2 is given by:

$$\Omega_1 = \left\{\left[0, W_1\right) \times \left[0, \infty\right]\right\} \cup \left\{\left[W_1, \infty\right] \times \left[0, U_1\right)\right\} \tag{11.50}$$

$$\Omega_2 = \left\{\left[W_1, W_2\right) \times \left[U_1, \infty\right]\right\} \cup \left\{\left[W_2, \infty\right] \times \left[U_1, U_2\right)\right\} \tag{11.51}$$

and the refund function is given by:

$$R(t, x \mid r) = \begin{cases} \left[1 - \text{Min}\left(\dfrac{t - W_1}{W_2 - W_1}, \dfrac{x - U_1}{U_2 - U_1}\right)\right] \times C_s & \text{if } (t, x) \in \Omega_2 \\ 0 & \text{otherwise} \end{cases} \tag{11.52}$$

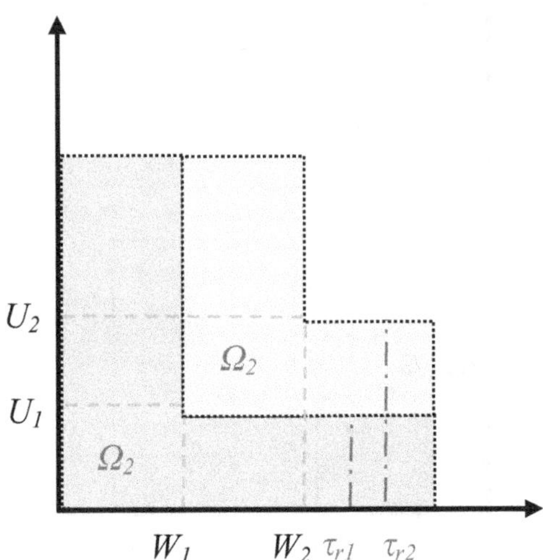

FIGURE 11.3
Warranty Regions for Policy 26(b) and Policy 27(b).

The expected warranty cost $EC_r(\tilde{\theta})$ is given by:

$$EC\left[\tilde{\theta}\right] = \int_{0}^{r_1} EC_r\left(W_1, W_2\right) dG(r) + \int_{r_1}^{\infty} EC_r\left(\tau_{r1}, \tau_{r2}\right) dG(r) \tag{11.53}$$

Example 11.5

Based on Data Set II (i) (see Section 6.4) the expected warranty costs determined from non-renewing FRW-PRW formulation for different warranty periods and usages are shown in Table 11.9. Table 11.10 shows the confidence intervals for the ARTO simulation runs. The example here considers a two-dimensional FRW-PRW policy for the remanufactured ACs with three different remaining lives (1 year, 2 years and 3 years), warranty periods (1 year, 2 years and 3 years) and usage (100 hours, 200 hours and 300 hours). The warranty expires when either the age or usage limit is reached. We assume that $W = U$ and consider values of $W = U = 1$, 2 and 3. These correspond to warranties of 1 year/100 hours, 2 years/200 hours and 3 years/300 hours, respectively.

Table 11.9 presents the expected cost for remanufactured ACs for the two-dimensional FRW-PRW policy. In Table 11.9, the expected cost to the remanufacturer includes the cost of supplying the original item, Cs. Thus, the expected cost of the warranty is calculated by subtracting Cs from the expected cost to the remanufacturer. For example, from Table 11.9, for $W = U= 1$ and $RL = 1$, the warranty cost for the remanufactured AC is \$16.99 and \$13.73 for Rectangular and Infinite Strips warranty shapes, respectively.

TABLE 11.9

The Expected Warranty Costs for 2D FRW-PRW Policy

				Expected Cost to Remanufacturer		
Two-Dimensional RFRW	**Rectangular**	*Item*	*W = U*	*RL = 1*	*RL = 2*	*RL = 3*
		AC	1.00	\$71.99	\$61.07	\$68.41
			2.00	\$75.12	\$75.94	\$71.62
			3.00	\$88.27	\$86.95	\$74.29
	Infinite Strips			Expected Cost to Remanufacturer		
		Item	*W = U*	*RL = 1*	*RL = 2*	*RL = 3*
		AC	1.00	\$68.73	\$65.93	\$65.31
			2.00	\$71.71	\$72.49	\$68.37
			3.00	\$84.26	\$83.01	\$70.92

For a one-year remaining life remanufactured AC sold with a one-year warranty, the ARTO system can claim with 90% confidence that the expected warranty cost is in the interval [\$65.51–\$80.88] and [\$62.54–\$77.21] for Rectangular and Infinite Strips warranty shapes, respectively, as shown in Table 11.23.

The expected warranty cost to the remanufacturer is increased by 2.97% compared to that of the FRW policy for a remanufactured AC component with Rectangular warranty region. The expected warranty cost to the remanufacturer is increased by 15.37% compared to that of the FRW policies with Infinite Strips warranty region. The expected warranty cost to the remanufacturer is reduced by 1.97% and 13.32% compared to that of the PRW with Rectangular and Infinite Strips warranty region, respectively.

11.2.3.2 Analysis of Two-Dimensional Renewing FRW-PRW Policy

POLICY 27 (COMBINED RENEWING FRW & RENEWING PRW POLICY): Under this policy, the remanufacturer replaces a failed item with a remanufactured one free of charge should failure occur in Ω1 and refunds a fraction of the selling price should failure occur in Ω2 Each replacement item comes with a new warranty identical to that of the original remanufactured item, and the refund is conditional, as it is tied to a replacement purchase and the amount refunded is given by the refund function R(t, x) if the remaining life and usage at failure are given (t, x).

Policy 27 (a): Rectangular Two-Dimensional RFRW-RPRW Warranty Region: The warranty region is given in Figure 11.2 with Ω_1 and Ω_2 given by (11.45) and (11.46) and the refund function given by (11.47). The expected warranty cost per item, $EC(\tilde{\theta})$, is given by:

TABLE 11.10

Standard Error and Confidence Interval on 2D FRW-PRW Policy

Two-Dimensional RFRW							Confidence Interval					
				Standard Error			*RL* = 1		*RL* = 2		*RL* = 3	
Rectangular	*Item*	*W* = *U*	*RL* = 1	*RL* = 2	*RL* = 3		*L limit*	*U limit*	*L limit*	*U limit*	*L limit*	*U limit*
	AC	1.00	0.71	1.05	1.59		$65.51	$80.88	$62.85	$75.97	$64.72	$76.86
		2.00	1.83	2.69	2.81		$68.36	$84.40	$61.10	$83.53	$67.76	$80.47
		3.00	3.53	4.03	4.64		$80.32	$91.16	$71.13	$95.65	$70.28	$83.46
							Confidence Interval					
				Standard Error			*RL* = 1		*RL* = 2		*RL* = 3	
Infinite Strips	*Item*	*W* = *U*	*RL* = 1	*RL* = 2	*RL* = 3		*L limit*	*U limit*	*L limit*	*U limit*	*L limit*	*U limit*
	AC	1.00	0.59	0.86	1.31		$62.54	$77.21	$60.00	$72.52	$61.78	$73.37
		2.00	1.51	2.21	2.32		$65.26	$80.57	$65.97	$71.74	$64.68	$76.81
		3.00	2.91	3.32	3.83		$76.68	$94.66	$75.54	$91.31	$67.09	$71.67

$$EC\left[\tilde{\theta}\right]=\int_{0}^{r_1}\left[cF(W_1|r)+\int_{W_1}^{W_2}\left\{C-\left(S-R(t,rt)\right)\right\}dF(t|r)\right]\Big/\left[1-F(W_2|r)\right]dG(r) \tag{11.54}$$

$$\int_{r_1}^{\infty}\left[cF(\tau_{r1}|r)+\int_{\tau_{r1}}^{\tau_{r2}}\left\{c-\left(S-R(t,rt)\right)\right\}dF(t|r)\right]\Big/\left[1-F(\tau_{r2}|r)\right]dG(r)$$

Policy 27 (b): Infinite Strips Two-Dimensional RFRW-RPRW Warranty Region: The warranty region is given in Figure 11.3 with Ω_1 and Ω_2 given by (11.50) and (11.51) and the refund function given by (11.52). The expected warranty cost, $EC(\tilde{\theta})$, is given by:

$$EC\left[\tilde{\theta}\right]=\int_{0}^{r_1}\left[cF(\tau_{r1}|r)+\int_{\tau_{r1}}^{\tau_{r2}}\left\{C-\left(S-R(t,rt)\right)\right\}dF(t|r)\right]\Big/\left[1-F(\tau_{r1}\ r)\right]dG(r)$$

$$\int_{r_1}^{\infty}\left[cF(W_1|r)+\int_{W_1}^{W_2}\left\{c-\left(S-R(t,rt)\right)\right\}dF(t|r)\right]\Big/\left[1-F(W_2\ r)\right]dG(r) \tag{11.55}$$

Example 11.6

Based on Data Set II (i) (see Section 6.4), the expected warranty costs determined from renewing the FRW-PRW formulation for different warranty periods and usages are shown in Table 11.11. Table 11.12 shows the confidence intervals for the ARTO simulation runs. The example here considers a two-dimensional RFRW-RPRW policy for the remanufactured AC product with three different remaining lives (1 year, 2 years and 3 years), warranty periods (1 year, 2 years and 3 years) and usage (100 hours, 200 hours and 300 hours). The warranty expires when either the age or usage limit is reached. We assume that $W = U$ and consider values of $W = U = 1, 2$ and 3. These correspond to warranties of 1 year/100 hours, 2 years/200 hours and 3 years/300 hours, respectively.

Table 11.11 presents the expected cost for a remanufactured AC for the two-dimensional RFRW-RPRW policy. In Table 11.11, the expected cost to the remanufacturer includes the cost of supplying the original item, Cs. Thus, the expected cost of the warranty is calculated by subtracting Cs from the expected cost to the remanufacturer. For example, from Table 11.11, for $W = U = 1$ and $RL = 1$, the warranty cost for the remanufactured AC is \$25.88 and \$22.21 for Rectangular and Infinite Strips warranty shapes respectively.

TABLE 11.11

The Expected Warranty Costs for 2D RFRW-RPRW Policy

				Expected Cost to Remanufacturer		
Two-Dimensional RFRW	**Rectangular**	*Item*	$W = U$	$RL = 1$	$RL = 2$	$RL = 3$
		AC	1.00	$80.88	$77.59	$76.86
			2.00	$84.40	$85.31	$80.47
			3.00	$911.16	$97.69	$83.46
				Expected Cost to Remanufacturer		
	Infinite Strips	*Item*	$W = U$	$RL = 1$	$RL = 2$	$RL = 3$
		AC	1.00	$77.21	$74.07	$73.37
			2.00	$80.57	$81.44	$76.81
			3.00	$94.66	$93.26	$711.67

For a one-year remaining-life remanufactured AC sold with a one-year warranty, the ARTO system can claim with 90% confidence that the expected warranty cost is in the interval [$73.60–$90.87] and [$70.26–$86.74] for Rectangular and Infinite Strips warranty shapes, respectively, as shown in Table 11.12.

The expected warranty cost to the remanufacturer is increased by 2.01% compared to that of the RFRW policy for a remanufactured AC component with Rectangular warranty region. The expected warranty cost to the remanufacturer is increased by 18.16% compared to that of the RFRW policies with Infinite Strips warranty region. The expected warranty cost to the remanufacturer is reduced by 1.93% and 15.37% compared to that of the RPRW with Rectangular and Infinite Strips warranty region, respectively.

11.3 Conclusions

In this chapter, six two-dimensional warranty policies, namely, Non-Renewing 2D Free-Replacement Warranty (2D FRW), Non-Renewing 2D Pro-Rata Warranty (2D PRW), Renewing 2D Free-Replacement Warranty (2D RFRW), Renewing 2D Pro-Rata Warranty (2D RPRW), Combination (2D FRW-PRW) and Combination (2D RFRW-RPRW), were discussed.

TABLE 11.12
Standard Error and Confidence Interval on 2D RFRW-RPRW Policy

							Confidence Interval					
			Standard Error				RL = 1		RL = 2		RL = 3	
Two-Dimensional RFRW												
Rectangular	*Item*	W = U	RL = 1	RL = 2	RL = 3		*L limit*	*U limit*	*L limit*	*U limit*	*L limit*	*U limit*
	AC	1.00	0.79	1.16	1.76		$73.60	$90.87	$70.61	$85.35	$72.71	$86.35
		2.00	1.98	3.25	3.24		$76.80	$94.82	$77.64	$93.85	$76.12	$90.40
		3.00	3.58	4.19	4.74		$90.24	$111.41	$88.90	$107.46	$78.95	$93.76
							Confidence Interval					
			Standard Error				RL = 1		RL = 2		RL = 3	
Infinite Strips	*Item*	W = U	RL = 1	RL = 2	RL = 3		*L limit*	*U limit*	*L limit*	*U limit*	*L limit*	*U limit*
	AC	1.00	0.65	0.96	1.45		$70.26	$86.74	$67.40	$81.48	$611.41	$82.43
		2.00	1.63	2.68	2.67		$73.32	$90.51	$74.11	$81.59	$72.67	$86.30
		3.00	2.95	3.45	3.91		$86.14	$106.35	$84.86	$102.58	$75.37	$81.51

12

Conclusion

The importance of warranty and preventive maintenance for remanufactured products is increasing because consumers are becoming more and more demanding of the quality of remanufactured products and future costs of replacement/repair in case of product failures. Therefore, warranty and preventive maintenance management can be very important to remanufacturers. They need to estimate the warranty cost to factor it into the price structure. Failure to do so can result in the remanufacturer incurring a loss, as opposed to profit, with the sale of remanufactured items. Analysis of warranty cost for remanufactured products is more complex when compared to new products because of the uncertainties in usage and maintenance history. Moreover, warranty policies similar to new and secondhand products may not be economically acceptable to the remanufacturer. Therefore, it is necessary to show how warranties could be applied to remanufactured products and estimate the expected warranty costs associated with these policies.

This book addressed the issues that arise in implementing warranty policies to remanufactured products. The book introduced 27 different warranty policies for remanufactured products with a preventive maintenance strategy. They ranged from non-renewing to renewing, simple to combined, as well as one-dimensional to two-dimensional policies. Mathematical models were presented to analyze warranty costs with preventive maintenance for the remanufactured products when failures occurred at either the system or component level. A representative remanufacturing facility, called the Advanced Remanufacture-To-Order (ARTO) system, was introduced and considered to analyze the performance of various policies considered throughout the book.

The primary purpose of this book was to elucidate the warranty and preventive maintenance application to remanufactured products and articulate quantitative assessment of the effect of offering warranties, which covers the cost of remanufacturing from the remanufacturers' perspective, as well as an appealing price from the buyer's perspective. While there are studies on the development of warranty policies for new products and a few on secondhand products, studies which evaluate the potential benefits of warranties on remanufactured products in a quantitative and comprehensive fashion are lacking. This book fills that gap and addresses the issues that arise in implementing various warranty policies on remanufactured products. The issues addressed in this book may serve as foundations for the analysis of new and creative warranty proposals for remanufactured products.

References

Abbey, J. D., & Guide Jr, V. D. R. (2017). Closed-loop supply chains: a strategic overview. In: *Sustainable Supply Chains* (pp. 375–393). Springer International Publishing.

Addelman, S. (1962). Orthogonal main-effect plans for asymmetrical factorial experiments. *Technometrics*, **4**(1), 21–46.

Agrawal, S., Rajesh, K. S., & Murtaza, Q. (2015). A literature review and perspectives in reverse logistics. *Resources, Conservation and Recycling*, **97**, 76–92.

Ait-Kadi, D., & Cléroux, R. (1988). Optimal block replacement policies with multiple choice at failure. *Naval Research Logistic*. 35, 99–110.

Akcali, E., & Çetinkaya, S. (2011). Quantitative models for inventory and production planning in closed-loop supply chains. *International Journal of Production Research*, **49**(8), 2373–2407.

Akcali, E., Çetinkaya, S., & Üster, H. (2009). Network design for reverse and closed-loop supply chains: an annotated bibliography of models and solution approaches. *Networks*, **53**(3), 231–248.

Aksezer, C. S. (2011). Failure analysis and warranty modeling of used cars. *Engineering Failure Analysis*, **18**(6), 1520–1526.

Aksoy, H. K., & Gupta, S. M. (2005). Buffer allocation plan for a remanufacturing cell. *Computers & Industrial Engineering*, **48**(3), 657–677.

Alqahtani, A. Y., & Gupta, S. M. (2017a). Optimizing two-dimensional renewable warranty policies for sensor embedded remanufacturing products. *Journal of Industrial Engineering and Management*, **10**(2), 73–89.

Alqahtani, A. Y., & Gupta, S. M. (2017b). One-dimensional renewable warranty management within sustainable supply chain. *Resources*, **6**(2), 16–41.

Alqahtani, A. Y., & Gupta, S. M. (2017c). Warranty and maintainability analysis for sensor embedded remanufactured products in reverse supply chain environment. *International Journal of Supply Chain Management*, **6**(4), 22–42.

Alqahtani, A. Y., & Gupta, S. M. (2017d). Warranty and preventive maintenance analysis for sustainable reverse supply chains. *Journal of Management Science and Engineering*, **2**(1), 69–94.

Alqahtani, A. Y., & Gupta, S. M. (2017e). Evaluating two-dimensional warranty policies for remanufactured products. *Journal of Remanufacturing*, **7**(1), 19–47.

Alqahtani, A. Y., & Gupta, S. M. (2017). Warranty as a marketing strategy for remanufactured products. *Journal of Cleaner Production*, **161**(1), 1294–1307.

Alqahtani, A. Y., & Gupta, S. M. (2018). Money-back guarantee warranty policy with preventive maintenance strategy for sensor-embedded remanufactured products. *Journal of Industrial Engineering International*, **14**(1), 1–16.

Alqahtani, A. Y., Gupta, S. M., & Nakashima, K. (2014). Performance analysis of advanced remanufacture-to-order, disassembly-to-order and refurbishment-to-order system. *Innovation and Supply Chain Management*, **8**(4), 140–149.

Amezquita, T., & Bras, B. (1996). Lean remanufacture of an automobile clutch. In Proceedings of *First International Working Seminar on Reuse*, Eindhoven, The Netherlands.

Anityasari, M., Kaebernick, H., & Kara, S. (2007). The role of warranty in the reuse strategy. *Advances in Life Cycle Engineering for Sustainable Manufacturing Businesses* (pp. 335–340). Springer London.

Arnold, B. C., & Huang, J. S. (1995). Characterization. In: *The Exponential Distribution: Theory, Methods and Application*. (Eds., N. Balakrishnan and A. P. Basu) (pp. 185–203). Gordon and Breach Science Publishers, Newark, New Jersey.

Ayres, R., Ferrer, G., & Van Leynseele, T. (1997). Eco-efficiency, asset recovery and remanufacturing. *European Management Journal*, **15**(5), 557–574.

Baik, J., Murthy, D. N. P., & Jack, N. (2004). Two-dimensional failure modeling with minimal repair. *Naval Research Logistics (NRL)*, **51**(3), 345–362.

Balachander, S. (2001). Warranty signalling and reputation. *Management Science*, **47**(9), 1282–1289.

Bandivadekar, A. P., Kumar, V., Gunter, K. L., & Sutherland, J. W. (2004). A model for material flows and economicexchanges within the US automotive life cycle chain. *Journal of Manufacturing Systems*, **23**(1), 22–29.

Barange, S., & Agarwal, S. (2016). Green supply chain management–a review. *International Journal of Innovative Research and Advanced Studies*, **3**(4), 48–50.

Barlow, R., & Hunter, L. (1960). Optimum preventive maintenance policies. *Operations Research*, **8**(1), 90–100.

Basaly, N. A., & Billatos, S. B. (1997). *Green Technology and Design for the Environment*. CRC Press.

Ben Mabrouk, A., Chelbi, A., & Radhoui, M. (2016). Optimal imperfect preventive maintenance policy for equipment leased during successive periods. *International Journal of Production Research*, **54**(17), 5095–5110.

Berke, T. M., & Zaino, N. A. (1991). Warranties: what are they? What do they really cost? In *Reliability and Maintainability Symposium, 1991. Proceedings, Annual* (pp. 326–331). IEEE.

Bevilacqua, M., Braglia, M., Carmignani, G., & Zammori, F. A. (2007a). Life cycle assessment of pasta production in Italy. *Journal of Food Quality*, **30**(6), 932–952.

Bevilacqua, M., Ciarapica, F. E., & Giacchetta, G. (2007b). Development of a sustainable product lifecycle in manufacturing firms: a case study. *International Journal of Production Research*, **45**(18–19), 4073–4098.

Billatos, S. B., & Basaly, N. A. (1997). Challenges and solutions to design for recycling. *International Journal of Environmentally Conscious Design and Manufacturing*, **6**, 1–12.

Blackburn, J. D., Guide Jr, V. D. R., Souza, G. C., & Van Wassenhove, L. N. (2004). Reverse supply chains for commercial returns. *California Management Review*, **46**(2), 6–22.

Blischke, W. R. (1995). *Product Warranty Handbook*. CRC Press.

Blischke, W. R. (Ed.). (1993). *Warranty Cost Analysis*. CRC Press.

Blischke, W. R., & Murthy, D. N. P. (1992). Product warranty management—I: a taxonomy for warranty policies. *European Journal of Operational Research*, **62**(2), 127–148.

Blischke, W. R. & Murthy, D. N. P. (1993). *Warranty Cost Analysis*. CRC Press, Boca Raton, FL.

Blischke, W. R., & Murthy, D. N. P. (2011). *Reliability: Modeling, Prediction, and Optimization*. John Wiley & Sons.

Blischke, W. R., Karim, M. R., & Murthy, D. N. P. (2011). *Warranty Data Collection and Analysis*. Springer Science & Business Media.

Bogue, R. (2007). Design for disassembly: a critical twenty-first century discipline. *Assembly Automation*, **27**(4), 285–289.

Boks, C., & Stevels, A. (2007). Essential perspectives for design for environment. Experiences from the electronics industry. *International Journal of Production Research*, **45**(18–19), 4021–4039.

Boon, J. E., Isaacs, J. A., & Gupta, S. M. (2000). Economic impact of aluminum-intensive vehicles on the US automotive recycling infrastructure. *Journal of Industrial Ecology*, **4**(2), 117–134.

Boon, J. E., Isaacs, J. A., & Gupta, S. M. (2003). End-of-life infrastructure economics for "clean vehicles" in the United States. *Journal of Industrial Ecology*, **7**(1), 25–45.

Boudhar, H., Dahane, M., & Rezg, N. (2014). New dynamic heuristic for the optimization of opportunities to use new and remanufactured spare part in stochastic degradation context. *Journal of Intelligent Manufacturing*, 1–18.

Bouguerra, S., Chelbi, A., & Rezg, N. (2012). A decision model for adopting an extended warranty under different maintenance policies. *International Journal of Production Economics*, **135**(2), 840–849.

Bovea, M. D., & Wang, B. (2003). Identifying environmental improvement options by combining life cycle assessment and fuzzy set theory. *International Journal of Production Research*, **41**(3), 593–609.

Bovea, M. D., & Wang, B. (2007). Redesign methodology for developing environmentally conscious products. *International Journal of Production Research*, **45**(18–19), 4057–4072.

Bras, B., & Hammond, R. (1996). Towards design for remanufacturing—metrics for assessing remanufacturability. In Proceedings of the *1st International Workshop on Reuse* (pp. 5–22). Eindhoven, The Netherlands.

Bras, B., & McIntosh, M. W. (1999). Product, process, and organizational design for remanufacture–an overview of research. *Robotics and Computer-Integrated Manufacturing*, **15**(3), 167–178.

Brennan, L., Gupta, S. M., & Taleb, K. N. (1994). Operations planning issues in an assembly/disassembly environment. *International Journal of Operations & Production Management*, **14**(9), 57–67.

Carter, C. R., & Ellram, L. M. (1998). Reverse logistics: a review of the literature and framework for future investigation. *Journal of Business Logistics*, **19**(1), 85.

Cederberg, C., & Mattsson, B. (2000). Life cycle assessment of milk production—a comparison of conventional and organic farming. *Journal of Cleaner production*, **8**(1), 49–60.

Chan, J. W., & Tong, T. K. (2007). Multi-criteria material selections and end-of-life product strategy: grey relational analysis approach. *Materials & Design*, **28**(5), 1539–1546.

Chang, W. L., & Lin, J. H. (2012). Optimal maintenance policy and length of extended warranty within the life cycle of products. *Computers & Mathematics with Applications*, **63**(1), 144–150.

Chang, W. L., & Lo, H.-C. (2011). Joint determination of lease period and preventive maintenance policy for leased equipment with residual value. *Computers & Industrial Engineering*, **61**(3), 489–496.

Chanintrakul, P., Coronado Mondragon, A. E., Lalwani, C., & Wong, C. Y. (2009). Reverse logistics network design: a state-of-the-art literature review. *International Journal of Business Performance and Supply Chain Modelling*, **1**(1), 61–81.

Chari, N., Diallo, C., & Venkatadri, U. (2013). Optimal unlimited free-replacement warranty strategy using reconditioned products. *International Journal of Performability Engineering*, **9**(2), 191–200.

Chari, N., Diallo, C., Venkatadri, U., & Ait-Kadi, D. (2012). EOL warranty and spare parts manufacturing strategy using new and reconditioned parts. In Proceedings of the *54th Annual Conference of the Canadian Operational Research Society* and the *10th International Conference on Multiple Objective Programming and Goal Programming* CORS/MOPGP, Niagara Falls, Canada.

Charter, M., & Gray, C. (2008). Remanufacturing and product design. *International Journal of Product Development*, **6**(3–4), 375–392.

Chattopadhyay, G. N., & Murthy, D. N. P. (2000). Warranty cost analysis for second-hand products. *Mathematical and Computer Modelling*, **31**(10), 81–88.

Chattopadhyay, G. N., & Murthy, D. N. P. (2001). Cost sharing warranty policies for second-hand products. *International Transactions in Operational Research*, **8**(1), 47–60.

Chattopadhyay, G. N., & Murthy, D. N. P. (2004). Optimal reliability improvement for used items sold with warranty. *International Journal of Reliability and Applications*, **5**(2), 47–58.

Chattopadhyay, G. N., & Rahman, A. (2008). Development of lifetime warranty policies and models for estimating costs. *Reliability Engineering & System Safety*, **93**(4), 522–529.

Chen, J. A., & Chien, Y. H. (2007). Renewing warranty and preventive maintenance for products with failure penalty post-warranty. *Quality and Reliability Engineering International*, **23**(1), 107–121.

Cheng, F. T., Huang, G. W., Chen, C. H., & Hung, M. H. (2004). A generic embedded device for retrieving and transmitting information of various customized applications. In Proceedings of the *International Conference on Robotics and Automation*, ICRA (pp. 978–983).

Cheng, Z. H., Yang, Z. Y., Zhao, J. M., Wang, Y. B., & Li, Z. W. (2015). Preventive maintenance strategy optimizing model under two-dimensional warranty policy. *Eksploatacja i Niezawodność*, 17.

Chien, Y. H. (2005). Determining optimal warranty periods from the seller's perspective and optimal out-of-warranty replacement age from the buyer's perspective. *International Journal of Systems Science*, **36**(10), 631–637.

Chien, Y. H. (2008). A general age-replacement model with minimal repair under renewing free-replacement warranty. *European Journal of Operational Research*, **186**(3), 1046–1058.

Chien, Y. H. (2010). Optimal age for preventive replacement under a combined fully renewable free replacement with a pro-rata warranty. *International Journal of Production Economics*, **124**(1), 198–205.

Chukova, S., & Johnston, M. R. (2006). Two-dimensional warranty repair strategy based on minimal and complete repairs. *Mathematical and Computer Modelling*, **44**(11), 1133–1143.

Chukova, S., & Shafiee, M. (2013). One-dimensional warranty cost analysis for second-hand items: an overview. *International Journal of Quality & Reliability Management*, **30**(3), 239–255.

Chun, Y. H. (1992). Optimal number of periodic preventive maintenance operations under warranty. *Reliability Engineering & System Safety*, **37**(3), 223–225.

Chun, Y. H., & Lee, C. S. (1992). Optimal replacement policy for a warrantied system with imperfect preventive maintenance operations. *Microelectronics Reliability*, **32**(6), 839–843.

Corbu, D., Chukova, S., & O'Sullivan, J. (2008). Product warranty: modelling with 2D-renewal process. *International Journal of Reliability and Safety*, **2**(3), 209–220.

Correia, E., Carvalho, H., Azevedo, S. G., & Govindan, K. (2017). Maturity models in supply chain sustainability: a systematic literature review. *Sustainability*, **9**(1), 64.

Cox, D. R. (1962). Further results on tests of separate families of hypotheses. *Journal of the Royal Statistical Society. Series B (Methodological)*, 406–424.

Cox, J. F., & Blackstone, J. H. (Eds.). (2002). *APICS Dictionary*. Amer Production & Inventory.

Curkovic, S., & Sroufe, R. (2016). A literature review and taxonomy of environmentally responsible manufacturing. *American Journal of Industrial and Business Management*, **6**(3), 323.

Darghouth, M. N., Chelbi, A., & Ait-Kadi, D. (2015). On reliability improvement of second-hand products. *IFAC-PapersOnLine*, **48**(3), 2158–2163.

Darghouth, M. N., Chelbi, A., & Ait-Kadi, D. (2017). Investigating reliability improvement of second-hand production equipment considering warranty and preventive maintenance strategies. *International Journal of Production Research*, 1–19.

Desai, A., & Mital, A. (2003). Review of literature on disassembly algorithms and design for disassembly guidelines for product design. *International Journal of Industrial Engineering-Theory Applications and* Practice, **10**(3), 244–255.

Diallo, C., Venkatadri, U., Khatab, A., & Bhakthavatchalam, S. (2016). State of the art review of quality, reliability and maintenance issues in closed-loop supply chains with remanufacturing. *International Journal of Production Research*, **55**(5), 1–20.

Djamaludin, I., Murthy, D. N. P., & Kim, C. S. (2001). Warranty and preventive maintenance. *International Journal of Reliability, Quality and Safety Engineering*, **8**(2), 89–107.

Dong, J., & Arndt, G. (2003). A review of current research on disassembly sequence generation and computer aided design for disassembly. In Proceedings of the *Institution of Mechanical Engineers, Part B: Journal of Engineering Manufacture*, **217**(3), 299–312.

Dong, Y., Kaku, I., & Tang, J. (2005). Inventory management in reverse logistics: a survey. In Proceedings of the *International Conference on Services Systems and Services Management* ICSSSM (pp. 352–356).

Ehrlich, P. R., & Ehrlich, A. H. (1991). *Healing the Planet: Strategies for Resolving the Environmental Crisis*. Addison Wesley, Reading, Massachusetts.

Ehrlich, P. R., Ehrlich, A. H., & Daily, G. C. (1993). Food security, population and environment. *Population and Development Review*, **19**(1), 1–32.

Esmaeilian, B., Behdad, S., & Wang, B. (2016). The evolution and future of manufacturing: a review. *Journal of Manufacturing Systems*, **39**, 79–100.

Fang, H. C., Ong, S. K., & Nee, A. Y. C. (2015). Use of embedded smart sensors in products to facilitate remanufacturing. In *Handbook of Manufacturing Engineering and Technology* (pp. 3265–3290). Springer London.

Feldmann, K., Meedt, O., Trautner, S., Scheller, H., & Hoffman, W. (1999). The green design advisor: a tool for design for environment. *Journal of Electronics Manufacturing*, **9**(1), 17–28.

Ferguson, N., & Browne, J. (2001). Issues in end-of-life product recovery and reverse logistics. *Production Planning & Control*, **12**(5), 534–547.

Ferrer, G., Heath, S. K., & Dew, N. (2011). An RFID application in large job shop remanufacturing operations. *International Journal of Production Economics*, **133**(2), 612–621.

Fiksel, J. R. (1996). *Design for Environment: Creating Eco-Efficient Products and Processes*. McGraw-Hill Professional Publishing.

Fiksel, J., & Wapman, K. (1994). How to design for environment and minimize life cycle cost. In Proceedings of the *International Symposium on Electronics and the Environment, ISEE* (pp. 75–80).

Fisher, M., Hammond, J., Obermeyer, W., & Raman, A. (1997). Configuring a supply chain to reduce the cost of demand uncertainty. *Production and Operations Management*, **6**(3), 211–225.

Fleischmann, M., Bloemhof-Ruwaard, J. M., Dekker, R., Van der Laan, E., Van Nunen, J. A., & Van Wassenhove, L. N. (1997). Quantitative models for reverse logistics: a review. *European Journal of Operational Research*, **103**(1), 1–17.

Fleischmann, M., Krikke, H. R., Dekker, R., & Flapper, S. D. P. (2000). A characterisation of logistics networks for product recovery. *Omega*, **28**(6), 653–666.

Gal-Or, E. (1989). Warranties as a signal of quality. *Canadian Journal of Economics*, 50–61.

Garg, A., & Deshmukh, S. G. (2006). Maintenance management: literature review and directions. *Journal of Quality in Maintenance Engineering*, **12**(3), 205–238.

General Motors (2014). 2014 annual report of the General Motors Company. Retrieved from https://www.gm.com/content/dam/gm/en_us/english/Group4/InvestorsPDFDocuments/2014_GM_Annual_Report.pdf.

Geyer, R., & Jackson, T. (2004). Supply loops and their constraints: the industrial ecology of recycling and reuse. *California Management Review*, **46**(2), 55–73.

Giudice, F., La Rosa, G., & Risitano, A. (2005). Materials selection in the life-cycle design process: a method to integrate mechanical and environmental performances in optimal choice. *Materials & Design*, **26**(1), 9–20.

Giudice, F., La Rosa, G., & Risitano, A. (2006). *Product Design for the Environment: A Life Cycle Approach*. CRC Press.

Govindan, K., & Soleimani, H. (2017). A review of reverse logistics and closed-loop supply chains: a Journal of Cleaner Production focus. *Journal of Cleaner Production*, **142**(1), 371–384.

Govindan, K., Fattahi, M., & Keyvanshokooh, E. (2017). Supply chain network design under uncertainty: a comprehensive review and future research directions. *European Journal of Operational Research*, https://doi.org/10.1016/j.ejor.2017.04.009

Govindan, K., Soleimani, H., & Kannan, D. (2015). Reverse logistics and closed-loop supply chain: a comprehensive review to explore the future. *European Journal of Operational Research*, **240**(3), 603–626.

Grote, C. A., Jones, R. M., Blount, G. N., Goodyer, J., & Shayler, M. (2007). An approach to the EuP Directive and the application of the economic eco-design for complex products. *International Journal of Production Research*, **45**(18–19), 4099–4117.

Guerriero, F., Frugiuele, M., & Furfari, A. (2010). Forecasting models for manufacturer warranty returns: a case study. *Journal of Statistics and Management Systems*, **13**(6), 1363–1398.

Guide Jr, V. D. R. (2000). Production planning and control for remanufacturing: industry practice and research needs. *Journal of Operations Management*, **18**(4), 467–483.

Guide Jr, V. D. R., Jayaraman, V., & Srivastava, R. (1999). Production planning and control for remanufacturing: a state-of-the-art survey. *Robotics and Computer-Integrated Manufacturing*, **15**(3), 221–230.

Güngör, A., & Gupta, S. M. (1999). Issues in environmentally conscious manufacturing and product recovery: a survey. *Computers & Industrial Engineering*, **36**(4), 811–853.

Güngör, A., & Gupta, S. M. (2001). A solution approach to the disassembly line balancing problem in the presence of task failures. *International Journal of Production Research*, **39**(7), 1427–1467.

Guo, R., Ascher, H., & Love, E. (2001). Towards practical and synthetical modelling of repairable systems. *Economic Quality Control*, **16**(1), 147–182.

Gupta, S. M., Imtanavanich, P., & Nakashima, K. (2009). Using neural networks to solve a disassembly-to-order problem. *International Journal of Biomedical Soft Computing and Human Sciences*, *15*(1), 67–71.

Harjula, T., Rapoza, B., Knight, W. A., & Boothroyd, G. (1996). Design for disassembly and the environment. *CIRP Annals-Manufacturing Technology*, **45**(1), 109–114.

Heal, G. (1977). Guarantees and risk-sharing. *The Review of Economic Studies*, 549–560.

Holloway, L. (1998). Materials selection for optimal environmental impact in mechanical design. *Materials & Design*, **19**(4), 133–143.

Horvath, A., Hendrickson, C. T., Lave, L. B., McMichael, F. C., & Wu, T. S. (1995). Toxic emissions indices for green design and inventory. *Environmental Science & Technology*, **29**(2), 86A–90A.

Huang, Y. S., & Yen, C. (2009). A study of two-dimensional warranty policies with preventive maintenance. *IIE Transactions*, **41**(4), 299–308.

Huang, Y. S., Lo, H.-C., & Ho, J. W. (2008). Design of effective inspection schema for imperfect production systems. *International Journal of Production Research*, **46**(16), 4537–4551.

Ilgin, M. A., & Gupta, S. M. (2010). Environmentally conscious manufacturing and product recovery (ECMPRO): a review of the state of the art. *Journal of Environmental Management*, **91**(3), 563–591.

Ilgin, M. A., & Gupta, S. M. (2011a). Evaluating the impact of sensor-embedded products on the performance of an air conditioner disassembly line. *International Journal of Advanced Manufacturing Technology*, **53**(9–12), 1199–1216.

Ilgin, M. A., & Gupta, S. M. (2011b). Recovery of sensor embedded washing machines using a multi-kanban controlled disassembly line. *Robotics and Computer-Integrated Manufacturing*, **27**(2), 318–334.

Ilgin, M. A., & Gupta, S. M. (2012a). Physical programming: a review of the state of the art. *Studies in Informatics and Control*, **21**(4), 349–366.

Ilgin, M. A., & Gupta, S. M. (2012b). *Remanufacturing Modeling and Analysis*. CRC Press.

Ilgin, M. A., Gupta, S. M., & Battaïa, O. (2015). Use of MCDM techniques in environmentally conscious manufacturing and product recovery: state of the art. *Journal of Manufacturing Systems*, **37**, 746–758.

Imtanavanich, P., & Gupta, S. M. (2006). Calculating disassembly yields in a multi-criteria decision-making environment for a disassembly-to-order system. In *Applications of Management Science: In Productivity, Finance, and Operations* (pp. 109–125). Emerald Group Publishing Limited.

Inderfurth, K., & Langella, I. M. (2006). Heuristics for solving disassemble-to-order problems with stochastic yields. *OR Spectrum*, **28**(1), 73–99.

Isaacs, J. A., & Gupta, S. M. (1997). Economic consequences of increasing polymer content for the US automobile recycling infrastructure. *Journal of Industrial Ecology*, **1**(4), 19–33.

Iskandar, B. P., & Murthy, D. N. P. (2003). Repair-replace strategies for two-dimensional warranty policies. *Mathematical and Computer Modelling*, **38**(11–13), 1233–1241.

ISO, 1997. Standard on Environmental Management: Life Cycle Assessment, DIS 14040. International Organisation for Standardisation.

Jack, N., & Dagpunar, J. S. (1994). An optimal imperfect maintenance policy over a warranty period. *Microelectronics Reliability*, **34**(3), 529–534.

Jack, N., & Murthy, D. N. P. (2002). A new preventive maintenance strategy for items sold under warranty. *IMA Journal of Management Mathematics*, **13**(2), 121–129.

Jack, N., & Van der Duyn Schouten, F. (2000). Optimal repair–replace strategies for a warranted product. *International Journal of Production Economics*, **67**(1), 95–100.

Jack, N., Iskandar, B. P., & Murthy, D. N. P. (2009). A repair–replace strategy based on usage rate for items sold with a two-dimensional warranty. *Reliability Engineering & System Safety*, **94**(2), 611–617.

Jacobsson, N. (2000). Emerging product strategies: selling services of remanufactured products. Licenciate thesis at the *International Institute for Industrial Environmental Economics* (IIIEE), Lund University, Sweden.

Jafar Raam, B., & Mahsa, S. N. (2015). Comparative studies of three types of product policies (remanufactured, refurbished and new products) on warranty cost and profitability. In UniMap Library, Digital Repository. *International Journal of Business and Technopreneurship.*

Jain, M., & Maheshwari, S. (2006). Discounted costs for repairable units under hybrid warranty. *Applied Mathematics and Computation*, **173**(2), 887–901.

Jayaraman, V. (2006). Production planning for closed-loop supply chains with product recovery and reuse: an analytical approach. *International Journal of Production Research*, **44**(5), 981–998.

Jayaraman, V., Guide Jr, V. D. R., & Srivastava, R. (1999). A closed-loop logistics model for remanufacturing. *Journal of the Operational Research Society*, **50**(5), 497–508.

Jena, S. K., & Sarmah, S. P. (2016). Price and service co-opetiton under uncertain demand and condition of used items in a remanufacturing system. *International Journal of Production Economics*, **173**, 1–21.

Jung, K. M., Park, M., & Park, D. H. (2010). System maintenance cost dependent on life cycle under renewing warranty policy. *Reliability Engineering & System Safety*, **95**(7), 816–821.

Jung, M., & Bai, D. S. (2007). Analysis of field data under two-dimensional warranty. *Reliability Engineering & System Safety*, **92**(2), 135–143.

Karlsson, B. (1997). A distributed data processing system for industrial recycling. In Proceedings of *IEEE Instrumentation and Measurement Technology Conference.* 197–200.

Karlsson, B. (1998). Fuzzy handling of uncertainty in industrial recycling. In Proceedings of *IEEE Instrumentation and Measurement Technology Conference.* 832–836.

Kempthorne, O. (1979). *The Design and Analysis of Experiments*. Oxford, England: Wiley

Khatab, A., Ait-Kadi, D., & Rezg, N. (2014). Availability optimisation for stochastic degrading systems under imperfect preventive maintenance. *International Journal of Production Research*, **52**(14), 4132–4141.

Kijima, M. (1989). Some results for repairable systems with general repair. *Journal of Applied Probability*, **26**(01), 89–102.

Kijima, M., Morimura, H., & Suzuki, Y. (1988). Periodical replacement problem without assuming minimal repair. *European Journal of Operational Research*, **37**(2), 194–203.

Kim, C. S., Djamaludin, I., & Murthy, D. N. P. (2004). Warranty and discrete preventive maintenance. *Reliability Engineering & System Safety*, **84**(3), 301–309.

Kim, H. G., & Rao, B. M. (2000). Expected warranty cost of two-attribute free-replacement warranties based on a bivariate exponential distribution. *Computers & Industrial Engineering*, **38**(4), 425–434.

Kim, H. J., Lee, D. H., & Xirouchakis, P. (2007). Disassembly scheduling: literature review and future research directions. *International Journal of Production Research*, **45**(18–19), 4465–4484.

Kim, K., Song, I., Kim, J., & Jeong, B. (2006). Supply planning model for remanufacturing system in reverse logistics environment. *Computers & Industrial Engineering*, **51**(2), 279–287.

Kim, M. J., Jiang, R., Makis, V., & Lee, C. G. (2011). Optimal Bayesian fault prediction scheme for a partially observable system subject to random failure. *European Journal of Operational Research*, **214**(2), 331–339.

Kiritsis, D., Bufardi, A., & Xirouchakis, P. (2003). Research issues on product lifecycle management and information tracking using smart embedded systems. *Advanced Engineering Informatics*, **17**(3), 189–202.

Klausner, M., Grimm, W. M., & Hendrickson, C. T. (1998a). Reuse of electric motors in consumer products. *Journal of Industrial Ecology*, **2**(2), 89–102.

Klausner, M., Grimm, W. M., & Horvath, A. (1999). Integrating product takeback and technical service. In Proceedings of the *International Symposium on Electronics and the Environment* (ISEE). 48–53.

Klausner, M., Grimm, W. M., Hendrickson, C. T., & Horvath, A. (1998b). Sensor-based data recording of use conditions for product takeback. In Proceedings of the *IEEE International Symposium on Electronics and the Environment (ISEE)*. 138–143.

Knight, W. A., & Sodhi, M. S. (2000). Design for bulk recycling: analysis of materials separation. *CIRP Annals-Manufacturing Technology*, **49**(1), 83–86.

Knight, W. A., & Curtis, M. (2002). Measuring your ecodesign [end-of-life disassembly]. *Manufacturing Engineer*, **81**(2), 64–69.

Kongar, E., & Gupta, S. M. (2002). A multi-criteria decision making approach for disassembly-to-order systems. *Journal of Electronics Manufacturing*, **11**(2), 171–183.

Kongar, E., & Gupta, S. M. (2006a). Disassembly sequencing using genetic algorithm. *International Journal of Advanced Manufacturing Technology*, **30**(5–6), 497–506.

Kongar, E., & Gupta, S. M. (2006b). Disassembly to order system under uncertainty. *Omega*, **34**(6), 550–561.

Kongar, E., & Gupta, S. M. (2009a). A multiple objective tabu search approach for end-of-life product disassembly. *International Journal of Advanced Operations Management*, **1**(2–3), 177–202.

Kongar, E., & Gupta, S. M. (2009b). Solving the disassembly-to-order problem using linear physical programming. *International Journal of Mathematics in Operational Research*, **1**(4), 504–531.

Kriwet, A., Zussman, E., & Seliger, G. (1995). Systematic integration of design-for-recycling into product design. *International Journal of Production Economics*, **38**(1), 15–22.

Kuik, S. S., Kaihara, T., & Fujii, N. (2015). Stochastic decision model of the remanufactured product with warranty. In Proceedings of the *International MultiConference of Engineers and Computer Scientists* (IMECS). Hong Kong.

Kulkarni, A., Ralph, D., & McFarlane, D. (2007). Value of RFID in remanufacturing. *International Journal of Services Operations and Informatics*, **2**(3), 225–252.

Lam, Y., & Lam, P. K. W. (2001). An extended warranty policy with options open to consumers. *European Journal of Operational Research*, **131**(3), 514–529.

Lambert, A. J. (2003). Disassembly sequencing: a survey. *International Journal of Production Research*, **41**(16), 3721–3759.

Lambert, A. J. D., & Gupta, S. M. (2005). *Disassembly Modeling for Assembly, Maintenance, Reuse, and Recycling*. Boca Raton, FL: CRC Press.

Lambert, A. J. D. (1999). Linear programming in disassembly/clustering sequence generation. *Computers & Industrial Engineering*, **36**(4), 723–738.

Lambert, A. J. D., & Gupta, S. M. (2002). Demand-driven disassembly optimization for electronic products package reliability. *Journal of Electronics Manufacturing*, **11**(02), 121–135.

Lambert, A. J. D., & Gupta, S. M. (2008). Methods for optimum and near optimum disassembly sequencing. *International Journal of Production Research*, **46**(11), 2845–2865.

Langella, I. M. (2007). Heuristics for demand-driven disassembly planning. *Computers & Operations Research*, **34**(2), 552–577.

Lee, D. H., Kang, J. G., & Xirouchakis, P. (2001). Disassembly planning and scheduling: review and further research. In Proceedings of the *Institution of Mechanical Engineers, Part B: Journal of Engineering Manufacture*, **215**(5), 695–709.

Liao, B. F., Li, B. Y., & Cheng, J. S. (2015). A warranty model for remanufactured products. *Journal of Industrial and Production Engineering*, **32**(8), 551–558.

Lo, H.-C., Yeh, R. H., Kurniati, N., & Lin, J.-J. (2013). The impact of used products on channel coordination and quality decision for warranted products. *Proceedings of the 19th ISSAT International Conference on Reliability and Quality in Design*, Honolulu, HI, 131–135.

Lund, R. (1998). Remanufacturing: an American resource. In Proceedings of the *Fifth International Congress Environmentally Conscious Design and Manufacturing*, Rochester Institute of Technology, Rochester, NY. 16–17.

Lutz, N. A., & Padmanabhan, V. (1995). Why do we observe minimal warranties? *Marketing Science*, **14**(4), 417–441.

Lye, S. W., Lee, S. G., & Khoo, M. K. (2002). ECoDE–An environmental component design evaluation tool. *Engineering with Computers*, **18**(1), 14–23.

Mabee, D. G., Bommer, M., & Keat, W. D. (1999). Design charts for remanufacturing assessment. *Journal of Manufacturing Systems*, **18**(5), 358–366.

Madu, C. N., Kuei, C., & Madu, I. E. (2002). A hierarchic metric approach for integration of green issues in manufacturing: a paper recycling application. *Journal of Environmental Management*, **64**(3), 261–272.

Manna, D. K., Pal, S., & Sinha, S. (2006). Optimal determination of warranty region for 2D policy: a customers' perspective. *Computers & Industrial Engineering*, **50**(1), 161–174.

Manna, D. K., Pal, S., & Sinha, S. (2007). A use-rate based failure model for two-dimensional warranty. *Computers & Industrial Engineering*, **52**(2), 229–240.

Manna, D. K., Pal, S., & Sinha, S. (2008). A note on calculating cost of two-dimensional warranty policy. *Computers & Industrial Engineering*, **54**(4), 1071–1077.

Marsaglia, G., & Tubilla, A. (1975). A note on the "lack of memory" property of the exponential distribution. *The Annals of Probability*, **3**(2), 353–354.

Martorell, S., Sanchez, A., & Serradell, V. (1999). Age-dependent reliability model considering effects of maintenance and working conditions. *Reliability Engineering & System Safety*, **64**(1), 19–31.

Masanet, E., & Horvath, A. (2007). Assessing the benefits of design for recycling for plastics in electronics: A case study of computer enclosures. *Materials & Design*, *28*(6), 1801–1811.

Masui, K., Sakao, T., Kobayashi, M., & Inaba, A. (2003). Applying quality function deployment to environmentally conscious design. *International Journal of Quality & Reliability Management*, **20**(1), 90–106.

Matsumoto, M., Yang, S., Martinsen, K., & Kainuma, Y. (2016). Trends and research challenges in remanufacturing. *International Journal of Precision Engineering and Manufacturing-Green Technology*, **3**(1), 129–142.

Mazhar, M. I., Kara, S., & Kaebernick, H. (2005, February). Reusability assessment of components in consumer products—a statistical and condition monitoring data analysis strategy. In Proceedings of the *4th Australian LCA Conference*, Sydney. 1–8.

Mazhar, M. I., Kara, S., & Kaebernick, H. (2007). Remaining life estimation of used components in consumer products: life cycle data analysis by Weibull and artificial neural networks. *Journal of Operations Management*, **25**(6), 1184–1193.

McGovern, S. M., & Gupta, S. M. (2007). A balancing method and genetic algorithm for disassembly line balancing. *European Journal of Operational Research*, **179**(3), 692–708.

McGovern, S. M., & Gupta, S. M. (2011). *The Disassembly Line: Balancing and Modeling*, McGraw Hill, New York, NY.

McGuire, E. P. (1980). *Industrial Product Warranties: Policies and Practices*. Conference Board Inc., New York, NY.

Mehta, C., & Wang, B. (2001). Green quality function deployment III: a methodology for developing environmentally conscious products. *Journal of Design and Manufacturing Automation*, **1**(1–2), 1–16.

MIL-STD-721B, *Military Standard: Definition of Terms for Reliability and Maintainability*, 05 Dec 1995.

Mitra, A., & Patankar, J. G. (2006a). Warranty costs for repairable products with a two-attribute policy: impact of warranty execution. *International Journal of Operational Research*, **1**(4), 363–381.

Mitra, A., & Patankar, J. G. (2006b). A two-dimensional minimal-repair warranty policy. In *Applications of Management Science: In Productivity, Finance, and Operations*. Emerald Group Publishing Limited. 12, 235–251.

Mitra, S. (2007). Revenue management for remanufactured products. *Omega*, **35**(5), 553–562.

Mok, H. S., Kim, H. J., & Moon, K. S. (1997). Disassemblability of mechanical parts in automobile for recycling. *Computers & Industrial Engineering*, **33**(3), 621–624.

Montgomery, D. C. (2008). *Design and Analysis of Experiments*. John Wiley & Sons, Chicago, IL.

Montgomery, D. C., Runger, G. C., & Hubele, N. F. (2009). *Engineering Statistics*. John Wiley & Sons, Chicago, IL.

Moore, K. E., Güngör, A., & Gupta, S. M. (1998). A petri net approach to disassembly process planning. *Computers & Industrial Engineering*, **35**(1), 165–168.

Moore, K. E., Güngör, A., & Gupta, S. M. (2001). Petri Net Approach to disassembly process planning for products with complex AND/OR precedence relationships. *European Journal of Operational Research*, 135(2), 428–449.

Morgan, S. D., & Gagnon, R. J. (2013). A systematic literature review of remanufacturing scheduling. *International Journal of Production Research*, **51**(16), 4853–4879.

Moskowitz, H., & Chun, Y. H. (1994). A poisson regression model for two-attribute warranty policies. *Naval Research Logistics (NRL)*, **41**(3), 355–376.

Moyer, L. K., & Gupta, S. M. (1997). Environmental concerns and recycling/disassembly efforts in the electronics industry. *Journal of Electronics Manufacturing*, **7**(1), 1–22.

Murthy, D. N. P. (2006). Product warranty and reliability. *Annals of Operations Research*, **143**(1), 133–146.

Murthy, D. N. P., & I. Djamaludin. (2002). New product warranty: a literature review. *International Journal of Production Economics*, **79**(3): 231–260.

Murthy, D. N. P., & Jack, N. (2003). Warranty and maintenance. In *Handbook of Reliability Engineering*. Springer, London. 305–316.

Murthy, D. N. P., Rausand, M., & Osteras, T. (2008). *Product Reliability: Performance and Specifications*. Springer, London.

Murthy, D. N. P., & Blischke, W. R. (2006). *Warranty Management and Product Manufacture*. Springer Science & Business Media, London.

Murthy, D. N. P., Page, N. W., & Rodin, E. Y. (1990). *Mathematical Modelling: A Tool for Problem Solving in Engineering, Physical, Biological, and Social Sciences*. Oxford, UK, Pergamon press.

Murthy, D. N. P., & R. Wilson. (1991). Modeling 2-Dimensional Failure Free Warranties. In Proceedings of the *Fifth Symposium on Applied Stochastic Models and Data Analysis*, Granada, Spain, 481–492.

Musa, A., & Dabo, A. A. A. (2016). A review of RFID in supply chain management: 2000–2015. *Global Journal of Flexible Systems Management*, **17**(2), 189–228.

Naini, S. G. J., & Shafiee, M. (2011). Joint determination of price and upgrade level for a warranted remanufactured product. *The International Journal of Advanced Manufacturing Technology*, **54**, 1187–1198.

Nakagawa, T. (1981). A summary of periodic replacement with minimal repair at failure. *Journal of the Operations Research Society of Japan*, **24**(3), 213–227.

Nakagawa, T. (2006). *Maintenance Theory of Reliability*. Springer Science & Business Media.

Nakagawa, T. (2008). *Advanced Reliability Models and Maintenance Policies*. Springer Science & Business Media.

Nakagawa, T., & Kowada, M. (1983). Analysis of a system with minimal repair and its application to replacement policy. *European Journal of Operational Research*, **12**(2), 176–182.

Nasr, N., & Thurston, M. (2006). Remanufacturing: a key enabler to sustainable product systems. In Key Notes of the *13th CIRP International Conference on Life Cycle Engineering*, Rochester Institute of Technology.

Nguyen, D. G., & Murthy, D. N. P. (1984). Cost analysis of warranty policies. *Naval Research Logistics Quarterly*, **31**(4), 525–541.

Nguyen, D. G., & Murthy, D. N. P. (1986). An optimal policy for servicing warranty. *Journal of the Operational Research Society*, **37**(11), 1081–1088.

Nguyen, D. G., & Murthy, D. N. P. (1989). Optimal replace-repair strategy for servicing products sold with warranty. *European Journal of Operational Research*, **39**(2), 206–212.

Noh, B., & Borges, A. (2015). The paradox of a warranty: can no warranty really signal higher quality? *Psychology & Marketing*, **32**(11), 1049–1060.

Ondemir, O., & Gupta, S. M. (2012). Optimal management of reverse supply chains with sensor-embedded end-of-life products. In *Applications of Management Science*. Emerald Group Publishing Limited. 109–129.

Ondemir, O., & Gupta, S. M. (2013a). Advanced remanufacturing-to-order and disassembly-to-order system under demand/decision uncertainty. In *Reverse Supply Chains: Issues and Analysis*. CRC Press. 203–228.

Ondemir, O., & Gupta, S. M. (2013b). Quality assurance in remanufacturing with sensor embedded products. In *Quality Management in Reverse Logistics*. Springer, London. 95–112.

Ondemir, O., & Gupta, S. M. (2014). A multi-criteria decision making model for advanced repair-to-order and disassembly-to-order system. *European Journal of Operational Research*, **233**(2), 408–419.

Ondemir, O., Ilgin, M. A., & Gupta, S. M. (2012). Optimal end-of-life management in closed-loop supply chains using RFID and sensors. *IEEE Transactions on Industrial Informatics*, **8**(3), 719–728.

O'Shea, B., Grewal, S. S., & Kaebernick, H. (1998). State of the art literature survey on disassembly planning. *Concurrent Engineering*, **6**(4), 345–357.

Ovchinnikov, A. (2011). Revenue and cost management for remanufactured products. *Production and Operations Management*, **20**(6), 824–840.

Özceylan, E., Kalayci, C. B., Güngör, A., & Gupta, S. M. (2018). Disassembly line balancing problem: a review of the state of the art and future directions. *International Journal of Production Research*, 1–23.

Padmanabhan, V. (1995). *Extended Warranties*. New York, NY: Marcel Dekker. 439–452.

Pan, L., & Zeid, I. (2001). A knowledge base for indexing and retrieving disassembly plans. *Journal of Intelligent Manufacturing*, **12**(1), 77–94.

Parkinson, H. J., & Thompson, G. (2003). Analysis and taxonomy of remanufacturing industry practice. In Proceedings of the *Institution of Mechanical Engineers, Part E: Journal of Process Mechanical Engineering*, **217**(3), 243–256.

Parlikad, A. K., & McFarlane, D. (2007). RFID-based product information in end-of-life decision making. *Control Engineering Practice*, **15**(11), 1348–1363.

Pascual, R., & Ortega, J. H. (2006). Optimal replacement and overhaul decisions with imperfect maintenance and warranty contracts. *Reliability Engineering & System Safety*, **91**(2), 241–248.

Pecht, M. (2008). *Prognostics and Health Management of Electronics*. John Wiley & Sons, Ltd.

Petriu, E. M., Georganas, N. D., Petriu, D. C., Makrakis, D., & Groza, V. Z. (2000). Sensor-based information appliances. *IEEE Instrumentation & Measurement Magazine*, **3**(4), 31–35.

Pham, H., & Wang, H. (1996). Imperfect maintenance. *European Journal of Operational Research*, **94**(3), 425–438.

Plackett, R. L., & Burman, J. P. (1946). The design of optimum multifactorial experiments. *Biometrika*, **33**(4), 305–325.

Pochampally, K. K., Gupta, S. M., & Govindan, K. (2009). Metrics for performance measurement of a reverse/closed-loop supply chain. *International Journal of Business Performance and Supply Chain Modelling*, **1**(1), 8–32.

Pokharel, S., & Mutha, A. (2009). Perspectives in reverse logistics: a review. *Resources, Conservation and Recycling*, **53**(4), 175–182.

Pongpech, J., Murthy, D. N. P., & Boondiskulchock, R. (2006). Maintenance strategies for used equipment under lease. *Journal of Quality in Maintenance Engineering*, **12**(1), 52–67.

Prahinski, C., & Kocabasoglu, C. (2006). Empirical research opportunities in reverse supply chains. *Omega*, **34**(6), 519–532.

Priyono, A., Ijomah, W., & Bititci, U. (2016). Disassembly for remanufacturing: a systematic literature review, new model development and future research needs. *Journal of Industrial Engineering and Management*, **9**(4), 899.

Raghavarao, D. (1971). *Constructions and combinatorial problems in design of experiments*. Wiley.

Rahman, A., & Chattopadhyay, G. N. (2015). Long term warranty and after sales service. In *Long Term Warranty and After Sales Service* (pp. 1–15). Springer, Cham.

Raja Jayaraman, B. S. (2008). *On Minimizing Expected Warranty Costs in 1-dimension and 2-dimensions with Different Repair Options*. Doctoral dissertation, Texas Tech University.

Ramani, K., Ramanujan, D., Bernstein, W. Z., Zhao, F., Sutherland, J. W., Handwerker, C., Choi, J. K., Kim, H., & Thurston, D. (2010). Integrated sustainable life cycle design: a review. *Journal of Mechanical Design*, **132**(9), 091004.

Ross, S. M. (1970). Average cost semi-Markov decision processes. *Journal of Applied Probability*, 7(3), 649–656.

Ross, S. M. (1997). *Introduction to Probability Models*. Academic press.

Rubio, S., & Jiménez-Parra, B. (2017). Reverse logistics: concept, evolution and marketing challenges. In: *Optimization and Decision Support Systems for Supply Chains*. (Eds., A. Póvoa, A. Corominas, and J. de Miranda) *Lecture Notes in Logistics*. Springer International Publishing.

Rubio, S., & Corominas, A. (2008). Optimal manufacturing–remanufacturing policies in a lean production environment. *Computers & Industrial Engineering*, **55**(1), 234–242.

Ryding, S. O. (1999). ISO 14042 Environmental management-life cycle assessment-life cycle impact assessment. *The International Journal of Life Cycle Assessment*, **4**(6), 307–307.

Saidi-Mehrabad, M., Noorossana, R., & Shafiee, M. (2010). Modeling and analysis of effective ways for improving the reliability of second-hand products sold with warranty. *International Journal of Advanced Manufacturing Technology*, **46**(1–4), 253–265.

Sakao, T. (2007). A QFD-centred design methodology for environmentally conscious product design. *International Journal of Production Research*, **45**(18–19), 4143–4162.

San, G. S., & Pujawan, I. N. (2012). *Closed-Loop Supply Chain with Remanufacturing: A Literature Review*, Doctoral dissertation, Petra Christian University.

Sarada, Y., & Mubashirunnissa, M. (2011). Warranty cost analysis for second-hand products using bivariate approach. *International Journal of Operational Research*, **12**(1), 34–55.

Sasikumar, P., & Kannan, G. (2008a). Issues in reverse supply chains, part I: end-of-life product recovery and inventory management–an overview. *International Journal of Sustainable Engineering*, **1**(3), 154–172.

Sasikumar, P., & Kannan, G. (2008b). Issues in reverse supply chains, part II: reverse distribution issues–an overview. *International Journal of Sustainable Engineering*, **1**(4), 234–249.

Sasikumar, P., & Kannan, G. (2009). Issues in reverse supply chain, part III: classification and simple analysis. *International Journal of Sustainable Engineering*, **2**(1), 2–27.

Sbihi, A., & Eglese, R. W. (2007). Combinatorial optimization and green logistics. *4OR: A Quarterly Journal of Operations Research*, **5**(2), 99–116.

Scheidt, L., & Zong, S. (1994). An approach to achieve reusability of electronic modules. In Proceedings of the *International Symposium on Electronics and the Environment* (*ISEE*). 331–336.

Schluter, F. (2001). On the integration of environmental aspects into early product development-life cycle design structure matrix. *LicEng Thesis*, Royal Institute of Technology, Stockholm, Sweden.

Seaver, W. B. (1994). Design considerations for remanufacturability, recyclability and reusability of user interface modules. In Proceedings of the *International Symposium on Electronics and the Environment* (*ISEE*). 241–245.

Seiden, E. (1954). On the problem of construction of orthogonal arrays. *The Annals of Mathematical Statistics*, **25**(1), 151–156.

Seitz, M. A., & Peattie, K. (2004). Meeting the closed-loop challenge: the case of remanufacturing. *California Management Review*, **46**(2), 74–89.

Shafiee, M., & Chukova, S. (2013a). Maintenance models in warranty: a literature review. *European Journal of Operational Research*, **229**(3), 561–572.

Shafiee, M., & Chukova, S. (2013b). Optimal upgrade strategy, warranty policy and sale price for second-hand products. *Applied Stochastic Models in Business and Industry*, **29**(2), 157–169.

Shafiee, M., Chukova, S., Yun, W. Y., & Niaki, S. T. A. (2011). On the investment in a reliability improvement program for warranted second-hand items. *IIE Transactions*, **43**(7), 525–534.

Shafiee, M., Finkelstein, M., & Zuo, M. J. (2013c). Optimal burn-in and preventive maintenance warranty strategies with time-dependent maintenance costs. *IIE Transactions*, **45**(9), 1024–1033.

Shahanaghi, K., Noorossana, R., Jalali-Naini, S. G., & Heydari, M. (2013). Failure modeling and optimizing preventive maintenance strategy during two-dimensional extended warranty contracts. *Engineering Failure Analysis*, **28**, 90–102.

Sharma, A., Yadava, G. S., & Deshmukh, S. G. (2011). A literature review and future perspectives on maintenance optimization. *Journal of Quality in Maintenance Engineering*, **17**(1), 5–25.

Sheu, S. H., & Griffith, W. S. (2002). Extended block replacement policy with shock models and used items. *European Journal of Operational Research*, **140**(1), 50–60.

Shu, L. & Flowers, W. (1999). Application of a design-for-remanufacture framework to the selection of product life-cycle fastening and joining methods. *International Journal of Robotics and Computer Integrated Manufacturing* (Special Issue: Remanufacturing), 15(3), 179–190.

Simon, M., Bee, G., Moore, P., Pu, J. S., & Xie, C. (2001). Modelling of the life cycle of products with data acquisition features. *Computers in Industry*, **45**(2), 111–122.

Simon, M., Pu, J. S., & Moore, P. (1998). The WHITEBOX-capturing and using product life cycle data. In Proceedings of the *5th CIRP Seminar on Life Cycle Design*, Stockholm. 161–170.

Soberman, D. A. (2003). Simultaneous signaling and screening with warranties. *Journal of Marketing Research*, **40**(2), 176–192.

Sodhi, M. S., Young, J., & Knight, W. A. (1999). Modelling material separation processes in bulk recycling. *International Journal of Production Research*, **37**(10), 2239–2252.

Souza, G. C. (2013). Closed-loop supply chains: a critical review, and future research. *Decision Sciences*, **44**(1), 7–38.

Spence, M. (1977). Consumer misperceptions, product failure and producer liability. *The Review of Economic Studies*, **44**(3), 561–572.

Srivastava, S. K. (2007). Green supply-chain management: a state-of-the-art literature review. *International Journal of Management Reviews*, **9**(1), 53–80.

Su, C., & Shen, J. (2012). Analysis of extended warranty policies with different repair options. *Engineering Failure Analysis*, **25**, 49–62.

Su, C., & Wang, X. (2014). Optimizing upgrade level and preventive maintenance policy for second-hand products sold with warranty. In Proceedings of the *Institution of Mechanical Engineers, Part O: Journal of Risk and Reliability*, **228**(5), 518–528.

Su, C., & Wang, X. (2016). Optimal upgrade policy for used products sold with two-dimensional warranty. *Quality and Reliability Engineering International.* **32**(8), 2889–2899.

Subramoniam, R., Huisingh, D., & Chinnam, R. B. (2009). Remanufacturing for the automotive aftermarket-strategic factors: literature review and future research needs. *Journal of Cleaner Production*, **17**(13), 1163–1174.

Sutherland, J. W., Adler, D. P., Haapala, K. R., & Kumar, V. (2008). A comparison of manufacturing and remanufacturing energy intensities with application to diesel engine production. *CIRP Annals-Manufacturing Technology*, **57**(1), 5–8.

Taguchi, G. (1987). *System of Experimental Design: Engineering Methods to Optimize Quality and Minimize Costs.* White Plains, New York, NY: UNIPIB, and Dearborn, MI: American Supplier Institute.

Tang, Y., Zhou, M., Zussman, E., & Caudill, R. (2002). Disassembly modeling, planning, and application. *Journal of Manufacturing Systems*, **21**(3), 200–217.

Tarakci, H. (2016). Two types of learning effects on maintenance activities. *International Journal of Production Research*, **54**(6), 1721–1734.

Teng, T. L., Chu, Y. A., Chang, F. A., Shen, B. C., & Cheng, D. S. (2008). Development and validation of numerical model of steel fiber reinforced concrete for high-velocity impact. *Computational Materials Science*, **42**(1), 90–99.

Thöni, A., & Tjoa, A. M. (2017). Information technology for sustainable supply chain management: a literature survey. *Enterprise Information Systems*, **11**(6), 828–858.

Thorpe, J. F., & Middendorf, W. H. (1979). *What every engineer should know about product liability*. CRC Press, Boca Raton, FL.

Tong, P., Liu, Z., Men, F., & Cao, L. (2014). Designing and pricing of two-dimensional extended warranty contracts based on usage rate. *International Journal of Production Research*, **52**(21), 6362–6380.

Vadde, S., Kamarthi, S. V., Gupta, S. M., & Zeid, I. (2008). Product life cycle monitoring via embedded sensors. In *Environment Conscious Manufacturing*. (Eds., S. M. Gupta and A. J. D. Lambert) (pp. 91–104). CRC Press.

Van Nunen, J. A., & Zuidwijk, R. A. (2004). E-enabled closed-loop supply chains. *California Management Review*, **46**(2), 40–54.

Veerakamolmal, P., & Gupta, S. M. (1998). Optimal analysis of lot-size balancing for multiproducts selective disassembly. *International Journal of Flexible Automation and Integrated Manufacturing*, **6**(3), 245–269.

Veerakamolmal, P., & Gupta, S. M. (2000). Design for disassembly, reuse and recycling. In *Green Electronics/Green Bottom Line: Environmentally Responsible Engineering*, 69–82.

Veerakamolmal, P., & Gupta, S. M. (2001). Optimizing the supply chain in reverse logistics. In Proceedings of the *SPIE International Conference on Environmentally Conscious Manufacturing*, vol. 4193, 157–166.

Villalba, G., Segarra, M., Chimenos, J. M., & Espiell, F. (2004). Using the recyclability index of materials as a tool for design for disassembly. *Ecological Economics*, **50**(3), 195–200.

Villalba, G., Segarra, M., Fernandez, A. I., Chimenos, J. M., & Espiell, F. (2002). A proposal for quantifying the recyclability of materials. *Resources, Conservation and Recycling*, **37**(1), 39–53.

Wang, H. (2002). A survey of maintenance policies of deteriorating systems. *European Journal of Operational Research*, **139**(3), 469–489.

Wang, Y., Liu, Z., & Liu, Y. (2015). Optimal preventive maintenance strategy for repairable items under two-dimensional warranty. *Reliability Engineering & System Safety*, **142**, 326–333.

Warranty Week. 2015. *Automotive Warranty Report*. http://www.warrantyweek.com/archive/ww20150326.html

Whiteman, G., & Cooper, W. H. (2000). Ecological embeddedness. *Academy of Management Journal*, **43**(6), 1265–1282.

Williams, J. A. S. (2006). A review of electronics demanufacturing processes. *Resources, Conservation and Recycling*, **47**(3), 195–208.

Williams, J. A. S. (2007). A review of research towards computer integrated demanufacturing for materials recovery. *International Journal of Computer Integrated Manufacturing*, **20**(8), 773–780.

Wu, J., Xie, M., & Ng, T. S. A. (2011). On a general periodic preventive maintenance policy incorporating warranty contracts and system ageing losses. *International Journal of Production Economics*, **129**(1), 102–110.

Wu, S., & Longhurst, P. (2011). Optimising age-replacement and extended non-renewing warranty policies in lifecycle costing. *International Journal of Production Economics*, **130**(2), 262–267.

Wu, S., & Zuo, M. J. (2010). Linear and nonlinear preventive maintenance models. *IEEE Transactions on Reliability*, **59**(1), 242–249.

Xie, W., H. Liao, & X. Zhu. (2014). Estimation of gross profit for a new durable product considering warranty and post-warranty repairs. *IIE Transactions*, **46**(2), 87–105.

Yang, D., He, Z., & He, S. (2016). Warranty claims forecasting based on a general imperfect repair model considering usage rate. *Reliability Engineering & System Safety*, **145**, 147–154.

Yang, S. C., & Nachlas, J. A. (2001). Bivariate reliability and availability modeling. *IEEE Transactions on Reliability*, **50**(1), 26–35.

Yang, X., Moore, P., & Chong, S. K. (2009a). Intelligent products: from lifecycle data acquisition to enabling product-related services. *Computers in Industry*, **60**(3), 184–194.

Yang, X., Moore, P., Pu, J. S., & Wong, C. B. (2009b). A practical methodology for realizing product service systems for consumer products. *Computers & Industrial Engineering*, **56**(1), 224–235.

Yazdian, S. A., Shahanaghi, K., & Makui, A. (2014). Joint optimisation of price, warranty and recovery planning in remanufacturing of used products under linear and non-linear demand, return and cost functions. *International Journal of Systems Science*, **47**(5), 1155–1175.

Yazdian, S. A., Shahanaghi, K., & Makui, A. (2016). Joint optimisation of price, warranty and recovery planning in remanufacturing of used products under linear and non-linear demand, return and cost functions. *International Journal of Systems Science*, **47**(5), 1155–1175.

Yeh, R. H., & Chen, C. K. (2006b). Periodical preventive-maintenance contract for a leased facility with Weibull life-time. *Quality and Quantity*, **40**(2), 303–313.

Yeh, R. H., & Chen, T. H. (2006a). Optimal lot size and inspection policy for products sold with warranty. *European Journal of Operational Research*, **174**(2), 766–776.

Yeh, R. H., & H.-C. Lo. (2001). Optimal preventive-maintenance warranty policy for repairable products. *European Journal of Operational Research* **134**(1), 59–69.

Yeh, R. H., Chen, G. C., & Chen, M. Y. (2005). Optimal age-replacement policy for nonrepairable products under renewing free-replacement warranty. *IEEE Transactions on Reliability*, **54**(1), 92–97.

Yeh, R. H., Chen, M. Y., & Lin, C. Y. (2007). Optimal periodic replacement policy for repairable products under free-repair warranty. *European Journal of Operational Research*, **176**(3), 1678–1686.

Yeh, R. H., Kao, K. C., & Chang, W. L. (2009). Optimal preventive maintenance policy for leased equipment using failure rate reduction. *Computers & Industrial Engineering*, **57**(1), 304–309.

Yeh, R. H., Lo, H.-C., & Yu, R. Y. (2011). A study of maintenance policies for second-hand products. *Computers & Industrial Engineering*, **60**(3), 438–444.

Yu, J., Xi, L., & Zhou, X. (2009). Identifying source (s) of out-of-control signals in multivariate manufacturing processes using selective neural network ensemble. *Engineering Applications of Artificial Intelligence*, **22**(1), 141–152.

Yun, W. Y., Murthy, D. N. P., & Jack, N. (2008). Warranty servicing with imperfect repair. *International Journal of Production Economics*, **111**(1), 159–169.

Zeid, I., Kamarthi, S. V. & Gupta, S. M. (2004) Product Take-Back: Sensors-Based Approach. In Proceedings of the *SPIE International Conference on Environmentally Conscious Manufacturing IV*, Philadelphia, Pennsylvania, pp. 200–206, October 26–27.

Zhang, H. C., Kuo, T. C., Lu, H., & Huang, S. H. (1997). Environmentally conscious design and manufacturing: a state-of-the-art survey. *Journal of Manufacturing Systems*, **16**(5), 352.

Zhang, Y. (1999). Green QFD-II: a life cycle approach for environmentally conscious manufacturing by integrating LCA and LCC into QFD matrices. *International Journal of Production Research*, **37**(5), 1075–1091.

Zhou, X., Li, Y., Xi, L., & Lee, J. (2015). Multi-phase preventive maintenance policy for leased equipment. *International Journal of Production Research*, **53**(15), 4528–4537.

Author Index

Subject Index